Louis Carlos Bernal

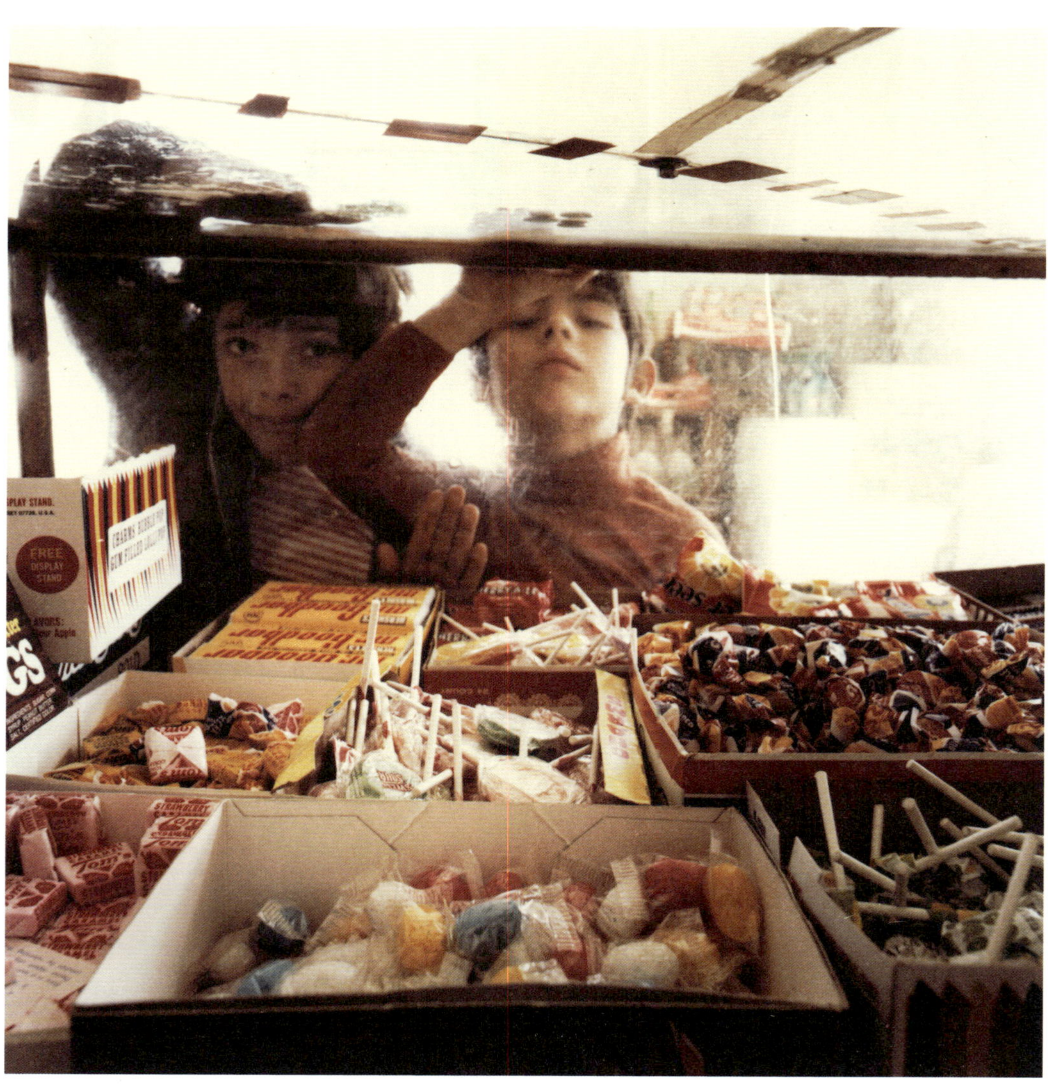

Martinez Brothers in Candy Store, Douglas, Arizona, 1978

Elizabeth Ferrer

MONOGRAFÍA   Louis Carlos Bernal

aperture   **CCP** Center for Creative Photography

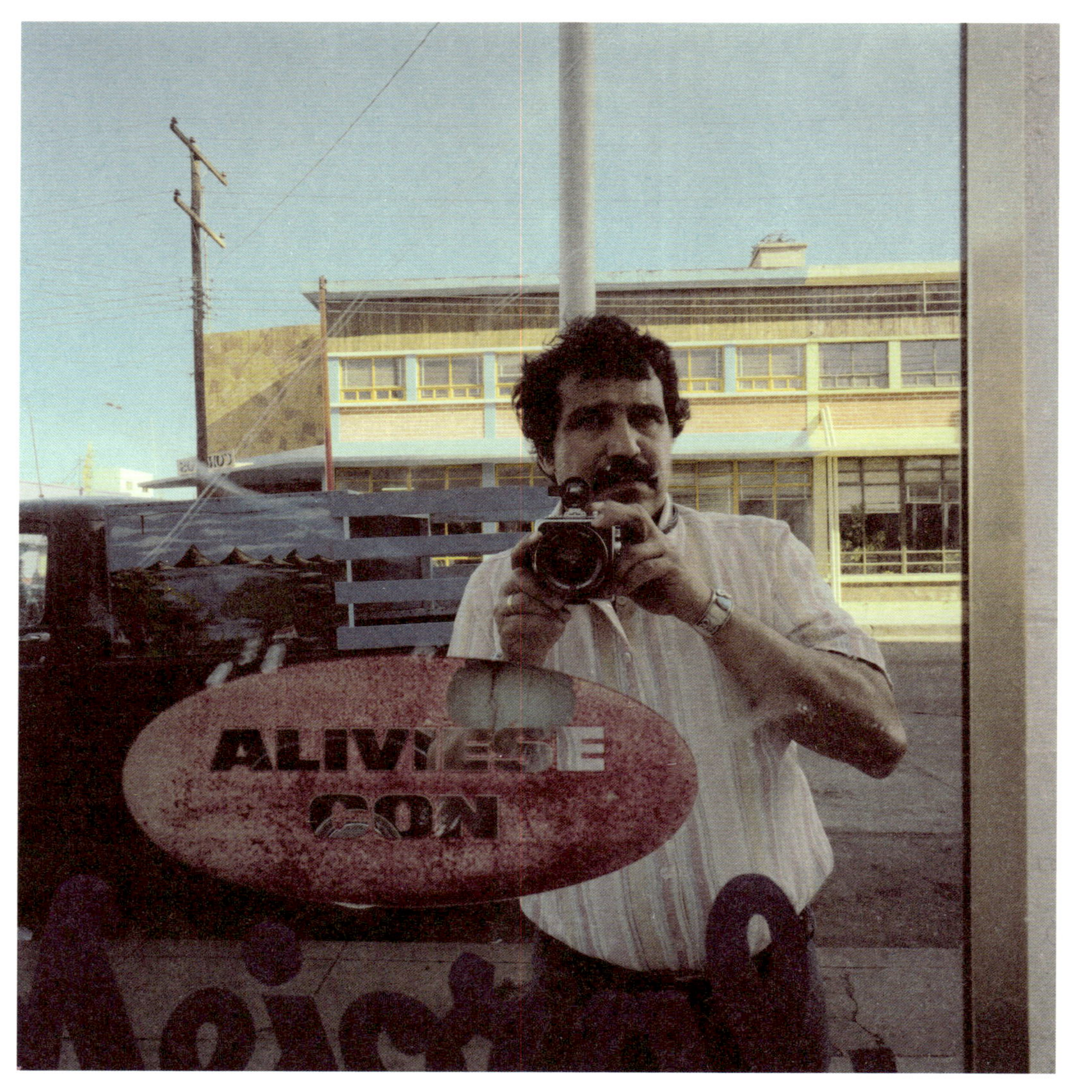

Self-Portrait, ca. 1977

CONTENTS / CONTENIDOS

FOREWORD / PRÓLOGO
Andrew Schulz

Vice President for the Arts / Vicepresidente de Artes
Dean, College of Fine Arts / Decano, Facultad de Bellas Artes
University of Arizona

Louis Carlos Bernal is a homegrown Arizona photographic celebrity. Referred to as the father of Chicano art photography, he is important beyond the distinctive and innovative photographs he made. Over his too-brief five decades, he had a tremendous impact on the network of photographers who were his colleagues, peers, students, and mentees. The mention of his name—even thirty years after his passing—brings forth fond recollections. So very many people knew and appreciated his warmth, collegiality, and passion for photography.

The Center for Creative Photography (CCP) at the University of Arizona, Tucson, is perfectly situated to produce the excellent research that has resulted in a traveling exhibition and this publication. In 2014, Louis Carlos Bernal's daughters, Lisa Bernal Brethour and Katrina Bernal, gifted his archive, consisting primarily of photographic prints, contact sheets, negatives, and transparencies, with some related biographical materials, to CCP. This group joined 110 photographic prints by Bernal already in the Center's collection through a combination of purchases and gifts. That the archive did not immediately come to the Center following Bernal's passing in 1993 suggests the precarity of so many archives of artists and photographers who have been neglected within the canons of art history. Fortunately, CCP is now home to Bernal's important archive, and this project is the culmination of a long effort by the Bernal family, together with photographer and head of the photography program at Pima Community College, Ann Simmons-Myers, to ensure these research materials are both preserved and accessible. We extend our profound gratitude to Lisa Bernal Brethour, Katrina Bernal, and Ann Simmons-Myers for their patience, generosity, and trust.

The success of this project relies on three other critical components. The first is major financial support from the Henry Luce Foundation. The Center for Creative Photography is deeply grateful for the grant monies that allow for the components necessary to make our work possible: a guest curator, a community advisory council, research support, exhibition materials and production, publication subvention, rights and licensing fees, and digitization services. This backing has allowed the Center's expert staff to support the creation of this monographic survey of Louis Carlos Bernal, which is sure to be the first of many serious scholarly studies of his important body of work.

The second acknowledgment is to our guest curator Elizabeth Ferrer. We are incredibly fortunate to be working with a scholar of her depth and expertise and are furthermore lucky that she was not only able to take on this project at this time, but also eager to turn her research attention to the life and work of Louis Carlos Bernal. It felt like a "stars aligning" moment—something Ferrer has noted has happened more than once during this process—which perhaps suggests that the universe is helping smooth the way for the project's success. Ferrer's expansive research is rooted in the archive at CCP, but it also involved her following various leads and conducting interviews with many of the people who knew, worked alongside, or studied with Bernal. She has discovered materials—through his friends who kept his every letter, clipping, and announcement for over thirty years—that point to what a beloved figure he is. Her thoughtful and thorough essay, her selection of images, and the understanding of Bernal's context, built by a lifetime of scholarship, make this a critical contribution to American photography and art.

Our partnership with Aperture also deserves special mention. Aperture is a mainstay in photographic publishing, and we are delighted to work with its team to bring this critical book to the public. The challenges of an increasingly complicated, resource-strapped, and dynamic world make it essential to work with the best and most skilled collaborators, and we find that with our colleagues at Aperture. Their continued dedication to producing beautiful, compelling, and accessible publications, with an eye to inclusion and amplifying underrepresented voices, made for a perfect fit for this project. We are proud to have teamed up with them.

I want to extend additional thanks to George Luna-Peña, who researched, wrote, and beautifully illustrated the chronology that graces this volume. This kind of resource, which allows us to better understand the elements and progression of Bernal's life, is invaluable to students, scholars, and members of the broader community. Gratitude also goes to the Center's chief curator, Rebecca Senf, whose essay on the relationship of Bernal's artworks to vernacular photography opens a way to think about his unique style and photographic goals within a larger photographic history. Finally, I want to acknowledge the CCP staff, especially CCP's director, Todd J. Tubutis, and say that without your deep investment, continued efforts, and top-notch professionalism, projects of this quality would just not be possible.

Louis Carlos Bernal es una celebridad fotográfica de Arizona. Conocido como el padre de la fotografía artística chicana, su importancia va más allá de las fotografías distintivas e innovadoras que realizó. A lo largo de sus demasiado breves cinco décadas tuvo un enorme impacto en la red de fotógrafos que fueron sus colegas, compañeros, alumnos y discípulos. La mención de su nombre —aún treinta años después de su fallecimiento— me trae gratos recuerdos. Muchísimas personas conocieron y apreciaron su calidez, su compañerismo y su pasión por la fotografía.

The Center for Creative Photography (El Centro para la Fotografía Creativa, o CCP) de la Universidad de Arizona en Tucson está perfectamente situado para producir una excelente investigación que ha dado lugar a una exposición itinerante y a esta publicación. En 2014, las hijas de Louis Carlos Bernal, Lisa Bernal Brethour y Katrina Bernal, donaron al CCP su archivo, compuesto principalmente por impresiones fotográficas, hojas de contacto, negativos y transparencias, con algunos materiales biográficos relacionados. Ello se aunó a las 110 impresiones fotográficas de Bernal que ya formaban parte de la colección del Centro a través de una combinación de compras y donaciones. El hecho de que el archivo no haya llegado inmediatamente al Centro tras el fallecimiento de Bernal en 1993 sugiere la precariedad de tantos archivos de artistas y fotógrafos que han quedado en el olvido dentro de los cánones de la historia del arte. Afortunadamente, el CCP alberga ahora este archivo tan importante de Bernal; este proyecto es, pues, la culminación del gran esfuerzo de la familia Bernal junto con la fotógrafa y directora del programa de Fotografía de Pima Community College, Ann Simmons-Myers, para garantizar que estos materiales de investigación se conserven y sean accesibles. Extendemos nuestra profunda gratitud a Lisa Bernal Brethour, Katrina Bernal y Ann Simmons-Myers por su paciencia, generosidad y confianza.

El éxito de este proyecto depende de otros tres componentes fundamentales. El primero es el gran apoyo financiero del Henry Luce Foundation. The Center for Creative Photography está profundamente agradecido por la subvención económica que permite contar con los elementos necesarios para realizar nuestro trabajo: una curadora invitada, un consejo asesor comunitario, apoyo a la investigación, materiales y producción de exposiciones, la subvención para la publicación, las tarifas de derechos y licencias, y los servicios de digitalización. Este respaldo ha permitido al personal experto del Centro apoyar la creación de este estudio monográfico sobre Louis Carlos Bernal, que sin duda será el primero de muchos estudios académicos importantes acerca de su gran obra.

El segundo reconocimiento es para nuestra curadora invitada Elizabeth Ferrer. Nos sentimos increíblemente afortunados de trabajar con una académica de tal profundidad y experiencia y, además, de que no solo haya sido capaz de asumir este proyecto en este momento, sino que también haya sido interesada en centrar su atención investigadora en la vida y obra de Louis Carlos Bernal. Fue como si los astros se alinearan —algo que Ferrer señala que ocurrió más de una vez durante este proceso—, lo que quizá indica que el universo está allanando el camino para el éxito del proyecto. La amplia investigación de Ferrer se basa en el archivo del CCP, pero también la ha llevado a seguir varias pistas y a entrevistar a muchas de las personas que conocieron, trabajaron o estudiaron con Bernal. Ha descubierto material a través de sus amigos, quienes guardaron todas sus cartas, recortes y anuncios durante más de treinta años, algo que demuestra lo querido que es. Su ensayo reflexivo y minucioso, su selección de imágenes y la comprensión del contexto de Bernal, construida gracias a toda una vida de erudición, hacen de esta obra una contribución fundamental a la fotografía y el arte norteamericano.

Nuestra colaboración con Aperture también merece una mención especial. Aperture es un pilar de la edición fotográfica y estamos encantados de trabajar con su equipo para hacer llegar al público este libro crítico. Los retos de un mundo cada vez más complicado, dinámico y con menos recursos hacen que sea esencial trabajar con los mejores y más capacitados colaboradores, algo que distingue a nuestros colegas de Aperture. Su dedicación constante a la producción de publicaciones hermosas, cautivadoras y accesibles, que tomen en cuenta la inclusión y la amplificación de las voces marginalizadas, resonó perfectamente con este proyecto. Estamos orgullosos de nuestra colaboración.

También quisiera extender mi agradecimiento a George Luna-Peña, que investigó, escribió e ilustró preciosamente la cronología que adorna este volumen. Este tipo de recurso, que nos permite conseguir una comprensión mayor de los elementos y la evolución de la vida de Bernal, tiene un valor incalculable para estudiantes, académicos y miembros de la comunidad en general. También queremos agradecer a la curadora del CCP, Rebecca Senf, cuyo ensayo sobre la vinculación de las obras de Bernal con la fotografía vernácula abre un camino para pensar en su estilo único y sus objetivos fotográficos en un espectro histórico y fotográfico más amplio. Por último, quiero agregar mi propio reconocimiento al personal del CCP en especial a su director, Todd J. Tubutis, así como mencionar que sin su profunda participación, sus esfuerzos continuos y su profesionalismo de primer orden, proyectos de esta calidad simplemente no serían posibles.

PLATES / LÁMINAS

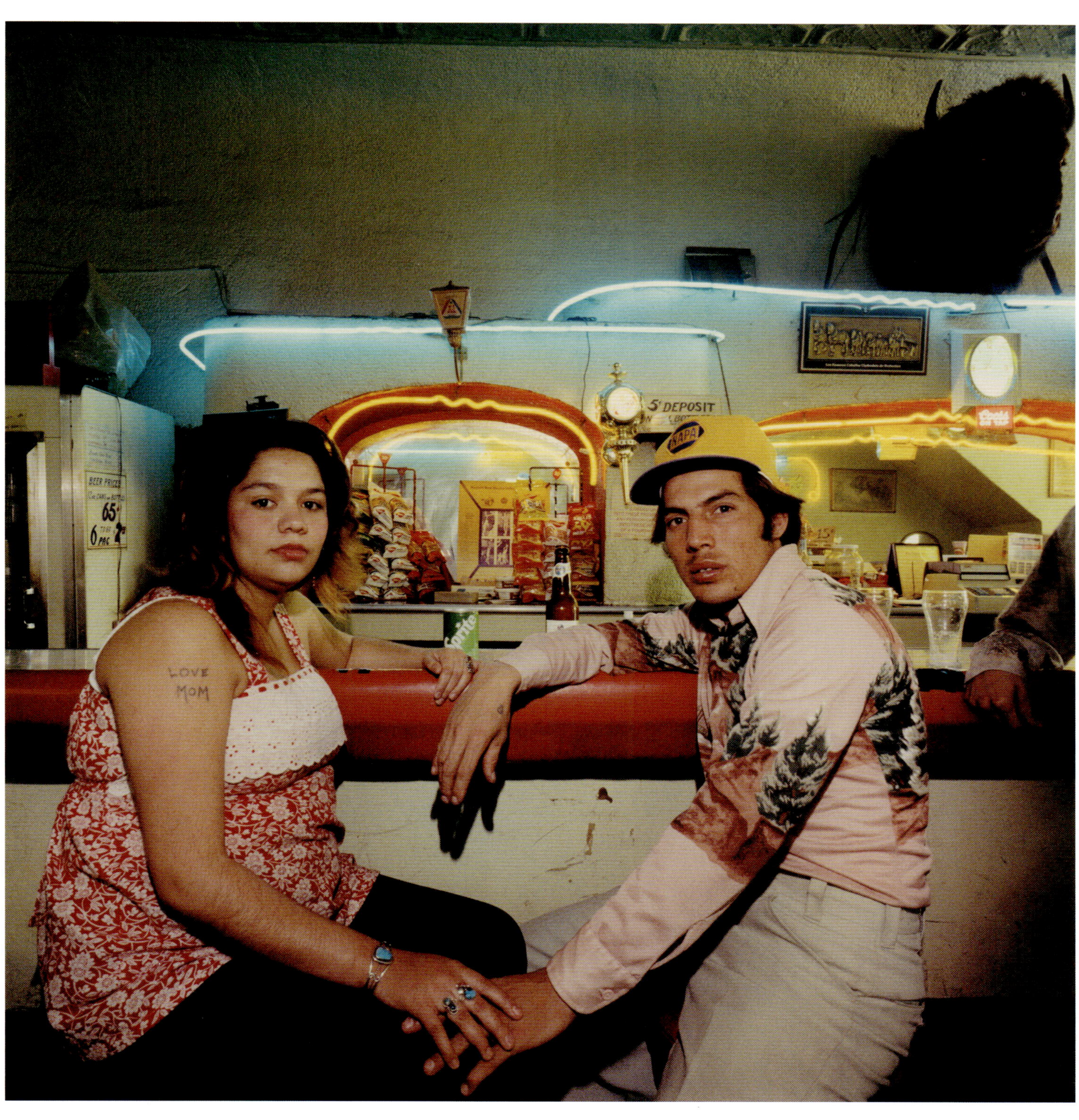

11   *Albert y Lynn Morales, Silver City, New Mexico,* 1978

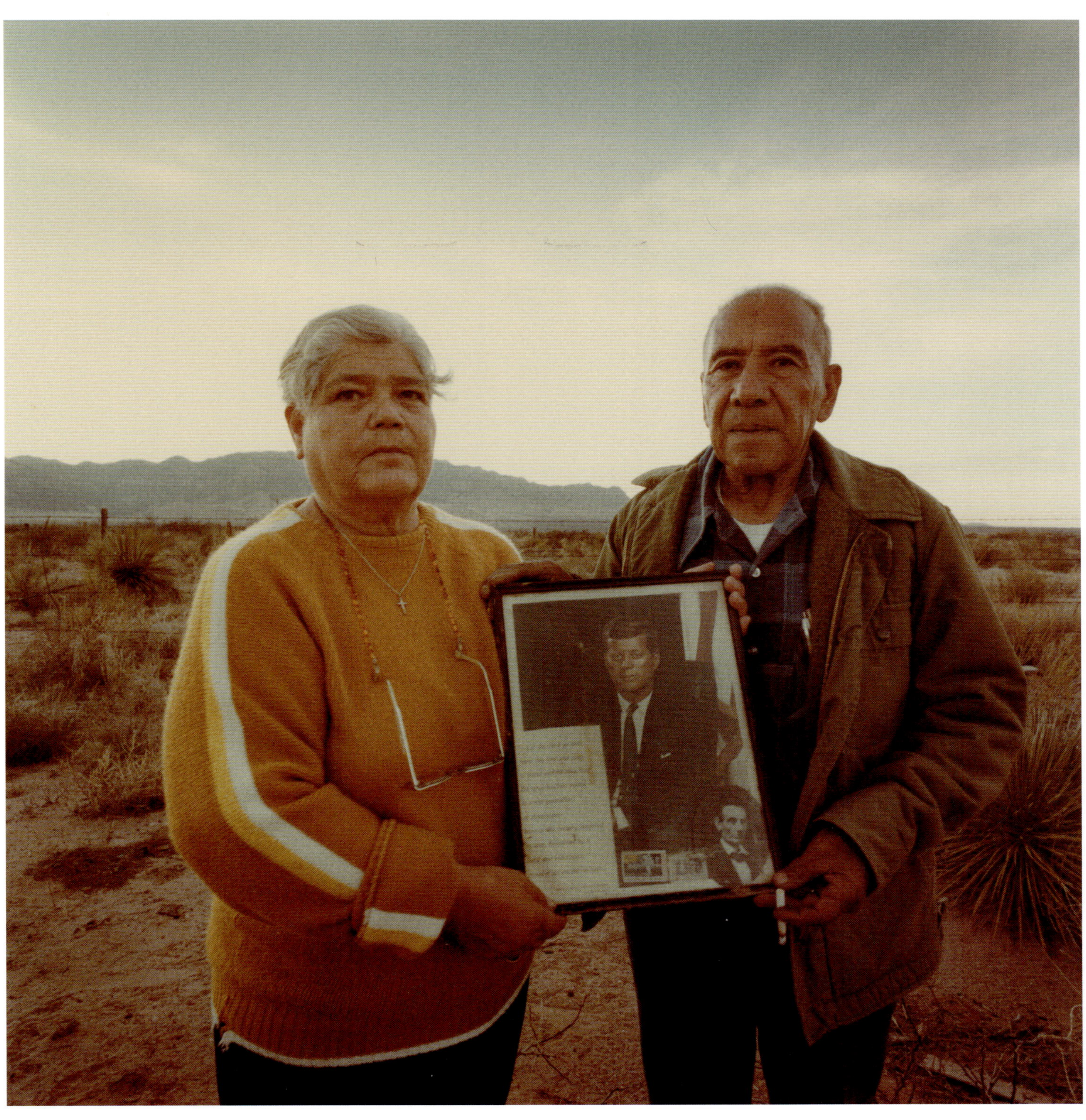

13   *Untitled*, 1978

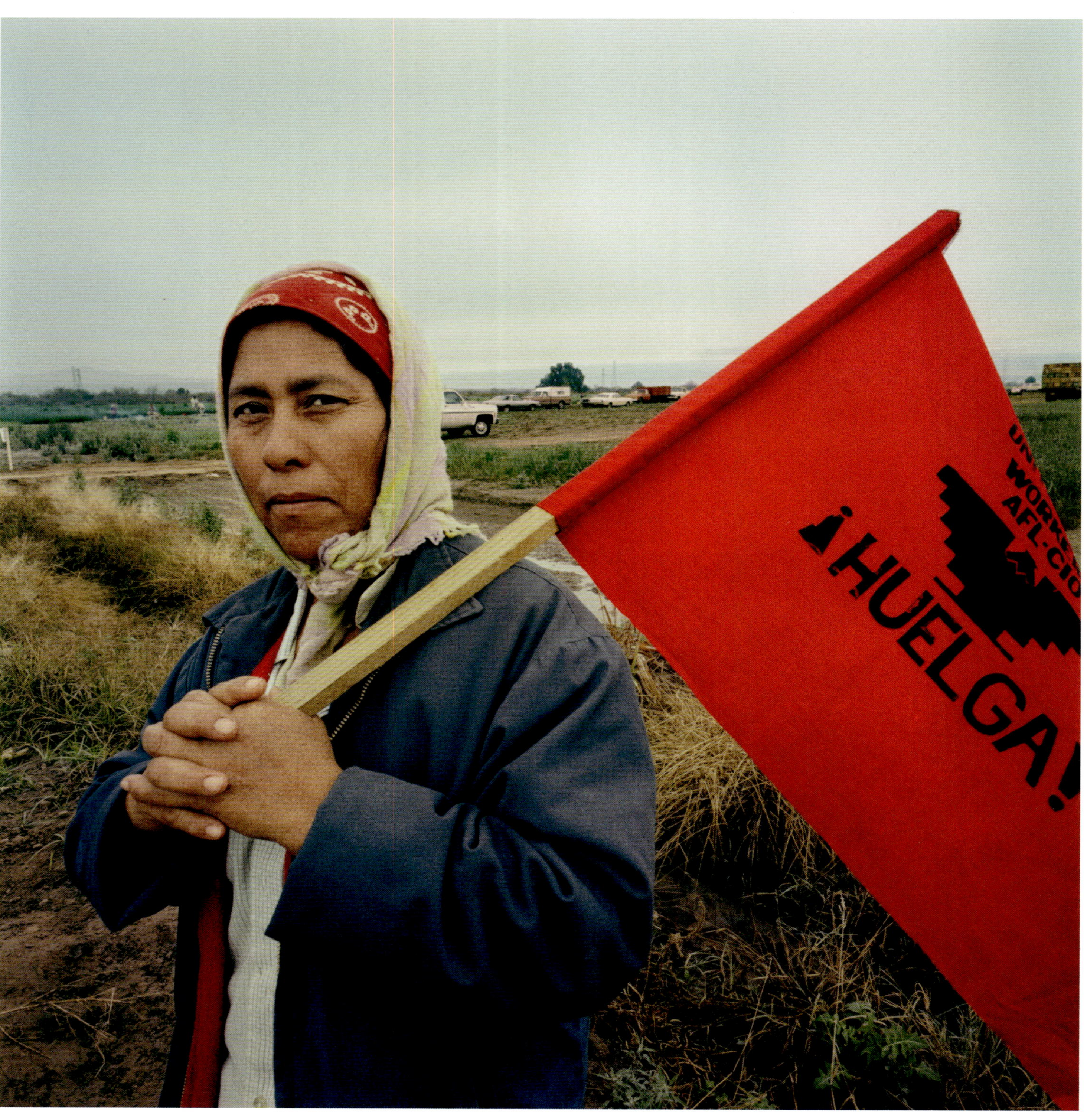

14   *Untitled (female striker)*, late 1970s

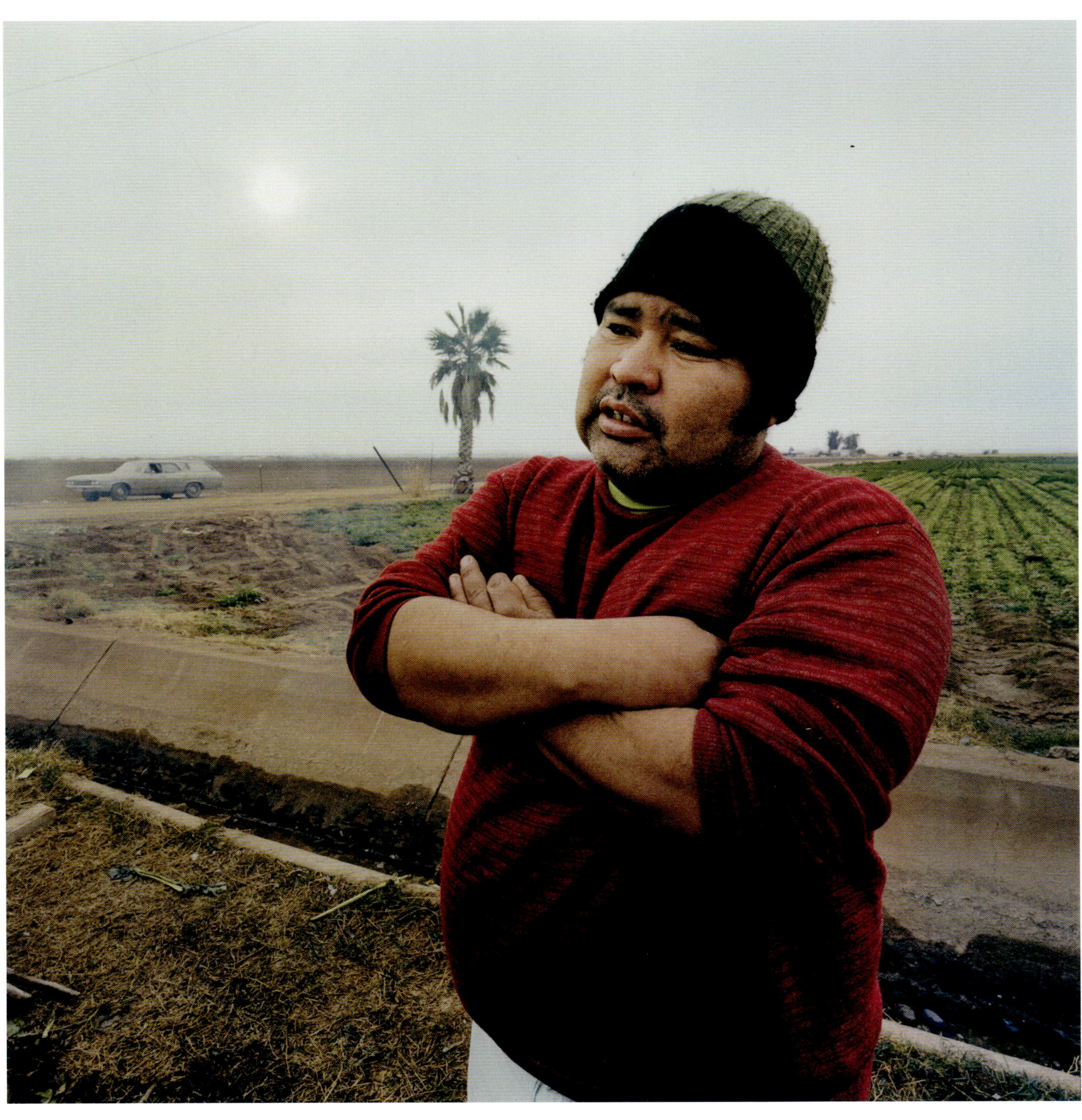

15   *Untitled (farmworker),* late 1970s

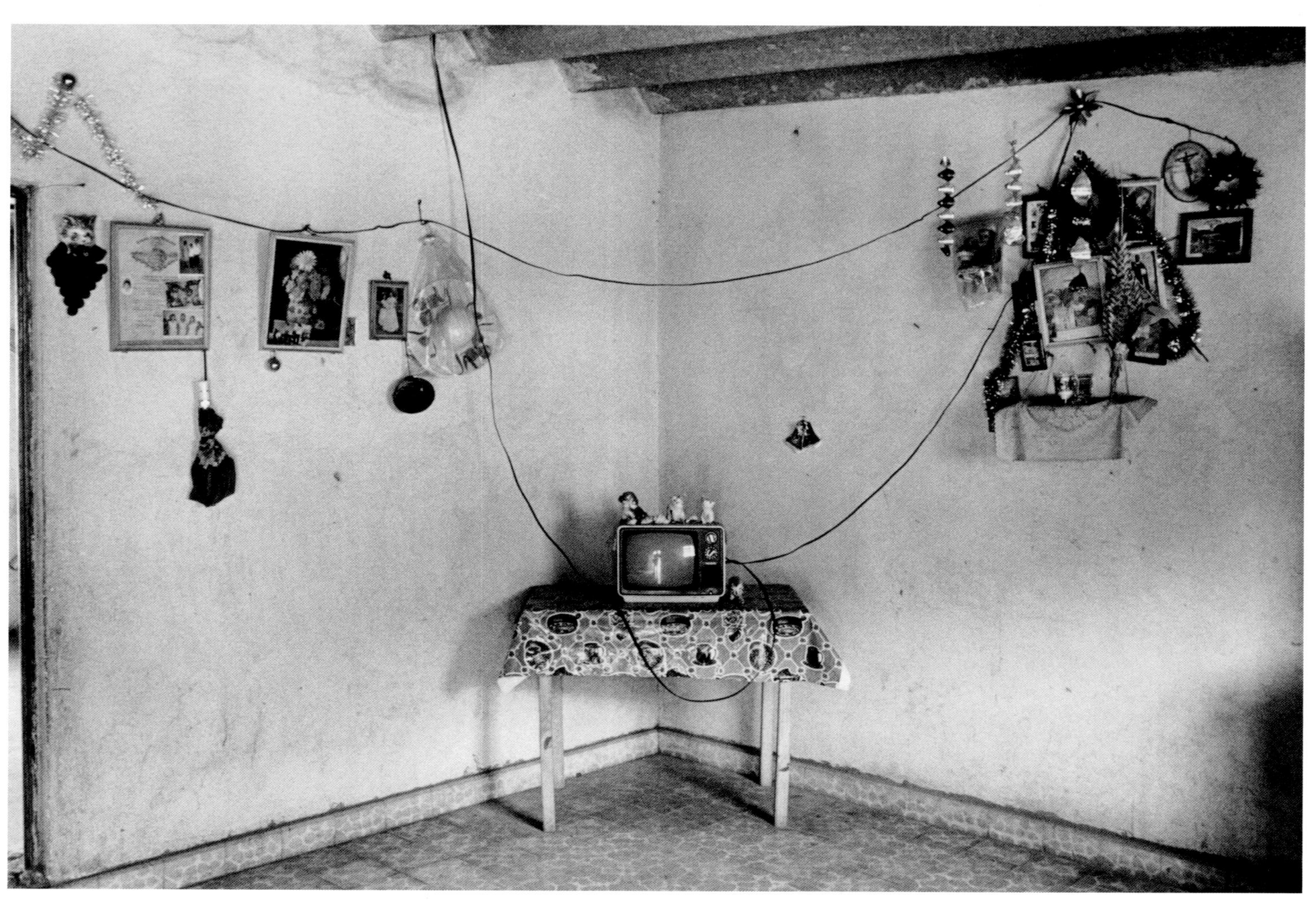

16   *Santos y Television, Mexico*, 1981

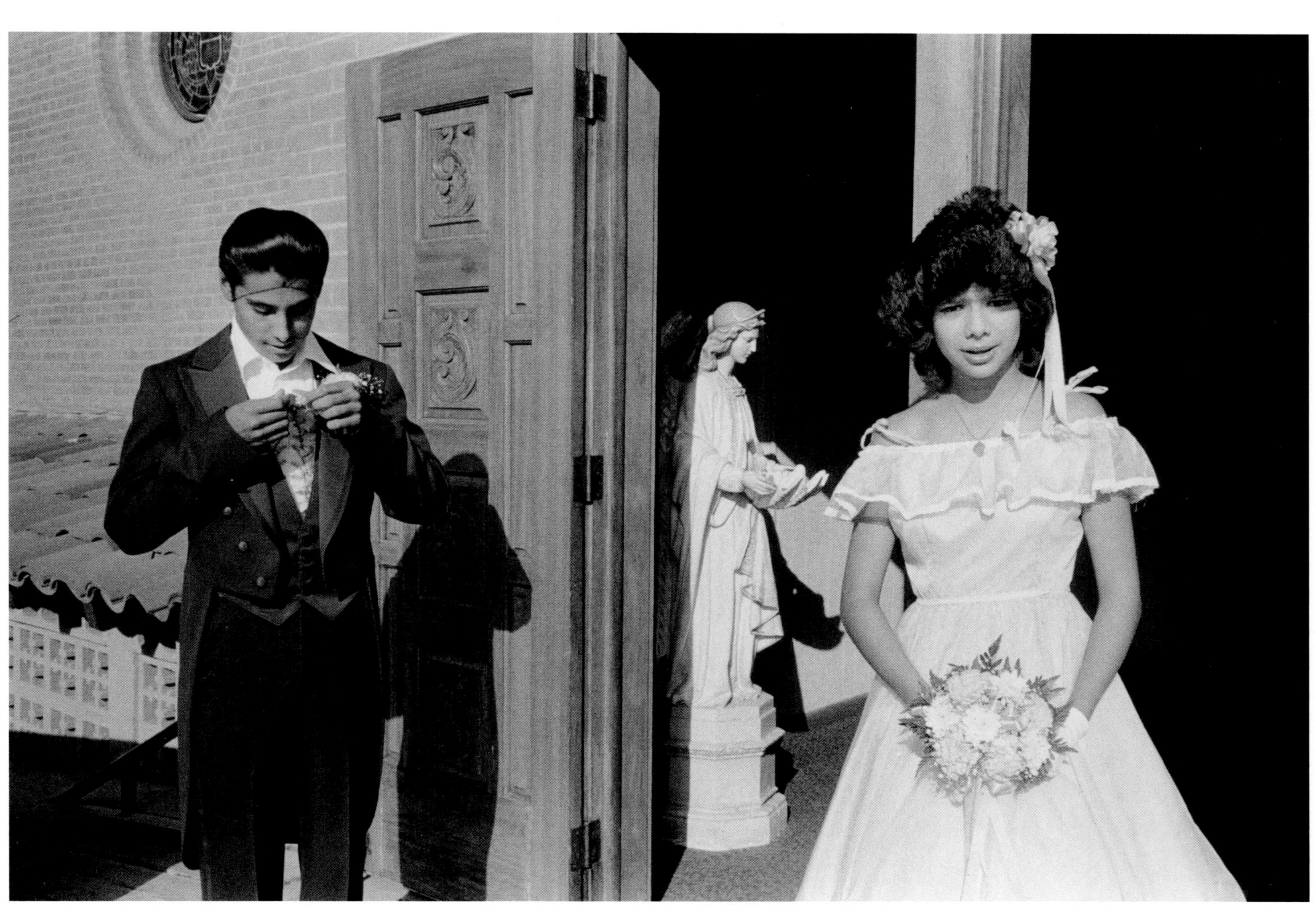

17   *Quinceañera, Phoenix, Arizona,* 1981

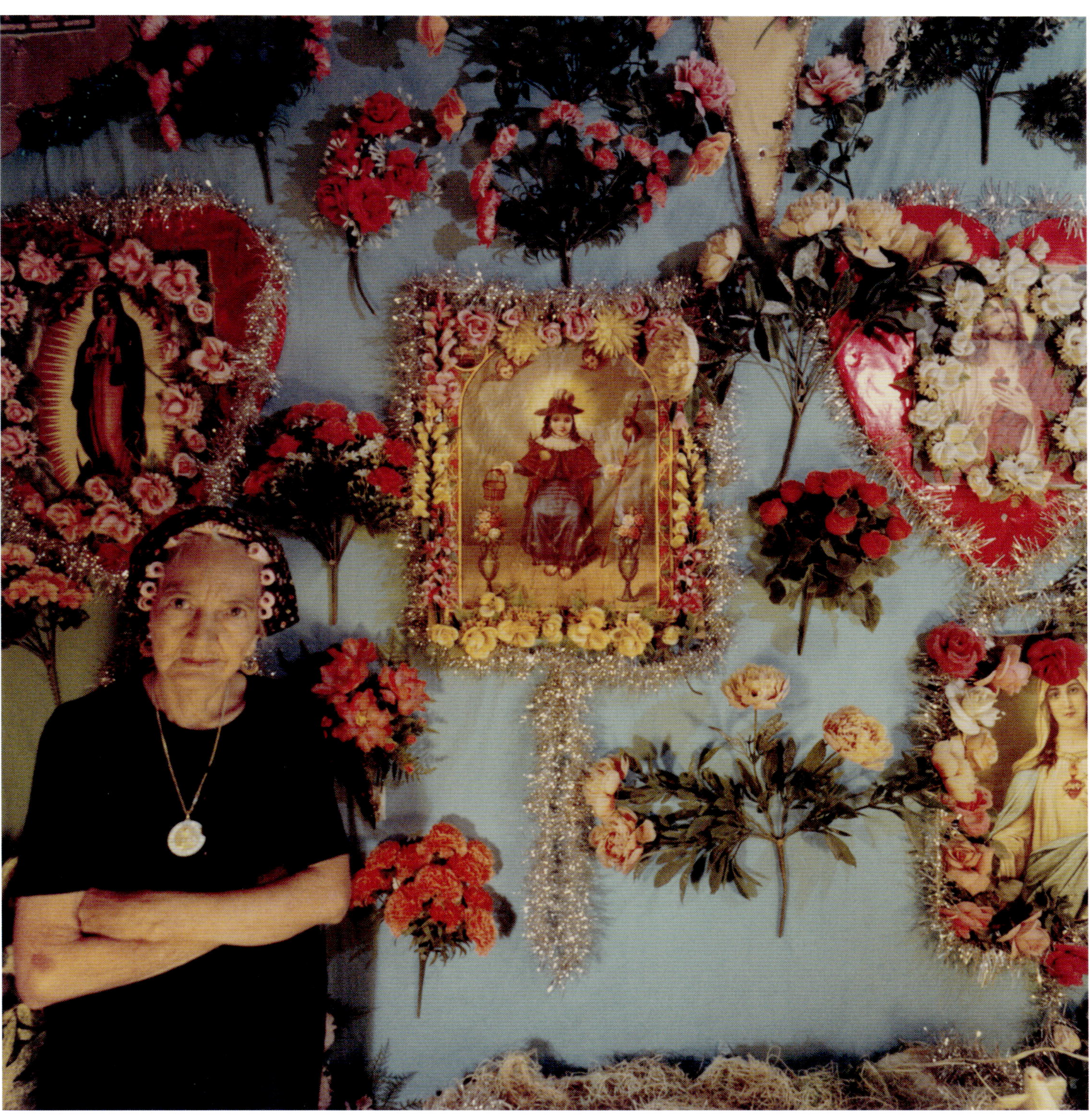

19   *Juanita Serrano with Santo Niño de Atocha,* 1978

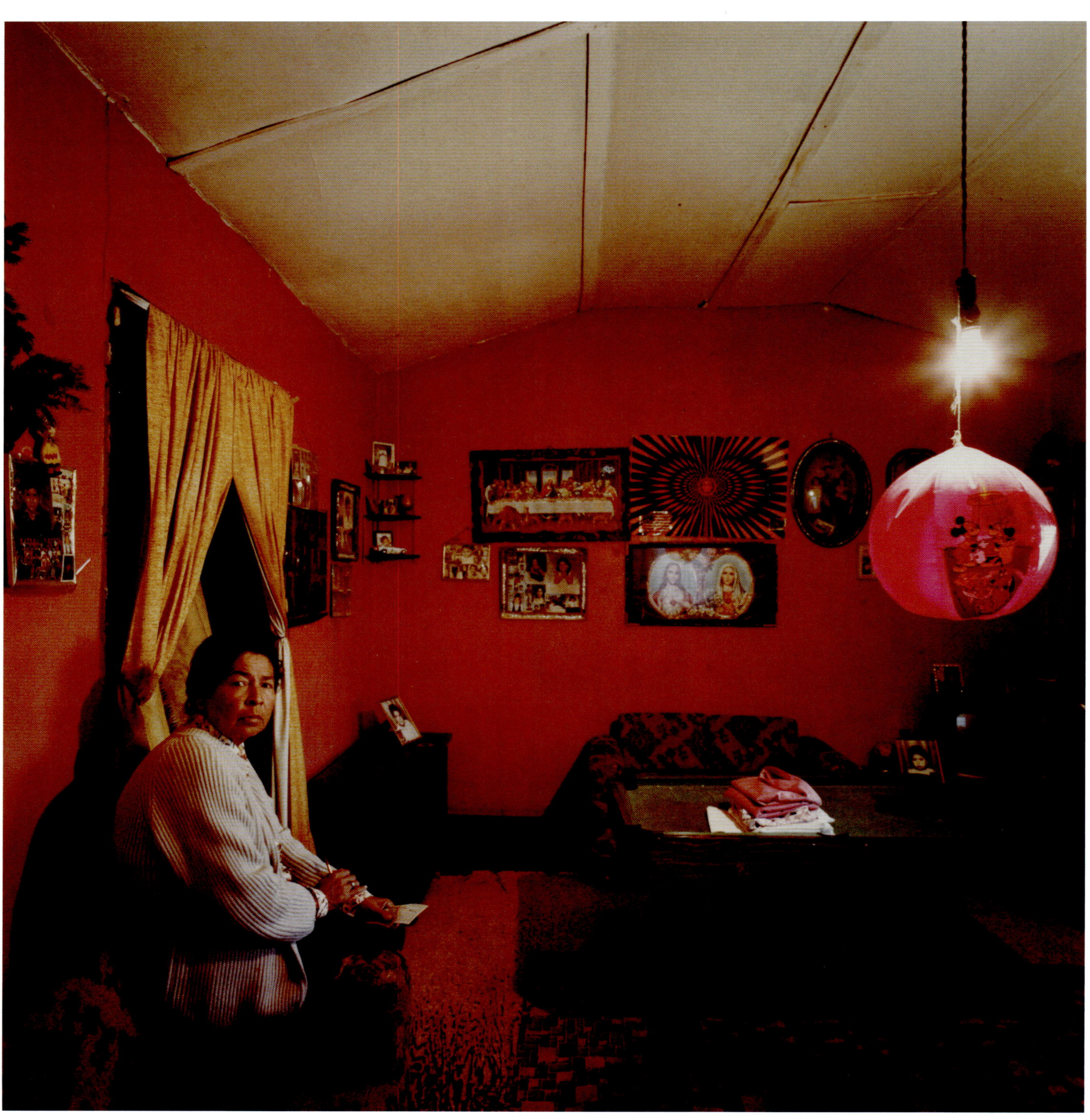

20   *Nanita Mendibles, Barrio Anita*, 1978

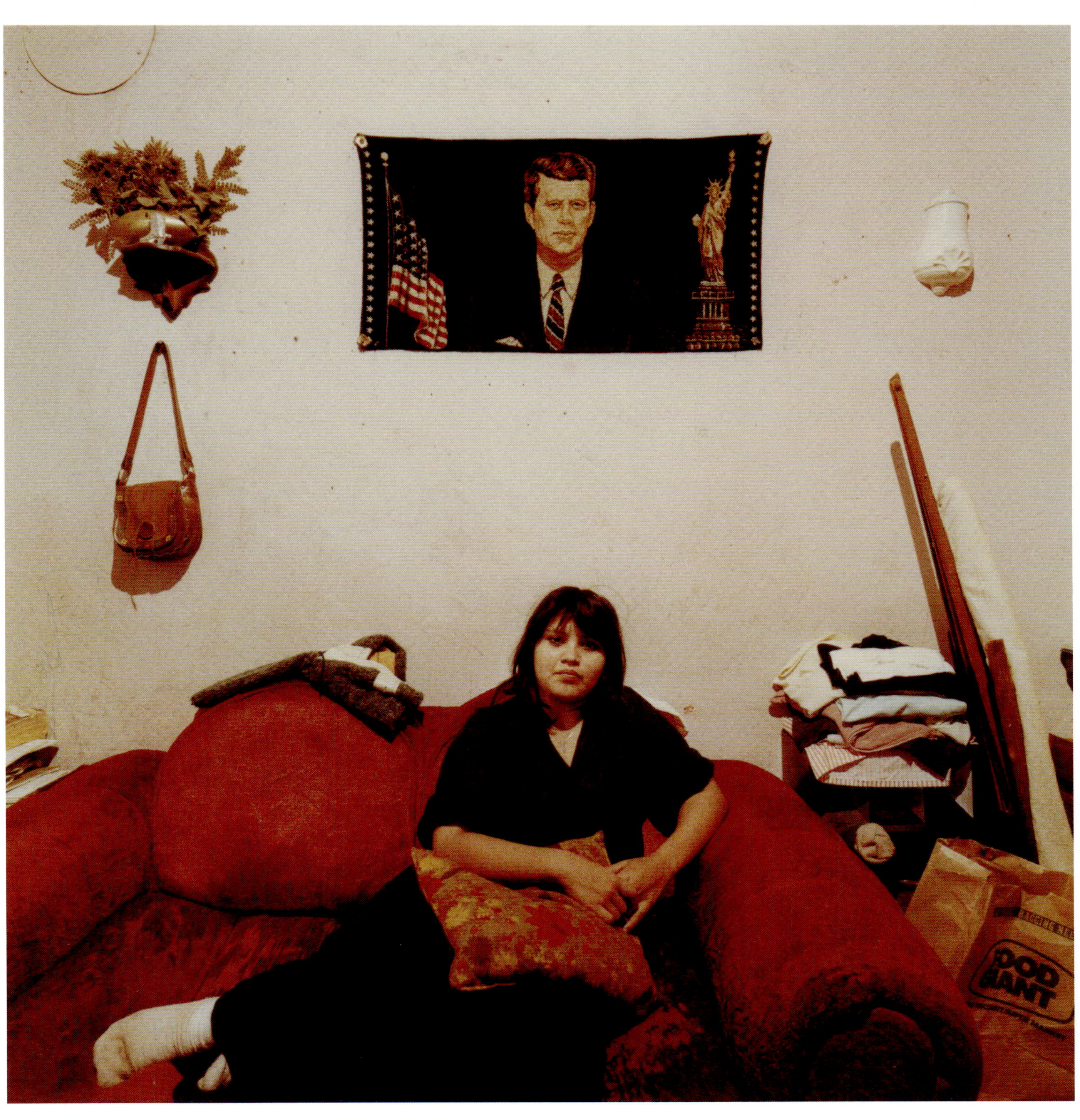

    Rosie Siqueiros, Barrio Anita, Tucson, Arizona, 1978

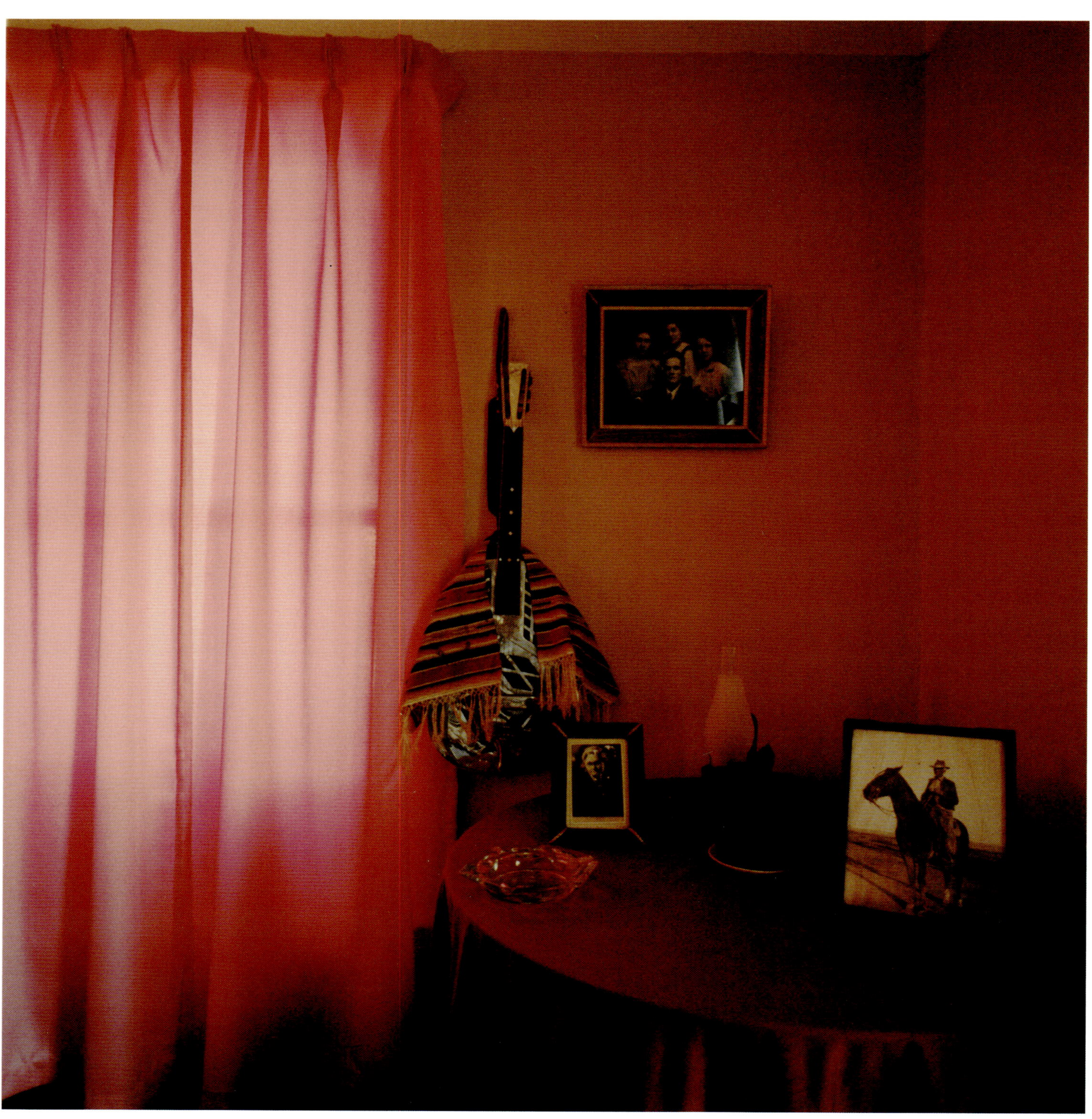

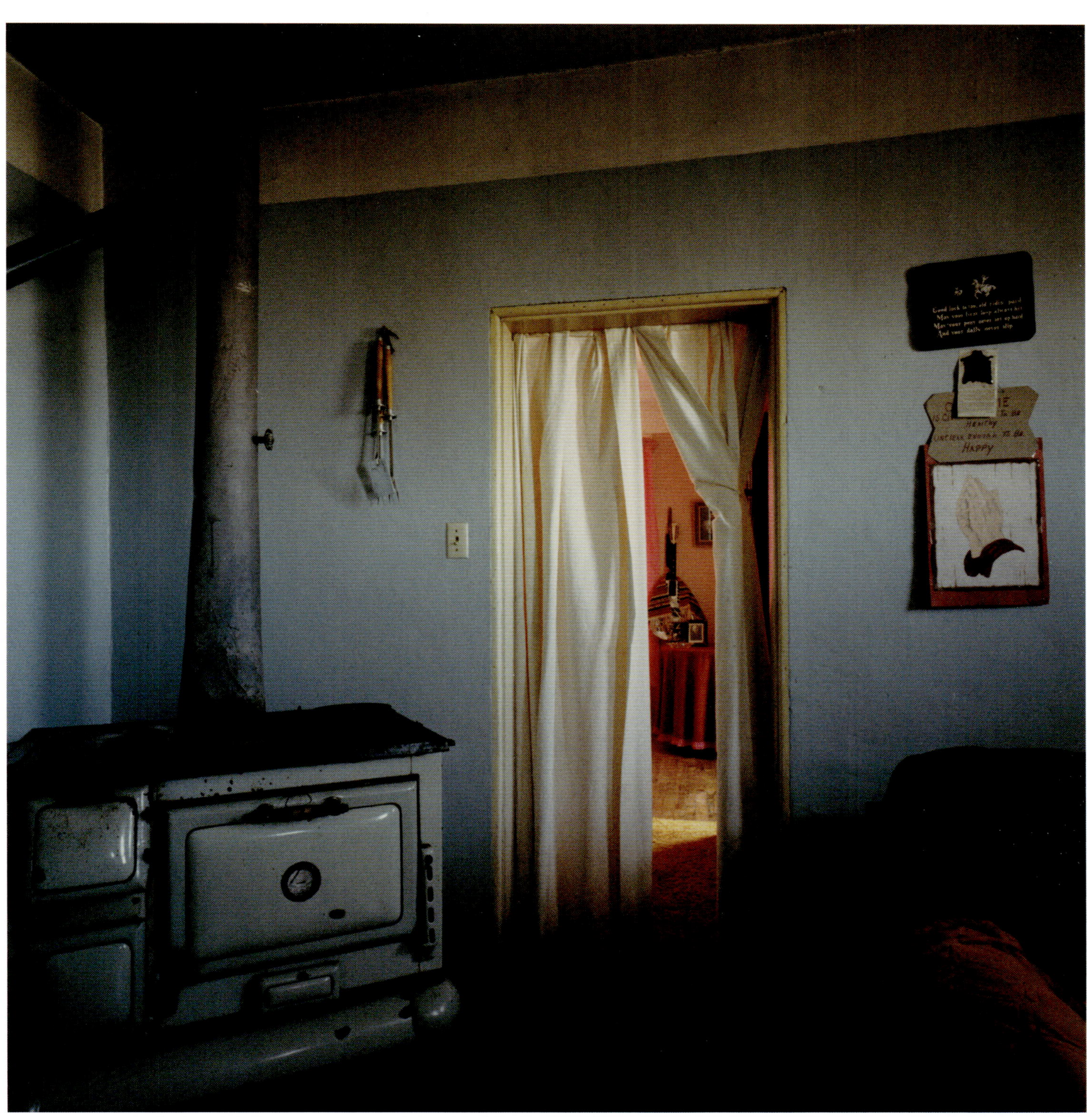

    San Pedro Ranch, Animas, New Mexico, 1978

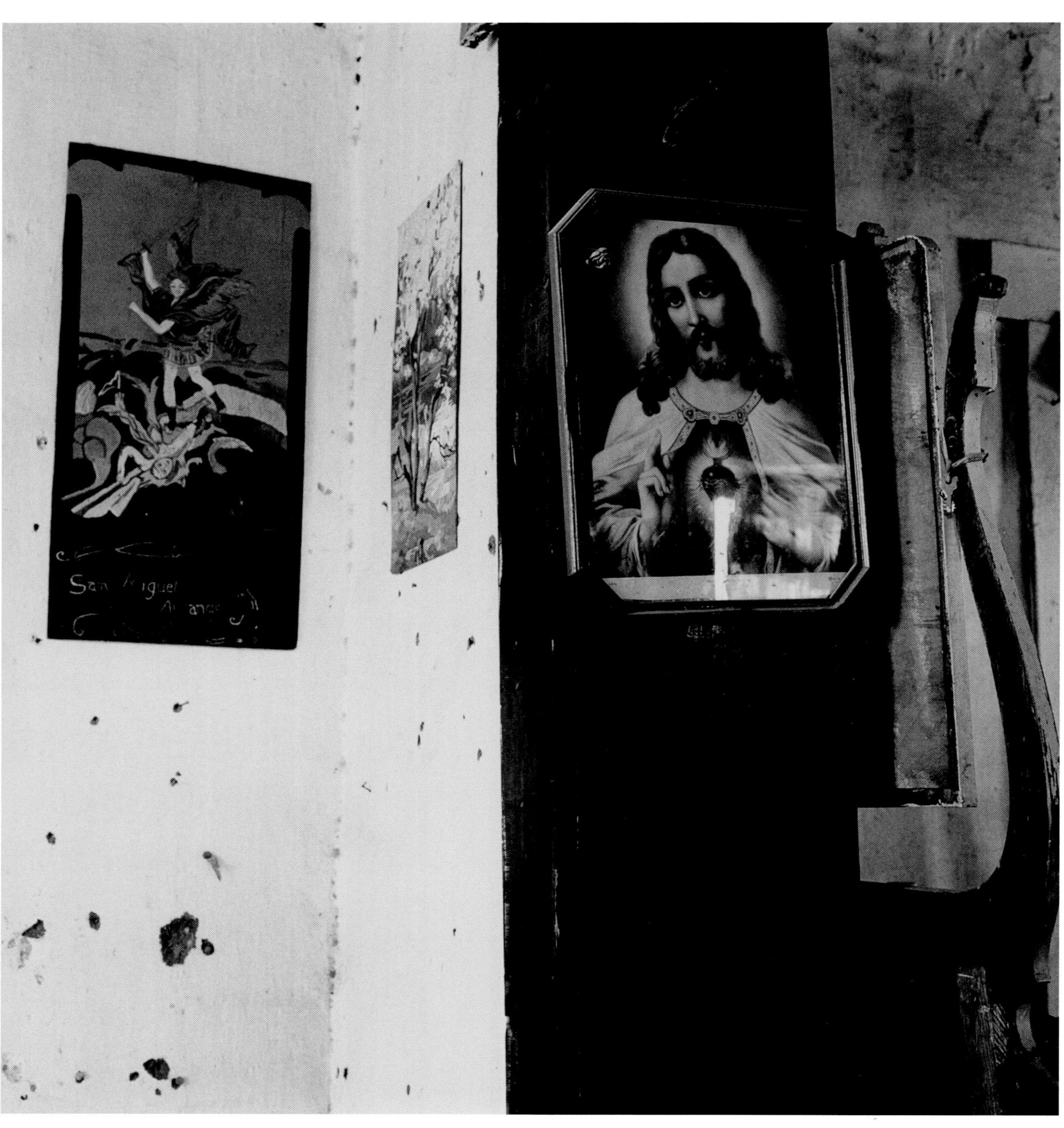

24   *Corazón de Jesús*, 1977; from the series *Benitez Suite*

LOUIS CARLOS BERNAL: LIFE AND WORK

Elizabeth Ferrer

Dedicated to the memory of Gilbert C. Ferrer

Louis Carlos Bernal was born in 1941 in Douglas, Arizona, a small border town in a region known for cattle ranching and copper min ng. His modest upbringing as the Mexican American son of a maid and a boilermaker played a decisive role in his formation as a Chicano and as a photographer. The family moved to Phoenix

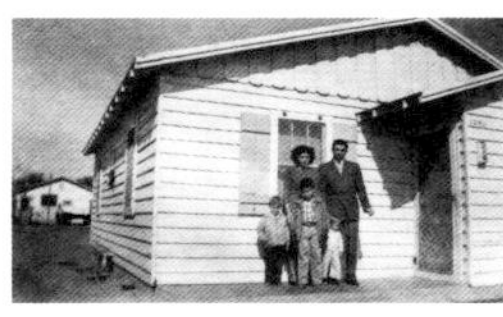

when he was six, where the children (Louis was the oldest of three sons) would receive a better education (fig. 1, page 47). When he was eleven, Bernal received a camera as a gift from an aunt, and he soon became infatuated with cameras and the chemical process of producing an image, even turning a home bathroom into an improvised dark-

1

room. But he did not initially envision this as a professional pursuit; in any case, a creative path would have been deemed impractical for the son of an upwardly mobile Mexican American family in the 1950s and '60s.

In Phoenix, Bernal experienced the overt racism that was common in the years prior to the passage of the Civil Rights Acts of the 1960s. The city had a large white majority, segregated schools, and ne ghborhoods known as "sundown towns," where people of color could work but not live. Bernal himself recalled seeing restaurants with separate entrances for whites and "Mexicans" (once meant as a disparaging epithet, even if one was born in the US), and, as a high-school athlete, being restricted from hotels where fellow team members stayed.[1] In defiance of the limited expectations of Mexican Americans imposed by society, he aimed for college, initially planning to study Spanish with the goal of teaching. But Bernal continued to pursue photography, covering athletic events for his high-school and college newspapers. In fact, the camera became such a ubiquitous accessory in his life that he became known as "Shutterbug Louie."[2] By the mid-1960s, when Bernal was completing his undergraduate studies at Arizona State University (ASU) in Tempe, he resolved to study photography seriously and become an artist.

In 1966, Bernal received his undergraduate degree, was drafted into the army, and married Sandra Jean Anderson, an artist who had previously modeled for him. The conflict in Vietnam was escalating, but he avoided deployment to Southeast Asia when he received a posting to Berlin, where he was assigned work as a photographer. His closest college friend, Tom Eckert, calls Bernal's military service a kind of pause; he rarely spoke about it, but in a journal entry written during that period, Bernal expressed frustration at needing more time and freedom to create photographs and to work toward fulfillment as an artist.[3] He returned to Phoenix two years later "fired up" and ready to pursue his passion.[4]

Bernal entered graduate school at ASU in 1968 and spent a formative period between 1970 and 1972 under the tutelage of the renowned but reclusive photographer Frederick Sommer (1905–1999), who was based in Prescott, Arizona. In 1972 Bernal received his MFA in photography and moved with his family to Tucson after Pima Community College hired him to launch its photography department. Although he traveled widely throughout the Southwest and Mexico, Tucson remained his home until his death in 1993. He recounted the move to Tucson in a 1984 interview:

> During the physical move I also began a spiritual move back to the barrio and a new attitude toward life—Chicanismo. Mexican-American is the term used

Editors' note:
This publication uses both the inclusive, gender-neutral terms Latinx and Chicanx in the English texts, as well as Chicano, the latter reflecting the era of the Chicano civil rights movement and Louis Carlos Bernal's own use of the term.

1. Katrina and Lisa Bernal, phone interview with the author, August 26, 2021.

2. Marietta Bernstorff, interview with the author, December 29, 2021.

3. Louis Carlos Bernal, journal entry, May 27, 1968. I am grateful to Marietta Bernstorff for sharing this information.

4. Tom Eckert, interview with the author, January 14, 2022.

to describe a person who is of American birth but whose cultural soul derives from Mexico. This dual reality has been a burden which has clouded our identity. Chicanismo allows us to accept our history but also gives us a new reality to deal with the present and the future. To be a Chicano means to be involved in controlling your life. Chicanismo represents a new sense of pride, a new attitude and a new awareness . . . The Chicano artist cannot isolate himself from the community but finds himself in the midst of his people creating art of and for the people. My images speak of the religious and family ties that I have expressed as a Chicano. I have concerned myself with the mysticism of the Southwest and the strength of the spiritual and cultural values of the barrios.[5]

Bernal came of age as a photographer in the early 1970s, amid the Chicano civil rights movement. This broad-based social justice struggle was rooted in the labor-organizing efforts that César Chávez and Dolores Huerta had led in California's central agricultural valley in the 1960s to support farmworkers who toiled under harsh conditions for minimal pay. The movement galvanized a young generation of Mexican Americans, many of whom traveled to Delano,

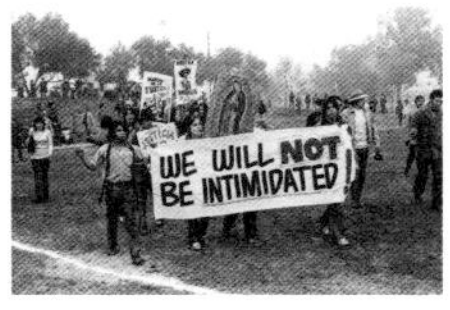

2

Salinas, and Sacramento, to join protest marches, coordinate drives to deliver food and clothing to farmworkers, organize boycotts, and document the movement. Members of this generation began referring to themselves as Chicanos, reclaiming and redefining what was once an ethnic slur as an empowering term grounded in solidarity and self-determination. *El movimiento*, as it was known, expanded to confront numerous social justice issues: the Vietnam War, which was being fought by a disproportionate number of Brown and Black men; the poor quality of public-school education in Mexican American neighborhoods; the lack of economic opportunity; and myriad other manifestations of racism (fig. 2, page 47).

The articulation of cultural and spiritual values that reflected pride in one's race and heritage—Chicanismo—was central to the movement. An iconography centering on pre-Columbian deities and culture; the Virgin of Guadalupe (Mexico's patron saint) and the Sacred Heart of Jesus (an emblem of love and compassion); and popular heroes of the Mexican Revolution served to link Chicanxs to histories and values apart from and well beyond the Eurocentric construct of American exceptionalism. Moreover, new articulations around the concept of Aztlán, the ancestral home of the Aztecs in the American Southwest, became a rallying cry for Chicanxs claiming sovereignty over the colonized lands of the region.[6] Although it does not appear that Bernal ever spoke of Aztlán, the arc of his life and travels as a photographer, beginning in the border town of Douglas and extending to states throughout the Southwest and to Mexico, evokes a similar quest: a search for ancestral roots, for a sovereign homeland, and for a coalescence of personal and creative fulfillment.

Bernal began to express his awakening Chicano identity as a student, at the same time he was grappling with the development of his artistic voice. The two threads were becoming intertwined. As he wrote, "I have felt a great deal of anger and anxiety in my life and I have used photography as an outlet for these frustrations. My images have always dealt with the inner battle of my soul."[7] And although his formative years as an artist coincided with the years of the Chicano civil rights movement, he more directly expressed his sense of Chicanismo in spiritual and cultural, rather than political, terms. It appears that he did not participate in the student-activist-led demonstrations that took place in Tucson in the

5. Louis Carlos Bernal, in *Awards in the Visual Arts 3* (Winston-Salem, NC: Southeastern Center for Contemporary Art, 1984), p. 16.

6. See Shifra M. Goldman, "The Iconography of Chicano Self-Determination: Race, Ethnicity, and Class," special issue, *Art Journal: Depictions of the Dispossessed* 49, no. 2 (Summer 1990): pp. 167–73; and Rodolfo Gonzales and Alurista [pseud.], "El plan espiritual de Aztlán," *El Grito del Norte* 2, no. 9 (July 6, 1969): p. 5. Chicano poet Alurista (Alberto Baltazar Urista Heredia) read "El plan espiritual de Aztlán," a manifesto announcing these concepts, at the National Chicano Youth Liberation Conference held in Denver in 1969.

7. Timothy Troy, "Louis Carlos Bernal," in *Original Sources. Art and Archives at the Center for Creative Photography*, eds. Amy Rule and Nancy Solomon (Tucson: Center for Creative Photography, University of Arizona, 2002), pp. 53–55.

late 1960s, and he took on explicitly political themes in his work only occasionally, and primarily early in his career. Nevertheless, Bernal was an early beneficiary of the broader civil rights movement and the new opportunities it afforded, especially to students. He was among the first wave of Mexican Americans to enter graduate programs at ASU in the late 1960s, and the racist attitudes he experienced as a child had dissipated to the extent that he was enthusiastically hired to teach at Pima Community College in 1972.

As Bernal pondered his *artistic* identity in the early 1970s, he became intrigued by the new approaches to the medium that had come to the fore in recent years, including abstract and conceptual modes that challenged the purist dicta of preceding generations devoted to so-called straight photography. Some photographers were staging compositions and devising nontraditional darkroom processes; others were creating photomontages, often appropriating images from mass media or combining words and pictures to produce loaded political statements. Even the documentary tradition was undergoing a sea change. Photographers like Lee Friedlander, Diane Arbus, and Garry Winogrand were ushering in a personally inflected form of social documentation, with images that could seem at times snapshot-like or incidental while often functioning as trenchant social commentaries.[8]

Bernal's early work reflects his enthusiasm for nonconventional modes of photography. At Phoenix College he studied with Allen A. Dutton (1922–2017), known for surrealist landscapes and desert nudes, and, at ASU, with Jack Stuler (1932–2015), who created surreal abstractions out of natural forms and collaged imagery.[9] Both likely inspired Bernal to approach his medium as an art form and with a sense of freedom. In 1970, he sought out the internationally known photographer Frederick Sommer, with whom he worked for two years. Born in Italy and raised in Brazil, Sommer was a maverick known for distinct bodies of work: intensely detailed desert landscapes with no visible horizon, nudes, macabre and surreal still lifes, and collages often built from found images. Sommer's example encouraged Bernal to broadly consider the possibilities of the medium, even if his resulting work was at times overly indebted to the older artist.

For one series of constructed images, Bernal made eerie arrangements and constructions out of old doll parts, some seeming to emerge from the brittle pages of ancient newsprint, and others cut open to display their mechanical insides. These images, as well as others that employ vintage toys, are reminiscent of photographs Sommer made decades earlier of dolls scavenged from local dumps.

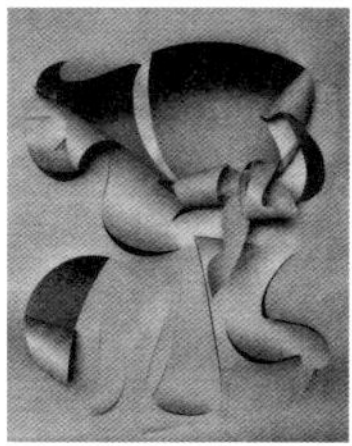

3

This approach to picture-making was a temporary source of fascination to Bernal, but it did play into a genuine personal interest: throughout his life he collected small toys and objects that he assembled into still lifes for the occasional photograph. Sommer's influence is also clearly seen in Bernal's black-and-white abstract photographs of cut butcher paper arranged into elaborate curvilinear forms (fig. 3, page 47). Sommer had developed this technique in the 1960s and realized numerous compositions in this style, which ingeniously combined elements of drawing, sculpture, and photography. Bernal also used these lengths of paper as an extravagant, if provocative, costume for female nudes whom he photographed in a studio in this period.

Ultimately, it was Sommer himself, not his work, that had a more enduring effect on the young Bernal. In a journal entry, Bernal wrote admiringly about Sommer's intellect, his knowledge of the history of photography, and his mastery

8. See Rebecca Senf's essay in this publication for a discussion on the relationship of Bernal's work to the snapshot aesthetic associated with these photographers.

9. I am grateful to photographer Robert Buitrón for pointing out to me the significance of Dutton to Bernal's early career, and to artist Tom Eckert, for information on Jack Stuler.

of cameras and technique. Reflecting on the example that Sommer set, as an artist who brought the full weight of his being and intellect to the creation of work, he recalled: "Somehow I felt upon meeting him that I've been moving toward this encounter for a long time."[10]

In the early 1970s Bernal realized several small bodies of politically oriented work. What bound them was his interest in television and the mass media's role in 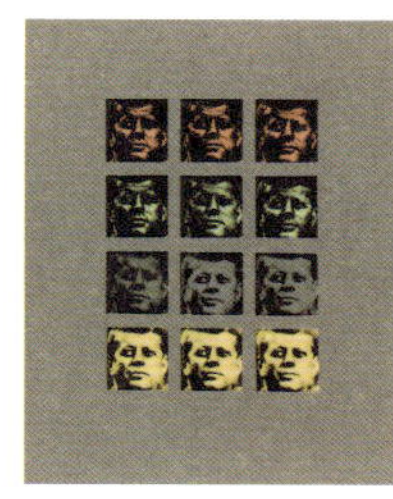 promulgating mainstream American values, even in a period of political dissent and growing cultural diversity. These works also suggest his new artistic influences, including Robert Heinecken (1931–2006), the Los Angeles–based conceptualist who specialized in appropriating and reassembling images from the media. One small series features the repeated, high-contrast portrait of President John F. Kennedy as photographed from a television screen—another Heinecken technique (fig. 4, page 48). Here, Bernal also nods to Andy Warhol (1928–1987), who had become renowned in the previous decade for silkscreen prints depicting serial repetitions of iconic imagery and his own attraction to the Kennedys.[11] In another small group of works, Bernal collaged his own photographs of TV screens over images he found in magazines. In one example, a screen showing the somber faces of women of color in mourning during the televised funeral of Robert F. Kennedy is laid over a larger scene of two white children in a pastoral landscape (fig. 5, page 48).

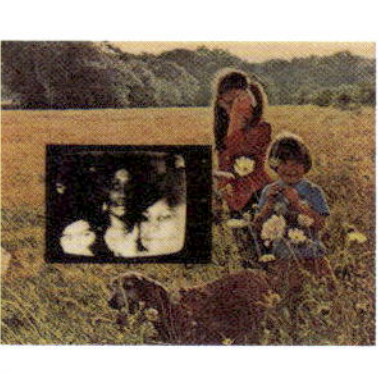
5

Bernal made his series *An American Fairy Tale* (1974–75, pages 77–85) shortly after receiving his MFA and in the wake of the Watergate hearings, live coverage of which he followed closely in 1973. He was inspired by the power of the media to foster idealized or demonized views of public figures. In the early and mid-1970s, President Richard Nixon was widely satirized and presented as a disgraced figure of scorn, in stark contrast to more sympathetic and idealized portrayals of John F. Kennedy after his assassination. For his series of staged images, Bernal recruited his young daughters and strangers to hold masks of Nixon's face over their own and pose in incongruous settings—in the desert surrounded by tall saguaro cacti, in front of a modest boarding home for senior citizens, or nearly camouflaged by a trash heap they stand in.[12] These images are unique in his oeuvre, both as staged compositions and for their biting sense of humor.

BARRIOS

Bernal found the voice truest to his vision within a more traditional form of picture-making, linking his embrace of Chicanismo with a creative mode that enabled him to memorialize everyday Mexican American people. In 1973, before completing *An American Fairy Tale*, he made his initial forays into the Tucson barrios to photograph locals in their domestic spaces. The barrios, among the city's most historic neighborhoods, were then largely populated by families who could trace their lineage in southern Arizona over generations.[13] The oldest of the barrios and a handful of surviving homes date to when Arizona was still Mexican territory.[14] But these neighborhoods near Tucson's downtown had faced the threats of redevelopment and "urban renewal" since the 1960s. In fact, Bernal began the series not long after the construction of a large convention

10. Louis Carlos Bernal, journal entry, November 23, 1970. For a comprehensive study of Frederick Sommer see Keith F. Davis, *The Art of Frederick Sommer: Photography, Drawing, Collage* (Prescott, AZ: Frederick and Frances Sommer Foundation, 2005).

11. Warhol made prints with appropriated portraits of both John F. Kennedy and First Lady Jacqueline Bouvier Kennedy.

12. Bernal had also planned a culminating group photo of nude models holding these masks, an idea that was nixed when too many of his subjects decided against participating. Related by Bernal in Ben "Easy" Rider, "An Informal Chat with Louis Carlos Bernal," 1982, from Louis Carlos Bernal Archive, Center for Creative Photography, video, 1:03:34.

13. Historically, the barrios were exceptionally diverse. They were home to *Tucsonenses*, or Mexican Americans whose families lived in southern Arizona before it became a part of the United States; and African Americans and Chinese Americans who settled in these neighborhoods in the late nineteenth century. See Cynthia Radding, *Wandering Peoples: Colonialism, Ethnic Spaces, and Ecological Frontiers in Northwestern Mexico, 1700–1850* (Durham, NC: Duke University Press, 1997).

14. Arizona became the forty-eighth state in the Union in 1912.

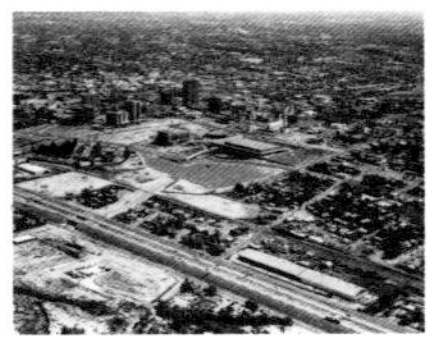

center, which severely diminished the size of the Barrio Viejo, displacing over three hundred families and more than one thousand homes (fig. 6, page 48).[15] He was interested in photographing those who remained: people who were poor but resilient, symbols of the precarity and invisibility of the city's Mexican American population. Bernal's goal was to speak as an insider, as the first Mexican American photographing his own people, and to reveal the dignity, cultural richness, and spiritual tenor of members of these communities.[16]

Bernal's decision to focus on the barrios presented a personal challenge: he knew he had the technical skills necessary to undertake such a project, but he was less confident about approaching people and asking if he could enter and photograph their homes. As he explained, "Even though I'm a Mexican American, I had not grown up in the barrios of Tucson—I grew up middle-class in Phoenix."[17] And at the time, he was living comfortably in a Tucson suburb. But Bernal—warm, gregarious, and fluent in Spanish—was familiar with these kinds of environments and the ways of life they represented. He also had a gift for knowing who to approach, "for reading peoples' spiritual barometers," in the words of a former student.[18] Bernal produced nineteen photographs, all in black and white, for his first *Barrios* series, limited by his natural inclination to shoot film sparingly as well as by financial constraints. He called such works "snapshot-like." His most memorable images were still to come, but these early efforts taught him how to compose in tight domestic settings, to make the most of natural or limited light, and to work with people outside his circle of family and friends. In his 1974 portrait of the elderly Doña Rita Mendoza, for example, a woman stands in her bedroom beside a home altar. A curtain has been pulled to one side and billows softly, illuminating his subject and casting bands of light and shadow along the room, creating a scene suffused with an intimate spirituality (page 161).

Bernal was developing his own mode and reaching toward a new kind of photographic aesthetic. Just a few years earlier, "Chicano photography" referred to documentary images by mostly young activist photographers who used their cameras in the service of the civil rights movement. These photographers, often volunteers learning on the job, chronicled the long struggle led by Chávez and

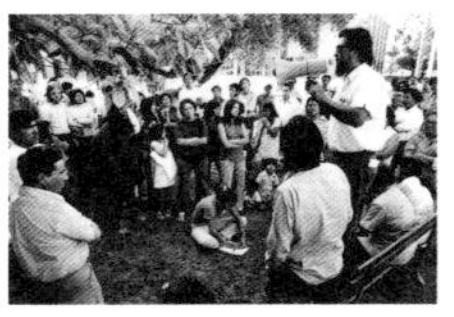

Huerta to unionize farm workers, anti-Vietnam War protests, and high-school student walkouts (fig. 7, page 49). Bernal was surely familiar with the scenes of union organizing and demonstrations that were published in the mainstream press as well as in student newspapers and alternative publications. They may not have directly influenced his work, but as Colin Gunckel has stated, "The more conceptual implications of the Chicano/a photographic have their foundations in Chicano movement photojournalism and documentary photography."[19] Indeed, when Louis Carlos Bernal peered into the lives of common Mexican American people, he was drawing from the same well of empathy and deep desire for social justice that informed the pioneering generation of civil rights photographers, to give visibility to those with little agency and to conjure histories and traditions that have been subject to political and cultural erasure.

In a relatively early body of color photographs, Bernal did, in fact, take up the concerns of his contemporaries who documented the California farmworkers' struggle. Likely compelled by labor strikes in the local news, he photographed at

15. See Juan Gomez-Novy and Stefanos Polyzoides, "A Tale of Two Cities: The Failed Urban Renewal of Downtown Tucson in the Twentieth Century," *Journal of the Southwest* 45, no. 1/2 (2003): pp. 87–119. http://www.jstor .org/stable/40170251; and Jane Kay, "Home Is Disappearing," in "Tucson's Barrio's: A Report from the Inside," *Arizona Daily Star*, July 16, 1978. http://www.barriostories.org/wp-content /uploads/2015/11/Tucson-Barrios-Section -ADS-1978.pdf.

16. For a moving, first-hand account of life in a Tucson barrio in the 1960s and early 1970s, see Lydia R. Otero, *In the Shadows of the Freeway: Growing Up Brown & Queer* (Tucson: Planet Earth Press, 2019).

17. Bernal, in Rider, "An Informal Chat."

18. Camille Bonzani, in "Louis Bernal," *Arizona Illustrated* segment, aired January 24, 1990, on KUAT-TV, 29:34.

19. Colin Gunckel, "The Chicano/a Photographic: Art as Social Practice in the Chicano Movement," *American Quarterly* 67, no. 2 (June 2015): pp. 377–412.

two farms in Maricopa County, portraying striking laborers at one and the primitive living conditions at the other (pages 14–15).[20] This small group of images, however, moves beyond documentation. Bernal demonstrated his ability to draw out the specificities of each individual he approached and to convey the strength and personal qualities of people with little means. Here, on his own, more personal terms, Bernal revealed a side of his work that was quietly political. These images made clear that even when making photographs that were more topical in subject matter, he maintained an artistic stance that was in service less to a movement or ideology than to individuals and communities.

Throughout the 1970s, Bernal developed his mature style melding documentation with portraiture, still life, and elements of staged photography. This adherence to traditional photographic genres might have been difficult for someone who had once been drawn to abstract and conceptual approaches to the medium and who deeply wanted to be seen, first and foremost, as an artist. But only by hewing to more direct forms of representation could he most fully realize his goal of making art rooted in the ideals of Chicanismo. Conscious of his aesthetic choices, he once said, "My work is not documentation in the technical sense, there are elements of it there, but basically my work is my own viewpoint about a particular set of circumstances or conditions that people live under, and their emotions as they react to that."[21] He saw his artistic mission as a kind of moral imperative, to speak for his community and to act as a bridge, to uphold his culture to the larger world. "The Chicano artist," he stated, "cannot isolate himself from the community but finds himself in the midst of his people creating art of and for the people."[22] And to realize these ideals, Bernal brought his whole self to the creation of this work: his childhood memories of racism and poverty, his education and thorough training in photography, and his personal and political values. Before making a photo, he would devote time to walking, thinking, writing, and talking to people he encountered in a neighborhood. When he clicked the shutter of his camera, he had fully readied himself for the moment of making an image that would crystallize an individual life.

Bernal experienced an apotheosis of sorts in 1977 when he came upon a small barrio house, its front door slightly ajar. He knocked several times and then entered. Once inside he discovered that this was an abandoned residence; a thick layer of dust coated every surface. The house, he later learned, was once the home of Mary Benitez, an elderly woman who had been hospitalized three years earlier and was living in a nursing home. "There were only three rooms to the entire house," Bernal later described, "but it was filled with a treasure of visual and spiritual imagery that glowed in the quiescent light transmitted by the white curtains covering the windows. I moved cautiously, studying the images while making a conscious effort not to touch anything since I felt I was trespassing in the spiritual space of another human being."[23]

The seven black-and-white photographs comprising the *Benitez Suite* (1977, pages 24, 104–11), include images of a dresser top covered with an array of personal possessions and a photo, perhaps of Mary Benitez as a child with a sibling; a tabletop shrine with dead flowers and pictures of Pope Pius XII and the Infant Jesus of Prague; and memorably, a bedroom bathed in soft light streaming in from a curtained window. The title of this last image, *Calendario*, refers to the calendar hanging on the bedroom's doorway. It dates to 1951 and is illustrated with the face of Jesus Christ—a reminder of the temporal and the eternal realms that Mary Benitez would have beheld daily for over two decades.

20. Bernal produced some of these photographs at Goldmar, a citrus farm partly owned by former US Senator Barry Goldwater. At the time, Goldmar had signed what was believed to be the first contract with undocumented workers, reflecting, in the words of a *Washington Star* reporter, "the growing militancy of illegal aliens." See "Mexicans Who Had Led Strikes Sign Contract with a Goldwater." *New York Times*, February 4, 1979, p. 38.

21. Louis Carlos Bernal, in "Luis [*sic*] Bernal, Espejos del Alma," *Latina*, February 1986, p. 52.

22. *Awards in the Visual Arts 3*, p. 16.

23. Louis Carlos Bernal, "Benitez Suite," in *Chicanismo: Photographs by Louis Carlos Bernal* (Rochester, NY: International Museum of Photography at George Eastman House, 1992). Bernal later met Mary Benitez, and she granted him permission to exhibit these photographs.

What we know about Mary Benitez we learn from Bernal's photographs: she was poor, she was deeply religious, and she lived in a world of memory. She surrounded herself with holy pictures and family portraits, including one of a handsome young man in an oval frame who may have been her husband. This constellation of imagery forms the nexus of a single life, representing Benitez's history, her loved ones, and her abiding faith. For *Ahora* (Now, 1977; page 107), Bernal assembled, over a picture of the Archangel Michael, the plethora of receipts, prayers, and notes—each beginning with the word *ahora*—he found scattered on the floor of Benitez's residence. Here, Bernal poetically evokes a confluence of the everyday and the spiritual, suggesting how even life's quotidian moments are touched with grace.

ESPEJO

The mid-1970s were fruitful and busy for Bernal. He and his wife had two daughters, Lisa Marie and Katrina Ann, born in 1969 and 1972, respectively. He relished his work at Pima Community College, where he earned a reputation as a dedicated and generous but also demanding teacher. In 1974, he received one of his first grants, from the Arizona Commission on the Arts and Humanities, as well as even wider recognition in the form of a Time-Life Yearbook Discovery Award naming him one of fifty outstanding young photographers in the world. He exhibited his work locally and nationally—at the Smithsonian Institution in Washington, DC, Galería de la Raza in San Francisco, and with the Latinx photographers' collective En Foco in New York. And notably, in 1977, the documentary photographer Morrie Camhi (1928–1999) invited Bernal to create a body of work for a major photographic project on the Mexican American experience in the Southwest.

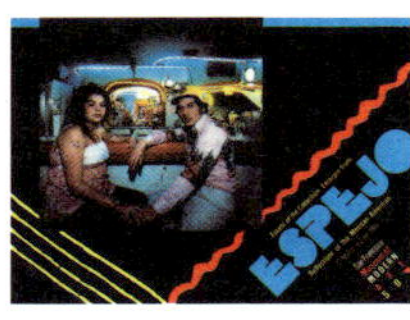
8

Espejo: Reflections of the Mexican American was sponsored by the Mexican American Legal Defense and Educational Fund (MALDEF), a leading civil rights organization, in commemoration of its tenth anniversary. With substantial financial support from the National Endowment for the Arts, *Espejo* received broad exposure, both as a traveling exhibition and publication (fig. 8, page 49). Camhi, a socially committed photographer based in northern California, had spent significant time earlier that decade documenting migrant farm workers and the Chicano civil rights movement; he also invited Abigail Heyman, Roger Minick, and Neal Slavin to contribute portfolios to the project. Each brought their own perspective: Heyman, as a pioneering feminist photographer and the first female member of Magnum; Minick, as a longtime and incisive chronicler of the American landscape; and Slavin, as an early practitioner of color photography who was known for large group portraits. But Bernal was the only Chicano in the group and the only photographer depicting his own community.

The commission's timing could not have been more fortuitous. Bernal was deeply committed to his *Barrios* series and wanted to go deeper. "The MALDEF project," he wrote, "allowed me to explore the essence of my being. I wanted to convey what I found—the new sense of pride, the new awareness that is flowering both within myself and within the community."[24] In other words, Bernal had arrived at a point where the work he was undertaking had personal and cultural dimensions in equal measure. He was also keenly aware that these photographs would have much broader exposure than his previous work, and he therefore

24. Troy, "Louis Carlos Bernal," p. 53.

took on the assignment with a special sense of responsibility. Bernal spoke frankly about his singular status as a Chicano involved in the project. "I am a perfectionist," he wrote, "constantly driven by the need to create a more perfect image, to excel in a world where I do not have the luxury of being average. I have felt a great deal of anger and anxiety in my life, and I have used photography as an outlet for these frustrations."[25]

Espejo gave Bernal the opportunity to advance his goal of exploring barrio neighborhoods beyond Tucson. He also worked in Douglas and Phoenix, as well as through a swath of southern New Mexico, where he photographed in the small towns of Canutillo, Silver City, and Animas. Through this travel, he believed, he could narrate a broader story of Mexican American life. In Douglas, he photographed the middle-aged Juan Mejia in black and white, in a spartan setting that projects an enduring loneliness (page 101). In contrast, in Tucson's Barrio Anita, he pictured Nanita Mendibles in color, capturing a living room decorated with a wall hanging of Leonardo da Vinci's *The Last Supper*, family portraits, and, incongruously, a psychedelic poster and a Mickey Mouse balloon (page 20).

The project also allowed Bernal to work in color, which became a hallmark of his practice. He was a master black-and-white printer, but he saw color as a means of deepening the psychological impact of his portraits. This was a bold decision at the time, when only a handful of American photographers, principally William Eggleston, Joel Meyerowitz, and Stephen Shore, were working in color.[26] Bernal had used color film sparingly in the past but was reluctant to use it with any consistency given the non-archival nature of printing papers in use at that time and his own limited resources. With the six-thousand-dollar fee he received (an amount he called "huge"), he could pay for film, processing, and materials, and explore image-making in a new way.[27] He had discussed his earlier black-and-white *Barrio* photographs as "environmental portraits"; with *Espejo*, he aimed to lay bare the interiority of barrio residents and to describe the barrio in a psychological and spiritual sense.[28]

One of Bernal's best-known images emerged from this project: *Dos Mujeres* (Two women), *Douglas, Arizona* (1978, page 121). It pictures in the foreground a seated girl, Maricella Martínez, then twelve years old, peering up shyly from her sewing. An older woman, Patricia Lopez, is visible through a doorway, seated on a bed in a farther room. This is Bernal's coming-of-age image. The two figures—their relationship is unclear—seem to inhabit separate worlds, a point the photographer underscores by the distinct spaces each occupies. But they are united by their lack of reserve—each presents herself openly and without pretense, simply as she is. Bernal may not have known these women, but he was exceptionally gifted at putting people at ease and gaining the confidence of strangers. Moreover, he skillfully composed the image, capturing the light passing through the translucent curtain to illuminate the faces of both women, falling more softly on the younger Maricella.

In *Dos Mujeres*, color is not only descriptive but crucial to the image's emotional charge. Similarly, in *Albert y Lynn Morales, Silver City, New Mexico* (1978, page 11), a neon-soaked color palette vividly evokes the gaudy setting where Bernal discovered this couple in a Silver City, New Mexico, bar. Bernal's gift for composition is also evident here. The two figures create a tightly enclosed world; their arms and hands are arranged in the shape of a heart, and they are framed by lines of neon. Color itself is the primary subject matter of the more

25. Louis Carlos Bernal, in *Espejo: Reflections of the Mexican American* (Oakland, CA: Oakland Museum, 1978), n.p.

26. See Senf, this volume.

27. Bernal, in Rider, "An Informal Chat." The amount is worth over $25,000 in today's dollars.

28. The colors of Bernal's original prints have significantly degraded. The exhibition that coincides with this publication contains examples of these vintage prints as well as prints based on high-resolution captures of Bernal's negatives that demonstrate the rich color he intended the images to have. Ernesto Esquer, working under the director of Bernal's friend and colleague Ann Simmons-Myers, made these digital reproductions and printed them full frame to respect Bernal's intentions.

minimal *Retrato de Boda Rosa* (Rosa's wedding portrait, 1978; page 123), in which Bernal gives over the majority of the frame to the modulations of pink on a worn plaster wall. The inclusion of the small wedding portrait that gives the image its title seems almost incidental in comparison.

Bernal had developed a nuanced sense of composition, confidently staging his subjects and spaces during this period. He took liberties in arranging a room and would often position curtains and doors to enhance lighting or provide a view into adjacent spaces. Bernal often posed his subjects, as he did to create the nuanced symmetry of *Dos Mujeres* or in his emblematic portrait of male adolescence, *Stephen Quiñonez, Douglas, Arizona* (1979, page 135), whose titular subject sits cross-legged on a bed wearing a Playboy Bunny T-shirt and holding barbells, precisely centered between posters of bathing-suit-clad models. And while most of the photographs for *Espejo* are indoor scenes, Bernal also photographed people outside their homes. *Barrio Portrait, H Avenue Cuadra, Douglas, Arizona* (1978, page 134) is a family scene, with three small children in front of their home, their parents at the entrance. The father stands beside the doorway while a young woman poses just inside. It is unclear how carefully Bernal arranged each figure, but the composition is not incidental. He often worked with his subjects in a collaborative manner, or as the critic Mark Johnstone wrote, "in collaborative acquiescence" here, to painstakingly construct an idealized scene of a Mexican American family.[29]

Bernal also recognized signs of change in the barrios. While he frequently portrayed elders and their traditional, if fading, ways of life, he also captured signs of change and of modernity, as in his portrait of the youthful Stephen Quiñonez or in *Los Vatos Locos* (The crazy guys), *Douglas, Arizona* (1978, page 136), a casual scene of young men hanging out around a car. Recalling some of his early efforts as a photographer, many of these photographs prominently feature the television. *El Show de Rosita* (Rosita's Show), *Barrio Anita* (1978, page 119) pictures a television set airing a popular Spanish-language variety show; only the show's title on the screen indicates that we are inside the residence of a Mexican American family. But Bernal recognized that such a scene would clearly signal the ascendance of the Spanish-speaking population in the United States. If television and mass media had promoted the assimilationist, melting-pot ethos of the 1950s and '60s, this kind of entertainment—by and for Latinxs—exemplified the growing clout of this demographic, whose members now expected entertainment and culture on their own terms.

BERNAL IN THE 1980s

Following the *Espejo* project, Bernal continued to extend his *Barrio* series and remained fully immersed in illuminating Mexican American life. In the early 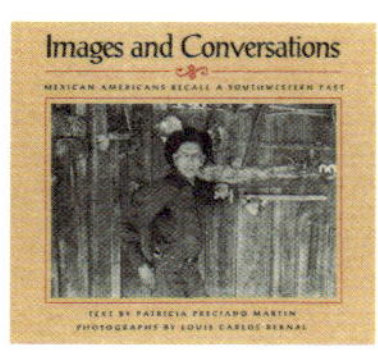 1980s, the writer and historian Patricia Preciado Martin invited him to contribute images to a volume of oral histories of Mexican Americans with deep roots in Arizona. *Images and Conversations: Mexican Americans Recall a Southwestern Past* was one of several public scholarship initiatives in Tucson during this period, and it meant to address the striking omission of materials related to this population from local libraries and historical societies (fig. 9, page 49).[30] The project gave Bernal the opportunity to meet Tucsonans with long

9

29. Mark Johnstone, "Observations in a Social Environment," *Artweek* 16, no. 30 (May 18, 1985): p. 12.

30. See Patricia Preciado Martin and Louis Carlos Bernal, *Images and Conversations: Mexican Americans Recall a Southwestern Past* (Tucson: University of Arizona Press, 1983).

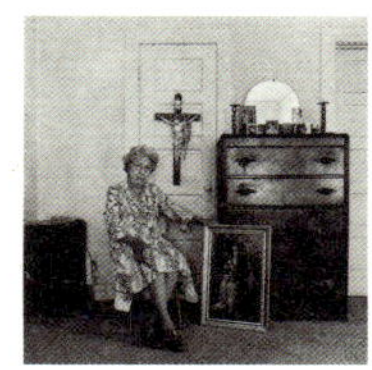

10

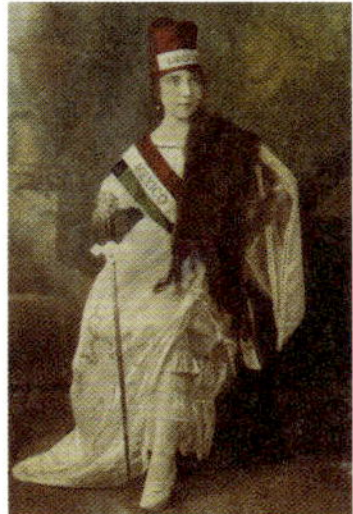

11

histories as well as to travel through a more rural Arizona, where he visited old ranches that had remained in families over generations. Among his subjects was María Soto Audelo, who in one photograph sits proud and dignified beside a large crucifix festooned with a rosary and palms, and a chest holding family photos and saints' images (fig. 10, page 50; see also page 125). A large, framed photo of Soto Audelo taken in 1917 for Tucson's Independence Day celebration is propped against the chest. In it, she is an adolescent with dark hair flowing well past her waist, elaborately dressed as an allegorical personification of Mexico (fig. 11, page 50).[31] In the accompanying oral history, Soto Audelo relates that her family traces its origins in Tucson to 1774, and that her father was born in 1860. For Bernal, a portrait embodying the long history of Mexican Americans in Arizona would have been implicitly political: it denotes their colonized status in the Southwest and their sovereign ties to the land. And while Bernal infrequently photographed landscapes, for *Images and Conversations* he pictured cottonwood trees and corrals, working ranches, and small rural cemeteries—scenes that bespeak the centrality of land to Mexican Americans in this region. When Bernal focused on the land itself, he was looking at it through the eyes of subjects who recognized it as an inextricable part of their identity and ancestral history.[32]

Bernal was also expanding his artistic network in these years and becoming a more integral part of the Chicanx community in Arizona. In 1978 he attended the Festival Flor y Canto at his alma mater, Arizona State University. This was the fifth edition in a series of influential "oral literary symposia," as they were termed, held throughout that decade in Los Angeles, Austin, San Antonio, Albuquerque, and Milwaukee. Its purpose, in the words of its organizers, was to present a collective portrait of the mestizo aesthetic in the United States through presentations from emerging and established Chicanx and Indigenous poets, writers, artists, and musicians from the Southwest.[33] Festival Flor y Canto was as much political as cultural, providing platforms for artistic voices as well as a meeting place where activists from throughout the region could congregate and establish bonds of solidarity. It inspired the Arizona-based contingent to found an organization in 1978 that they named Ariztlán, a portmanteau for Arizona and Aztlán, the mythic homeland of Aztecs. An artist-led support organization, Ariztlán organized exhibitions, artist talks, workshops on practical matters for artists, and cultural exchange programs with Mexico. Bernal was president of the group in the 1980s, and he worked to challenge the invisibility of Chicanx artists in the local art scene and in the marketplace.[34] In promoting Ariztlán's work in the local press, he summed up his frustration about this lack of attention, saying, "The white culture is interested in our food, our architecture, and our language, but not our people."[35]

In the 1980s, Bernal was spending more time outside of Tucson. He traveled to California, New Mexico, Texas, Cuba, and Mexico, where he made photographs, took part in exhibitions, spoke at conferences, and developed friendships with Chicanx and Mexican artists.[36] These relationships formed a crucial support system for the photographer, who long suffered from insecurity about his place in the art world at large, and who was relatively isolated in Tucson compared to Chicanxs based in cities like Los Angeles or San Francisco. As his partner Marietta Bernstorff noted, Bernal never really felt like he was part of the established photo

31. Tucson had a tradition of elaborate Fourth of July celebrations even before its 1877 incorporation as a city. They featured processions with bands, triumphal carts, speeches, choral singing, and dramatic readings of the Declaration of Independence. See, for example, Ruthann Grace, "Don Pedro Pellón: Tucson's Pioneer Actor and Activist," *Journal of Arizona History* 57, no. 2 (Summer 2016): p. 159.

32. At the conclusion of the Mexican American War (1846–48), Mexico ceded over half its territory to the United States. While the Treaty of Guadalupe Hidalgo provided constitutional rights and protections for landowners north of the new border line, many Mexican Americans were dispossessed of their land interests. The Treaty effectively relegated outsider status to a native people and impoverished land-grant descendants. In the early years of the Chicano movement, ancient concepts of Aztlán, the mythic homeland, as well as of sovereignty and self-determination, acted as crucial guideposts for emerging leaders of activists. See Rodolfo Acuña, *Occupied America: A History of Chicanos*, 3rd ed. (New York: Harper Collins, 1987), p. 115; and Rudolfo A. Anaya, Francisco A. Lomelí, and Enrique R. Lamadrid, *Aztlán: Essays on the Chicano Homeland*, rev. ed. (Albuquerque: University of New Mexico Press, 2017).

33. See Arnoldo Carlos Vento, "The *Flor y Canto* and *Canto al Pueblo* Festivals," in *Mestizo: The History, Culture and Politics of the Chicano and Mexican* (Lanham, MD: University Press of America, 1997), pp. 237–42; and *Flor y Canto IV and V: An Anthology of Chicano Literature from the Festivals Held in Albuquerque, New Mexico, 1977 and Tempe, Arizona, 1978* (Albuquerque: Pajarito Publications, 1980).

34. I am grateful to artists Jim Covarrubias and Joseph Sánchez for providing me with information about Ariztlán.

35. Louis Carlos Bernal, in Roberta Tubis, "Photographer Seeks to Promote Hispanic Arts," *El Independiente* (Tucson), October 30, 1981.

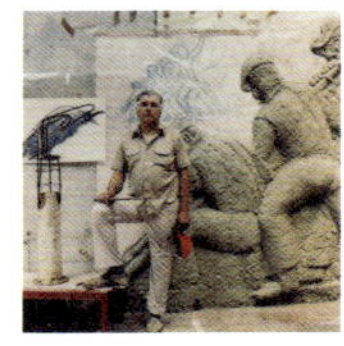
12

community. He knew he was a good photographer, but he felt more connected to working-class people and to Chicanxs, in great part because of the discrimination he experienced in his youth.[37] Among his most important friends was Luis Jiménez (1940–2006), who was based in Hondo, New Mexico, and was a nationally known artist by the early 1970s (fig. 12, page 50). Although their work was very different—Jiménez worked largely with polychrome fiberglass to create sculptures that were often monumental in scale—Bernal deeply respected the artist, an intellectual and a perfectionist with an unwavering sense of himself as a Chicano. It was Jiménez, in fact, who encouraged Bernal to see Chicanismo as central to his artistic identity.[38]

In Los Angeles, Bernal exhibited with some frequency at spaces such as the Los Angeles Center for Photographic Studies and Los Angeles Contemporary Exhibitions. He developed convivial relationships with members of the city's large community of Chicanx artists and photographers and became part of a coterie that met for conversations and mentoring at Cityscape Foto Gallery in Pasadena,

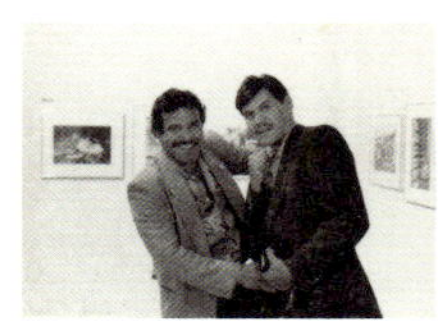
13

one of the area's few Chicano-owned galleries, run by collector and cultural promoter Lorenzo Hernandez. Among them was Ricardo Valverde (1946–1998), a fellow photographer who likewise understood the importance of capturing barrio life and focusing on his own community—in his case, East Los Angeles (fig. 13, page 50). Valverde experimented widely with the medium, scratching or painting his prints to add a surreal dimension to the people and places he photographed. Another Los Angeles friend of Bernal's, the painter Roberto Gil de Montes (b. 1950), lived in Mexico City during the 1980s when he became an important conduit for Chicanx artists between Los Angeles and Mexico, and he helped introduce Bernal's work to the Mexican art world.

Travel also allowed Bernal to expand the scope of his work. In 1980, on a trip to San Diego, he photographed the cholos and cholas who represented a significant, if often scorned, aspect of Chicanx youth culture in Southern California. In an iconic work made in Barrio Logan, he portrays two young men standing beneath a bridge overpass, flanked by monumental murals painted on the bridge's concrete pylons (page 126). This is a politically charged statement: The area under and around the bridge had been designated as a park in 1971 after years of pressure by activists who protested the destruction of much of their neighborhood due to highway construction. Chicano Park soon became a veritable museum of large-scale murals, and Bernal's portrait of the men—one displaying his gang affiliation with hand symbols—suggests both a defiance of mainstream cultural norms and a territorial claim to this land and the art that surrounds them.

Bernal visited Cuba in 1982 to take part in the Premio de Fotografía Cubana, and in 1984, as an invited guest of the Tercer Coloquio Latinoamericana de Fotografía, the third edition of a major gathering of Latin American photographers, critics, and historians for panel discussions, workshops, and exhibitions. He was one of only a few US citizens in attendance at the Havana edition, and the only one to present a workshop.[39] His was on the zone system, a technique standardized by Ansel Adams and Fred Archer in the late 1930s to determine the optimal exposures to yield black-and-white prints with rich tonal values.[40] Bernal also made some of his finest street photographs in Cuba. This was a mode of working he pursued only sporadically in the United States given his proclivity for

36. Among the exhibitions Bernal participated in during these years was *Fotografía Latinoamericana del Suroeste/USA*, held in 1981 at La Casa de Fotografía, Mexico City. Bernal's work was shown alongside that of other pioneering figures like Don Gregorio Antón, Isabel Castro, Harry Gamboa Jr., Luis C. Garza, and Ricardo Valverde, all then based in Los Angeles. In 1990, he participated in a historic, critically lauded exhibition, *Chicano Art: Resistance and Affirmation*, or CARA. Organized by the Wight Gallery at UCLA, it presented some 180 works of art dating from 1964 to 1985 by about 140 Chicanx artists working in varied media. The exhibition traveled to museums in ten cities in the early 1990s and was accompanied by an extensive catalog. Through *CARA*, Bernal's work was introduced to tens of thousands of people throughout the United States. See Richard Griswold del Castillo, Teresa McKenna, and Yvonne Yarbro-Bejarano, eds., *Chicano Art: Resistance and Affirmation 1965–1985* (Los Angeles: Wight Art Gallery, University of California Los Angeles, 1991).

37. Marietta Bernstorff, interview with the author, Oaxaca, Mexico, November 2002.

38. Marietta Bernstorff, phone interview with the author, December 29, 2021. Jiménez and Bernal remained lifelong friends, and Jiménez was often at Bernal's side when he lay in a coma after his 1989 accident. Luis Jiménez died in 2006 in a tragic accident, when a portion of a large sculpture fell on him in his studio.

39. Other Americans in attendance included photo historians Amy Conger and Keith McElroy, photographers Esther Parada, and Walter Rosenblum, and historian and photographer Max Kozloff.

40. I am grateful to Armando Cristeto for information on Bernal's travels to Havana.

careful control of his compositions. Working in black and white, he captured denizens of downtown Havana, busy shop fronts, graffiti, and the city's neoclassical architecture. He seemed especially enamored of the uniformed school children he encountered along one crumbling, unpaved street, whom he depicted playing and mugging for his camera (page 177). Bernal recognized the significance of these images; he discussed his hopes of assembling them into a book, a project he was never able to realize.[41]

In 1983, Bernal was invited to teach a session on documentary photography as part of a workshop organized by the nonprofit Friends of Photography in Carmel, California.[42] Others were seeking him out as an instructor and speaker. As the late Bill Jay, a former ASU professor of photography noted, "He has this special ability to stimulate, excite, and infuse his pupils, and at the same time tell them they have a long way to go."[43] The Carmel workshop was another of Bernal's career benchmarks, putting him in contact with photographers from throughout the United States, including Ansel Adams, who founded Friends of Photography. Bernal drove to Northern California with Tucson photo dealer Terry Etherton, who recalled Bernal's enthusiasm at meeting fellow instructors Mary Ellen Mark, Danny Lyon, and Burk Uzzle. But according to Etherton, the event also underscored Bernal's professional insecurities and reminded him of his white peers' advanced standing compared to his own at the time.[44]

Changes were also taking place in Bernal's personal life. In 1985 he and Sandy, his wife of nearly twenty years, divorced. He had begun a relationship with Marietta Bernstorff, a former student and then gallery owner in Tucson. Bernal had lived in a northwest Tucson suburb while photographing in the city's barrios for over a decade, and with Bernstorff, he moved into an adobe house in El Hoyo, one of the oldest barrios in Tucson. This move was a cultural and political decision, bringing him much closer to the people who formed the core of his work.[45]

PICTURES OF PICTURES

Bernal was long fascinated with not only the people who stood before his camera but also the objects and images they displayed in their homes. He repeatedly found his way into houses whose walls and tabletops held arrangements of holy pictures, family photographs, figurines, and *calendarios* (calendars), the kind handed out by bakeries and other stores in barrios at the end of each year. Many of these compositions are stunning depictions of Roman Catholic devotion. *Recámara de Catalina Olomos* (Catalina Olomos's bedroom), *Phoenix, Arizona* (1978, page 114), for example, centers on the small, densely filled shrine visible in the corner of a room above a bed. Pictures of the Virgin of Guadalupe, Our Mother of Perpetual Help, and the Santo Niño de Atocha hang above a shelf filled with other religious imagery and bric-a-brac.[46] The display attests to the profound role of faith in this woman's life; her place of rest is also a place of fervent devotion.

An even more elaborate exposition is seen in *Recámara de Blas y Pauline Flores* (Blas and Pauline Flores's bedroom, 1978; page 118), which focuses on a chest of drawers and a desk set in a corner, both covered with religious statuary, candles, and artificial flowers. This is a world unto itself, a humbling demonstration of faith that transforms the intimate space of the bedroom into a Catholic shrine. For Bernal, who rarely attended Mass as an adult, such spaces must have

41. "Espejos del Alma," p. 54.

42. Friends of Photography was founded by Ansel Adams in 1967 as an organization to promote the medium of photography through exhibitions, publications, and education. Bernal took part in one of the final programs in which Adams, who died in 1984, also participated.

43. Bill Jay, in "Espejos del Alma," p. 53.

44. Terry Etherton, interview with the author, September 10, 2021. In fact, Bernal was the only photographer of color to present at Friends of Photography's Carmel workshops that year. See James G. Alinder, ed., *Light Years: The Friends of Photography 1967–1987 (Untitled 43)* (Carmel, CA: Friends of Photography, 1987).

45. El Hoyo means "The Hole," so named because of the neighborhood's low elevation and propensity for flooding during rainstorms in the early twentieth century. The City of Tucson eventually installed a proper drainage system in the neighborhood.

46. The Santo Niño, or Holy Infant, de Atocha is the patron saint of prisoners and travelers and a popular devotional figure for Mexican Americans with ties to a distant homeland or with family histories marked by migration. The Christ Child, dressed as a pilgrim, brings aid to the needy and protects travelers.

felt both familiar and mystical, projecting a kind of unquestioning devotion to which he did not subscribe. But as his friend the photographer and photo historian Armando Cristeto noted, the religious displays Bernal witnessed in these homes would make him emotional—he understood the spiritual weight they held for his subjects.[47] They also became a central theme in his work, as expressions of Mexican American cultural identity that he pictured time and again throughout the Southwest.

Bernal also photographed shrines in his subjects' yards and gardens. In *Sr. Ernesto Villa, Barrio Hollywood* (1977, page 117), a man stands before his house, between two prickly-pear cacti and a grotto-like shrine dedicated to the Virgin of Guadalupe. It appears to be the holiday season, and Villa has transformed a cactus into a Christmas tree, decorating it with multicolored lights. Similarly, in a black-and-white photograph, Herminia Vargas sits under a big shade tree beside a shrine made out of an old refrigerator filled with statuary and flowers (page 99). Bernal captured such expressions of religiosity, whether elaborate or improvised, wherever he found them. He photographed at El Tiradito, a wishing shrine and historic site in Barrio Viejo that dates to the 1870s, and elsewhere around Tucson, where he came upon storefront altars or images of the Virgin of Guadalupe.[48] In his singular image *La Reina de Mi Vida* (Queen of my life, 1983; page 131), a man raises his shirt to reveal a large tattoo of the Virgin of Guadalupe covering his back—a transformation of the body itself into a shrine or *ofrenda*. Imprinting the skin with the image of this brown-skinned Virgin—common among working-class Mexican American men, including those who have been incarcerated—signals pride in one's mestizo (mixed race) identity. Bernal saw these various manifestations of faith as a form of creative expression, a folk art that sprung from the barrio neighborhoods of Tucson.[49]

Bernal could sometimes approach his subjects with less reverence. In *Juanita Serrano with Santo Niño de Atocha* (1978, page 19), a woman, her hair carefully set in pink rollers, stands beside an elaborate wall of flower-framed religious pictures. He often entered homes to find symbols of faith intermingled with portraits of John F. Kennedy, the first Catholic president who was beloved among many Mexican Americans, or of pop stars or cartoon characters, such as the occasional Mickey Mouse. In *Kennedy Cocio Altar* (1980, page 97), the president's portrait, adorned with a cross and a heart, dominates a wall that also holds images of the Holy Trinity and St. Martín de Porres. The Chicana artist and writer Amalia Mesa-Bains has described these kinds of domestic assemblages of disparate elements, ranging from "images of Walt Disney, Mexican cinema, and mass media advertising, and even Mexican *calendario* graphics and American Pop Art," as "an encounter of two worlds [that] could only be negotiated through the sensibility of rasquachismo"—an irreverent underdog philosophy of reusing and improvising with what is at hand, of challenging standards of so-called good taste, and of appropriating objects and symbols to one's end.[50]

The photograph itself is another common element in Bernal's interior scenes, and it makes certain works function as pictures of pictures. We frequently see walls with photographs of ancestors, the *ancianos* known only through large, hand-tinted or hand-toned prints set in heavy frames, as in the *Benitez Suite*, or in tabletop portraits, as in the photograph *San Pedro Ranch, Animas, New Mexico* (1978, page 22). Contemporary family photos, pictures from graduations or weddings, and military portraits also appear—images that mark rites of passage and act as testimony to extended families over time. In an essay on photography and

47. Armando Cristeto, interview with the author, Mexico City, 2002.

48. *El tiradito* means "the little outcast," and the site is so named for a young man supposedly buried there after being caught in an affair and murdered. Visitors still leave candles and notes carrying prayers or expressions of gratitude for wishes granted at the site.

49. I am grateful for the insights of Bernal's friend and neighbor Antonio Solisgomez regarding the photographer's interests in vernacular artistic expressions in Tucson's barrios.

50. The Chicano art historian Tomás Ybarra-Frausto articulated the concept of *rasquachismo* in "Rasquachismo: A Chicano Sensibility," in *Chicano Aesthetics: Rasquachismo* (Phoenix: Movimiento Artístico del Rio Salado, 1989), p. 5. Amalia Mesa-Bains added an important Chicana perspective to his theories in "'Domesticana': The Sensibility of Chicana Rasquache," *Aztlán: A Journal of Chicano Studies* 24, no. 2 (Fall 1999): p. 159.

African American life, bell hooks notes the camera's value among Black people, who have used it as a tool for refuting negative representations of themselves that emerge from "racist White imaginations."[51] The same can be said for the assemblages of photographs Bernal recorded: they were veritable museums of family histories and accomplishments. In focusing on these displays, he also reflected the value Mexican Americans placed on photography, long before the era of camera phones and social media. Photographs, whether hung on walls or stored in albums or old shoeboxes, acted as *recuerdos*, remembrances, of ancestors and family members left behind once individuals migrated to the United States. When Bernal was making photographs of photographs, he was bearing witness to the specificities of a family history and, more broadly, evoking the centrality of family to Chicanx life, including those of a more distant past who brought one to this time and place.[52]

Photographs of interior spaces, even if absent of the human figure, also became another form of portraiture for Bernal. He had created these kinds of representations of individuals early on with the *Benitez Suite*, when he came upon an abandoned home filled with belongings and remembrances. In later images, like *Retrato de Boda Rosa* (Rosa's wedding portrait, 1978), *Boda de Luz* (Wedding of light, 1978), and *Santos y Televisión* (1981, pages 123, 100, 16)—more intentional portraits of interiors and possessions—Bernal vividly evokes the lives of their inhabitants. Tellingly, *Recámara de Mis Padres* (My parents' bedroom), *Phoenix, Arizona* (1978, page 140), alternately titled *Retrato de Mis Padres* (Portrait of my parents), which depicts a corner of a bedroom in the family home, is Bernal's only work dedicated to his parents. It centers on a lampshade imprinted with his parents' wedding portrait, signaling the value he placed on such symbolic portraits.[53] The warm glow from the lamp adds another layer of meaning; he conveys his parents' essence in both physical and emotional terms. Bernal once called this an image of a feeling and place. In other words, it is an image capable of expressing the same kind of personal impact made by representations of people.[54]

MEXICO

Bernal had a long, sometimes conflicted, but ultimately nurturing relationship with Mexico—its language, cultures, and members of its photography community. In his youth, long before he visited Mexico, the Spanish language held a central place in his consciousness. Growing up in the border town of Douglas where bilingual households were the norm, his parents primarily spoke Spanish, while emphasizing the importance of speaking both English and Spanish properly. But once the family moved to Phoenix, he was "knuckled" by the nuns for his lack of English proficiency, a punishment that compelled him to improve in this language. Likewise, his parents, although English speakers, studied to refine their own use of the language. The family home was filled with a remarkable number of English-Spanish dictionaries, and each family member used language as a form of self-advancement, whether toward assimilation or as a return to roots. Ultimately, Bernal's Spanish fluency served him well, giving him an easy rapport with the principal subjects of his photographs, the barrio residents who allowed him into their homes.[55] And in Mexico, he was able to lecture and fully engage in intellectual discourse with members of the photographic community who became his friends.

51. bell hooks, "In Our Glory: Photography and Black Life," *Art on My Mind: Visual Politics* (New York: New Press, 1998), p. 59.

52. Mesa-Bains, "Domesticana," pp. 157–67.

53. I am grateful to Ann Simmons-Myers, who succeeded Bernal as head of the photography program at Pima Community College, for providing me with information about this photograph.

54. Louis Carlos Bernal, "Comentario," *1er Coloquio Nacional de Fotografía* (Pachuca, Hidalgo, Mexico: Gobierno del Estado de Hidalgo; Mexico City: Instituto Nacional de Bellas Artes and Consejo Mexicano de Fotografía, 1984).

55. Katrina and Lisa Bernal, phone interview with the author, January 7, 2022, and email correspondence, November 2022.

In 1962, at the age of twenty-one, Bernal traveled to Mexico City, where he enrolled at Mexico City College (now known as the Universidad de las Américas), with the objective of improving his Spanish and preparing for a career as a language teacher. This may have been the practical goal, but his passion for art and photography was growing. He found early success with the medium not long after his return to Arizona, exhibiting his work in a solo show at Arizona State University in 1964 and in a group exhibition at the prestigious George Eastman House in Rochester, New York, the following year. By the time he was drafted into the military in 1966, he had abandoned his plan to teach Spanish, but his devotion to Mexican culture endured. He visited Mexico throughout his life for both personal and professional reasons.

Among the earliest photograph in the Bernal archives, *Chiclets, Cuernavaca*, dates to 1963, when Bernal first visited Mexico (page 167). The scene, showing a shoeless boy, a street vendor who seems very willing to pose for the camera, is one he must have come upon frequently during that stay. The child's sense of innocence and level of poverty clearly struck Bernal; in fact, his close friend, Armando Cristeto, noted that Bernal would have had a special empathy for a child like this, given his own challenges growing up in Douglas.[56] And he would return to the theme of poverty on future trips. As much as he loved Mexico, he disdained its highly visible social inequalities.

Bernal took an extended trip to Mexico by train with his wife and children in 1980, following the classic itinerary that many Mexican Americans have made in the quest to become more familiar with their heritage. They visited the immense Museo Nacional de Antropología, Chapultepec Park, and the house museums of Diego Rivera and Frida Kahlo, and attended Ballet Folklórico performances at the Palacio de Bellas Artes. Bernal relished introducing his daughters to Mexican history and traditions, but a family trip afforded him little time to think about photography. This changed in 1981, when Bernal was invited to participate in the Segundo Coloquio Latinoamericano de Fotografía, the second colloquium of Latin American photography, and to exhibit at the Palacio de Bellas Artes, the same institution he had visited with his family a year earlier. Organized by the Consejo Mexicano de Fotografía and the Instituto Nacional de Bellas Artes, the Coloquia were watershed events for Latin American photographers of that era. Prior to their establishment, no consciousness of "Latin American photography" had existed, only the knowledge of a small number of photographers (especially the Mexican Manuel Álvarez Bravo, the Brazilian Sebastião Salgado, and the Peruvian Martín Chambi), who had been singled out for broader international exposure by publishers or museums. These photographers had little opportunity to know one another, and they were hardly visible within a photography world dominated by Americans and Europeans.[57]

Organizers of the second colloquium made a concerted effort to include Chicanx photographers, among them Bernal, Robert Buitrón, Isabel Castro, Harry Gamboa Jr., Luis C. Garza, Roberto Gil de Montes, and Kathy Vargas. As Cristeto noted, "The colloquia activated a flow of communications between creators and countries that resulted in exhibitions and trips to Mexico on the part of Chicano photographers, including Louis Carlos Bernal."[58] Bernal arrived in Mexico City as the leading Chicano photographer in the United States, and he relished the opportunity to represent his community at such a historic gathering (fig. 14, page 51).

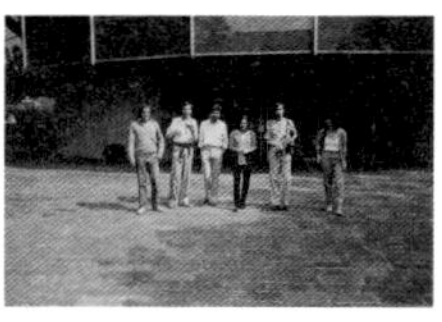

14

56. Armando Cristeto, email exchange with the author, November 3, 2021.

57. See Leticia Rigat, "Los Coloquios Latinoamericanos de Fotografía y la reconfiguración de las prácticas fotográficas," *Dixit* no.32 (2020); and Pablo Ortiz Monasterio, "Close to the Boom," *VIST*, October 5, 2021, https://vist projects.com/en/close-to-the-boom.

58. Armando Cristeto, in Elizabeth Ferrer, "First Encounters: Latino Artists at the Colloquiums of Latin American Photography," paper presented at the Latino Art Now Conference, University of Illinois, Chicago, 2016.

The discussions and debates on the ideological role and responsibility of the Latin American photographer would have held special relevance for Bernal, who grappled with the same issues as a Chicano photographer. In his keynote address, Pedro Meyer, a leading Mexican photographer and the influential head of the Consejo, noted that photographic art should respond to the characteristics of the society from which it emanates. He argued that in Latin America, whose recent history had been marked by immense social struggles and repression, the photographer had a responsibility to act as witness and integral participant. Bernal himself delivered a paper titled "La fotografía como reflejo de las estructuras sociales" (Photography as a reflection of social structures), in which he called the US photography world a "microcosm of North American society." He noted the elite nature of the field—the years of education required and the expensive nature of the medium—while also underscoring the crucial role of photographers of color in confronting the invisibility of underrepresented communities, populations he termed the "Third World of the United States." Bernal advocated for Chicanx, Puerto Rican, and Cuban American photographers to take part in workshops, present at conferences like those organized by the Society for Photographic Education, and apply for grants. While acknowledging the discrimination and exclusion that fellow Latinx photographers faced, he declared that it was time to "stop blaming everyone for our problems . . . and start taking responsibility for ourselves."[59]

In 1984, Bernal was invited to attend a national photography conference, the Primer Coloquio Nacional de Fotografía. It was held in Pachuca, a historic mining town about sixty miles north of Mexico City where a colonial-era convent was being repurposed as a national photography archive and museum. His paper, part of the panel "¿Para quién y para qué se fotografía?" (For whom does one photograph and why does one photograph?), responded to Pedro Meyer's keynote remarks. Bernal presented images by a wide range of photographers,

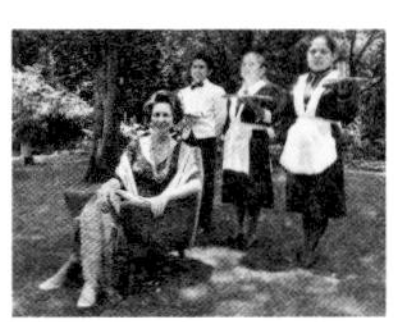

including Eugène Atget, Ansel Adams, and Joel-Peter Witkin, by means of discussing the value reflected in photographic images. He then brought up Meyer's well-known photograph *La señora y sus sirvientes* (The lady and her servants, 1978; fig. 15, page 51), which he had seen at an exhibition at the Center for Creative Photography at the University of Arizona.[60] He stated that he later learned that Meyer made this portrait of his mother, a fact that caused him some consternation. The class division between the two photographers could not have been more stark, and Bernal was struck by this representation of immense wealth. Was this a class critique? And who among Bernal's Mexican colleagues could have had access to a person of such privilege? He noted how issues of distortion and misunderstanding can influence the reading of a photo, but one can also sense Bernal's disapprobation in encountering a level of class difference that he would not have imagined existed in Mexico.[61]

15

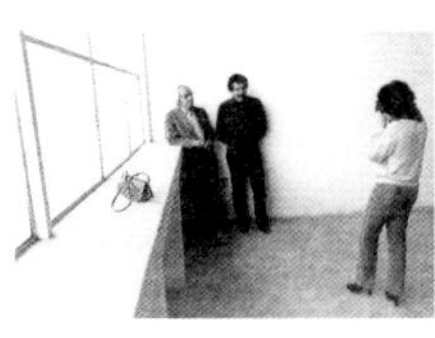

In this and other visits to Mexico in the 1980s, Bernal met photographers ranging from such legendary figures as Manuel Álvarez Bravo and Lola Álvarez Bravo, to his contemporaries Graciela Iturbide and Rogelio Villarreal. These were significant encounters, especially because Bernal did not move in similarly influential circles in the United States (fig. 16, page 51). Like his relationships with Chicanx artists, this network of Mexican peers provided him with a sense of validation and comradeship, as well as an artistic context

16

59. To underscore his own uncommon position as a Chicanx photographer, Bernal noted his experience at the Society for Photographic Education conference in 1980. Among six hundred attendees, four were African American and three were Latinx. See Luis [*sic*] Carlos Bernal, "La fotografía como reflejo de las estructuras sociales," *Hecho en Latinoamérica: Segundo Coloquio Latinoamericano de Fotografía.* (Mexico City: Consejo Mexicano de Fotografía, 1981), pp. 92–94.

60. In 1978 the Center for Creative Photography presented an exhibition of recent Mexican photography, including work by Meyer as well as by Graciela Iturbide, José Ángel Rodríguez, Jesús Sánchez Uribe, Lázaro Blanco, Colette Álvarez Urbajtel, Manuel Álvarez Bravo, Rafael Doniz, and Antonio Reynoso Castañeda. See Terrence Pitts, *Contemporary Photography in Mexico: 9 Photographers* (Tucson: Center for Creative Photography, University of Arizona, 1978).

61. Louis Carlos Bernal, "Comentario," *1er Coloquio Nacional de Fotografía* (Pachuca, Mexico: Gobierno del Estado de Hidalgo; Mexico City: Instituto Nacional de Bellas Artes and Consejo Mexicano de Fotografía, 1984), pp. 114–17.

that he lacked in Tucson. Bernal soon became a respected member of the photo world in Mexico, exhibiting there frequently and maintaining close relationships with many of these photographers throughout his lifetime.

Bernal also came under the spell of the Mexican aesthetic tradition, then still dominated by black-and-white documentary and street photography focusing on Indigenous people and the urban poor. His 1980 image *La Pelona* pictures a man who has placed his hand to his mouth, suppressing a bemused smirk as he stands at the entrance of a coffin store (page 172). The composition feels like an allegory and is reminiscent of Manuel Álvarez Bravo's depictions of inci-

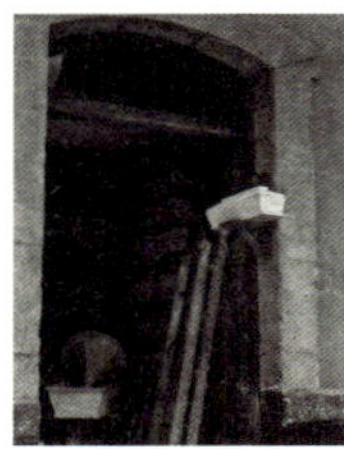

17

dental moments or quotidian objects in the urban milieu that are laden with philosophical or spiritual meaning. Indeed, *La Pelona* responds to Álvarez Bravo's photograph *Ladder of Ladders* (1931), which offers a view into a storefront workshop with leaning ladders at its entrance and stacked coffins in the background— symbols of ascension and mortality (fig. 17, page 52). In other images, Bernal depicted scenes of impoverishment and indifference that were common in Mexico City. With *Cristo de la Calle* (1988, page 175), he imagines a blind beggar as a Christ of the streets, a figure enduring his own Calvary. The image stands in contrast to *El Diablo* (ca. 1985, page 174), a photograph of a well-dressed man displaying contempt for a destitute figure in the background—an earthbound personification of the devil.

It was Bernal's color photographs that made him an influential figure in some quarters of Mexico's photo world. In the 1980s, a rising generation of photographers in Mexico City was challenging long-held conventions, undertaking various forms of darkroom manipulation, staging images, and focusing on such themes as youth culture and the increasingly visible queer community, and the impact

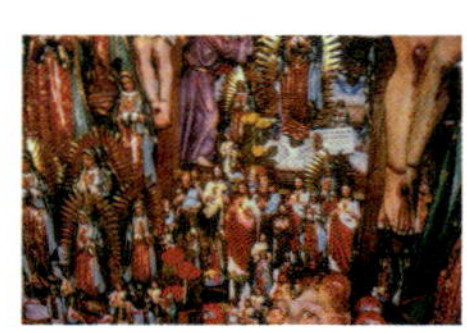

18

of globalism on the city and countryside. Rubén Ortiz-Torres (b. 1964), who was photographing Mexico's punk scene in black and white, got to know Bernal at the 1981 Coloquio and later wrote about his impact: "His color photography would influence countless Mexican and Latin American photographers," he noted, giving the example of Adolfo Patiño (1954–2005), who went by the moniker Adolfotográfo. Patiño, who was working with Polaroid cameras, a diaristic approach, and snapshot aesthetics, was struck by Bernal's use of color "not only as an aesthetic effect, but as a cultural signifier."[62] Ortiz-Torres himself moved from black-and-white to color photography to make a series on border culture in garish color, citing Bernal as his model (fig. 18, page 52).[63]

BERNAL GOES TO THE OLYMPICS

Bernal received a high-profile commission to photograph at the 1984 Summer Olympics in Los Angeles under the auspices of the Olympics Arts Festival. The US had last hosted the Summer Olympics in 1932, also in Los Angeles, and there was palpable excitement in the city surrounding the Games' return. This was new territory for Bernal. Although he had experience in high school photographing student athletes, the Olympics were in a completely different league, as much spectacle as competition. And while Bernal was familiar with Los Angeles, he had never photographed there. At the time, LA's population exceeded three million, nearly a third of which, per the US census nomenclature of the time, identified as Hispanic.

62. Rubén Ortiz-Torres, "¡!El Pachuco Actual Se Nueva A Morir!," *Mex/L.A.: "Mexican" Modernism(s) in Los Angeles, 1930–1985.* (Berlin: Hatje Cantz and Long Beach, CA: Museum of Latin American Art, 2011): 31.

63. Rubén Ortiz-Torres, "De cómo el color migro al sur desde Aztlán en busca de una águila devorando a una serpiente en una penca de maguey," *Luna Córnea* 34 (2013): pp. 397–401.

Bernal laid out a clear plan: he would approach the assignment from the perspective of a Chicano. "My job," he wrote, "will not only be that of a photographer of athletes. In addition, I shall leave behind the record that the photographic lens of an Hispanic registered the comings and goings of ordinary people during those two months."[64] He did precisely this, photographing in vivid color at the official Olympics site, then visiting the city's Mexican American districts with black-and-white film in his camera.

Bernal had a unique take on the Olympics. He left it up to others to document the competitions and star athletes, while he focused on gate attendants, security staff, and souvenir vendors—in other words, the working-class people who made the enterprise run and who were otherwise ignored (pages 185–87). The rich color he captured seems to align with his image of Los Angeles as a city of artifice and manufactured happiness.[65] In contrast, the black-and-white photographs he made illustrate a side of life in the city that was largely invisible except to its denizens (pages 188–91). As his friend, the writer Leslie Marmon Silko noted, "Lou soon found the elitism inside the Olympic pavilions so obnoxious that after a day or two he chose to photograph outside the Olympic park gates in the streets where multitudes of visitors and fans, unable to afford or obtain tickets, created a joyous spontaneous street fiesta."[66] In his forays outside the official sites, he found a more familiar world of norteño music, modest Mexican food counters, and working-class families attending to everyday tasks. While he rarely worked in the mode of the street photographer, it was in the busy streets of central LA where Bernal seemed to relish the opportunity to capture a version of American life that was largely ignored by street photographers of the era. He turned his lens on working-class people as well on the city's eccentrics, including fervent street preachers or a bikini-clad, high-heeled woman walking incongruously with a toddler along a boardwalk. To Bernal, Los Angeles must have seemed raucous, a city of contradictions where the banal and the bizarre existed side by side.

LUBBOCK

Bernal made one of his last series of photographs in 1987 and 1988 in the northwest Texas town of Lubbock, for a commission from Texas Tech University to portray the town's Mexican American community.[67] The project, conceived for an exhibition at the university, represented an important symbolic effort by a major institution in Lubbock, where Jim Crow laws and racial segregation had persisted well into the 1980s. It was also significant for Bernal, who was unfamiliar with the region but had long hoped to extend his *Barrios* series to Mexican American communities throughout the Southwest. Moreover, the resulting series includes portraits of Afro Latinxs, who are otherwise little represented in his oeuvre. Ultimately, Bernal made some of his most distinct and penetrating images in Lubbock.

In an unpublished statement about the series, Bernal elaborated on why he had sought to record life inside the homes of Mexican American people for well over a decade. He wrote about his subjects' "outer" and "inner" realities, as he termed them, the former concerning public matters and accommodation, and the latter encompassing private and familial life. It was this inner realm, he stated, that held "Hispanic culture and traditions, imbued with religious and spiritual values." Bernal aimed to convey this aspect of life—"the essence of the Chicano

64. Troy, "Louis Carlos Bernal."

65. For an analysis of Bernal's Olympics photographs see Josh Rios, "Race to the Periphery," *Dilettante Army*, n.d., https://dilettantearmy.com/articles/race-to-the-periphery#_edn13.

66. Leslie Marmon Silko, untitled essay in *Louis Carlos Bernal: Barrios* (Tucson: Pima Community College in association with University of Arizona Library, 2002), p. 31.

67. The exhibition, *Espiritu Mejicano: Lubbock*, was displayed at the Museum of Texas Tech University in 1988.

soul," as he put it—knowing that these realms were otherwise unknown to outsiders. Ultimately, he aimed to act as a bridge between Brown and white people and, through his work, foster understanding and respect between cultures.[68]

Bernal completed the series during two brief trips to Lubbock, where he wandered residential neighborhoods, looking for opportunities to photograph. His portraits include *Helen* (1988, page 199), named for the adolescent girl who peers expectantly at the photographer, and an untitled image of her younger sister, seen sprawling on a bed in a kind of bored acquiescence as she waits for Bernal to click the camera shutter (page 195). Although they had just met the photographer, he clearly allayed any discomfort they may have experienced with a stranger standing in their bedrooms, and each directly confronts the camera's gaze. Bernal also photographed outdoors in Lubbock, picturing members of a family arranged along the front porch of their house, and an older couple posing amiably in their lush garden, cradling a large bowl of freshly picked fruits (pages 200–1).

While in Lubbock, Bernal repeatedly heard about a well-known Cuban *curandera* (healer), Caridad Sanchez, and he arranged to meet her. As much as he wanted to photograph the woman, his superstitious nature made their meeting one of the most fraught encounters of his career In the photograph, Sanchez stands proudly next to a large home altar populated not only by the usual array of representations of Jesus and Mary, but also by the bust of a Native American, a large black doll resembling Sanchez, and a statue of the dark-skinned Martin de Porres, the patron saint of mixed-race people who is known for levitation, miraculous knowledge, and instantaneous cures (page 203). Bernal often photographed traditional Catholic shrines and altars, but this one was new to him, with its syncretic mix of Christian, African, and Indigenous Caribbean spiritual forms. As he was photographing, the *curandera* threw holy water on him and told him he would change many lives. As much as he was intrigued by spiritual practices beyond Catholicism, he felt a peculiar, discomforting energy in the room. He made a few exposures of the woman and then quickly left.[69]

CODA

Bernal made his final series of photographs in 1989, in Douglas, the town of his birth. His aunt Berta had died, and he returned to attend the funeral and photograph inside her home. He returned to a familiar mode, working in the kind of modest domestic environment that reminded him of his own upbringing. He produced a series of color photographs (pages 207–8) depicting such scenes as the worn furniture inside a bedroom, an old pair of shoes set on the floor, and cosmetics and face creams neatly lined up on a dresser. Bernal may not have conceived of himself as a photographer of still lifes, but he had a special gift for endowing the inanimate with reverence, for magnifying common possessions so they stood as expressions of one's sense of values and identity. He had manifested this tendency as early as 1977 with the *Benitez Suite*, when he lovingly photographed the threadbare rooms that were home to Mary Benitez. Bernal photographed those spaces in black and white, using the limited natural light to picture them with an air of melancholy and religiosity. His renditions of his aunt's personal spaces do not reflect the level of poverty visible in the *Benitez Suite*, but the two series share an enveloping loneliness, a sense that we are witnessing an ending.

68. I am grateful to Robert Buitrón for sharing "Espiritu Mejicano," Bernal's handwritten, undated statement about the series with me.

69. Bernal's companion Marietta Bernstorff accompanied him to Lubbock and provided recollections of this meeting. She noted that Bernal was unusually nervous while shooting and initially failed to remove the cap from his camera lens.

Bernal did not know that the photographs he made in Douglas, a meditation on life's last years and mortality, would mark another ending: that of his creative career. In fact, he never had a chance to see these images in print. But transitions, and perhaps even a sense of an ending, seemed to increasingly be on his mind in the late 1980s. His spiritual sensibility, one that intensified as he matured, encompassed the realms of dreams, psychic connections, and even premonitions. His encounter with the *curandera* Caridad Sanchez was one of several psychologically charged incidents that occurred in the year or so prior to the accident in October 1989 that eventually claimed his life. He offered intimations of his own death in this period—in his work, in communications with those close to him, and in events that transpired that year. In retrospect, to those who knew him well, this was hardly surprising. He had long been drawn to the supernatural, superstitions, and ghost stories like the Mexican folk legend of La Llorona.[70] Bernal's daughters have spoken of his interest in Carl Jung, as well as in theories of the collective unconscious and of rebirth.[71] He did not reject the Catholicism of his youth, and he was certainly familiar with Church-based rituals; scenes of baptisms, quinceañeras, and weddings all figure in his oeuvre. But Bernal, who referred to himself as a "fallen Catholic," was more genuinely interested in popular expressions of faith—faith tied to culture and to the everyday.[72]

Bernal made his last trip to Mexico in the summer of 1989 with Marietta Bernstorff and his old friend Armando Cristeto. While visiting Palenque, a complex of ancient Mayan ruins in southern Mexico, he nearly slipped into an open tomb structure and jokingly blamed the mishap on the shirt he was wearing decorated with *calaveras* (skeletons)—possibly offensive to the Mayan deities. But it rattled him. The past was preoccupying Bernal, which was unlike him, as was his future. Later in the trip, during a walk in Mexico City, he happened to pass by a house where he had lived as a student a quarter century earlier.[73] He also spoke to his companions about possibly moving away from photography. He was frustrated with the lack of respect the medium received compared to other art forms, and by his lack of sales from a recent gallery exhibition in Tucson. He thought he might turn to writing and perhaps return to Oaxaca to live for a while.[74]

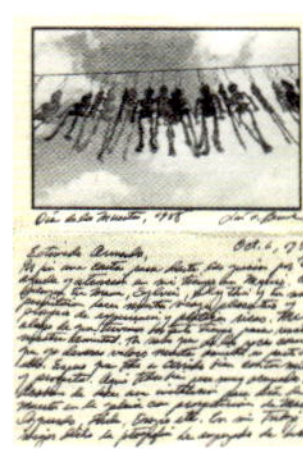

A frequent letter writer, Bernal was known for sending cartes de visite, illustrated with his photographs, to friends and acquaintances in the United States and Mexico. In his last few cards to Cristeto, he repeatedly sent an image titled *Día de los Muertos* (Day of the Dead, 1988) that depicts a row of *calaveras* hanging from a clothesline (fig. 19, page 52). And in his very last communication to Cristeto, dating to October 6, 1989, he wrote, "*Para rematar nuestra amistad*"—"to complete our friendship."[75] Eighteen days later in Tucson, he was hit by an automobile while riding his bike to Pima Community College. He suffered a brain-stem injury and fell into a long coma from which he never awoke. Bernal died on August 18, 1993—his fifty-second birthday.

19

For Bernal, the elaboration of an artistic language was an act of finely balancing concerns for aesthetics, culture, and community. As much as he followed photography's experimental and conceptual currents, he sought to produce images that would resonate with members of the very communities he celebrated and most deeply convey their values and spirituality. In speaking of his portrayals of Mexican Americans, he once stated, "I've tried to capture the spiritual and the religious aspect, photographing an ordinary situation and making it more than ordinary because it is more than ordinary. There is a sense of greatness, of

70. The story of La Llorona (The Weeping Woman) has many variations, but it is most typically associated with the story of a mother wailing at night for her lost or dead children, perhaps the victims of filicide.

71. Katrina and Lisa Bernal, phone interview with the author, January 7, 2022.

72. Ibid.

73. Marietta Bernstorff, interview with the author, Oaxaca, Mexico, November 2002.

74. Marietta Bernstorff, interview with the author, November 2002 and September 13, 2022.

75. Armando Cristeto, interview with the author, Mexico City, November 2002.

immortality in every one of us here . . . That attaches us to the larger events in life."[76] Where others might have seen people who were unremarkable or lesser than them, Bernal found beauty and a quiet grandeur. In a career spanning only two decades, he produced a body of work that constitutes a Chicanx imaginary, a worldview absent of discrimination and marginalization. Bernal mapped a borderless realm across the Southwest, to Mexico, and even to Cuba, where cultural identity was shaped foremost by family, community, and spirituality. He found a way to put Chicanx people at the center of this world, indelibly memorialized. His work may not have been on the cutting edge, but it went deep to the heart of Chicanismo, expressing an enduring pride and depth of spirit.

Bringing his *full self* to his work was Bernal's longstanding aspiration, and he understood the process of making a photograph as a complex synthesis of the physical and the mechanical, the visual and the psychological. "The most important is the trigger pull," he once said. "The intellectual and intuitive responses of a photographer come together when the shutter release is pressed. Camera, eye, mind, finger, through this sequence we arrive at the moment in time, a fraction of a second when we press the shutter release. This shutter impulse becomes an affirmation of what we believe."

76. Bernal, in Rider, "An Informal Chat."

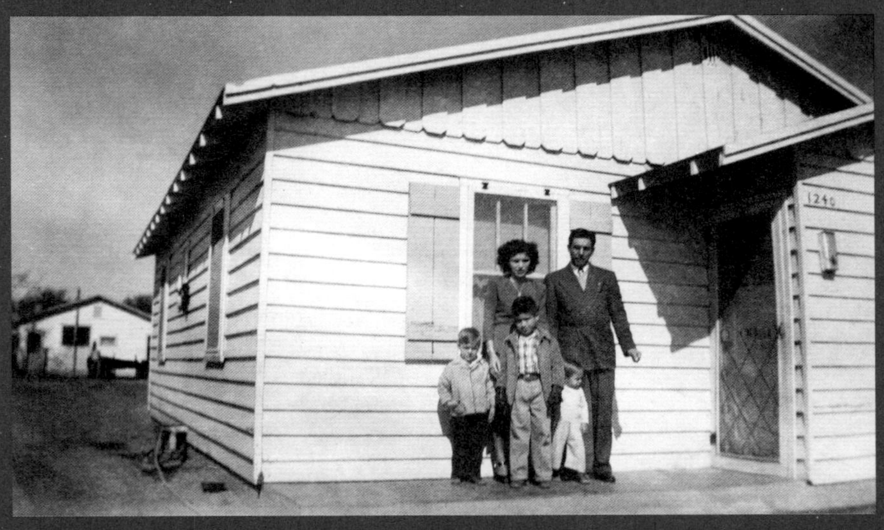

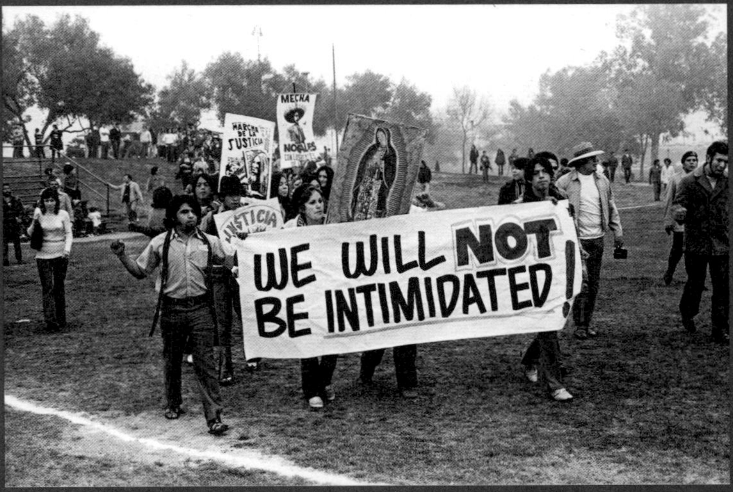

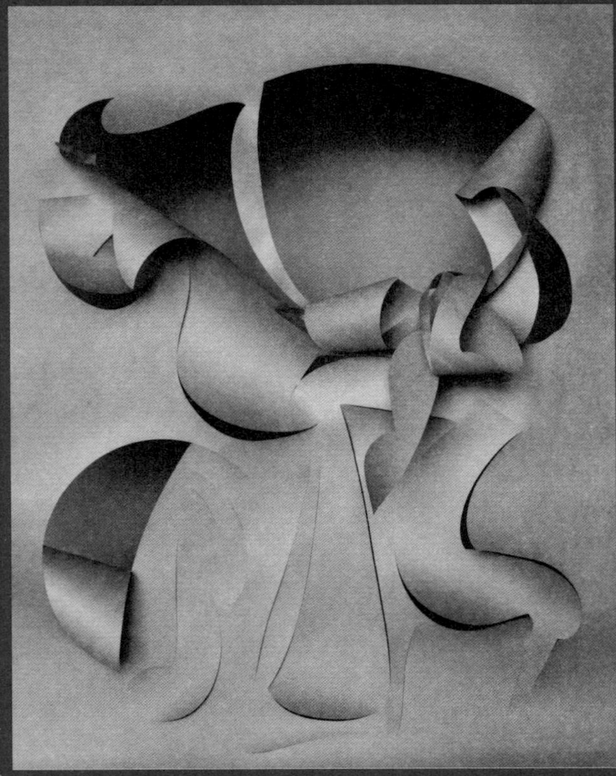

EN
1. Bernal family, Douglas, Arizona, mid-1940s
2. Luis C. Garza, *We Will Not Be Intimidated, Los Angeles, California*, 1971
3. Frederick Sommer, *Cut Paper*, 1970

ES
1. La familia Bernal, Douglas, Arizona, mediados de los 1940s
2. Luis C. Garza, *No seremos intimidados*, Los Ángeles, California, 1971
3. Frederick Sommer, *Papel cortado*, 1970

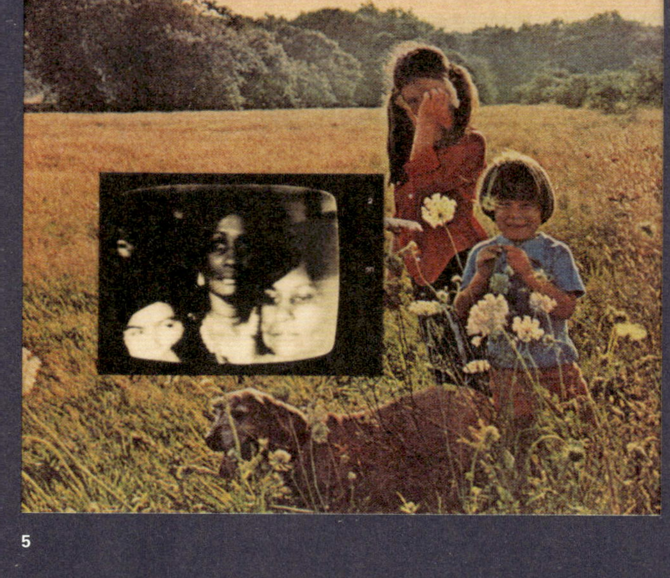

5

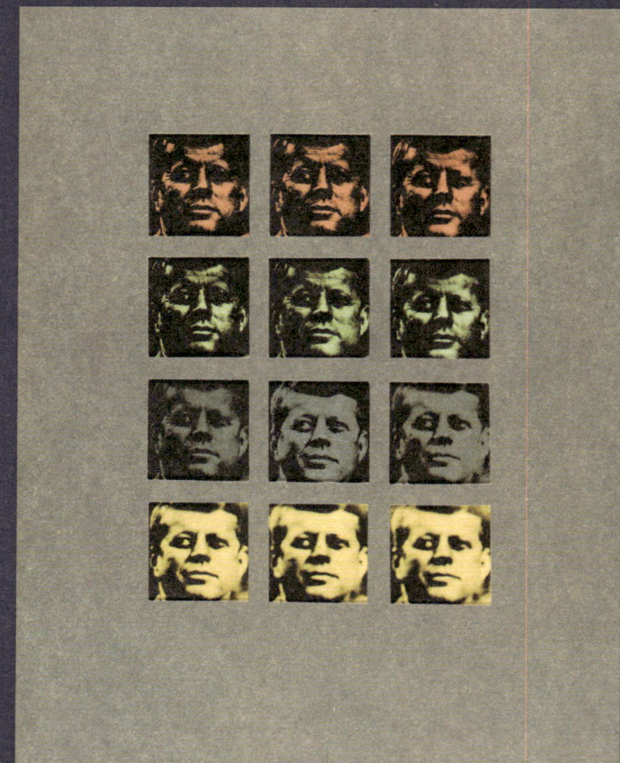

4

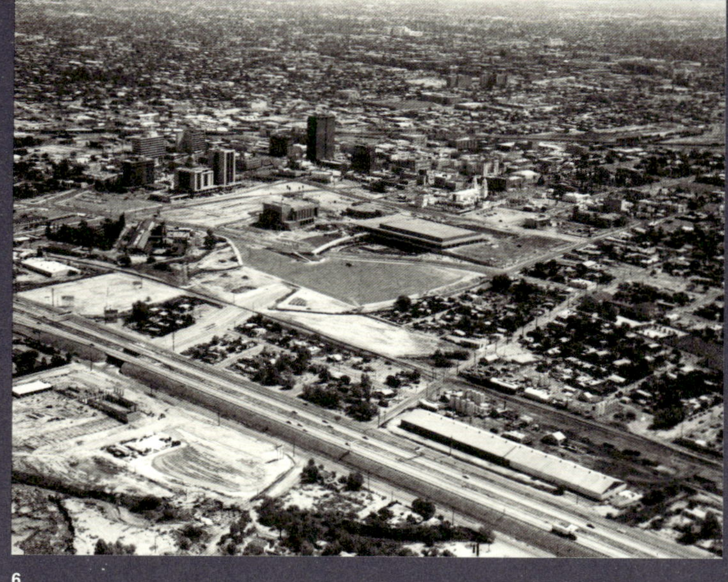

6

EN
4. Louis Carlos Bernal, *Untitled*, ca. 1970
5. Louis Carlos Bernal, *American Landscape*, 1970
6. Gene Magee, *Aerial View of Tucson*, ca. 1970

ES
4. Louis Carlos Bernal, *Sin título*, ca. 1970
5. Louis Carlos Bernal, *Paisaje americano*, 1970
6. Gene Magee, *Vista aérea de Tucson*, ca. 1970

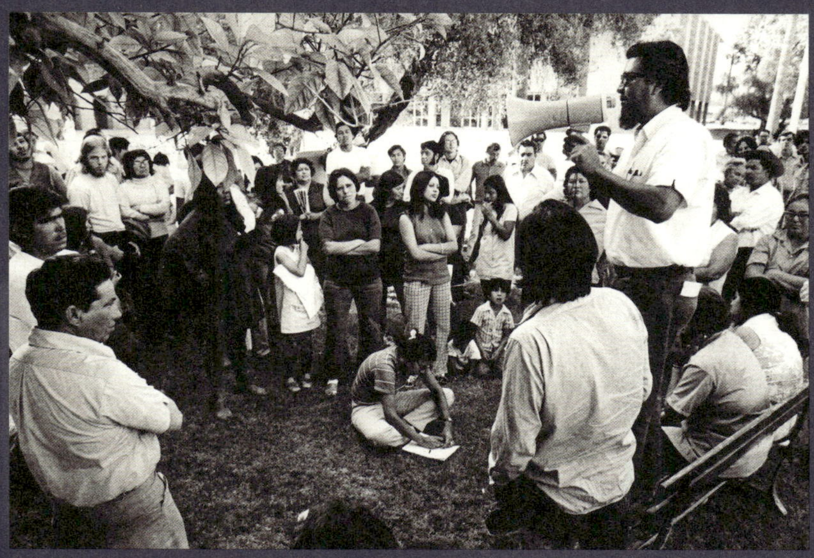

7

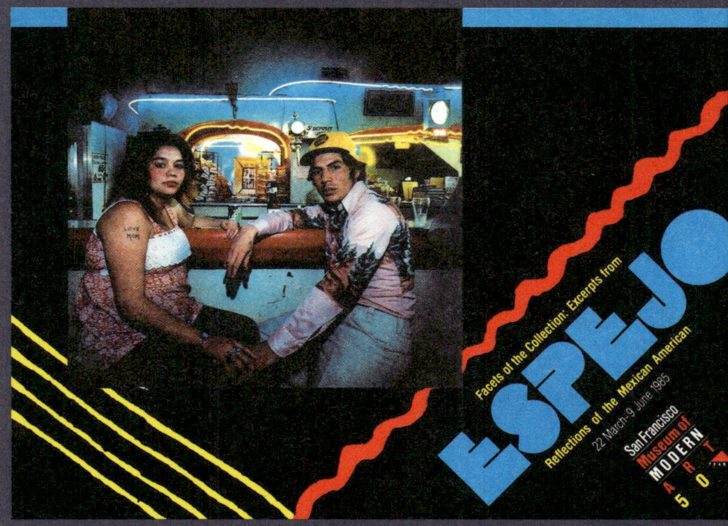

8

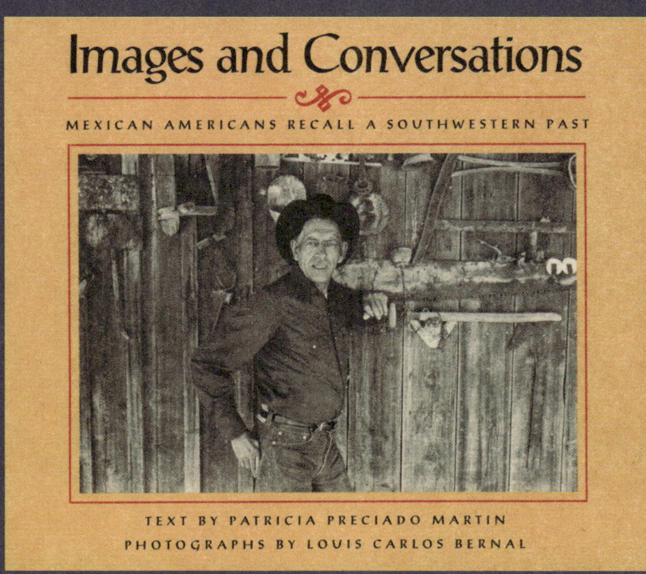

9

7. Richard Chávez, César Chávez's brother, speaks to a group at the Arizona State Capitol to protest HB 2134, a law that restricted workers' ability to organize, ca. early 1970s. Photograph by Nyle Leatham

8. Exhibition brochure for *Facets of the Collection: Excerpts from Espejo, Reflections of the Mexican American*, San Francisco Museum of Modern Art, 1985, with inset photograph by Louis Carlos Bernal

9. Cover of *Images and Conversations: Mexican Americans Recall a Southwestern Past* (1983), with photograph by Louis Carlos Bernal

7. Richard Chávez, hermano de César Chávez, habla a un grupo en el Capitolio del Estado de Arizona para protestar contra HB 2134, una ley que restringía el derecho de los trabajadores a organizarse, ca. principios de los 1970s. Fotografía por Nyle Leatham

8. Folleto de exposición para *Facetas de la Colección: Fragmentos de Espejo, Reflexiones del mexicano-americano*, San Francisco Museum of Modern Art, 1985, con fotografía añadida por Louis Carlos Bernal

9. Portada de *Imágenes y conversaciones: Mexicanos-americanos recuerdan su pasado del suroeste* (1983), con fotografía por Louis Carlos Bernal

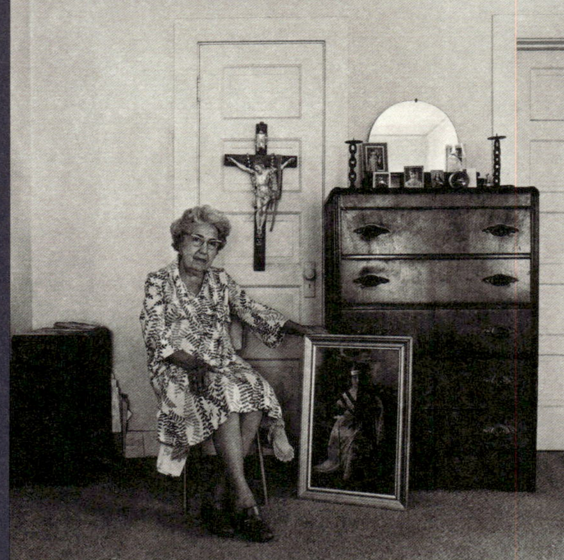

10

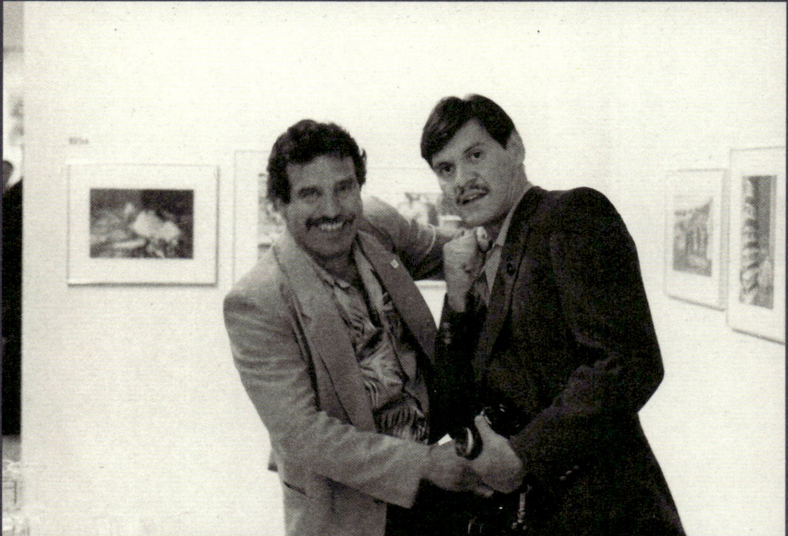

11

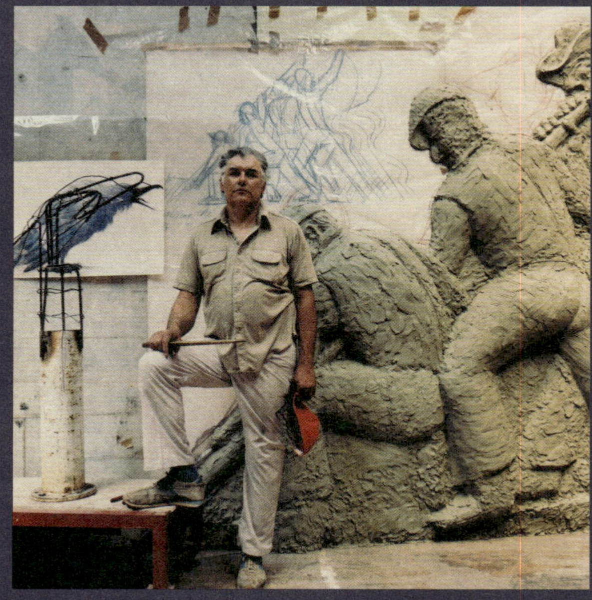

12

13

EN
10. Louis Carlos Bernal, *María Soto Audelo, Tucson, Arizona*, 1979
11. Photographer unknown, Portrait of María Soto Audelo, 1917
12. Louis Carlos Bernal, Portrait of the artist Luis Jiménez in his studio, Hondo, New Mexico, 1980s
13. Louis Carlos Bernal and Ricardo Valverde in Riverside, California, 1980s. Photograph by Adam Avila

ES
10. Louis Carlos Bernal, *María Soto Audelo, Tucson, Arizona*, 1979
11. Fotógrafo desconocido, Retrato de María Soto Audelo, 1917
12. Louis Carlos Bernal, Retrato del artista Luis Jiménez en su estudio, Hondo, Nuevo México, 1980s
13. Louis Carlos Bernal y Ricardo Valverde en Riverside, California, 1980s. Fotografía por Adam Avila

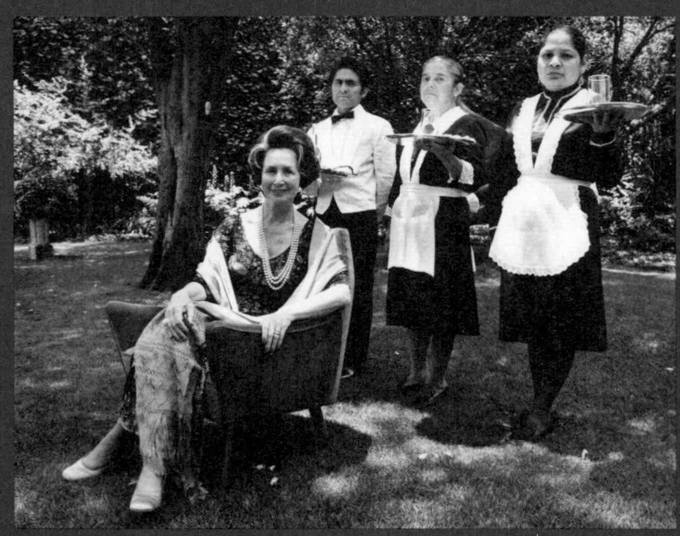

15

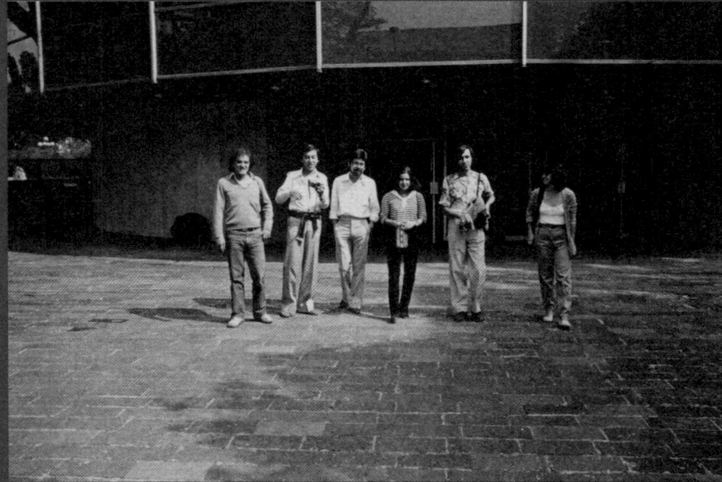

14

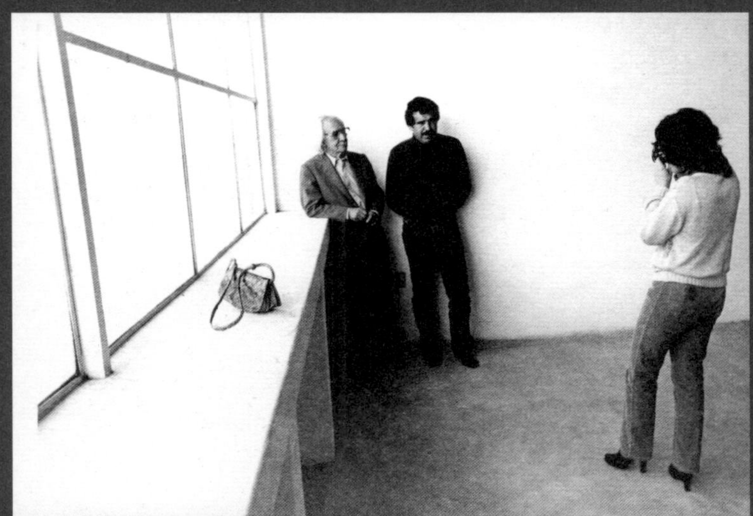

16

EN

14. Louis Carlos Bernal, Photographers Rogelio Villarreal (far left), Armando Cristeto (second from left), and Adolfo Patiño (second from right) with others at the Museo de Arte Moderno, Mexico City, ca. 1981–82

15. Pedro Meyer, *The Lady and Her Servants*, 1978

16. Manuel Álvarez Bravo and Louis Carlos Bernal photographed by Graciela Iturbide, Coyoacán, Mexico City, 1984. Photograph by Armando Cristeto

ES

14. Louis Carlos Bernal, Fotógrafos Rogelio Villarreal (más a la izq.), Armando Cristeto (segundo de la izq.), y Adolfo Patiño (segundo de la der.) con otros en el Museo de Arte Moderno, Ciudad de México, ca. 1981–82

15. Pedro Meyer, *La señora y sus sirvientes*, 1978

16. Manuel Álvarez Bravo y Louis Carlos Bernal fotografiados por Graciela Iturbide, Coyoacán, Ciudad de México, 1984. Fotografía por Armando Cristeto

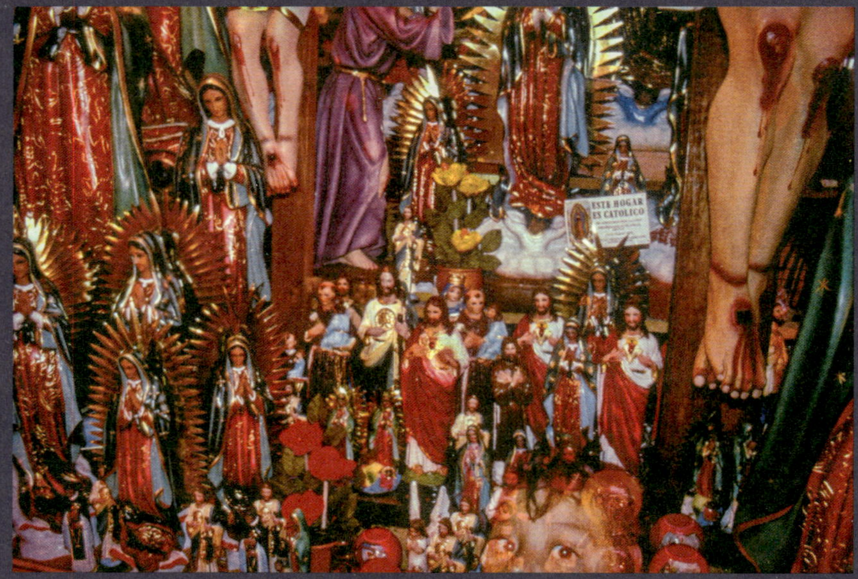

18

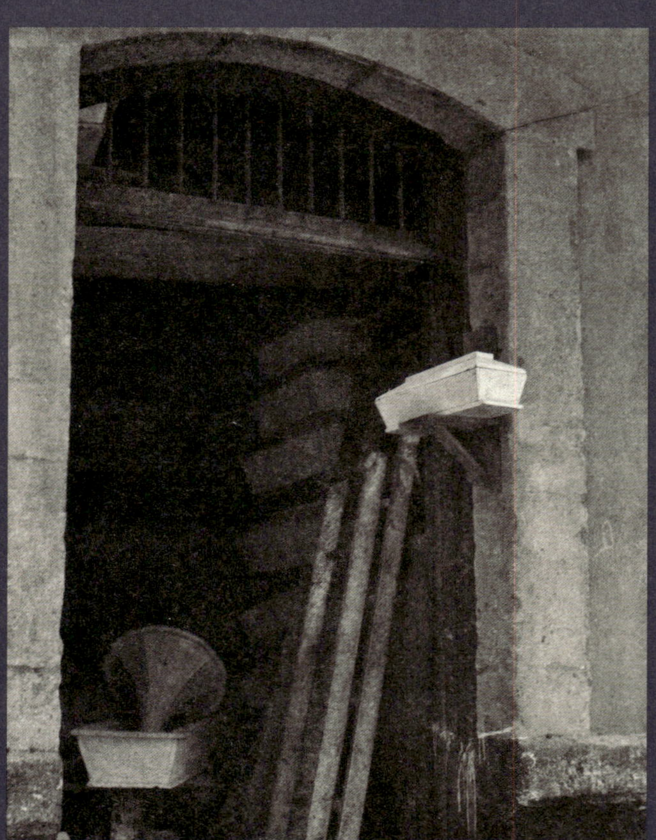

17

19

LOUIS CARLOS BERNAL: VIDA Y OBRA

Elizabeth Ferrer

Dedicado a la memoria de Gilbert C. Ferrer

COMIENZOS

Louis Carlos Bernal nació en 1941 en Douglas, Arizona, una pequeña ciudad fronteriza en una región conocida por la ganadería y la extracción de cobre. Su modesta educación como hijo mexicano-americano de una trabajadora del hogar y un calderero desempeñó un papel decisivo en su formación como chicano y 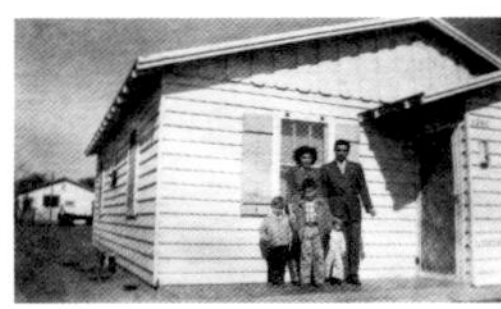 como fotógrafo. La familia se trasladó a Phoenix cuando él tenía seis años, donde los niños (Louis era el mayor de tres hijos) iban a recibir una mejor educación (fig. 1, página 47). Cuando tenía once años, Bernal recibió una cámara como regalo de una tía y pronto desarrolló una fascinación por las cámaras y el proceso químico de producción de una imagen; incluso, llegó a convertir el cuarto de baño de su casa en un cuarto oscuro improvisado. En cualquier caso, una trayectoria creativa habría sido poco práctica para el hijo de una familia mexicano-americana aspiracional en las décadas de 1950 y 1960.

En Phoenix, Bernal experimentó el racismo manifiesto que era habitual en los años anteriores a la aprobación de las Leyes de Derechos Civiles de la década de 1960. En la ciudad existían una gran mayoría de gente blanca, escuelas segregadas y barrios conocidos como *sundown towns*, donde la gente de color podía trabajar pero no vivir. El propio Bernal recordaba haber visto restaurantes con entradas separadas para blancos y "mexicanos" (lo que en su día se entendía como un epíteto despectivo, incluso si uno había nacido en EE.UU.) y, como atleta de escuela secundaria, se le negó la entrada a hoteles donde se alojaban sus compañeros de equipo.[1] Desafiando las limitadas expectativas de los mexicano-americanos impuestas por la sociedad, se fijó como objetivo ir a la universidad para, inicialmente, estudiar español con el propósito de enseñarlo. Pero Bernal siguió dedicándose a la fotografía y cubriendo eventos deportivos para los periódicos de su escuela secundaria y universidad. De hecho, la cámara se convirtió en un accesorio tan omnipresente en su vida que llegó a ser conocido como "Shutterbug Louie" —Louie, el cámara aficionado.[2] A mediados de la década de 1960, cuando Bernal finalizaba sus estudios universitarios en Arizona State University (la Universidad Estatal de Arizona o ASU) de Tempe, decidió tomarse en serio el estudio de la fotografía y convertirse en artista.

En 1966, Bernal se concluyó su licenciatura, lo reclutó el ejército y se casó con Sandra Jean Anderson, una artista que había trabajado con él como modelo. El conflicto de Vietnam se recrudecía, pero se salvó de que se le enviara al sudeste asiático al recibir una misión en Berlín, donde se le asignó trabajo como fotógrafo. Su mejor amigo de la universidad, Tom Eckert, califica el servicio militar de Bernal como una especie de pausa: rara vez hablaba de él, pero en una entrada de su diario escrita durante ese periodo, Bernal expresaba su frustración por necesitar más tiempo y libertad para crear fotografías y trabajar para realizarse como artista.[3] Regresó a Phoenix dos años después emocionado y dispuesto a seguir con su pasión.[4]

Bernal ingresó en la ASU en 1968 y pasó un período de formación entre 1970 y 1972 bajo la tutela de Frederick Sommer (1905–1999), renombrado pero solitario fotógrafo afincado en Prescott, Arizona. En 1972, Bernal obtuvo su maestría en fotografía y se trasladó con su familia a Tucson después de que el Pima Community College le contratara para poner en marcha su departamento de

Nota de los editores:
Esta publicación usa los términos inclusivos y neutrales al género Latinx y Chicanx en los textos en inglés, así como Chicano, este último mo reflejando la era del Movimiento de Derechos Civiles Chicanos y el propio uso del término por parte de Louis Carlos Bernal.

1. Katrina y Lisa Bernal, entrevista telefónica con la autora, 26 de agosto de 2021.

2. Marietta Bernstorff, entrevista con la autora, 29 de diciembre de 2021.

3. Louis Carlos Bernal, entrada de diario, 27 de mayo de 1968. Agradezco a Marietta Bernstorff que haya compartido esta información.

4. Tom Eckert, entrevista con la autora, 14 de enero de 2022.

fotografía. Aunque viajó mucho por el suroeste y México, Tucson siguió siendo su hogar hasta su muerte en 1993. En una entrevista de 1984 relató su traslado a Tucson:

> Durante el traslado físico también comencé un traslado espiritual de vuelta al barrio y una nueva actitud ante la vida: el chicanismo. Mexicano-americano es el término utilizado para describir a una persona nacida en Estados Unidos pero cuya alma cultural procede de México. Esta doble realidad ha sido una carga que ha nublado nuestra identidad. El chicanismo nos permite aceptar nuestra historia, pero también nos da una nueva realidad para afrontar el presente y el futuro. Ser chicano significa participar en el control de tu vida. El chicanismo representa un nuevo sentimiento de orgullo, una nueva actitud y conciencia [...] el artista chicano no puede aislarse de la comunidad, sino que se encuentra en medio de su pueblo creando arte de y para el pueblo. Mis imágenes hablan de los lazos religiosos y familiares que he expresado como chicano. Me he ocupado del misticismo del Suroeste y de la fuerza de los valores espirituales y culturales de los barrios.[5]

Bernal alcanzó la madurez como fotógrafo a principios de la década de 1970, en medio del movimiento chicano por los derechos civiles. Esta amplia lucha por la justicia social tenía sus raíces en los esfuerzos de organización laboral que César Chávez y Dolores Huerta habían liderado en el valle agrícola central de California los años 60 para apoyar a los trabajadores agrícolas que se desempeñaban en duras condiciones por un salario mínimo. El movimiento galvanizó a una generación joven de mexicano-americanos, muchos de los cuales viajaron a Delano, Salinas y Sacramento para unirse a las marchas de protesta, coordinar las campañas de entrega de alimentos y ropa a los trabajadores agrícolas, organizar boicots y documentar el movimiento. Los miembros de esta generación empezaron a referirse a sí mismos como chicanos y a reclamar y redefinir lo que antes era un insulto étnico como un término empoderador basado en la solidaridad y la autodeterminación. El

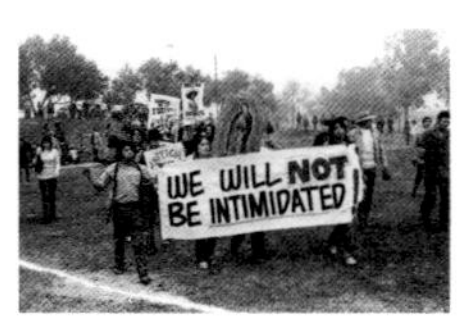

2

movimiento, como se le conocía, se expandió para hacer frente a numerosos problemas de justicia social: la guerra de Vietnam, en la que luchaban un número desproporcionado de hombres morenos y negros; la mala calidad de la educación en las escuelas públicas de los barrios mexicano-americanos; la falta de oportunidades económicas; y un sinnúmero de otras manifestaciones de racismo (fig. 2, página 47).

La articulación de valores culturales y espirituales que reflejaban el orgullo por la propia etnia y origen —el chicanismo— fue fundamental para el movimiento. Una iconografía centrada en las deidades y la cultura precolombinas; la Virgen de Guadalupe (patrona de México) y el Sagrado Corazón de Jesús (emblema del amor y la compasión); y los héroes populares de la Revolución mexicana sirvieron para vincular a la población chicana con historias y valores aparte y mucho más allá de la construcción eurocéntrica del excepcionalismo estadounidense. Además, las nuevas articulaciones en torno al concepto de Aztlán, el hogar ancestral de los aztecas en el Suroeste estadounidense, se convirtieron en un grito de guerra para los chicanos que reclamaban la soberanía sobre las tierras colonizadas de la región.[6]Aunque no parece que Bernal hablara nunca de Aztlán, la trayectoria de su vida y sus viajes como fotógrafo, que comienzan en la ciudad fronteriza de Douglas y se extienden por estados de todo el Suroeste y México,

5. Louis Carlos Bernal, en *Awards in the Visual Arts 3* (Winston-Salem, NC: Southeastern Center for Contemporary Art, 1984), p. 16.

6. Véase Shifra M. Goldman, "The Iconography of Chicano Self-Determination: Race, Ethnicity, and Class", número especial, *Art Journal: Depictions of the Dispossessed* 49, no. 2 (verano de 1990): pp. 167–73; y Rodolfo Gonzales y Alurista [seud.], "El plan espiritual de Aztlán", *El Grito del Norte* 2, no. 9 (6 de julio de 1969): p. 5. El poeta chicano Alurista (Alberto Baltazar Urista Heredia) leyó "El plan espiritual de Aztlán", un manifiesto que anunciaba estos conceptos, en la Conferencia Nacional de Liberación de la Juventud Chicana celebrada en Denver en 1969.

evoca una búsqueda similar: la de raíces ancestrales, de una patria soberana y de una fusión de realización personal y creativa.

Bernal comenzó a expresar su creciente identidad chicana como estudiante, al mismo tiempo que lidiaba con el desarrollo de su voz artística. Estos dos hilos se estaban entrelazando. Como él mismo escribió: "He sentido mucha rabia y ansiedad en mi vida y he utilizado la fotografía como válvula de escape para estas frustraciones. Mis imágenes siempre han tratado de la batalla interior de mi alma".[7] Aunque sus años de formación como artista coincidieron con los años del movimiento chicano por los derechos civiles, expresó su sentido del chicanismo de forma más directa en términos espirituales y culturales, más que políticos. Al parecer, no participó en las manifestaciones lideradas por activistas estudiantiles que tuvieron lugar en Tucson a finales de los sesenta y solo ocasionalmente —sobre todo al principio de su carrera— abordó temas explícitamente políticos en su obra. No obstante, Bernal fue uno de los primeros beneficiarios del movimiento por los derechos civiles y de las nuevas oportunidades que ofrecía, sobre todo para estudiantes. Formó parte de la primera oleada de mexicano-americanos que accedieron a los programas de posgrado de la ASU a finales de la década de 1960 y las actitudes racistas que experimentó de niño se habían disipado hasta el punto de que se lo contrataron con entusiasmo para enseñar en el Pima Community College en 1972.

Mientras Bernal reflexionaba sobre su identidad artística a principios de la década de 1970, se sintió intrigado por los nuevos enfoques del medio que habían surgido en los últimos años, incluidos los modos abstractos y conceptuales que desafiaban los dictados puristas de las generaciones precedentes dedicadas a la llamada fotografía directa. Algunos fotógrafos escenificaban composiciones e ideaban procesos no tradicionales en el cuarto oscuro; otros creaban fotomontajes, a menudo apropiándose de imágenes de los medios de comunicación o combinando palabras e imágenes para producir cargadas declaraciones políticas. Incluso la tradición documental estaba experimentando un cambio radical. Fotógrafos como Lee Friedlander, Diane Arbus y Garry Winogrand estaban introduciendo una forma de documentación social con influencias personales, con imágenes que a veces podían parecer instantáneas o incidentales, pero que a menudo funcionaban como comentarios sociales mordaces.[8]

Los primeros trabajos de Bernal reflejan su entusiasmo por los modos no convencionales de fotografía. En el Phoenix College estudió con Allen A. Dutton (1922–2017), conocido por sus paisajes surrealistas y sus desnudos desérticos; y en la ASU, con Jack Stuler (1932–2015), que creó abstracciones surrealistas a partir de formas naturales e imágenes collage.[9] Ambos inspiraron probablemente a Bernal a abordar su medio como una forma de arte y con un sentido de libertad. En 1970, buscó al fotógrafo de fama internacional Frederick Sommer, con quien trabajó durante dos años. Nacido en Italia y criado en Brasil, Sommer fue un inconformista conocido por sus distintas obras: paisajes desérticos intensamente detallados sin horizonte visible, desnudos, bodegones macabros y surrealistas y collages construidos a menudo a partir de imágenes encontradas. El ejemplo de Sommer animó a Bernal a considerar ampliamente las posibilidades del medio, aunque su obra resultante estuviera a veces demasiado en deuda con el artista mayor.

Para una serie de imágenes construidas, Bernal realizó arreglos inquietantes y construcciones a partir de piezas de muñecas viejas, algunas de las cuales parecían emerger de las páginas quebradizas de periódicos antiguos, mientras que otras se abrían para mostrar su interior mecánico. Estas imágenes, así como

7. Timothy Troy, "Louis Carlos Bernal", en *Original Sources. Art and Archives at the Center for Creative Photography*, eds. Amy Rule y Nancy Solomon (Tucson: Center for Creative Photography, University of Arizona, 2002), pp. 53–55.

8. Véase el ensayo de Rebecca Senf en esta publicación para una discusión sobre la relación de la obra de Bernal con la estética de la instantánea asociada a estos fotógrafos.

9. Agradezco al fotógrafo Robert Buitrón que me señalara la importancia de Dutton en los inicios de la carrera de Bernal, y al artista Tom Eckert, por la información sobre Jack Stuler.

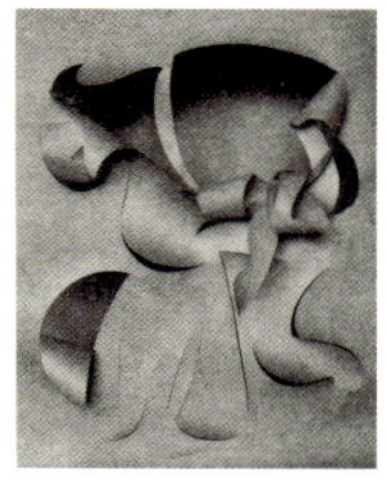

3

otras en las que se emplean juguetes antiguos, recuerdan a las fotografías que Sommer hizo décadas antes de muñecas rebuscadas en vertederos locales. Este enfoque de la creación de imágenes era una fuente temporal de fascinación para Bernal, pero respondía a un genuino interés personal: a lo largo de su vida coleccionó pequeños juguetes y objetos que ensamblaba en bodegones para alguna que otra fotografía. La influencia de Sommer también se aprecia claramente en las fotografías abstractas en blanco y negro de Bernal en papel de carnicero recortado dispuesto en elaboradas formas curvilíneas (fig. 3, página 47). Sommer había desarrollado esta técnica en la década de 1960 y realizado numerosas composiciones en este estilo, que combinaba ingeniosamente elementos del dibujo, la escultura y la fotografía. Bernal también utilizó estos trozos de papel como vestuario extravagante, aunque provocativo, para los desnudos femeninos que fotografió en su estudio en este periodo.

En última instancia, fue el propio Sommer —y no su obra— quien tuvo un efecto más duradero en Bernal de joven. En una entrada de su diario, Bernal escribió con admiración sobre el intelecto de Sommer, su conocimiento de la historia de la fotografía y su dominio de las cámaras y la técnica. Reflexionando sobre el ejemplo que Sommer dio, como artista que aportaba todo el peso de su ser y su intelecto a la creación de obras, recordó: "De alguna manera, al conocerlo sentí que llevaba mucho tiempo dirigiéndome hacia ese encuentro".[10]

A principios de la década de 1970, Bernal realizó varios pequeños trabajos de orientación política. Lo que les unía era su interés por la televisión y por el papel de los medios de comunicación en la promulgación de los valores estadounidenses dominantes, incluso en un periodo de disidencia política y creciente diversidad cultural. Estas obras también sugieren de sus nuevas influencias artísticas, entre ellas Robert Heinecken (1931–2006), el conceptualista afincado en Los Ángeles que se especializó en apropiarse y reensamblar imágenes de los medios de comunicación. Una pequeña serie muestra el retrato repetido y de alto contraste del presidente John F. Kennedy fotografiado desde una pantalla de televisión, otra técnica de Heinecken (fig. 4, página 48). Aquí, Bernal también hace un guiño a Andy Warhol (1928–1987), que se había hecho famoso en la década anterior por sus serigrafías con repeticiones en serie de imágenes icónicas y su propia atracción por los Kennedy.[11] En otro pequeño grupo de obras, Bernal hizo un collage de sus propias fotografías de pantallas de televisión sobre imágenes que encontró en revistas. En un ejemplo, una pantalla que muestra los rostros sombríos de mujeres de luto durante el funeral televisado de Robert F. Kennedy se coloca sobre una escena más amplia de dos niños blancos en un paisaje pastoral (fig. 5, página 48).

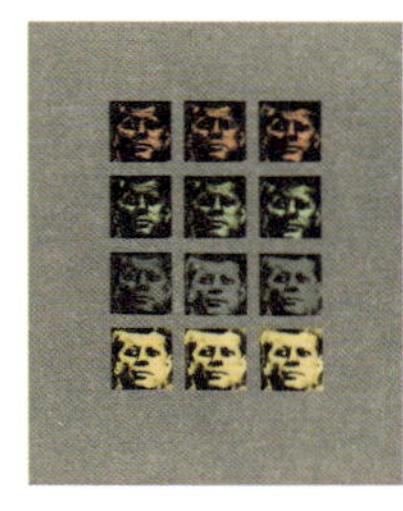

4

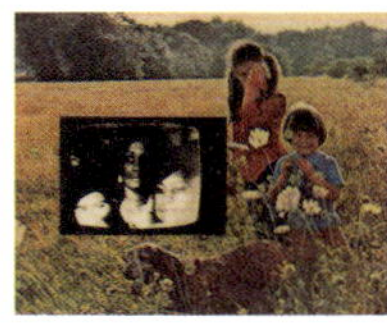

5

Bernal realizó su serie *An American Fairy Tale* (Un cuento de hadas americana, 1974–75; páginas 77–85) poco después de recibir su maestría en Bellas Artes y a raíz de las audiencias del Watergate, cuya cobertura en directo siguió de cerca en 1973. Se inspiró en el poder de los medios de comunicación para fomentar opiniones idealizadas o demonizadas de personajes públicos. A principios y mediados de la década de 1970, hubo una satirización generalizada del Presidente Richard Nixon, presentado como una figura despreciada

10. Louis Carlos Bernal, entrada de diario, 23 de noviembre de 1970. Para un estudio exhaustivo de Frederick Sommer, véase Keith F. Davis, *The Art of Frederick Sommer: Photography, Drawing, Collage* (Prescott, AZ: Frederick and Frances Sommer Foundation, 2005).

11. Warhol realizó grabados con retratos apropiados tanto de John F. Kennedy como de la Primera Dama Jacqueline Bouvier Kennedy.

y deshonrada, en contraste marcado con las representaciones más simpáticas e idealizadas de John F. Kennedy tras su asesinato. Para su serie de imágenes escenificadas, Bernal reclutó a sus hijas pequeñas y a desconocidos para que sostuvieran máscaras con el rostro de Nixon sobre el suyo propio y posaran en escenarios incongruentes: en el desierto rodeados de altos saguaros, frente a una modesta residencia de ancianos o casi camuflados en medio de un montón de basura.[12] Estas imágenes son únicas en su obra, tanto como composiciones escenificadas como por su mordaz sentido del humor.

BARRIOS

Bernal encontró la voz más fiel a su visión dentro de una forma más tradicional de hacer imágenes al vincular su acogida del chicanismo con un modo creativo que le permitía conmemorar a la gente mexicano-americana cotidiana. En 1973, antes de terminar *An American Fairy Tale*, hizo sus primeras incursiones en los barrios de Tucson para fotografiar a la gente en sus espacios domésticos. Los barrios, entre los más históricos de la ciudad, estaban entonces poblados en su mayoría por familias que podían rastrear su linaje en el sur de Arizona por generaciones.[13] El más antiguo de los barrios y un puñado de casas supervivientes datan de cuando

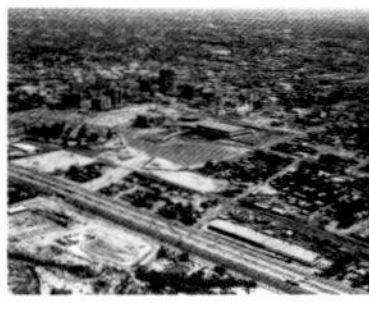
6

Arizona aún era territorio mexicano.[14] Pero estos barrios cercanos al centro de Tucson se habían enfrentado a las amenazas de la reurbanización y la llamada renovación urbana desde la década de 1960. De hecho, Bernal comenzó la serie poco después de la construcción de un gran centro de convenciones, que redujo gravemente el tamaño del Barrio Viejo, lo que desplazó a más de trescientas familias y más de mil viviendas (fig. 6, página 48).[15] Le interesaba fotografiar a quienes se quedaron: personas pobres pero resistentes, símbolos de la precariedad y de la invisibilidad de la población mexicano-americana de la ciudad. El objetivo de Bernal era hablar desde dentro, como el primer mexicano-americano que fotografiaba a su propio pueblo y revelar la dignidad, la riqueza cultural y el tenor espiritual de los miembros de esas comunidades.[16]

La decisión de Bernal de centrarse en los barrios supuso un reto personal: sabía que tenía el conocimiento técnico necesario para emprender un proyecto así, pero no se sentía tan seguro a la hora de acercarse a la gente y preguntarle si podía entrar en sus casas y fotografiarlas. Como él mismo explicó: "Aunque soy mexicano-americano, no crecí en los barrios de Tucson; crecí en la clase media de Phoenix".[17] Además, en ese momento, vivía cómodamente en un suburbio de Tucson. Pero Bernal —cariñoso, gregario y que hablaba español con fluidez— estaba familiarizado con este tipo de entornos y con las formas de vida que representaban. También tenía el don de saber a quién dirigirse, "de leer los barómetros espirituales de la gente", en palabras de un antiguo alumno.[18] Bernal produjo diecinueve fotografías, todas en blanco y negro, para su primera serie *Barrios*, limitado por su inclinación natural a rodar con moderación y por restricciones financieras. Calificó esas obras algo así como "instantáneas". Sus imágenes más memorables aún estaban por llegar, pero estos primeros esfuerzos le enseñaron a componer en entornos domésticos reducidos, a sacar el máximo partido de la luz natural o limitada y a trabajar con personas ajenas a su círculo familiar y de amigos. En su retrato de 1974 de la anciana Doña Rita Mendoza, por ejemplo, una mujer permanece de pie en su dormitorio junto a un altar casero.

12. Bernal también había planeado una foto de grupo culminante de modelos sin ropa sosteniendo estas máscaras, idea que se desechó cuando varias personas decidieron no participar. Relatado por Bernal en Ben "Easy" Rider, "An Informal Chat with Louis Carlos Bernal", 1982, del Louis Carlos Bernal Archive, Center for Creative Photography, vídeo, 1:03:34.

13. Históricamente, los barrios eran excepcionalmente diversos. En ellos vivieron; *tucsonenses* o mexicano-americanos cuyas familias vivían en el sur de Arizona antes de que formara parte de Estados Unidos; y afroamericanos y chino-americanos que se asentaron en estos barrios a finales del siglo XIX. Véase Cynthia Radding, *Wandering Peoples: Colonialism, Ethnic Spaces, and Ecological Frontiers in Northwestern Mexico, 1700–1850* (Durham, NC: Duke University Press, 1997).

14. Arizona se convirtió en el cuadragésimo octavo estado de la Unión en 1912.

15. Véase Juan Gómez-Novy y Stefanos Polyzoides, "A Tale of Two Cities: The Failed Urban Renewal of Downtown Tucson in the Twentieth Century", *Journal of the Southwest* 45, n° 1/2 (2003): pp. 87–119. http://www.jstor.org/stable/40170251; y Jane Kay, "Home is Disappearing", en "Tucson's Barrio's: A Report from the Inside", *Arizona Daily Star*, 16 de julio de 1978. http://www.barriostories.org/wp-content/uploads/2015/11/Tucson-Barrios-Section-ADS-1978.pdf.

16. Para un conmovedor relato de primera mano sobre la vida en un barrio de Tucson en los años sesenta y principios de los setenta, véase Lydia R. Otero, *In the Shadows of the Freeway: Growing Up Brown & Queer* (Tucson, AZ: Planet Earth Press, 2019).

17. Bernal, en Rider, "An Informal Chat".

18. Camille Bonzani, en "Louis Bernal", *Arizona Illustrated* segmento, emitido el 24 de enero de 1990, en KUAT-TV, 29:34.

Una cortina se ha corrido a un lado y ondea suavemente, iluminando a su sujeto y proyectando bandas de luz y sombra a lo largo de la habitación, lo que crea una escena impregnada de una espiritualidad íntima (página 161).

Bernal estaba desarrollando su propio modo y avanzando hacia un nuevo tipo de estética fotográfica. Solo unos años antes, la "fotografía chicana" hacía referencia a las imágenes documentales de fotógrafos activistas, en su mayoría jóvenes, que utilizaban sus cámaras al servicio del movimiento por los derechos civiles. Estos fotógrafos, a menudo voluntarios que aprendían sobre el traba-

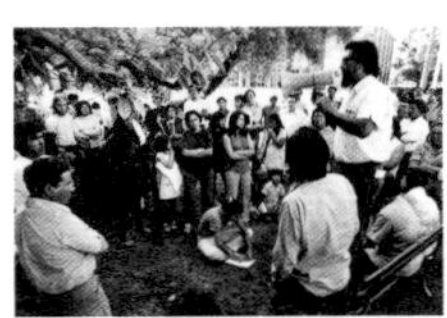

7

jo, hicieron la crónica de la larga lucha liderada por Chávez y Huerta para sindicalizar a los trabajadores agrícolas, las protestas contra la guerra de Vietnam y las huelgas de estudiantes de bachillerato (fig. 7, página 49). Bernal estaba seguramente familiarizado con las escenas de organización sindical y manifestaciones que se publicaban tanto en los medios convencionales como en periódicos estudiantiles y publicaciones alternativas. Puede que no hayan influido directamente en su obra, pero como ha afirmado Colin Gunckel, "Las implicaciones más conceptuales de la fotografía chicana tienen sus cimientos en el fotoperiodismo y la fotografía documental del movimiento chicano".[19] De hecho, cuando Louis Carlos Bernal se asomó a las vidas de la gente mexicano-americana, estaba recurriendo a la misma fuente de empatía y profundo deseo por la justicia social que motivó a la generación pionera de fotógrafas y fotógrafos de los derechos civiles a dar visibilidad a quienes tenían poca agencia y conjurar historias y tradiciones que han sido objeto de borrado político y cultural.

En un conjunto de fotografías a color de los inicios de su carrera, Bernal de hecho aceptó como suyas las preocupaciones de sus contemporáneos que documentaron la lucha de los trabajadores agrícolas de California. Probablemente motivado por las huelgas laborales en las noticias locales, tomó fotografías en dos granjas de Maricopa County en las que retrató a los trabajadores en huelga en una y las primitivas condiciones de vida en la otra (páginas 14–15).[20] Sin embargo, este pequeño grupo de imágenes va más allá de la documentación. Bernal demostró su capacidad para extraer las especificidades de cada individuo al que se acercó y transmitir la fuerza y las cualidades personales de individuos con pocos medios. Aquí, en sus propios términos más personales, Bernal reveló una faceta de su trabajo que era discretamente política. Estas imágenes dejaban claro que, incluso cuando hacía fotografías de temas más actuales, mantenía una postura artística que estaba menos al servicio de un movimiento o ideología que de los individuos y las comunidades.

A lo largo de la década de 1970, Bernal desarrolló un estilo maduro que combinaba la documentación con el retrato, la naturaleza muerta y elementos de la fotografía escenificada. Esta adhesión a los géneros fotográficos tradicionales podría haber sido difícil para alguien que antes se había sentido atraído por los enfoques abstractos y conceptuales del medio y que deseaba profundamente ser visto, ante todo, como un artista. Pero solo si se ceñía a formas de representación más directas podría alcanzar plenamente su objetivo de hacer un arte arraigado en los ideales del chicanismo. Consciente de sus elecciones estéticas, una vez dijo: "Mi trabajo no es documentación en el sentido técnico, hay elementos de ello, pero básicamente mi trabajo es mi propio punto de vista sobre un conjunto particular de circunstancias o condiciones en las que vive la gente y sus emociones al reaccionar ante ello".[21] Consideraba que su misión artística era

19. Colin Gunckel, "The Chicano/a Photographic: Art as Social Practice in the Chicano Movement", *American Quarterly* 67, no. 2 (junio de 2015): pp. 377–412.

20. Bernal realizó algunas de estas fotografías en Goldmar, una finca de cítricos propiedad en parte del ex senador estadounidense Barry Goldwater. En aquel momento, Goldmar había firmado lo que se creía que era el primer contrato con trabajadores indocumentados, lo que reflejaba, en palabras de un reportero del *Washington Star*, "la creciente militancia de los extranjeros ilegales". Véase "Mexicans Who Had Led Strikes Sign Contract with a Goldwater". *New York Times*, 4 de febrero de 1979, p. 38.

21. Louis Carlos Bernal, en "Luis [*sic*] Bernal, Espejos del Alma", *Latina*, febrero de 1986, p. 52.

una especie de imperativo moral: hablar en nombre de su comunidad y servir de puente, defender su cultura ante el resto del mundo. "El artista chicano", afirmó, "no puede aislarse de la comunidad, sino que se encuentra en medio de su pueblo creando arte de y para el pueblo".[22] Y para hacer realidad estos ideales, Bernal aportó todo su ser a la creación de esta obra: sus recuerdos infantiles de racismo y pobreza, su educación y formación exhaustiva en fotografía, así como sus valores personales y políticos. Antes de hacer una foto, dedicaba tiempo a pasear, pensar, escribir y hablar con la gente que encontraba en un barrio. Cuando pulsó el disparador de su cámara, se había preparado por completo para el momento de hacer una imagen que cristalizaría una vida individual.

Bernal experimentó una especie de apoteosis en 1977, cuando se topó con una pequeña casa de barrio cuya puerta principal estaba ligeramente entreabierta. Llamó a la puerta varias veces y entró. Cuando estaba dentro, descubrió que se trataba de una residencia abandonada. Una capa gruesa de polvo cubría todas las superficies. Más tarde se enteró de que la casa había sido el hogar de Mary Benítez, una anciana que había sido hospitalizada tres años antes y vivía en una residencia de ancianos. "Solo había tres habitaciones en toda la casa", describió Bernal más tarde, "pero estaba llena de un tesoro de imágenes visuales y espirituales que brillaban en la luz quiescente transmitida por las cortinas blancas que cubrían las ventanas. Me moví con cautela, estudiando las imágenes mientras hacía un esfuerzo consciente por no tocar nada, ya que sentía que estaba invadiendo el espacio espiritual de otro ser humano."[23]

Las siete fotografías en blanco y negro que componen la serie *Benítez Suite* (1977, páginas 24, 104–11), incluyen imágenes de una cómoda cubierta con una serie de objetos personales y una foto, tal vez de Mary Benítez de niña con un hermano; un relicario de sobremesa con flores muertas e imágenes del Papa Pío XII y el Niño Jesús de Praga; y memorablemente, un dormitorio bañado por una suave luz que entra por una ventana con cortinas. El título de esta última imagen, *Calendario*, hace referencia al calendario que cuelga en la puerta del dormitorio. Data de 1951 y está ilustrada con el rostro de Jesucristo, un recordatorio de los reinos temporal y eterno que Mary Benítez habría contemplado a diario durante más de dos décadas.

Lo que sabemos de Mary Benítez lo aprendemos de las fotografías de Bernal: era pobre, profundamente religiosa y vivía en un mundo de recuerdos. Se rodeaba de imágenes sagradas y retratos familiares, incluido uno de un apuesto joven en un marco ovalado que podría haber sido su marido. Esta constelación de imágenes forma el nexo de una sola vida, representando la historia de Benítez, sus seres queridos y su fe permanente. Para *Ahora* (1977, página 107), Bernal reunió sobre una imagen del Arcángel Miguel la plétora de recibos, oraciones y notas —cada una de las cuales empezaba por la palabra "ahora"— que encontró esparcidos por el suelo de la residencia de Benítez. Aquí, Bernal evoca poéticamente una confluencia de lo cotidiano y lo espiritual y sugiere cómo incluso los momentos cotidianos de la vida están tocados por la gracia.

ESPEJO

Los años setenta fueron fructíferos y ajetreados para Bernal. Él y su esposa tuvieron dos hijas, Lisa Marie y Katrina Ann, nacidas en 1969 y 1972, respectivamente. Disfrutaba de su trabajo en el Pima Community College, donde se

22. *Awards in the Visual Arts 3*, p. 16.

23. Louis Carlos Bernal, "Benítez Suite," in *Chicanismo: Photographs by Louis Carlos Bernal* (Rochester, NY: International Museum of Photography at George Eastman House, 1992). Bernal conoció más tarde a Mary Benítez y ella le dio permiso para exponer estas fotografías.

ganó la reputación de profesor dedicado y generoso, pero también exigente. En 1974, recibió una de sus primeras becas, de la Arizona Commission on the Arts and Humanities, así como un reconocimiento aún mayor en forma del premio Time-Life Yearbook Discovery, que le nombró uno de los cincuenta fotógrafos jóvenes más destacados del mundo. Expuso su obra a escala local y nacional, en el Instituto Smithsonian de Washington, en la Galería de la Raza de San Francisco y en el colectivo de fotógrafos latinos En Foco de Nueva York. En 1977, el fotógrafo documental Morrie Camhi (1928–1999) invitó a Bernal a crear un conjunto de obras para un importante proyecto fotográfico sobre la experiencia mexicano-americano en el Suroeste. *Espejo: Reflections of the Mexican American* (*Espejo: Reflejos del mexicano-americano*) se benefició del patrocinio

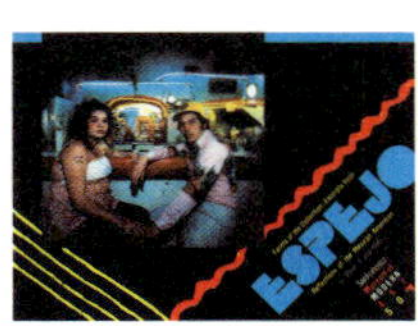

8

del Mexican American Legal Defense and Educational Fund (MALDEF, el Fondo Mexicano Americano de Defensa Legal y Educativo), una destacada organización de derechos civiles, con motivo de su décimo aniversario. Con un importante apoyo financiero del National Endowment for the Arts (el Fondo Nacional de las Artes), *Espejo* recibió una amplia difusión, tanto en forma de exposición itinerante como de publicación (fig. 8, página 49). Camhi, fotógrafo comprometido socialmente afincado en el norte de California, había dedicado mucho tiempo a principios de esa década a documentar a los trabajadores agrícolas migrantes y el movimiento chicano por los derechos civiles; también invitó a Abigail Heyman, Roger Minick y Neal Slavin a aportar portafolios al proyecto. Cada uno aportó su propia perspectiva: Heyman, como fotógrafa feminista pionera y primera mujer miembro de Magnum; Minick, como cronista incisivo y veterano del paisaje estadounidense; y Slavin, como uno de los primeros practicantes de la fotografía a color conocida por sus retratos de grandes grupos. Pero Bernal era el único chicano del grupo y el único fotógrafo que retrataba a su propia comunidad.

El momento elegido por la comisión no podía haber sido más fortuito. Bernal estaba profundamente comprometido con su serie *Barrios* y quería profundizar en ella. "El Proyecto MALDEF", escribió, "me permitió explorar la esencia de mi ser. Quería transmitir lo que he encontrado: el nuevo sentimiento de orgullo, la nueva conciencia que está floreciendo tanto en mí como en la comunidad".[24] En otras palabras, Bernal había llegado a un punto en el que el trabajo que estaba realizando tenía dimensiones personales y culturales a partes iguales. También era muy consciente de que estas fotografías tendrían una exposición mucho más amplia que sus trabajos anteriores, por lo que asumió el encargo con un especial sentido de responsabilidad. Bernal habló con franqueza de su singular condición de chicano implicado en el proyecto. "Soy un perfeccionista", escribió, "constantemente impulsado por la necesidad de crear una imagen más perfecta, de sobresalir en un mundo en el que no puedo permitirme el lujo de ser normal. He sentido mucha rabia y ansiedad en mi vida y he utilizado la fotografía como válvula de escape para estas frustraciones".[25]

Espejo dio Bernal la oportunidad de avanzar en su objetivo de explorar barrios más allá de Tucson. También trabajó en Douglas y Phoenix, así como en una franja del sur de Nuevo México, donde fotografió en los pequeños pueblos de Canutillo, Silver City y Animas. A través de este viaje, creía poder narrar una historia más amplia de la vida mexicano-americana. En Douglas, fotografió a Juan Mejía de mediana edad en blanco y negro, en un entorno espartano que proyecta una soledad perdurable (página 101). En cambio, en el Barrio Anita de

24. Troy, "Louis Carlos Bernal", página 53.

25. Louis Carlos Bernal, en *Espejo: Reflections of the Mexican American* (Oakland, CA: Oakland Museum, 1978), n.p.

Tucson, retrató a Nanita Mendibles a color, captando un salón decorado con un mural de *La Última Cena* de Leonardo da Vinci, retratos familiares y, de forma incongruente, un póster psicodélico y un globo de Mickey Mouse (página 20).

El proyecto también permitió a Bernal trabajar a color, lo que se convirtió en un sello distintivo de su práctica. Era un maestro de la impresión en blanco y negro, pero veía en el color un medio de profundizar en el impacto psicológico de sus retratos. Fue una decisión audaz en aquella época, en la que solo un puñado de fotógrafos estadounidenses, principalmente William Eggleston, Joel Meyerowitz y Stephen Shore, trabajaban a color.[26] Bernal había utilizado la película a color con moderación en el pasado, pero era reacio a utilizarla con cierta regularidad, dada la naturaleza no archivística de los papeles de impresión que se utilizaban en aquella época y sus propios recursos limitados. Con los seis mil dólares que recibió (una cantidad que él calificó como "enorme"), pudo pagar la película, el procesado y los materiales, así como explorar la creación de imágenes de una forma nueva.[27] Había calificado sus primeras fotografías en blanco y negro *Barrio* como "retratos ambientales"; con *Espejo*, pretendía exponer la interioridad de los habitantes del barrio y describirlo en un sentido psicológico y espiritual.[28]

De este proyecto surgió una de las imágenes más conocidas de Bernal: *Dos Mujeres, Douglas, Arizona* (1978, página 121). En primer plano se ve a una niña sentada, Maricella Martínez, que entonces tenía doce años y mira tímidamente hacia arriba mientras cose. A través de una puerta se ve a una mujer mayor, Patricia López, sentada en una cama en una habitación más alejada. Con esta imagen Bernal logró consagrarse. Las dos figuras —su relación no está clara— parecen habitar mundos separados, un punto que el fotógrafo subraya por los distintos espacios que ocupa cada una. Pero están unidas por su falta de reservas: cada una se presenta abiertamente y sin pretensiones, tal y como es. Puede que Bernal no conociera a estas mujeres, pero estaba excepcionalmente dotado para tranquilizar a la gente y ganarse la confianza de los extraños. Además, compuso la imagen con habilidad al captar la luz que atraviesa la cortina translúcida para iluminar los rostros de ambas mujeres, incidiendo más suavemente sobre la más joven, Maricella.

En *Dos Mujeres*, el color no solo es descriptivo, sino crucial para la carga emocional de la imagen. Del mismo modo, en *Albert y Lynn Morales, Silver City, New Mexico* (1978, página 11), una paleta de colores empapada de neón evoca vívidamente el llamativo escenario en el que Bernal descubrió a esta pareja en un bar. El don de Bernal para la composición también se hace evidente aquí. Las dos figuras crean un mundo estrechamente cerrado; sus brazos y manos están dispuestos en forma de corazón y están enmarcados por líneas de neón. El propio color es el tema principal del más minimalista *Retrato de Boda Rosa* (1978, página 123), en el que Bernal cede la mayor parte del encuadre a las modulaciones del rosa en una pared de yeso desgastado. La inclusión del pequeño retrato de boda que da título a la imagen parece casi incidental en comparación con ello.

Bernal se había desarrollado un sentido matizado de la composición, escenificando con seguridad sus temas y espacios durante este periodo. Se tomaba libertades a la hora de organizar una habitación y a menudo colocaba cortinas y puertas para potenciar la iluminación o proporcionar vistas a los espacios adyacentes. Bernal a menudo hacía posar a sus personajes, como hizo para crear la matizada simetría de *Dos Mujeres* o en su emblemático retrato de la adolescencia

26. Véase Senf, este volumen.

27. Bernal, en Rider, "An Informal Chat". La cantidad asciende a más de 25.000 dólares en la actualidad.

28. Los colores de las impresiones originales de Bernal se han degradado considerablemente. La exposición que coincide con esta publicación contiene ejemplos de estas impresiones de época, así como impresiones basadas en capturas de alta resolución de los negativos de Bernal que demuestran la riqueza cromática que él pretendía que tuvieran las imágenes. Ernesto Esquer, trabajando bajo la dirección de Ann Simmons-Myers, amiga y colega de Bernal, realizó estas reproducciones digitales y las imprimió a todo fotograma para respetar las intenciones de Bernal.

masculina, *Stephen Quiñonez, Douglas, Arizona* (1979, página 135), cuyo protagonista está sentado con las piernas cruzadas en una cama, con una camiseta de la conejita Playboy y unas pesas en la mano, exactamente centrado entre carteles de modelos en bañador. Y aunque la mayoría de las fotografías de *Espejo* son escenas de interior, Bernal también fotografió a personas fuera de sus casas. *Barrio Portrait, Avenida H Cuadra, Douglas, Arizona* (1978, página 134) es una escena familiar, con tres niños pequeños delante de su casa, sus padres en la entrada. El padre permanece de pie junto a la puerta mientras una joven posa justo dentro. No está claro con qué cuidado dispuso Bernal cada figura, pero la composición no es casual. A menudo trabajaba con sus sujetos de forma colaborativa o, como escribió el crítico Mark Johnstone, "en aquiescencia colaborativa" para construir minuciosamente una escena idealizada de una familia mexicano-americana.[29]

Bernal también reconoció signos de cambio en los barrios. Aunque con frecuencia retrataba a los ancianos y sus modos de vida tradicionales, aunque en vías de desaparición, también captaba signos de cambio y de modernidad, como en su retrato del joven Stephen Quiñonez o en *Los Vatos Locos, Douglas, Arizona* (1978, página 136), una escena desenfadada de jóvenes que pasan el rato alrededor de un coche. Recordando algunos de sus primeros esfuerzos como fotógrafo, muchas de estas fotografías tienen como protagonista al televisor. *El Show de Rosita, Barrio Anita* (1978, página 119) muestra una televisión que transmite un programa popular de variedades en español; solo el título del programa en la pantalla indica que estamos dentro de la residencia de una familia mexicano-americana. Pero Bernal reconoció que una escena así señalaría claramente el ascenso de la población hispanohablante en los Estados Unidos. Si la televisión y los medios de comunicación de masas habían promovido el espíritu asimilacionista del crisol de culturas de los años cincuenta y sesenta, este tipo de entretenimiento —por y para los latinos— ejemplificaba la influencia creciente de este grupo demográfico, cuyos miembros esperaban ahora entretenimiento y cultura en sus propios términos.

BERNAL EN LOS AÑOS 80

Tras el proyecto *Espejo*, Bernal continuó ampliando su serie *Barrio* y siguió plenamente inmerso en la iluminación de la vida mexicano-americana. A principios de la década de 1980, la escritora e historiadora Patricia Preciado Martin le invitó a contribuir con imágenes en un volumen de historias orales de mexicano-americanos con raíces profundas en Arizona. *Images and Conversations: Mexican Americans Recall a Southwestern Past* (*Imágenes y conversaciones: Mexicano-americanos recuerdan un pasado del Sudoeste*) fue una de varias iniciativas de becas públicas en Tucson durante este periodo, y pretendía abordar

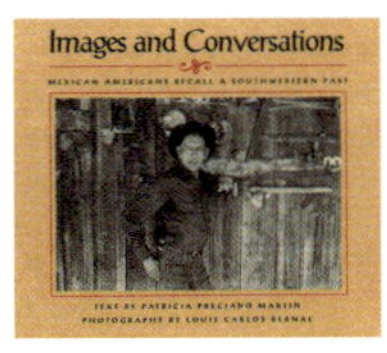

la sorprendente omisión de materiales relacionados con esta población en las bibliotecas y sociedades históricas locales (fig. 9, página 49).[30] El proyecto dio a Bernal la oportunidad de conocer a tucsonianos con una larga historia, así como de viajar por una Arizona más rural, donde visitó antiguos ranchos que habían permanecido en familias durante generaciones. Entre sus retratadas se encontraba María Soto Audelo, que en una fotografía aparece orgullosa y digna junto a un gran crucifijo adornado con un rosario y palmas y un cofre con fotos familiares e imágenes de santos (fig. 10, página 50). Una gran

9

29. Mark Johnstone, "Observations in a Social Environment", *Artweek* 16, no. 30 (18 de mayo de 1985): p. 12.

30. Véase Patricia Preciado Martin y Louis Carlos Bernal, *Images and Conversations: Mexican Americans Recall a Southwestern Past* (Tucson: University of Arizona Press, 1983).

31. Tucson tenía una tradición de celebraciones elaboradas el 4 de julio incluso antes de su constitución como ciudad en 1877. Hubo procesiones con bandas, carros triunfales, discursos, cantos corales y lecturas dramatizadas de la Declaración de Independencia. Véase, por ejemplo, Ruthann Grace, "Don Pedro Pellón: Tucson's Pioneer Actor and Activist", *Journal of Arizona History* 57, no. 2 (verano de 2016): p. 159.

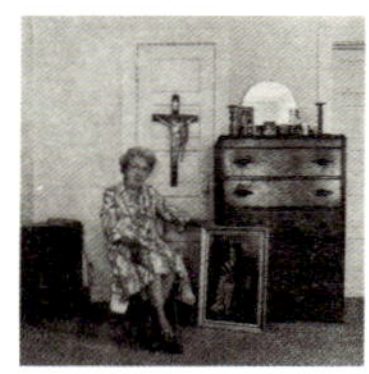

10

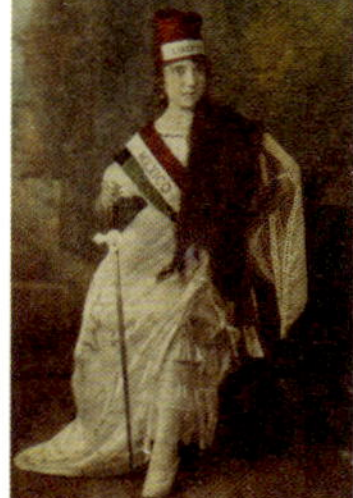

11

foto enmarcada de Soto Audelo tomada en 1917 para la celebración del Día de la Independencia en Tucson está apoyada contra el pecho. En ella, es una adolescente de cabello oscuro que le sobrepasa la cintura, vestida elaboradamente como una personificación alegórica de México (fig. 11, página 50; ver también página 125).[31] En la historia oral acompañante, Soto Audelo relata que los orígenes de su familia en Tucson se remontan a 1774 y que su padre nació en 1860. Para Bernal, un retrato que plasmara la larga historia de los mexicano-americanos en Arizona habría sido implícitamente político: denota su condición de colonizados en el Suroeste y sus vínculos soberanos con la tierra. Y aunque Bernal fotografiaba paisajes con poca frecuencia, para *Images and Conversations* retrató álamos y corrales, ranchos en funcionamiento y pequeños cementerios rurales, escenas que ponen de manifiesto la centralidad de la tierra para los mexicano-americanos de esta región. Cuando Bernal se centraba en la propia tierra, la miraba a través de los ojos de sujetos que la reconocían como parte inextricable de su identidad y de su historia ancestral.[32]

Bernal también estaba ampliando su red artística en estos años y convirtiéndose en una parte más integral de la comunidad chicana de Arizona. En 1978 asistió al Festival Flor y Canto de su alma mater, Arizona State University. Esta fue la quinta edición de una serie de influyentes "simposios literarios orales", como se les denominó, celebrados a lo largo de esa década en Los Ángeles, Austin, San Antonio, Albuquerque y Milwaukee. Su propósito, en palabras de sus organizadores, era presentar un retrato colectivo de la estética mestiza en Estados Unidos a través de presentaciones de poetas, escritores, artistas y músicos indígenas y chicanos emergentes y consagrados del Suroeste.[33] El Festival Flor y Canto era tanto político como cultural, ya que ofrecía plataformas para las voces artísticas, así como un lugar de encuentro donde los activistas de toda la región podían congregarse y establecer lazos de solidaridad. Inspiró al contingente de Arizona a fundar en 1978 una organización a la que llamaron Ariztlán, una palabra compuesta de Arizona y Aztlán, la patria mítica de los aztecas. Ariztlán, una organización de apoyo a los artistas, organizó exposiciones, charlas con artistas, talleres sobre cuestiones prácticas para éstos y programas de intercambio cultural con México. Bernal fue presidente del grupo en la década de 1980 y trabajó para desafiar la invisibilidad de los artistas chicanos en la escena artística local y en el mercado.[34] Al promocionar su trabajo en la prensa local, Ariztlán resumió su frustración por esta falta de atención diciendo: "La cultura blanca se interesa por nuestra comida, nuestra arquitectura y nuestra lengua, pero no por nuestra gente".[35]

En la década de 1980, Bernal pasaba más tiempo fuera de Tucson. Viajó a California, Nuevo México, Texas, Cuba y México, donde hizo fotografías, participó en exposiciones, habló en conferencias y entabló amistades con artistas chicanos y mexicanos.[36] Estas relaciones constituyeron un sistema de apoyo crucial para el fotógrafo, que durante mucho tiempo sufrió inseguridad sobre su lugar en el mundo del arte en general y que estaba relativamente aislado en Tucson en comparación con la población chicana afincada en ciudades como Los Ángeles o San Francisco. Como señaló su compañera Marietta Bernstorff, Bernal nunca se sintió realmente parte de la comunidad fotográfica establecida. Sabía que era un buen fotógrafo, pero se sentía más unido a la clase trabajadora y a la comunidad

32. Al concluir la Guerra México-Estados Unidos (1846–48), México cedió más de la mitad de su territorio a Estados Unidos. Aunque el Tratado de Guadalupe Hidalgo otorgaba derechos constitucionales y protecciones a los terratenientes al norte de la nueva línea fronteriza, muchos mexicano-americanos quedaron desposeídos de sus tierras. El Tratado relegó de hecho a la condición de forasteros a un pueblo nativo y a las personas empobrecidas descendientes de los terratenientes. En los primeros años del movimiento chicano, los antiguos conceptos de Aztlán, la patria mítica, así como de soberanía y autodeterminación, actuaron como guías cruciales para los líderes emergentes de activistas. Véase Rodolfo Acuña, *Occupied America: A History of Chicanos*, 3ª ed. (Nueva York: Harper Collins, 1987), p. 115; y Rudolfo A. Anaya, Francisco A. Lomelí y Enrique R. Lamadrid, *Aztlán: Essays on the Chicano Homeland*, rev. ed. (Albuquerque: University of New Mexico Press, 2017).

33. Véase Arnoldo Carlos Vento, "The *Flor y Canto* and *Canto al Pueblo* Festivals", en *Mestizo: The History, Culture and Politics of the Chicano and Mexican* (Lanham, MD: University Press of America, 1997), pp. 237–42; y *Flor y Canto IV y V: An Anthology of Chicano Literature from the Festivals Held in Albuquerque, New Mexico, 1977 and Tempe, Arizona, 1978* (Albuquerque: Pajarito Publications, 1980).

34. Agradezco a los artistas Jim Covarrubias y Joseph Sánchez que me hayan proporcionado información sobre Ariztlán.

35. Louis Carlos Bernal, en Roberta Tubis, "Photographer Seeks to Promote Hispanic Arts", *El Independiente* (Tucson), 30 de octubre de 1981.

36. Entre las exposiciones en las que participó Bernal durante estos años se encuentra *Fotografía Latinoamericana del Suroeste/USA*, celebrada en 1981 en La Casa de Fotografía de la Ciudad de México. La obra de Bernal se expuso junto a la de otras figuras pioneras como Don Gregorio Antón, Isabel Castro, Harry Gamboa Jr., Luis C. Garza y Ricardo Valverde, todos ellos afincados entonces en Los Ángeles. En 1990, participó en una exposición histórica, alabada por la crítica, *Chicano Art: Resistance and Affirmation* o *CARA*. Organizada por la Wight Gallery de la UCLA, presentó unas 180 obras de arte fechadas entre 1964 y 1985 de unos 140 artistas chicanos que trabajaban en diversos medios. La exposición viajó a museos de diez ciudades a principios de la década de 1990 y fue acompañada de un extenso catálogo. A través de *CARA*, la obra de Bernal se dio a conocer a decenas de miles de personas en todo Estados Unidos. Véase Richard Griswold del Castillo, Teresa McKenna e Yvonne Yarbro-Bejarano, editores, *Chicano Art: Resistance and Affirmation 1965–1985* (Los Angeles: Wight Art Gallery, University of California Los Angeles, 1991).

chicana, en gran parte debido a la discriminación que sufrió en su juventud.[37] Entre sus amigos más importantes se encontraba Luis Jiménez (1940–2006),

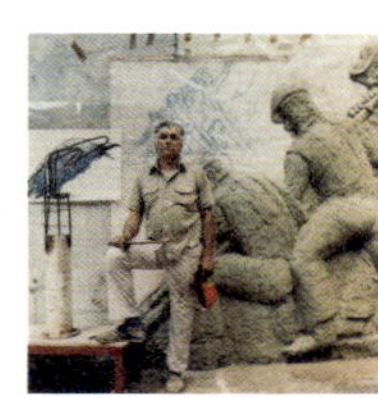

12

afincado en Hondo, Nuevo México, que a principios de la década de 1970 ya era un artista conocido en todo el país (fig. 12, página 50). Aunque sus obras eran muy diferentes —Jiménez trabajaba principalmente con fibra de vidrio policromada para crear esculturas a menudo de escala monumental—, Bernal respetaba profundamente al artista, un intelectual y perfeccionista con un inquebrantable sentido de sí mismo como chicano. Fue Jiménez, de hecho, quien animó a Bernal a ver el chicanismo como algo central en su identidad artística.[38]

En Los Ángeles, Bernal expuso con cierta frecuencia en espacios como el Los Angeles Center for Photographic Studies y Los Angeles Contemporary Exhibitions. Entabló relaciones cordiales con miembros de la gran comunidad de artistas y fotógrafos chicanos de la ciudad y pasó a formar parte de un grupo que se reunía para conversar y recibir asesoramiento en la Cityscape Foto Gallery de Pasadena, una de las pocas galerías de propiedad chicana de la

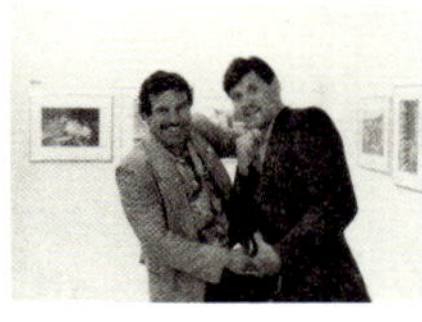

13

zona, dirigida por el coleccionista y promotor cultural Lorenzo Hernández. Entre ellos se encontraba Ricardo Valverde (1946–1998), un fotógrafo que también comprendió la importancia de captar la vida del barrio y de centrarse en su propia comunidad, en su caso, el este de Los Ángeles (fig. 13, página 50). Valverde experimentó ampliamente con el medio al rayar o

pintar sus grabados a fin de añadir una dimensión surrealista a las personas y los lugares que fotografiaba. Otro amigo de Bernal originario de Los Ángeles, el pintor Roberto Gil de Montes (n. 1950), vivió en la Ciudad de México durante la década de 1980, cuando se convirtió en un importante conducto para los artistas chicanos entre Los Ángeles y México y ayudó a introducir la obra de Bernal en el mundo del arte mexicano.

Los viajes también permitieron a Bernal ampliar el alcance de su trabajo. En 1980, en un viaje a San Diego, fotografió a los cholos y cholas que representaban un aspecto significativo, aunque a menudo despreciado, de la cultura juvenil chicana en el sur de California. En una obra icónica realizada en Barrio Logan, retrata a dos jóvenes de pie bajo el paso elevado de un puente, flanqueados por murales monumentales pintados en los pilones de hormigón del puente (página 126). Se trata de una afirmación con carga política: La zona debajo y alrededor del puente se había designado como parque en 1971 tras años de presión por parte de activistas que protestaban por la destrucción de gran parte de su barrio debido a la construcción de autopistas. Chicano Park pronto se convirtió en un especie de museo de murales a gran escala y el retrato de Bernal de los hombres —uno que muestra su afiliación a la banda con símbolos de manos— sugiere tanto un desafío a las normas culturales dominantes como una reivindicación territorial de esta tierra y del arte que los rodea.

Bernal visitó Cuba en 1982 para participar en el Premio de Fotografía Cubana y en 1984 como invitado del Tercer Coloquio Latinoamericano de Fotografía, la tercera edición de una importante reunión de fotógrafos, críticos e historiadores latinoamericanos para celebrar mesas redondas, talleres y exposiciones. Fue uno de los pocos ciudadanos estadounidenses que asistieron a la edición de La Habana y el único que ofreció un taller.[39] El suyo se basaba en el sistema de zonas, una técnica estandarizada por Ansel Adams y Fred Archer

37. Marietta Bernstorff, entrevista con la autora, Oaxaca, México, noviembre de 2002.

38. Marietta Bernstorff, entrevista telefónica con la autora, 29 de diciembre de 2021. Jiménez y Bernal siguieron siendo amigos de toda la vida; Jiménez estuvo a menudo al lado de Bernal cuando éste yacía en coma tras su accidente de 1989. Luis Jiménez murió en 2006 en un trágico accidente, cuando una parte de una gran escultura le cayó encima en su estudio.

39. Otros estadounidenses asistentes fueron los fotohistoriadores Amy Conger y Keith McElroy, los fotógrafos Esther Parada y Walter Rosenblum y el historiador y fotógrafo Max Kozloff.

a finales de la década de 1930 para determinar las exposiciones óptimas para obtener impresiones en blanco y negro con ricos valores tonales.[40] Bernal también realizó algunas de sus mejores fotografías callejeras en Cuba. Este modo de trabajar solo lo había practicado de manera esporádica en Estados Unidos, dada su propensión a controlar con cautela sus composiciones. Trabajando en blanco y negro, captó a los habitantes del centro de La Habana, las concurridas fachadas de las tiendas, los grafiti y la arquitectura neoclásica de la ciudad. Parecía mostrar una fascinación especial por unos niños uniformados que encontró sobre una calle en ruinas y sin pavimentar, a quienes retrató jugando y haciendo gestos para su cámara (página 177). Bernal reconoció la importancia de estas imágenes; habló de su esperanza de reunirlas en un libro, proyecto que nunca pudo realizar.[41]

En 1983, Bernal recibió una invitación a impartir una sesión sobre fotografía documental dentro de un taller organizado por la organización sin ánimo de lucro Friends of Photography (Amigos de la fotografía) en Carmel, California.[42] Otros lo buscaban como instructor y conferencista. Como señaló el difunto Bill Jay, antiguo profesor de fotografía de la ASU: "Tiene esa habilidad especial para estimular, emocionar y contagiar a sus alumnos y, al mismo tiempo, decirles que les queda mucho camino por recorrer".[43] El taller de Carmel fue otro de los puntos de referencia de la carrera de Bernal, ya que le puso en contacto con fotógrafos de todo Estados Unidos, entre ellos Ansel Adams, fundador de Friends of Photography. Bernal viajó al norte de California con Terry Etherton, un galerista de fotografía de Tucson, quien recordó el entusiasmo de Bernal al conocer a sus compañeros instructores Mary Ellen Mark, Danny Lyon y Burk Uzzle. Pero, según Etherton, el suceso también subrayó las inseguridades profesionales de Bernal y le recordó la posición avanzada de sus compañeros blancos en comparación con la suya en aquel momento.[44]

También se estaban produciendo cambios en la vida personal de Bernal. En 1985 él y Sandy, quien había sido su esposa durante casi veinte años, se divorciaron. Había iniciado una relación con Marietta Bernstorff, antigua alumna y luego galerista en Tucson. Bernal había vivido en un suburbio del noroeste de Tucson mientras tomaba fotografías en los barrios de la ciudad durante más de una década; con Bernstorff, se mudó a una casa de adobe en El Hoyo, uno de los barrios más antiguos de Tucson. Este traslado fue una decisión cultural y política que le acercó mucho más a las personas que constituían el núcleo de su obra.[45]

FOTOS DE FOTOS

Durante mucho tiempo, Bernal sintió una fascinación no solo por las personas que se ponían ante su cámara, sino también por los objetos e imágenes que éstas exhibían en sus hogares. A menudo entraba a casas cuyas paredes y mesas estaban decoradas con estampas, fotografías familiares, figuritas y calendarios de los que dan en las panaderías y otras tiendas de barrio cada fin de año. Muchas de estas composiciones son impresionantes representaciones de la devoción católica romana. *Recámara de Catalina Olomos, Phoenix, Arizona* (1978, página 114), por ejemplo, se centra en el pequeño relicario repleto que se ve en la esquina de una habitación, encima de una cama. Las imágenes de la Virgen de Guadalupe, Nuestra Madre del Perpetuo Socorro y el Santo Niño de Atocha cuelgan sobre una estantería llena de otras imágenes religiosas y chucherías.[46]

40. Agradezco a Armando Cristeto la información sobre los viajes de Bernal a La Habana.

41. "Espejos del Alma", p. 54.

42. Friends of Photography fue fundada por Ansel Adams en 1967 como una organización para promover el medio de la fotografía a través de exposiciones, publicaciones y educación. Bernal participó en uno de los últimos programas en los que también participó Adams, fallecido en 1984.

43. Bill Jay, en "Espejos del Alma", p. 53.

44. Terry Etherton, entrevista con la autora, 10 de septiembre de 2021. De hecho, Bernal fue el único fotógrafo de color que participó ese año en los talleres de Friends of Photography en Carmel. Véase James G. Alinder, ed., *Light Years: The Friends of Photography 1967–1987 (Untitled 43)* (Carmel, CA: Friends of Photography, 1987).

45. El Hoyo se llama así por la escasa elevación del barrio y su propensión a inundarse durante las tormentas de principios del siglo XX. Con el tiempo, la ciudad de Tucson instaló un sistema de drenaje adecuado en el barrio.

46. El Santo Niño de Atocha es el patrón de los presos y los viajeros y una figura de devoción popular entre los mexicano-americanos con lazos con una patria lejana o con historias familiares marcadas por la migración. El Niño Jesús, vestido de peregrino, lleva ayuda a los necesitados y protege a los viajeros.

La exposición atestigua el profundo papel de la fe en la vida de esta mujer; su lugar de descanso es también un lugar de ferviente devoción.

Una exposición aún más elaborada se observa en *Recámara de Blas y Pauline Flores* (1978, página 118), que se centra en una cómoda y un escritorio situados en un rincón, ambos cubiertos de estatuas religiosas, velas y flores artificiales. Es un mundo en sí mismo, una humilde demostración de fe que transforma el espacio íntimo del dormitorio en un santuario católico. Para Bernal, que de adulto apenas asistía a misa, esos espacios debían de resultarle familiares y místicos a la vez y proyectaban una especie de devoción incuestionable a que él no suscribía. Pero, como señaló su amigo el fotógrafo e historiador de la fotografía Armando Cristeto, las manifestaciones religiosas que Bernal presenciaba en estos hogares le emocionaban: comprendía el peso espiritual que tenían para quienes retrataba.[47] También se convirtieron en un tema central de su obra, como expresiones de la identidad cultural mexicano-americana que retrató una y otra vez por todo el Suroeste.

Bernal también fotografió santuarios en los patios y jardines de sus sujetos. En *Sr. Ernesto Villa, Barrio Hollywood* (1977, página 117), un hombre se encuentra ante su casa, entre dos nopales y un relicario en forma de gruta dedicado a la Virgen de Guadalupe. Parece que es época de vacaciones y Villa ha transformado un cactus en un árbol de Navidad al decorarlo con luces multicolores. Asimismo, en una fotografía blanco y negro, Herminia Vargas está sentada bajo un gran árbol de sombra junto a un altar hecho con un viejo refrigerador lleno de estatuas y flores (página 99). Bernal captaba esas expresiones de religiosidad, elaboradas o improvisadas, allí donde las encontraba. Tomó fotografías en El Tiradito, un santuario de los deseos y lugar histórico del Barrio Viejo que data de la década de 1870, y en otros lugares de Tucson, donde se topó con altares o imágenes de la Virgen de Guadalupe en escaparates.[48] En su singular imagen *La Reina de Mi Vida* (1983, página 131), un hombre se levanta la camisa para revelar un gran tatuaje de la Virgen de Guadalupe que cubre su espalda, una transformación del propio cuerpo en un santuario u ofrenda. Imprimirse en la piel la imagen de esta Virgen de piel morena —común entre los hombres mexicano-americanos de clase trabajadora, incluidos los que han sido encarcelados— es señal del orgullo por la propia identidad mestiza. Bernal veía estas diversas manifestaciones de fe como una forma de expresión creativa, un arte popular surgido de los barrios de Tucson.[49]

A veces, Bernal podía acercarse a sus temas con menos reverencia. En *Juanita Serrano with Santo Niño de Atocha* (1978, página 19), una mujer, con el pelo cuidadosamente recogido en rulos rosas, aparece junto a una pared decorada con imágenes religiosas enmarcadas con flores. A menudo entraba en las casas para encontrar símbolos de fe entremezclados con retratos de John F. Kennedy, el primer presidente católico querido entre muchos mexicano-americanos, o de estrellas del pop o personajes de dibujos animados, como el ocasional Mickey Mouse. En *Cocio Kennedy Altar* (1980, página 97), el retrato del presidente, adornado con una cruz y un corazón, domina una pared que también alberga imágenes de la Santísima Trinidad y San Martín de Porres. La artista y escritora chicana Amalia Mesa-Bains ha descrito este tipo de ensamblajes domésticos de elementos dispares que van desde "imágenes de Walt Disney, cine mexicano y publicidad en los medios de comunicación de masas e incluso gráficos del calendario mexicano y arte pop estadounidense" como "un encuentro de dos mundos [que] solo podía negociarse a través de la sensibilidad del rasquachismo", una filosofía

47. Armando Cristeto, entrevista con la autora, Ciudad de México, 2002.

48. *El tiradito* hace referencia a una persona marginada y se llama así por un joven supuestamente enterrado allí tras habérsele sorprendido en una aventura amorosa que le costó la vida. Los visitantes siguen dejando velas y notas con oraciones o expresiones de gratitud por los deseos cumplidos en el lugar.

49. Agradezco las apreciaciones de Antonio Solisgomez, amigo y vecino de Bernal, sobre el interés del fotógrafo por las expresiones artísticas vernáculas de los barrios de Tucson.

irreverente de reutilizar e improvisar con lo que se tiene a mano, de desafiar las normas del llamado buen gusto y de apropiarse de objetos y símbolos para su propio fin.[50]

La propia fotografía es otro elemento común en las escenas de interior de Bernal, lo que hace que ciertas obras funcionen como retratos de retratos. Vemos con frecuencia paredes con fotografías de antepasados, ancianos conocidos solo a través de grandes impresiones tintadas o entonadas a mano colocadas dentro de marcos pesados, como en la serie *Benítez Suite*; o en retratos de sobremesa, como en la fotografía *San Pedro Ranch, Animas, New Mexico* (1978, página 22). También aparecen fotos familiares contemporáneas, imágenes de graduaciones o bodas y retratos militares, imágenes que marcan ritos de paso y actúan como testimonio de familias extensas a través del tiempo. En un ensayo sobre la fotografía y la vida afroamericana, bell hooks señala el valor de la cámara entre los negros, que la han utilizado como herramienta para refutar las representaciones negativas de sí mismos que surgen de los "imaginarios racistas de los blancos".[51] Lo mismo puede decirse de los conjuntos de fotografías que Bernal grabó: eran auténticos museos de historias y logros familiares. Al centrarse en estas muestras, también reflejaba el valor que los mexicano-americanos concedían a la fotografía, mucho antes de la era de los teléfonos con cámara y las redes sociales. Las fotografías, ya estuvieran colgadas en las paredes o guardadas en álbumes o viejas cajas de zapatos, actuaban como *recuerdos*, remembranzas, de los antepasados y familiares que quedaban atrás una vez que las personas emigraban a Estados Unidos. Cuando Bernal hacía fotografías de fotografías, estaba dando testimonio de las especificidades de una historia familiar y, más ampliamente, evocando la centralidad de la familia en la vida chicana, incluyendo a aquellos de un pasado más lejano que nos trajeron a este tiempo y lugar.[52]

Las fotografías de espacios interiores, aunque en ausencia de la figura humana, también se convirtieron en otra forma de retrato para Bernal. Había creado este tipo de representaciones de individuos al principio con el *Benítez Suite*, cuando se topó con una casa abandonada llena de pertenencias y recuerdos. En imágenes posteriores como *Retrato de Boda Rosa* (1978), *Boda de Luz* (1978) y *Santos y Televisión* (1981, páginas 123, 100, 16) —retratos más intencionados de interiores y posesiones—, Bernal evoca vívidamente la vida de sus habitantes. Resulta revelador que *Recámara de Mis Padres, Phoenix, Arizona* (1978, página 140), titulada alternativamente *Retrato de Mis Padres*, que representa el rincón de un dormitorio de la casa familiar, es la única obra de Bernal dedicada a sus padres. Se centra en la pantalla de una lámpara con el retrato de boda de sus padres, lo que indica el valor que concedía a esos retratos simbólicos.[53] El cálido resplandor de la lámpara añade otra capa de significado; transmite la esencia de sus padres tanto en términos físicos como emocionales. Bernal se refirió a ella en una ocasión como la imagen de un sentimiento y de un lugar. En otras palabras, es una imagen capaz de expresar el mismo tipo de impacto personal que las representaciones de personas.[54]

MÉXICO

Bernal tuvo una larga relación, a veces conflictiva pero en última instancia enriquecedora, con México: su lengua, sus culturas y los miembros de su comunidad fotográfica. En su juventud, mucho antes de visitar México, la lengua española

50. El historiador del arte chicano Tomás Ybarra-Frausto articuló el concepto de *rasquachismo* en "Rasquachismo": A Chicano Sensibility", en *Chicano Aesthetics: Rasquachismo* (Phoenix: Movimiento Artístico del Río Salado, 1989), p. 5. Amalia Mesa-Bains añadió una importante perspectiva chicana a sus teorías en "'Domesticana': The Sensibility of Chicana Rasquache", *Aztlán: A Journal of Chicano Studies* 24, no. 2 (otoño 1999): p. 159.

51. bell hooks, "In Our Glory: Photography and Black Life", *Art on My Mind: Visual Politics* (Nueva York: New Press, 1998), p. 59.

52. Mesa-Bains, "Domesticana", pp. 157–67.

53. Agradezco a Ann Simmons-Myers, que sucedió a Bernal como directora del programa de fotografía del Pima Community College, que me facilitara información sobre esta fotografía.

54. Louis Carlos Bernal, "Comentario", *1er Coloquio Nacional de Fotografía* (Pachuca, Hidalgo, México: Gobierno del Estado de Hidalgo; México, D.F.: Instituto Nacional de Bellas Artes y Consejo Mexicano de Fotografía, 1984).

ocupaba un lugar central en su conciencia. Al crecer en la ciudad fronteriza de Douglas, donde los hogares bilingües eran la norma, sus padres hablaban principalmente español, al mismo tiempo que hacían hincapié en la importancia de hablar correctamente tanto inglés como español. Pero una vez que la familia se trasladó a Phoenix, las monjas le "dieron coscorrones" por su falta de dominio del inglés, un castigo que le obligó a mejorar en este idioma. Del mismo modo, sus padres, aunque eran angloparlantes, estudiaron para perfeccionar su propio uso del idioma. La casa familiar estaba repleta de un notable número de diccionarios inglés-español y cada miembro de la familia utilizaba el idioma como una forma de superación personal, ya fuera hacia la asimilación o como un retorno a las raíces. En última instancia, el dominio del español de Bernal le sirvió de mucho, ya que le facilitó la relación con los principales sujetos de sus fotografías, los vecinos del barrio que le permitieron entrar en sus casas.[55] En México pudo dar conferencias y entablar un diálogo intelectual con miembros de la comunidad fotográfica que se convirtieron en sus amigos.

En 1962, a los veintiún años, Bernal viajó a la Ciudad de México, donde se matriculó en el Mexico City College (ahora conocido como la Universidad de las Américas), con el objetivo de mejorar su español y prepararse para una carrera como profesor de idiomas. Puede que este fuera el objetivo práctico, pero su pasión por el arte y la fotografía estaban creciendo. Poco después de su regreso a Arizona, obtuvo su primer éxito con el medio, exponiendo su obra en una muestra individual en Arizona State University en 1964 y en una exposición colectiva en la prestigiosa George Eastman House de Rochester, Nueva York, al año siguiente. Cuando fue reclutado por el ejército en 1966, había abandonado su plan de enseñar español, pero su devoción por la cultura mexicana perduró. Visitó México a lo largo de su vida por motivos personales y profesionales.

Una de las fotografías de los archivos Bernal, *Chiclets, Cuernavaca*, data de 1963, cuando Bernal visitó México por primera vez (página 167). La escena, que muestra a un niño sin zapatos, un vendedor ambulante que parece muy dispuesto a posar para la cámara, es una con la que debió encontrarse a menudo durante aquella estancia. El sentimiento de inocencia del niño y su nivel de pobreza impresionaron a Bernal de manera contundente; de hecho, su amigo íntimo, Armando Cristeto, señaló que Bernal pudo haber sentido una empatía especial por aquel niño dadas las dificultades que él mismo enfrentó mientras crecía en Douglas.[56] Bernal volvería a tratar el tema de la pobreza en futuros viajes. Por mucho que amara a México, desdeñaba sus desigualdades sociales tan visibles.

Bernal hizo un largo viaje a México en tren con su esposa y sus hijas en 1980 con el itinerario clásico que muchos mexicano-americanos han seguido en esa búsqueda de familiarizarse más con sus orígenes. Visitaron el inmenso Museo Nacional de Antropología, el Parque de Chapultepec y las casas-museo de Diego Rivera y Frida Kahlo y asistieron a funciones del Ballet Folklórico en el Palacio de Bellas Artes. Bernal disfrutó mucho enseñar a sus hijas la historia y las tradiciones mexicanas, pero un viaje familiar le dejaba poco tiempo para pensar en la fotografía. Esto cambió en 1981, cuando Bernal recibió una invitación para participar en el Segundo Coloquio Latinoamericano de Fotografía y a exponer en el Palacio de Bellas Artes, la misma institución que había visitado con su familia un año antes. Organizados por el Consejo Mexicano de Fotografía y el Instituto Nacional de Bellas Artes, los coloquios marcaron un antes y un después para los fotógrafos latinoamericanos de la época. Antes de su creación, no existía

55. Katrina y Lisa Bernal, entrevista telefónica con la autora, 7 de enero de 2022 y correspondencia por correo electrónico, noviembre de 2022.

56. Armando Cristeto, intercambio de correos electrónicos con la autora, 3 de noviembre de 2021.

una conciencia de "fotografía latinoamericana", solo el conocimiento de un pequeño número de fotógrafos (en particular el mexicano Manuel Álvarez Bravo, el brasileño Sebastião Salgado y el peruano Martín Chambi), que habían sido seleccionados por editoriales o museos para una exposición internacional más amplia. Estos fotógrafos tuvieron pocas oportunidades de conocerse y apenas eran visibles dentro de un mundo fotográfico dominado por estadounidenses y europeos.[57]

Los organizadores del segundo coloquio hicieron un esfuerzo concertado para incluir a fotógrafas y fotógrafos chicanos, entre ellos Bernal, Robert Buitrón, 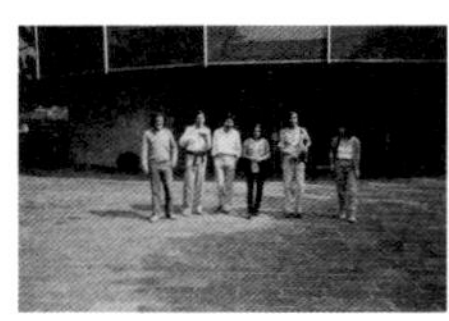 Isabel Castro, Harry Gamboa Jr., Luis C. Garza, Roberto Gil de Montes y Kathy Vargas. Como señaló Cristeto, "los coloquios activaron un flujo de comunicaciones entre creadores y países que se tradujo en exposiciones y viajes a México por parte de fotógrafos chicanos, entre ellos Louis Carlos Bernal".[58] Bernal llegó a la Ciudad de México como el principal fotógrafo chicano de Estados Unidos y le fascinó la oportunidad de representar a su comunidad en una reunión tan histórica (fig. 14, página 51).

14

Las discusiones y debates sobre el papel ideológico y la responsabilidad del fotógrafo latinoamericano habrían tenido una relevancia especial para Bernal, que se enfrentó a las mismas cuestiones como fotógrafo chicano. En su discurso inaugural, Pedro Meyer, destacado fotógrafo mexicano e influyente dirigente del Consejo, señaló que el arte fotográfico debe responder a las características de la sociedad de la que emana. Argumentó que en América Latina, cuya historia reciente había estado marcada por inmensas luchas sociales y represión, los que se dedican a la fotografía tenían la responsabilidad de actuar como testigos y participantes integrales. El propio Bernal presentó una ponencia titulada "La fotografía como reflejo de las estructuras sociales", en la que calificó el mundo de la fotografía estadounidense como "un microcosmos de la sociedad norteamericana". Señaló el carácter elitista de este campo —los años de formación necesarios y lo caro que era el medio—, al mismo tiempo que subrayó el papel crucial de los fotógrafos de color para enfrentar la invisibilidad de las comunidades marginalizadas, poblaciones a las que denominó el "Tercer Mundo de los Estados Unidos". Bernal abogó por que los fotógrafos chicanos, puertorriqueños y cubano-americanos participaran en talleres, presentaran ponencias en conferencias como las organizadas por la Society for Photographic Education y solicitaran subvenciones. Mientras reconocía la discriminación y exclusión a la que se enfrentaban sus colegas, otros fotógrafos latinos, declaró que "es tiempo de que dejemos de culpar a todos por nuestros problemas [...] y de que empecemos a tomar responsabilidad por nosotros mismos".[59]

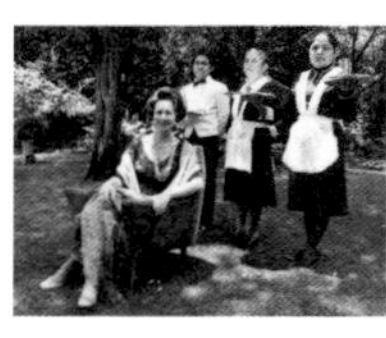 En 1984, a Bernal se le invitó a asistir a un congreso nacional de fotografía, el Primer Coloquio Nacional de Fotografía. El evento se celebró en Pachuca, una histórica ciudad minera a unos noventa y seis kilómetros al norte de la Ciudad de México, donde un convento de la época colonial se estaba reconvirtiendo en un archivo y museo nacional de fotografía. Su ponencia, como parte del panel "¿Para quién y para qué se fotografía?", respondió a las observaciones principales de Pedro Meyer. Bernal presentó imágenes de un amplio abanico de fotógrafos, entre ellos Eugène Atget, Ansel Adams y Joel-Peter Witkin, mediante el debate sobre el valor que reflejan las imágenes fotográficas. Entonces, trajo a colación la conocida fotografía de Meyer *La señora*

15

57. Véase Leticia Rigat, "Los Coloquios Latinoamericanos de Fotografía y la reconfiguración de las prácticas fotográficas", *Dixit* no. 32 (2020); y Pablo Ortiz Monasterio, "Close to the Boom", *VIST*, 5 de octubre de 2021, https://vistprojects.com/en/close-to-the-boom.

58. Armando Cristeto, en Elizabeth Ferrer, "First Encounters: Latino Artists at the Colloquiums of Latin American Photography", ponencia presentada en la Latino Art Now Conference, University of Illinois, Chicago, 2016.

59. Para subrayar su propia posición poco común como fotógrafo chicano, Bernal señaló su experiencia en la conferencia de la Society for Photographic Education en 1980. De los seiscientos asistentes, cuatro eran afroamericanos y tres latinos. Véase Luis [*sic*] Carlos Bernal, "La fotografía como reflejo de las estructuras sociales", *Hecho en Latinoamérica: Segundo Coloquio Latinoamericano de Fotografía*. (Ciudad de México: Consejo Mexicano de Fotografía, 1981), pp. 92–94.

y sus sirvientes (1978; fig. 15, página 51), que había visto en una exposición en el Center for Creative Photography.[60] Declaró que más tarde se enteró de que Meyer había hecho este retrato de su madre, un hecho que le causó cierta consternación. La división de clases entre los dos fotógrafos no podía ser más clara y a Bernal le llamó la atención esta representación de inmensa riqueza. ¿Fue una crítica de clase? ¿Y quién de entre sus colegas mexicanos podría haber tenido acceso a una persona de tales privilegios? Señaló cómo las cuestiones de distorsión y malentendido pueden influir en la lectura de una foto, pero uno también puede darse cuenta de la desaprobación de Bernal al encontrarse con un nivel de diferencia de clases que no habría imaginado que existiera en México.[61]

En ésta y otras visitas a México en la década de 1980, Bernal conoció a artistas de la fotografía que iban desde figuras tan legendarias como Manuel Álvarez Bravo y Lola Álvarez Bravo, hasta sus contemporáneos Graciela Iturbide y Rogelio Villarreal. Fueron encuentros significativos, sobre todo porque Bernal

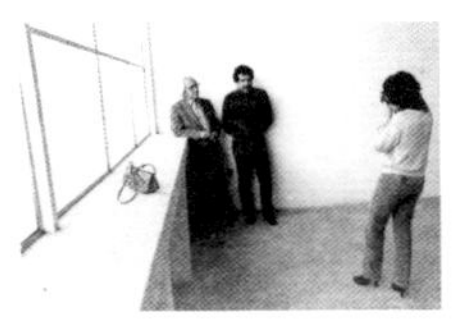

16

no se movía en círculos de influencia parecidos en Estados Unidos (fig. 16, página 51). Al igual que sus relaciones con colegas artistas chicanos, esta red de colegas mexicanos le proporcionó un sentimiento de validación y camaradería, así como un contexto artístico del que carecía en Tucson. Bernal pronto se convirtió en un miembro respetado del mundo de la fotografía en México y empezó a exponer allí con frecuencia y sostuvo relaciones estrechas con muchos de estos fotógrafos a lo largo de su vida.

Bernal también cayó bajo el hechizo de la tradición estética mexicana, en ese entonces aún dominada por la fotografía documental y callejera en blanco y negro centrada en los pueblos indígenas y la población urbana de gente pobre. Su imagen de 1980 *La Pelona* retrata a un hombre tapándose la boca con la mano, reprimiendo una mueca de perplejidad mientras está de pie a la entrada de una tienda de ataúdes (página 172). La composición parece una alegoría y recuerda

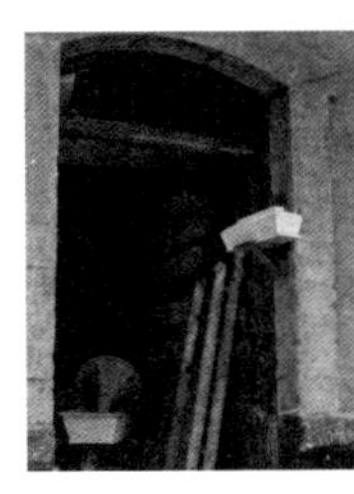

17

a las representaciones de Manuel Álvarez Bravo de momentos fortuitos u objetos cotidianos del entorno urbano cargados de significado filosófico o espiritual. En efecto, *La Pelona* responde a la fotografía de Álvarez Bravo *Escala de escalas* (1931), que ofrece una vista de un taller con escaleras inclinadas a la entrada y ataúdes apilados al fondo, símbolos de ascensión y mortalidad (fig. 17, página 52). En otras imágenes, Bernal retrató escenas de empobrecimiento e indiferencia bastante comunes en la Ciudad de México. Con *Cristo de la Calle* (1988, página 175), imagina a un mendigo ciego como un Cristo de la calle, una figura que vive su propio calvario. La imagen contrasta con *El Diablo* (ca. 1985, página 174), una fotografía de un hombre bien vestido que muestra desprecio por una figura indigente en el fondo, una personificación terrenal del diablo.

Fueron las fotografías a color de Bernal las que lo convirtieron en una figura influyente en algunos sectores del mundo fotográfico mexicano. En la década de 1980, una nueva generación de fotógrafas y fotógrafos emergentes en la Ciudad de México desafiaba las convenciones arraigadas al recurrir a formas diversas de manipulación en el cuarto oscuro, escenificar imágenes y centrarse en temas como la cultura juvenil y la comunidad queer, cada vez más visible, así como el impacto de la globalización en la ciudad y el campo. Rubén Ortiz-Torres (n. 1964), que fotografiaba la escena punk de México en blanco y negro, conoció a Bernal en el Coloquio de 1981 y más tarde escribió sobre sus

60. En 1978 el Center for Creative Photography presentó una exposición de fotografía mexicana reciente que incluía obra de Meyer, así como de Graciela Iturbide, José Ángel Rodríguez, Jesús Sánchez Uribe, Lázaro Blanco, Colette Álvarez Urbajtel, Manuel Álvarez Bravo, Rafael Doniz y Antonio Reynoso Castañeda. Véase Terrence Pitts, *Contemporary Photography in Mexico: 9 Photographers* (Tucson: Center for Creative Photography, University of Arizona, 1978.)

61. Louis Carlos Bernal, "Comentario", *1er Coloquio Nacional de Fotografía* (Pachuca, México: Gobierno del Estado de Hidalgo; México, D.F: Instituto Nacional de Bellas Artes y Consejo Mexicano de Fotografía, 1984), pp. 114–17.

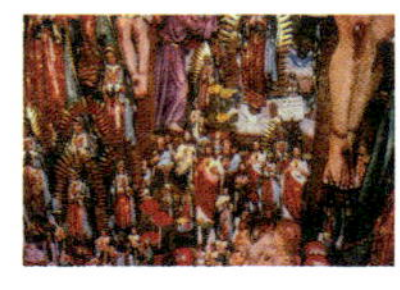

18

impresiones: "Su fotografía a color iba a influir a innumerables fotógrafos mexicanos y latinoamericanos", señaló, y puso como ejemplo a Adolfo Patiño (1954–2005), que se hizo llamar Adolfotógrafo. Patiño, que trabajaba con cámaras Polaroid, un enfoque diarístico y la estética de la instantánea, quedó impresionado por el uso que Bernal hacía del color "no sólo como un efecto estético sino también como un significante cultural".[62] El propio Ortiz-Torres pasó de la fotografía en blanco y negro a la fotografía a color para realizar una serie sobre la cultura fronteriza en colores chillones, citando a Bernal como modelo (fig. 18, página 52).[63]

BERNAL VA A LAS OLIMPIADAS

Bernal recibió el importante encargo de fotografiar los Juegos Olímpicos del verano de 1984 en Los Ángeles bajo los auspicios del Olympics Arts Festival. Estados Unidos había albergado por última vez los Juegos Olímpicos de verano en 1932, también en Los Ángeles, y en la ciudad se notaba un gran entusiasmo por el regreso de tal evento. Era un territorio nuevo para Bernal. Aunque tenía experiencia en el bachillerato fotografiando a estudiantes atletas, las Olimpiadas eran algo completamente distinto, ya que era tanto un espectáculo como una competición. Además, aunque Bernal conocía Los Ángeles, nunca había hecho fotografía ahí. En aquella época, la población de la cuidad superaba los tres millones de habitantes, casi un tercio de los cuales, según la nomenclatura del censo estadounidense de la época, se identificaban como hispanos.

Bernal trazó un plan claro: abordaría el encargo desde la perspectiva de un chicano. "Mi trabajo", escribió, "no será solo el de fotógrafo de atletas. Además de ello, dejaré constancia de que el objetivo fotográfico de un hispano registró las idas y venidas de la gente común durante esos dos meses."[64] Así lo hizo, fotografiando en vivos colores la sede oficial de los Juegos Olímpicos y visitando después a los barrios mexicano-americanos de la ciudad con película en blanco y negro en su cámara.

Bernal tenía una visión única de los Juegos Olímpicos. Dejó que otros documentaran las competiciones y atletas estrella, mientras él se centraba en la gente que fungía de asistente en las puertas, el personal de seguridad y la gente que vendía los souvenirs, es decir, la clase trabajadora que hacía funcionar el evento y a la que, de otro modo, fue ignorada (páginas 185–87). El rico colorido que captó parece alinearse con su imagen de Los Ángeles como ciudad de artificio y felicidad fabricada.[65] Por el contrario, las fotografías en blanco y negro que hizo ilustran una faceta de la vida en la ciudad que era en gran medida invisible salvo para sus habitantes (páginas 188–91). Como señaló su amiga, la escritora Leslie Marmon Silko, "Lou pronto pensó que el elitismo dentro de los pabellones olímpicos era tan detestable que al cabo de uno o dos días optó por empezar a tomar fotos fuera de las puertas del parque olímpico, en las calles, donde multitudes de visitantes y la afición, incapaces de permitirse pagar u obtener entradas, creaban una alegre fiesta callejera espontánea".[66] En sus incursiones fuera de los sitios oficiales, encontró un mundo más conocido de música norteña, modestos mostradores de comida mexicana y familias de clase trabajadora realizando tareas cotidianas. Aunque rara vez trabajó como fotógrafo callejero, fue en las concurridas calles del centro de

62. Rubén Ortiz-Torres, "¡El Pachuco Actual Se Nueva A Morir!", *Mex/L.A.: "Mexican" Modernism(s) in Los Angeles, 1930-1985*. (Berlín: HatjeCantz y Long Beach: Museum of Latin American Art, 2011): 30.

63. Rubén Ortiz-Torres, "De cómo el color migro al sur desde Aztlán en busca de una águila devorando a una serpiente en una penca de maguey", *Luna Córnea* 34 (2013): pp. 397–401.

64. Troy, "Louis Carlos Bernal".

65. Para un análisis de las fotografías olímpicas de Bernal, véase Josh Ríos, "Race to the Periphery", *Dilettante Army*, s.f., https://dilettantearmy.com/articles/race-to-the-periphery.

66. Leslie Marmon Silko, ensayo sin título en *Louis Carlos Bernal: Barrios* (Tucson: Pima Community College en asociación con la University of Arizona Library, 2002), p. 31.

Los Ángeles donde Bernal pareció disfrutar de la oportunidad de captar una versión de la vida estadounidense que los fotógrafos callejeros de la época ignoraban en gran medida. Dirigió su objetivo tanto hacia la clase trabajadora y a los excéntricos de la ciudad como a los fervientes predicadores callejeros o a una mujer en bikini y con tacones altos que caminaba de manera extraña con un niño por el paseo marítimo. A Bernal, Los Ángeles debía de parecerle una ciudad estridente, llena de contradicciones, en la que convivían lo banal y lo insólito.

LUBBOCK

Bernal realizó una de sus últimas series de fotografías en 1987 y 1988 en la ciudad de Lubbock, al noroeste de Texas, por encargo de Texas Tech University para retratar a la comunidad mexicano-americana de la ciudad.[67] El proyecto, concebido para una exposición en la universidad, representó un importante esfuerzo simbólico de una gran institución de Lubbock, donde las leyes de Jim Crow y la segregación racial habían persistido hasta bien entrada la década de 1980. También fue importante para Bernal, que desconocía la región pero llevaba tiempo esperando extender su serie *Barrios* a las comunidades mexicano-americanas de todo el Suroeste. Además, la serie resultante incluye retratos de afro-latinos, quienes estaban poco representados en su obra. En última instancia, Bernal realizó algunas de sus imágenes más nítidas y penetrantes en Lubbock.

En una declaración inédita sobre la serie, Bernal explicaba por qué había intentado registrar la vida en el interior de los hogares de la gente mexicano-americana durante más de una década. Escribía sobre las realidades "exteriores" e "interiores" de sus sujetos, como él las denominaba: las primeras se referían a los asuntos públicos y al alojamiento; y las últimas abarcaban la vida privada y familiar. Era este ámbito interior, afirmaba, el que albergaba "la cultura y las tradiciones hispanas, impregnadas de valores religiosos y espirituales". Bernal pretendía transmitir este aspecto de la vida —"la esencia del alma chicana", como él decía— sabiendo que estos ámbitos eran desconocidos para los forasteros. En última instancia, su objetivo era servir de puente entre la gente morena y la blanca y, a través de su obra, fomentar el entendimiento y el respeto entre culturas.[68]

Bernal completó la serie durante dos breves viajes a Lubbock, donde recorrió barrios residenciales en busca de oportunidades para fotografiar. Entre sus retratos se incluyen *Helen* (1988, página 199), llamado así por la adolescente que mira expectante al fotógrafo; y una imagen sin título de su hermana pequeña, que aparece tumbada en una cama en una especie de aburrida aquiescencia mientras espera a que Bernal haga clic en el obturador de la cámara (página 199). A pesar de que acababan de conocer al fotógrafo, éste disipó claramente cualquier incomodidad que pudieran haber sentido ante la presencia de un extraño en sus habitaciones y cada una de ellas se enfrenta de manera directa a la mirada de la cámara. Bernal también fotografió exteriores en Lubbock en donde retrató a los miembros de una familia dispuestos a lo largo del porche delantero de su casa, así como a una pareja mayor posando amistosamente en su jardín abundante, sosteniendo un gran cuenco de frutas recién recogidas (páginas 200–1).

Durante su estancia en Lubbock, Bernal oyó hablar en varias ocasiones de una conocida curandera cubana, Caridad Sánchez, y arregló para conocerla.

67. La exposición, *Espíritu Mejicano: Lubbock*, se expuso en el museo de Texas Tech University en 1988.

68. Agradezco a Robert Buitrón que haya compartido conmigo "Espíritu Mejicano", la declaración manuscrita y sin fecha de Bernal sobre la serie.

Por mucho que quisiera fotografiar a la mujer, su naturaleza supersticiosa hizo de su encuentro uno de los más tensos de su carrera. En la fotografía, Sánchez aparece orgullosa junto a un gran altar casero poblado no solo por el habitual conjunto de representaciones de Jesús y María, sino también por el busto de un indio americano, una gran muñeca negra parecida a Sánchez y una estatua del moreno Martín de Porres, el santo patrón de los mestizos conocido por la levitación, los conocimientos milagrosos y las curaciones instantáneas (página 203). Bernal fotografiaba a menudo santuarios y altares católicos tradicionales, pero éste era nuevo para él, con su mezcla sincrética de formas espirituales cristianas, africanas e indígenas caribeñas. Mientras la fotografiaba, la curandera le echó agua bendita y le dijo que cambiaría muchas vidas. Por mucho que le intrigaran las prácticas espirituales más allá del catolicismo, sintió una energía peculiar e incómoda en la sala. Hizo unas cuantas exposiciones de la mujer y luego se fue rápidamente.[69]

CODA

Bernal realizó su última serie de fotografías en 1989, en Douglas, su ciudad natal. Su tía Berta había muerto y volvió para asistir al funeral y fotografiar dentro de su casa. Regresó a un modo familiar, trabajando en el tipo de entorno doméstico modesto que le recordaba su propia educación. Produjo una serie de fotografías a color (páginas 207–8) que mostraban escenas como los muebles desgastados de un dormitorio, un par de zapatos viejos tirados en el suelo y cosméticos y cremas faciales ordenados en una cómoda. Puede que Bernal no se concibiera a sí mismo como un fotógrafo de naturalezas muertas, pero tenía un don especial para dotar a lo inanimado de reverencia, para magnificar las posesiones comunes de modo que se erigieran en expresiones del sentido de los valores y la identidad de cada ser. Ya había manifestado esta tendencia en 1977 con la serie *Benítez Suite*, en la que fotografió con cariño las raídas habitaciones en las que vivía Mary Benítez. Bernal hizo imágenes de esos espacios en blanco y negro, aprovechando la escasa luz natural para retratarlos con un aire de melancolía y religiosidad. Sus representaciones de los espacios personales de su tía no reflejan el nivel de pobreza visible en el *Benítez Suite*, pero las dos series comparten una soledad envolvente, la sensación de que somos testigos de un final.

Bernal no sabía que las fotografías que hizo en Douglas, una meditación sobre los últimos años de la vida y la mortalidad, marcarían otro final: el de su carrera creativa. De hecho, nunca tuvo la oportunidad de ver estas imágenes impresas. Pero las transiciones —y quizás incluso la sensación de un final— parecían estar cada vez más presentes en su mente a finales de la década de 1980. Su sensibilidad espiritual, que se intensificó a medida que maduraba, abarcaba los reinos de los sueños, las conexiones psíquicas e incluso las premoniciones. Su encuentro con la curandera Caridad Sánchez fue uno de varios incidentes de gran carga psicológica ocurridos aproximadamente un año antes del accidente en octubre de 1989 que acabó costándole la vida. En este periodo, en su trabajo, en las comunicaciones con sus allegados y en los acontecimientos que tuvieron lugar ese año, dio indicios de su propia muerte. En retrospectiva, para quienes lo conocían bien, esto no era sorprendente. Hacía tiempo que se sentía atraído por lo sobrenatural, las supersticiones y las historias de fantasmas, como la leyenda popular mexicana de La Llorona.[70] Las hijas de Bernal han hablado de su interés

69. Marietta Bernstorff, compañera de Bernal, le acompañó a Lubbock y aportó recuerdos de este encuentro. Señaló que Bernal estaba inusualmente nervioso mientras disparaba y que al principio no retiró la tapa del objetivo de su cámara.

70. La historia de La Llorona tiene muchas variantes, pero lo más típico es asociarla a la historia de una madre que llora por la noche por sus hijos perdidos o muertos, quizá víctimas de un filicidio.

por Carl Jung, así como por las teorías del inconsciente colectivo y del renacimiento.[71] No rechazó el catolicismo de su juventud y, sin duda, estaba familiarizado con los rituales eclesiásticos; escenas de bautizos, quinceañeras y bodas figuran en su obra. Pero Bernal, que se definía a sí mismo como un "católico caído", estaba más genuinamente interesado en las expresiones populares de la fe, una fe ligada a la cultura y a lo cotidiano.[72]

Bernal realizó su último viaje a México en el verano de 1989 con Marietta Bernstorff y su viejo amigo Armando Cristeto. Mientras visitaba Palenque, un complejo de antiguas ruinas mayas en el sur de México, estuvo a punto de resbalar en una estructura de tumba abierta y, bromeando, culpó del percance a la camisa que llevaba decorada con calaveras, posiblemente ofensiva para las deidades mayas. Sin embargo, esto lo puso nervioso. El pasado, al igual que su futuro, empezaba a preocupar a Bernal, cosa que no era habitual en él. Más adelante en el viaje, durante un paseo por la Ciudad de México, pasó por casualidad por una casa en la que había vivido como estudiante un cuarto de siglo antes.[73] También habló con sus compañeros de la posibilidad de alejarse de la fotografía. Estaba frustrado por la falta de respeto que recibía el medio en comparación con otras formas de arte y por su falta de ventas en una reciente exposición en una galería de Tucson. Pensó que podría dedicarse a escribir y quizá volver a Oaxaca a vivir una temporada.[74]

Bernal escribía cartas con frecuencia y se le conocía por enviar *cartes de visite* ilustradas con sus fotografías a amistades y conocidos de Estados Unidos y México. 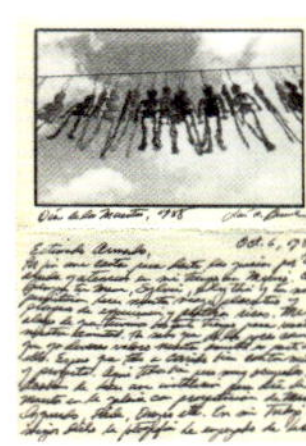 En sus últimas cartas a Cristeto, envió repetidamente una imagen titulada *Día de los Muertos* (1988) que representa una hilera de calaveras colgadas de un tendedero (fig. 19, página 52). En su última comunicación a Cristeto, fechada el 6 de octubre de 1989, escribió: "*Para rematar nuestra amistad*".[75] Dieciocho días después, en Tucson, un automóvil lo atropelló cuando iba en bicicleta al Pima Community College. Sufrió una lesión en el tronco encefálico y quedó en un largo coma del que nunca despertó. Bernal murió el 18 de agosto de 1993, el día en que cumplió 52 años.

19

Para Bernal, la elaboración de un lenguaje artístico era un acto de fino equilibrio entre la estética, la cultura y la comunidad. Igual que seguía las corrientes experimentales y conceptuales de la fotografía, buscaba producir imágenes que resonaran entre los miembros de las mismas comunidades que celebraba y que transmitieran más profundamente sus valores y espiritualidad. Al hablar de sus retratos de mexicano-americanos, declaró en una ocasión: "He intentado captar el aspecto espiritual y religioso al fotografiar una situación ordinaria y hacerla más que ordinaria porque es, justamente, más que ordinaria. Hay un sentimiento de grandeza, de inmortalidad en cada uno de los que estamos aquí [...] que nos une a los grandes acontecimientos de la vida".[76] Donde otros podrían haber visto personas anodinas o inferiores a ellos, Bernal encontró una belleza y una grandeza serena. En tan solo dos décadas de carrera, produjo una obra que constituye un imaginario chicano, una cosmovisión ausente de discriminación y marginalización. Bernal trazó un mapa sin fronteras a través del Suroeste, México e incluso Cuba, donde la identidad cultural estaba determinada principalmente por la familia, la comunidad y la espiritualidad. Encontró la manera de poner a la gente chicana en el centro de este mundo e inmortalizarla permanentemente. Su obra puede no haber estado a la vanguardia, pero caló hondo en el corazón del chicanismo al expresar un orgullo y una profundidad de espíritu perdurables.

71. Katrina y Lisa Bernal, entrevista telefónica con la autora, 7 de enero de 2022.

72. Ibid.

73. Marietta Bernstorff, entrevista con la autora, Oaxaca, México, noviembre de 2002.

74. Marietta Bernstorff, entrevista con la autora, noviembre de 2002 y 13 de septiembre de 2022.

75. Armando Cristeto, entrevista con la autora, Ciudad de México, noviembre de 2002.

76. Bernal, en Rider, "An Informal Chat".

Aportarle a su obra la totalidad de su ser fue el perseverante propósito de Bernal, ya que entendía el proceso de hacer una fotografía como una compleja síntesis de lo físico y lo mecánico, lo visual y lo psicológico. "Lo más importante es tirar del gatillo", dijo una vez. "Las respuestas intelectuales e intuitivas de un fotógrafo se unen cuando se pulsa el disparador. Cámara, ojo, mente, dedo, a través de esta secuencia llegamos al momento en el tiempo, una fracción de segundo en la que oprimimos el botón. Este impulso del obturador se convierte en una afirmación de aquello en lo que creemos".

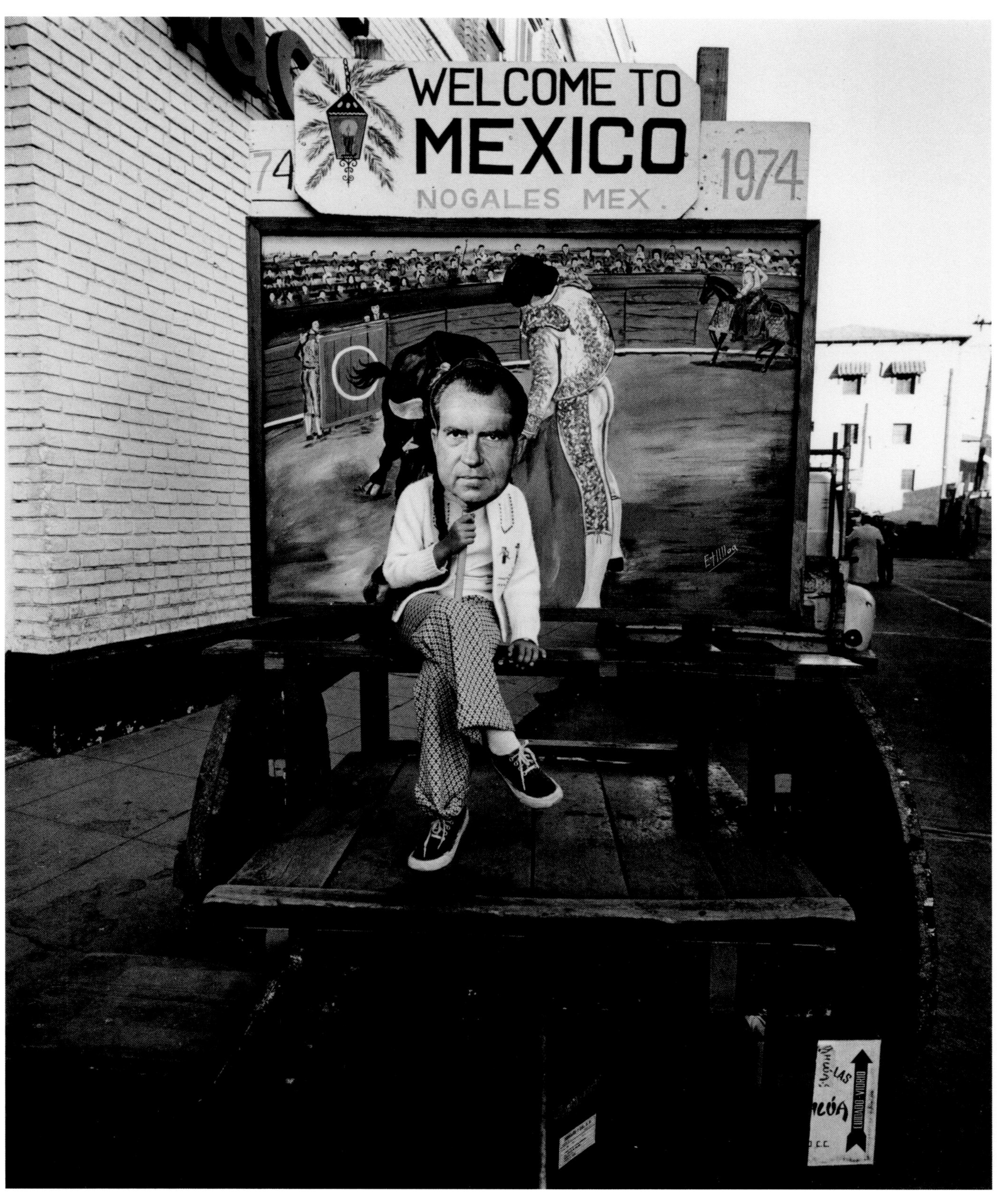

    Mexican Escapade, 1974; from the series *An American Fairy Tale*

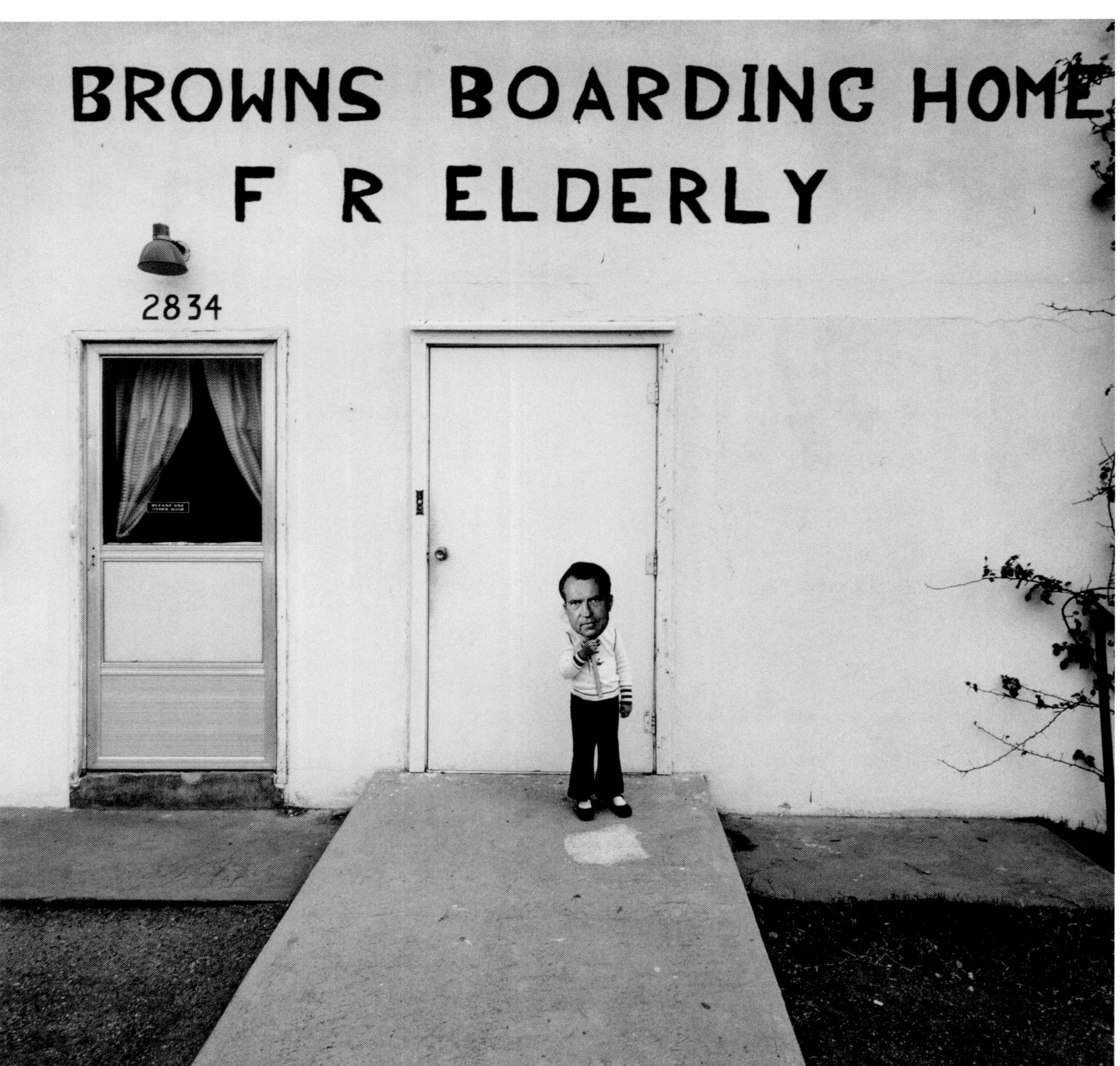

   Untitled (Browns Boarding House), 1975; from the series *An American Fairy Tale*

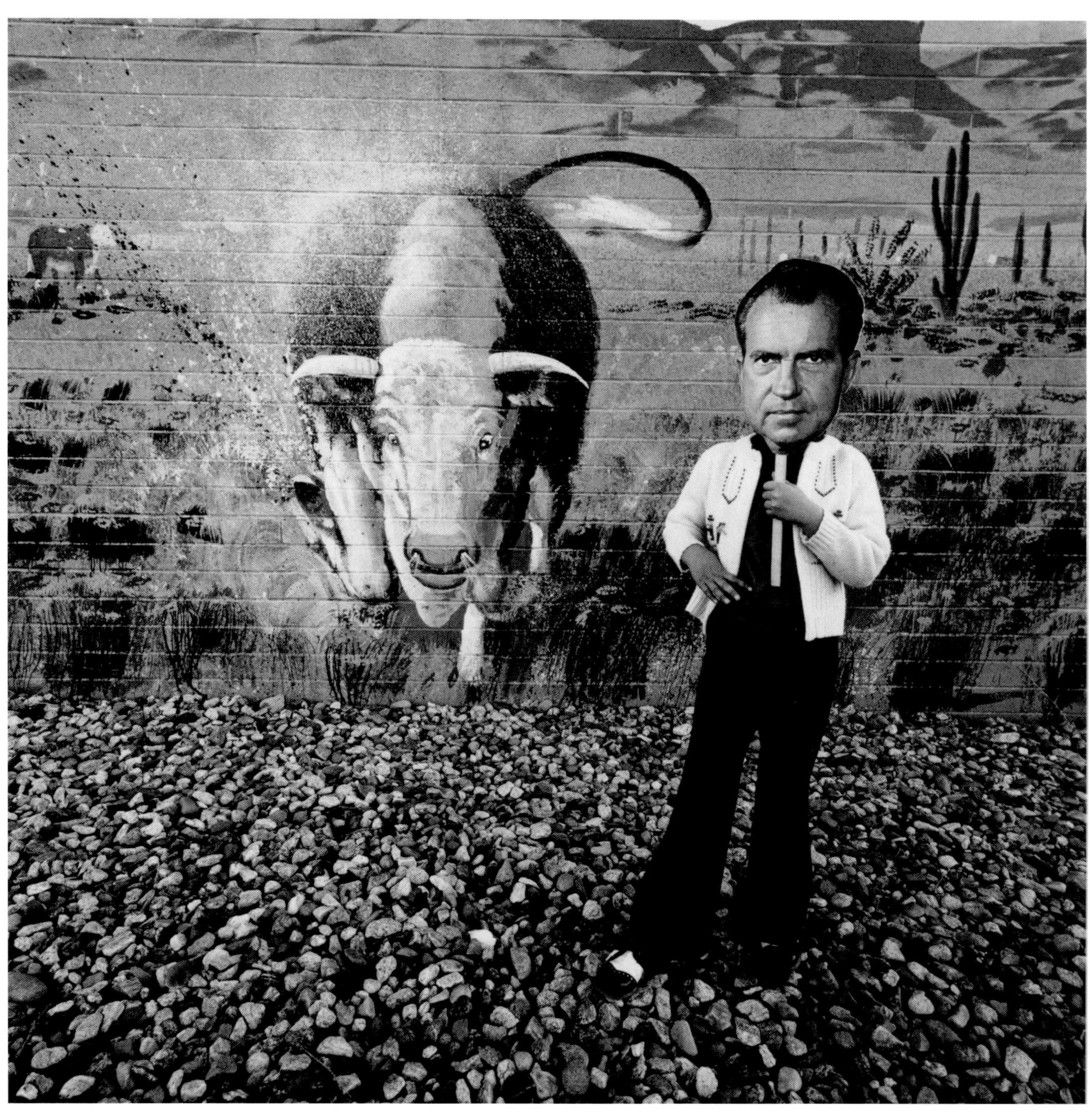

79   *A Lot of Bull,* 1975; from the series *An American Fairy Tale*

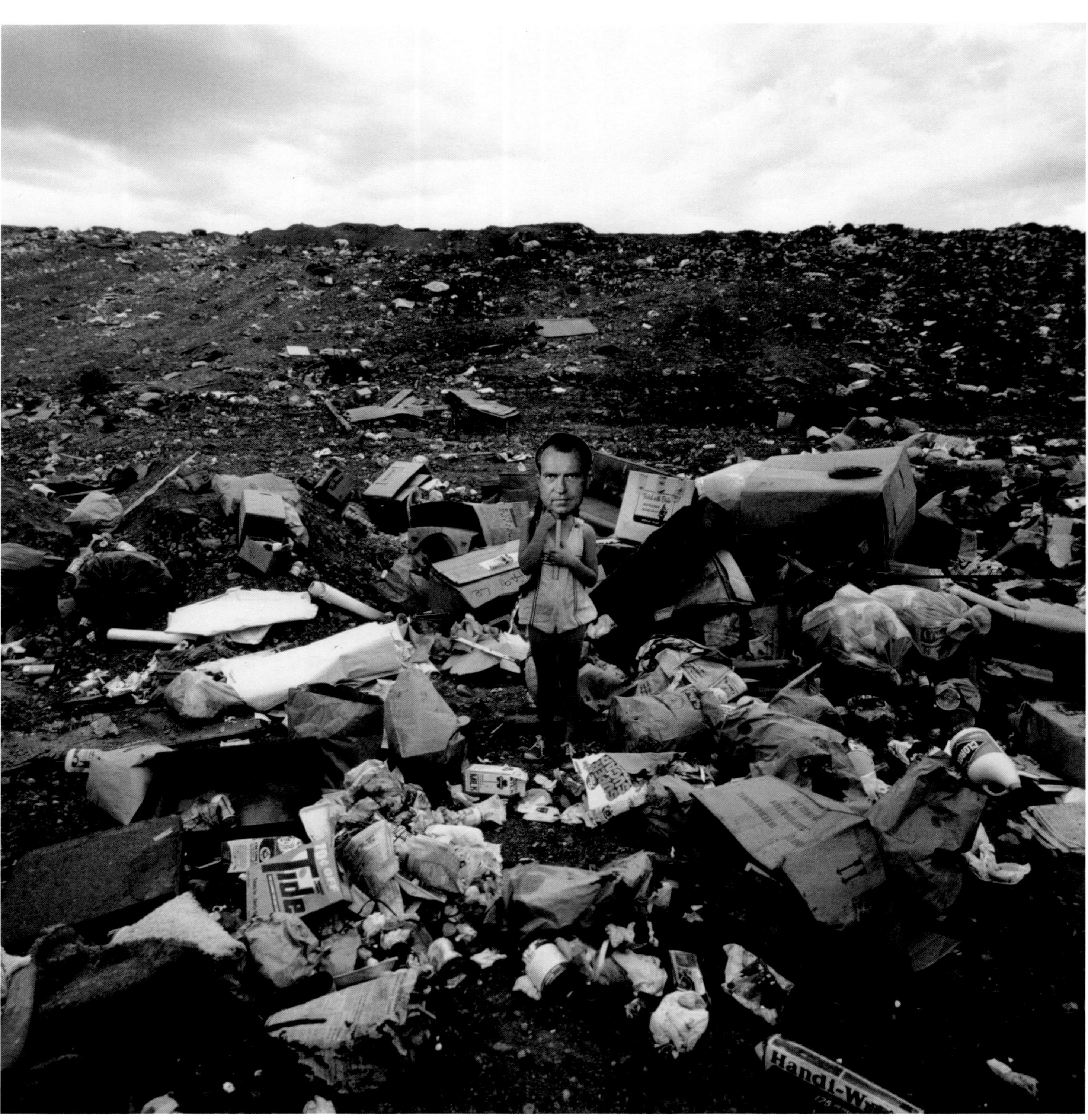

80   *Tide, Handiwipes, and Richard Millhouse,* 1974; from the series *An American Fairy Tale*

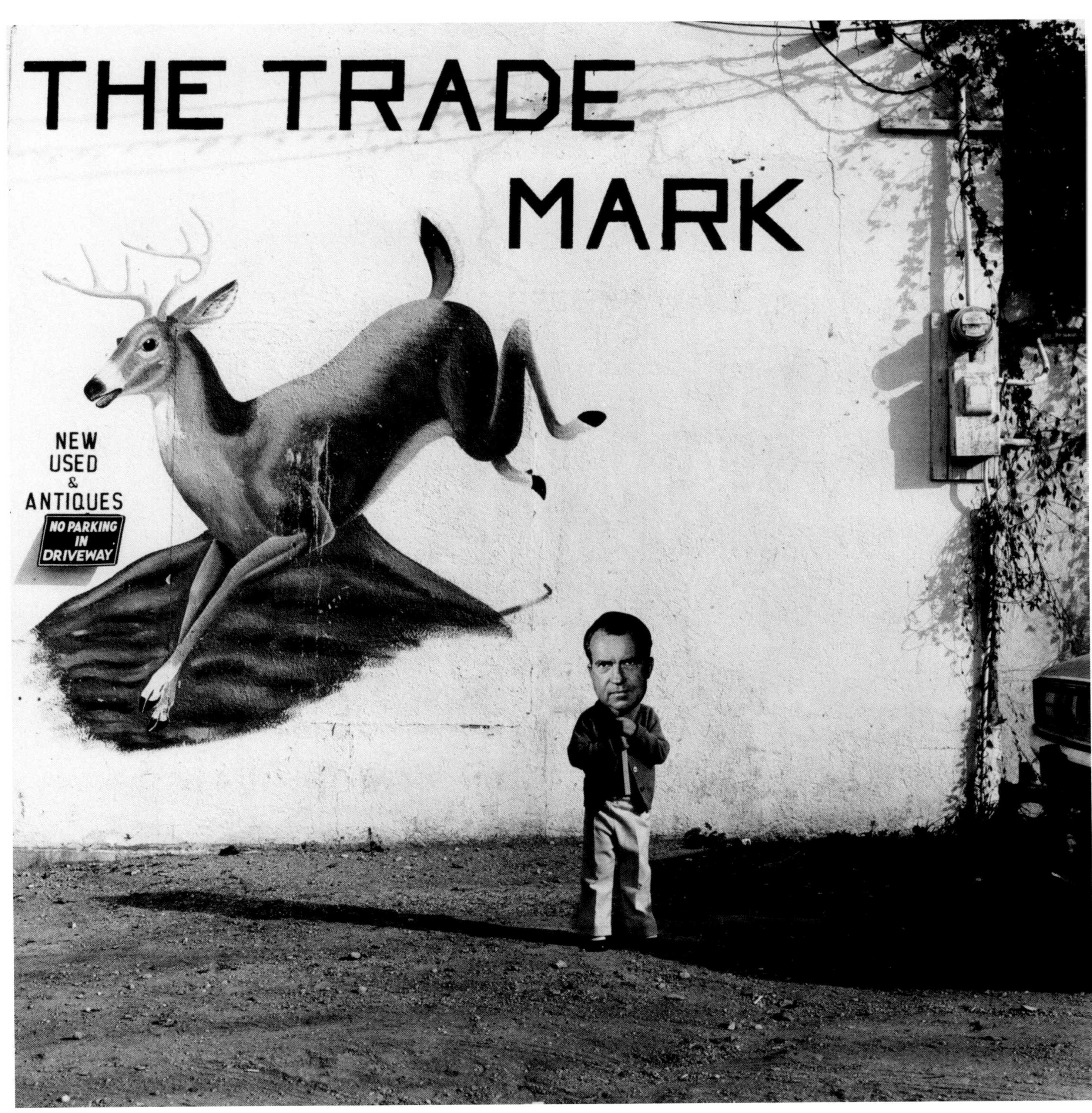

    I'm Not a Crook, 1974; from the series *An American Fairy Tale*

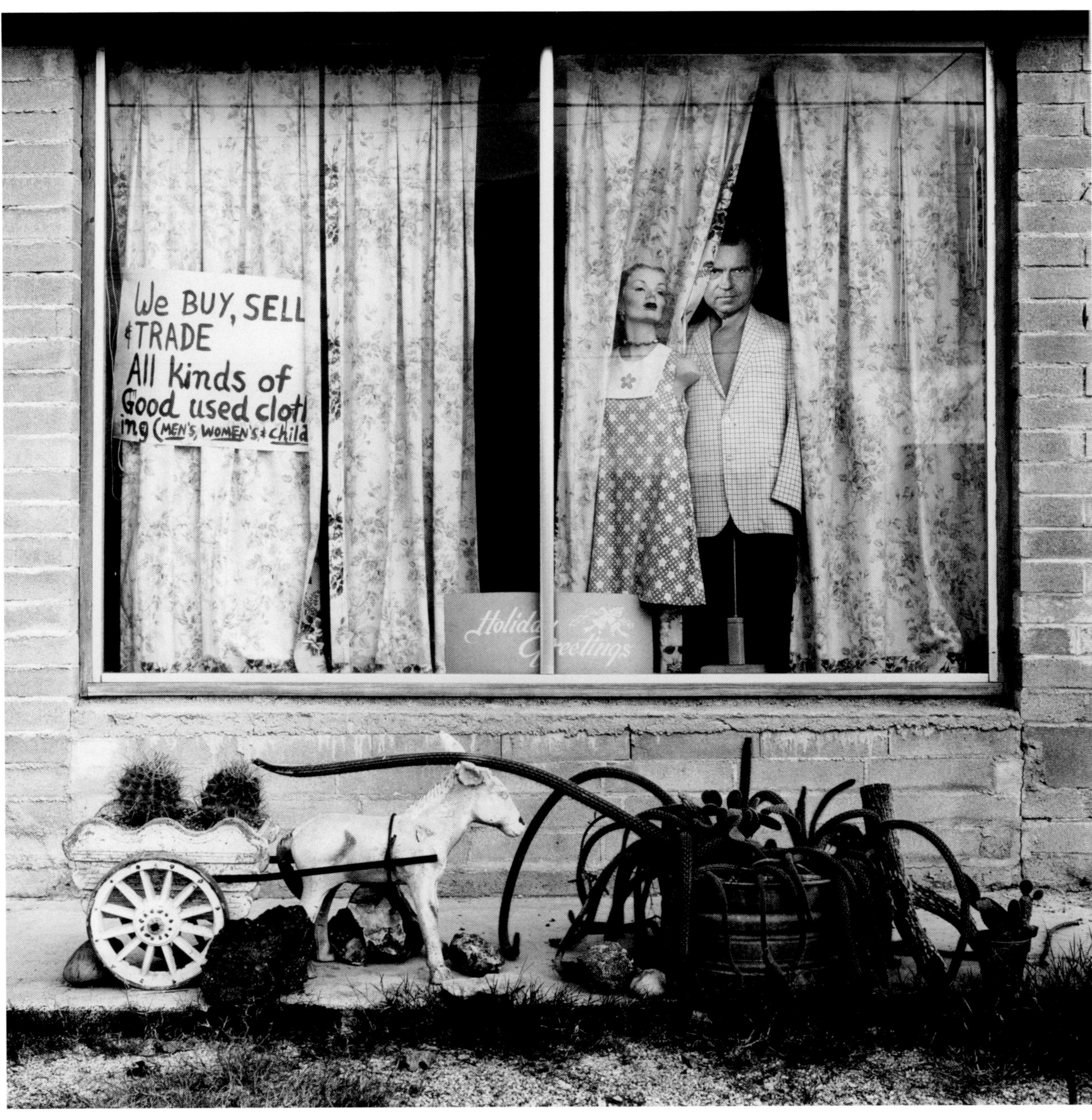

83   *Old Clothes, New Faces*, 1974; from the series *An American Fairy Tale*

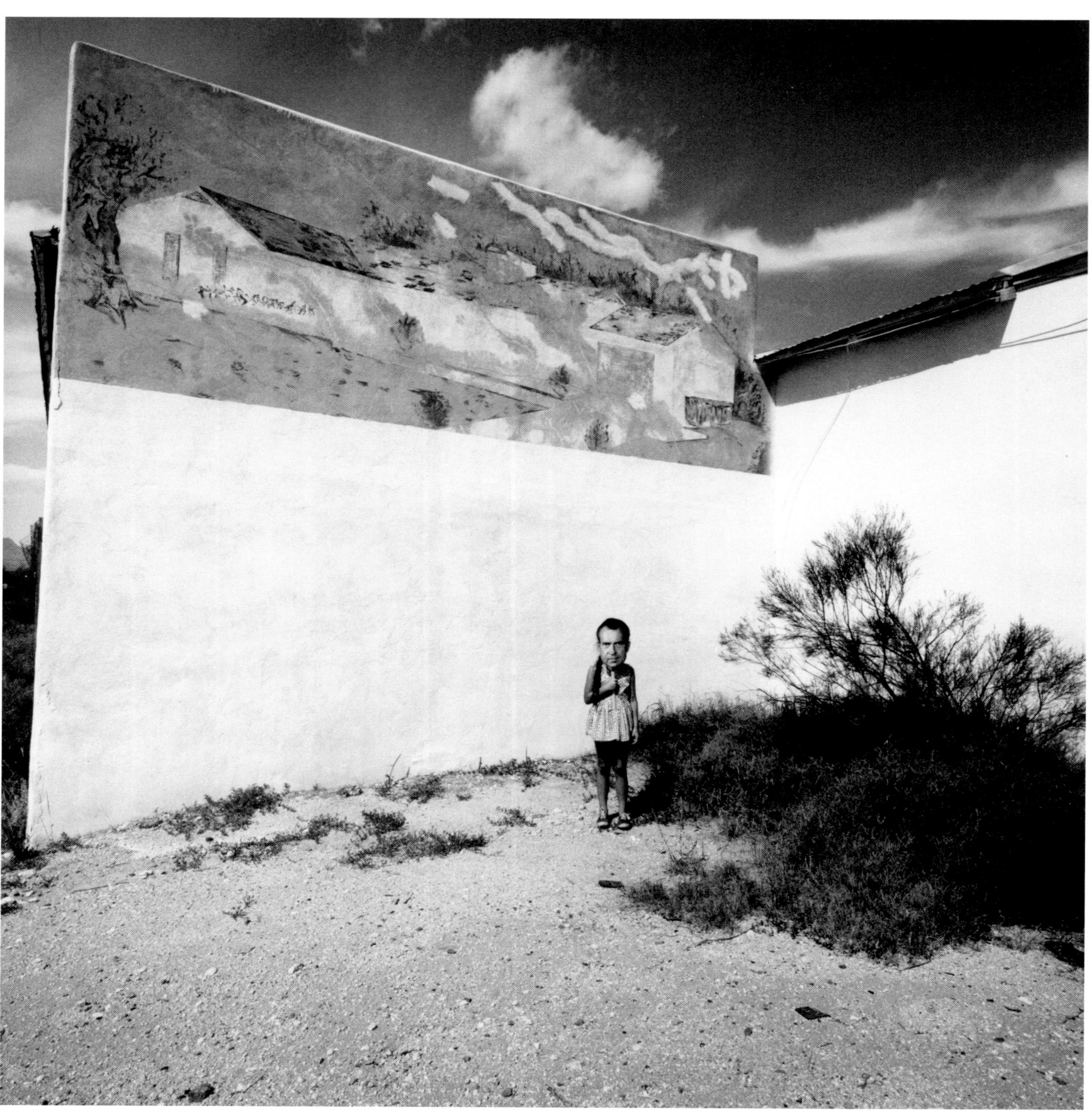

84   *White House, Blue Skies*, 1974; from the series *An American Fairy Tale*

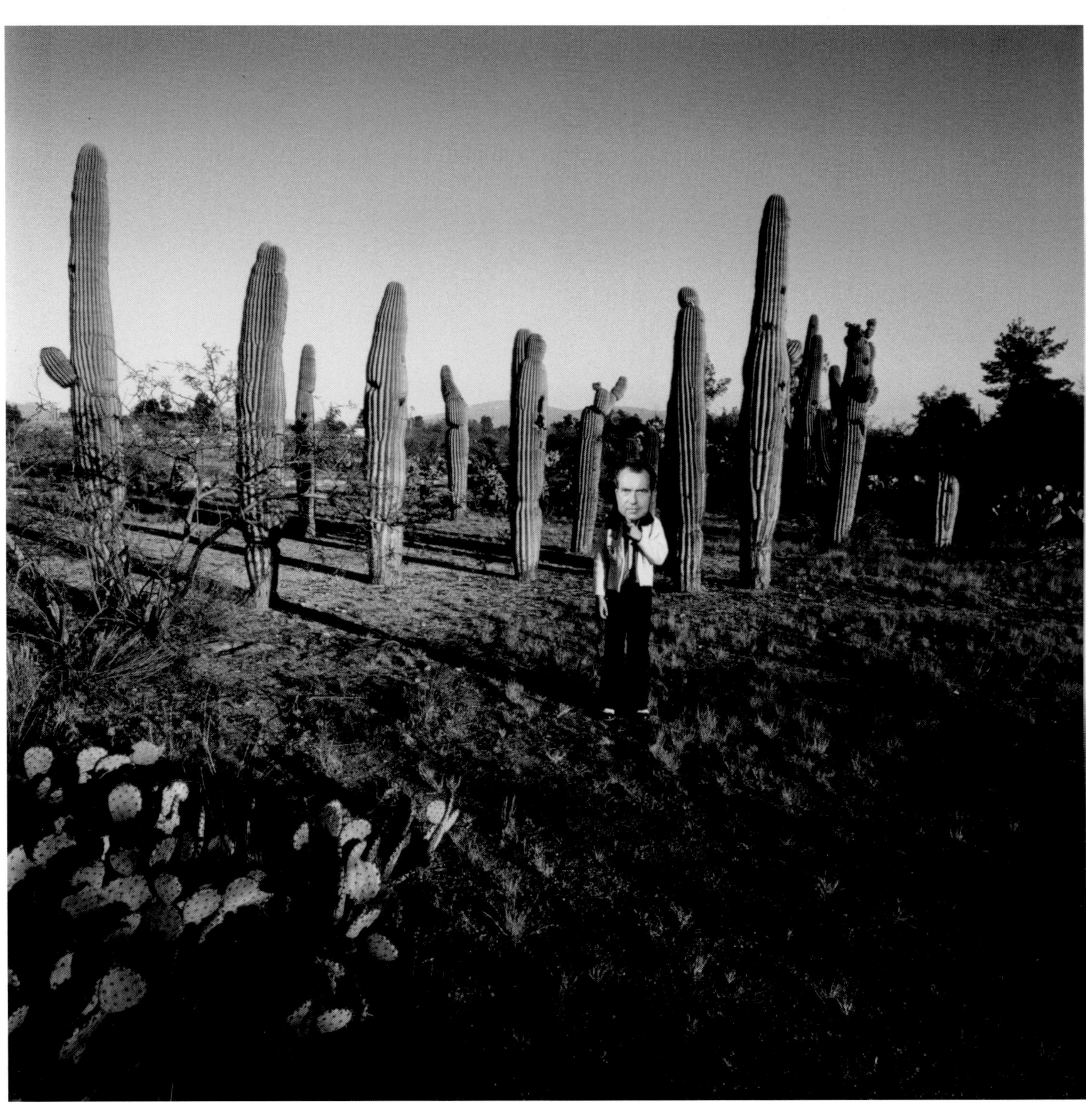

85   *Sticking Together*, 1974; from the series *An American Fairy Tale*

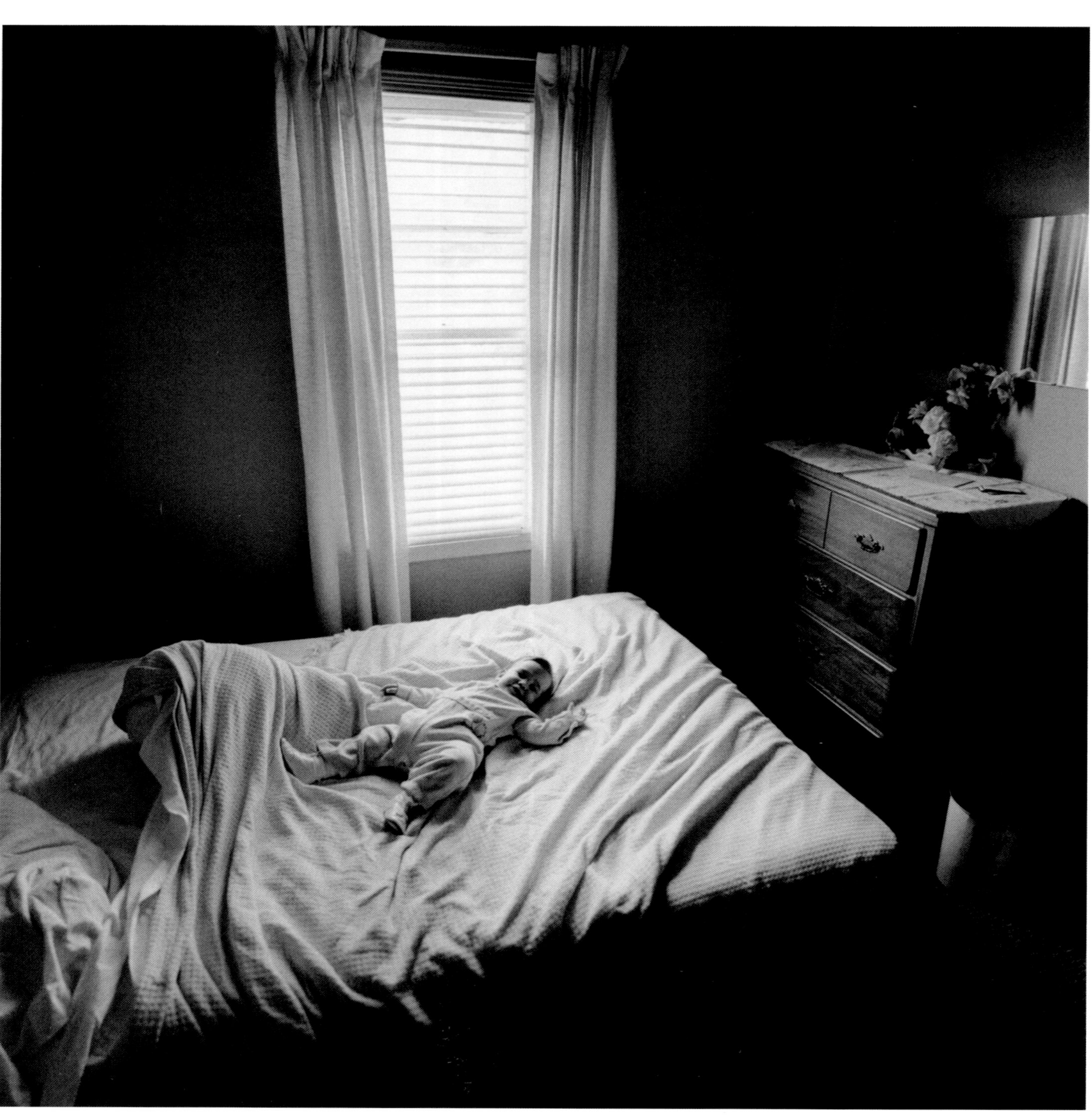

86   *Untitled (Katrina Bernal)*, 1972

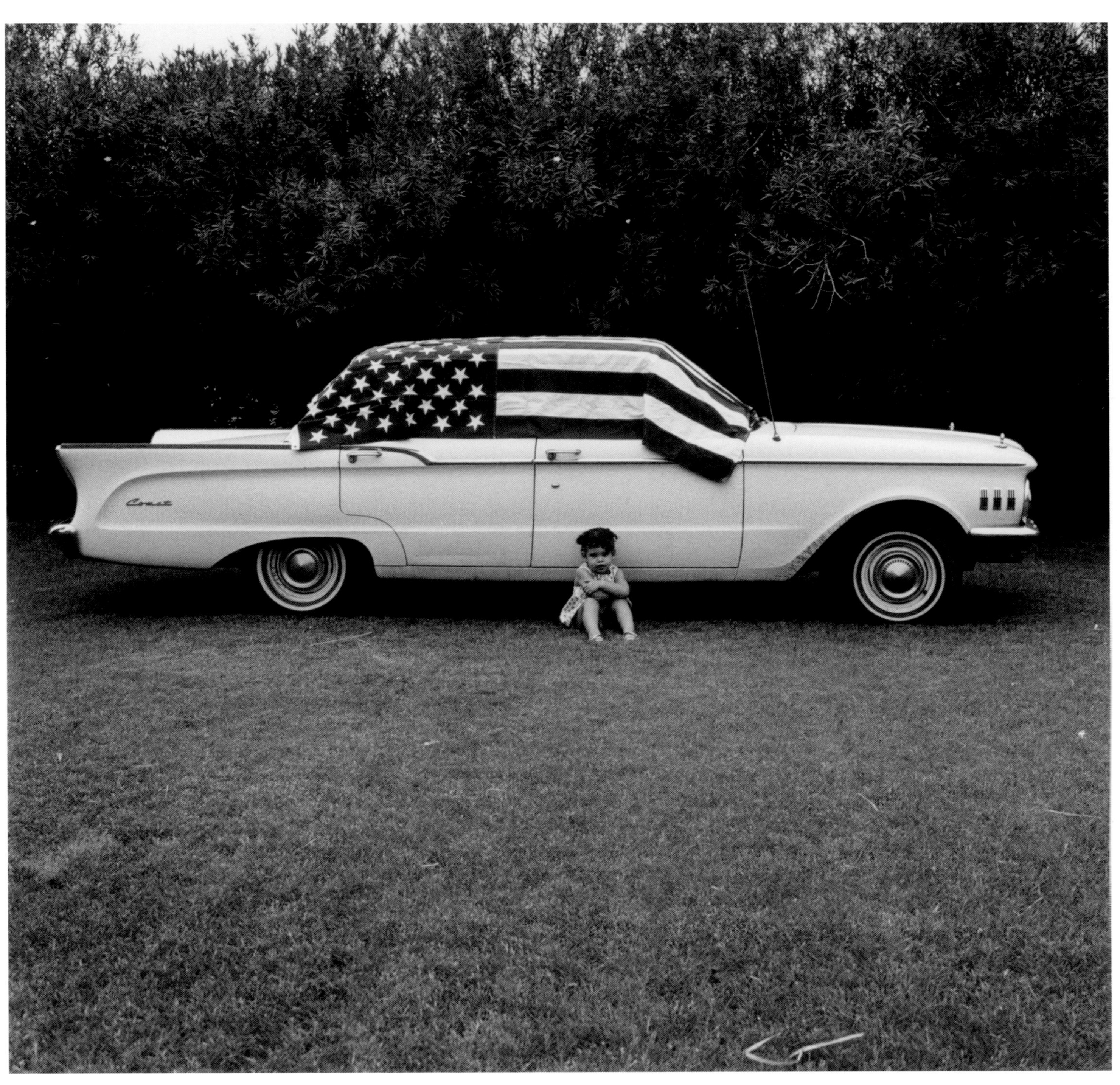

87   *Untitled (Lisa Bernal)*, 1970

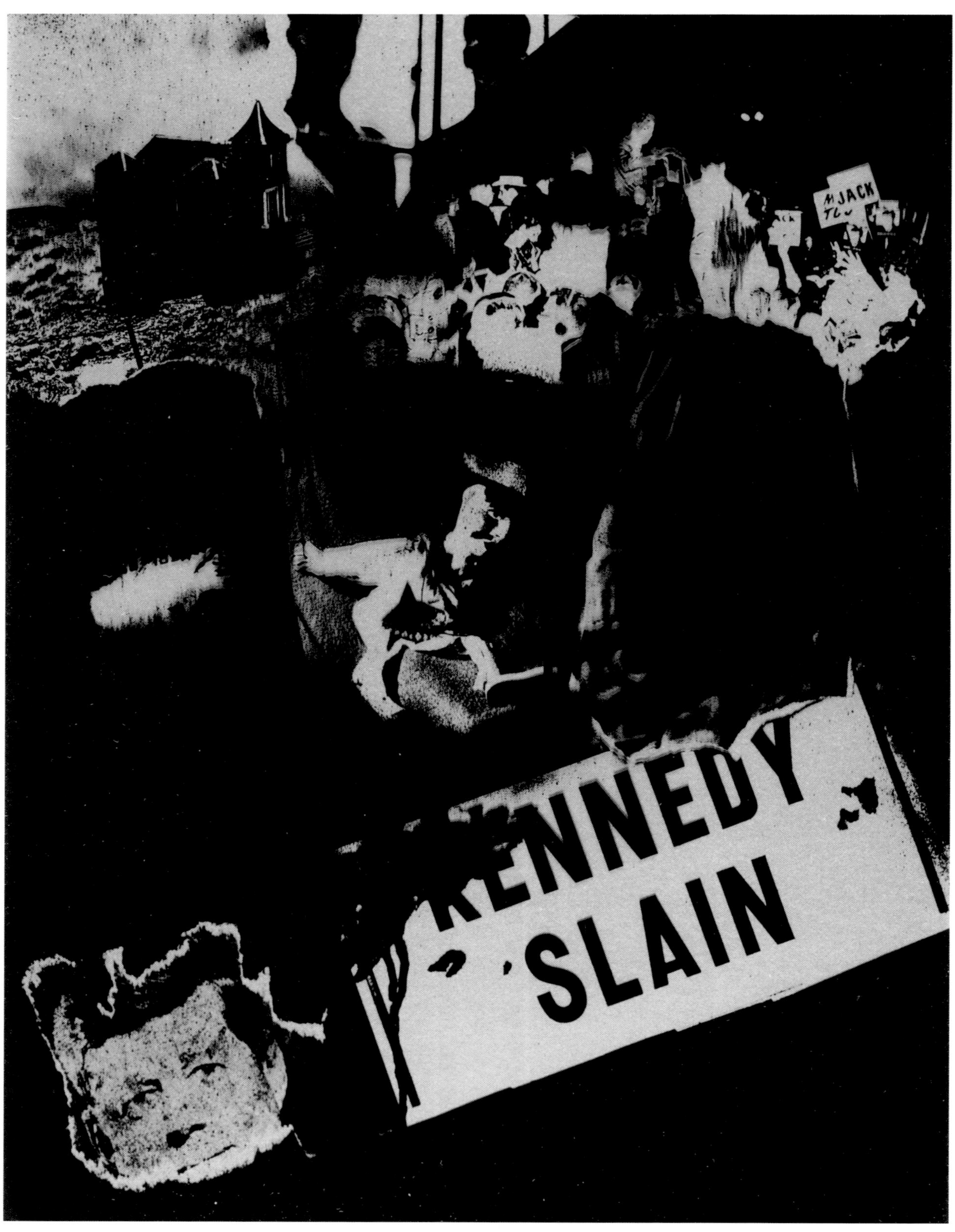

88   *Untitled,* 1970

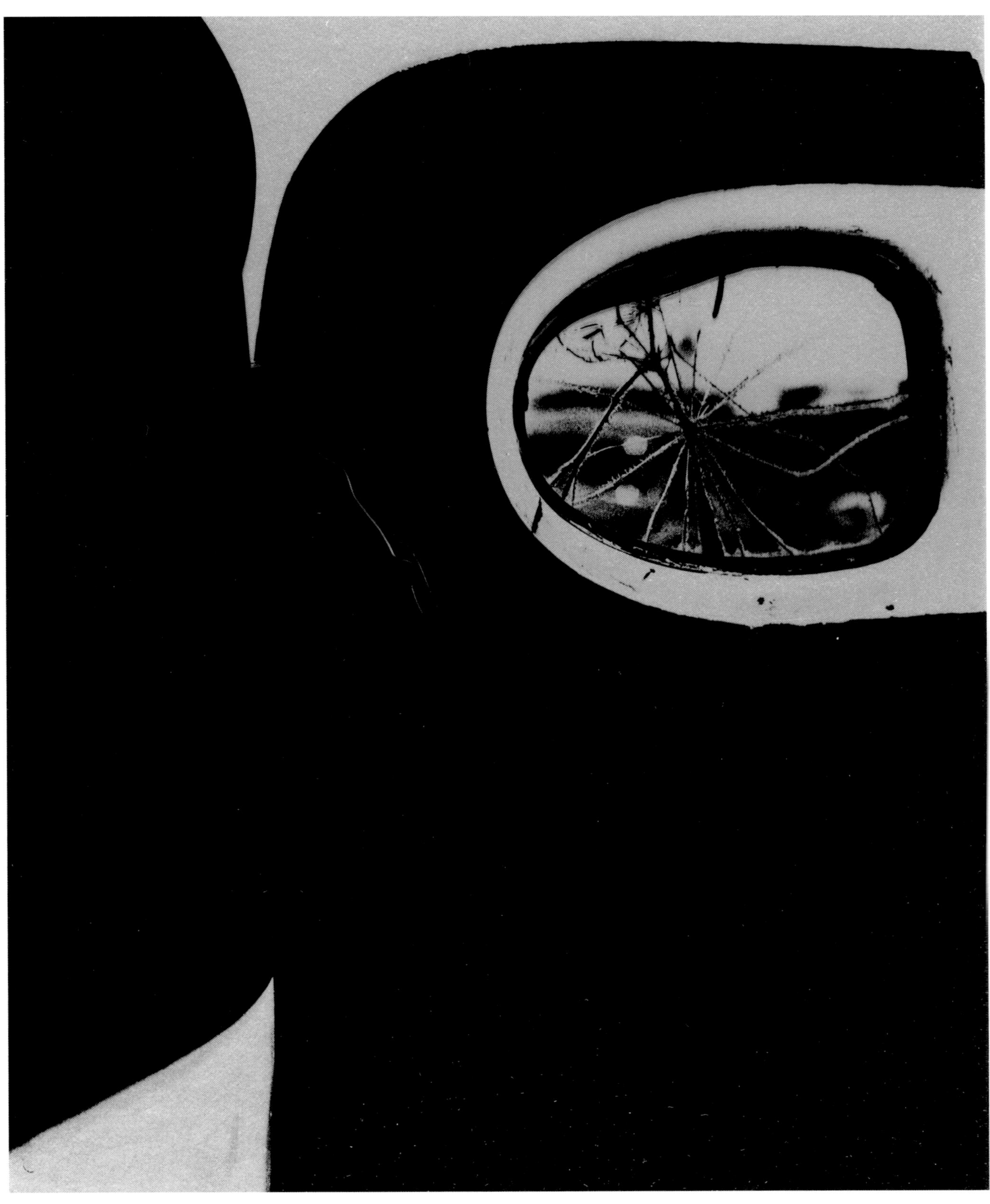

89   *Untitled*, 1970

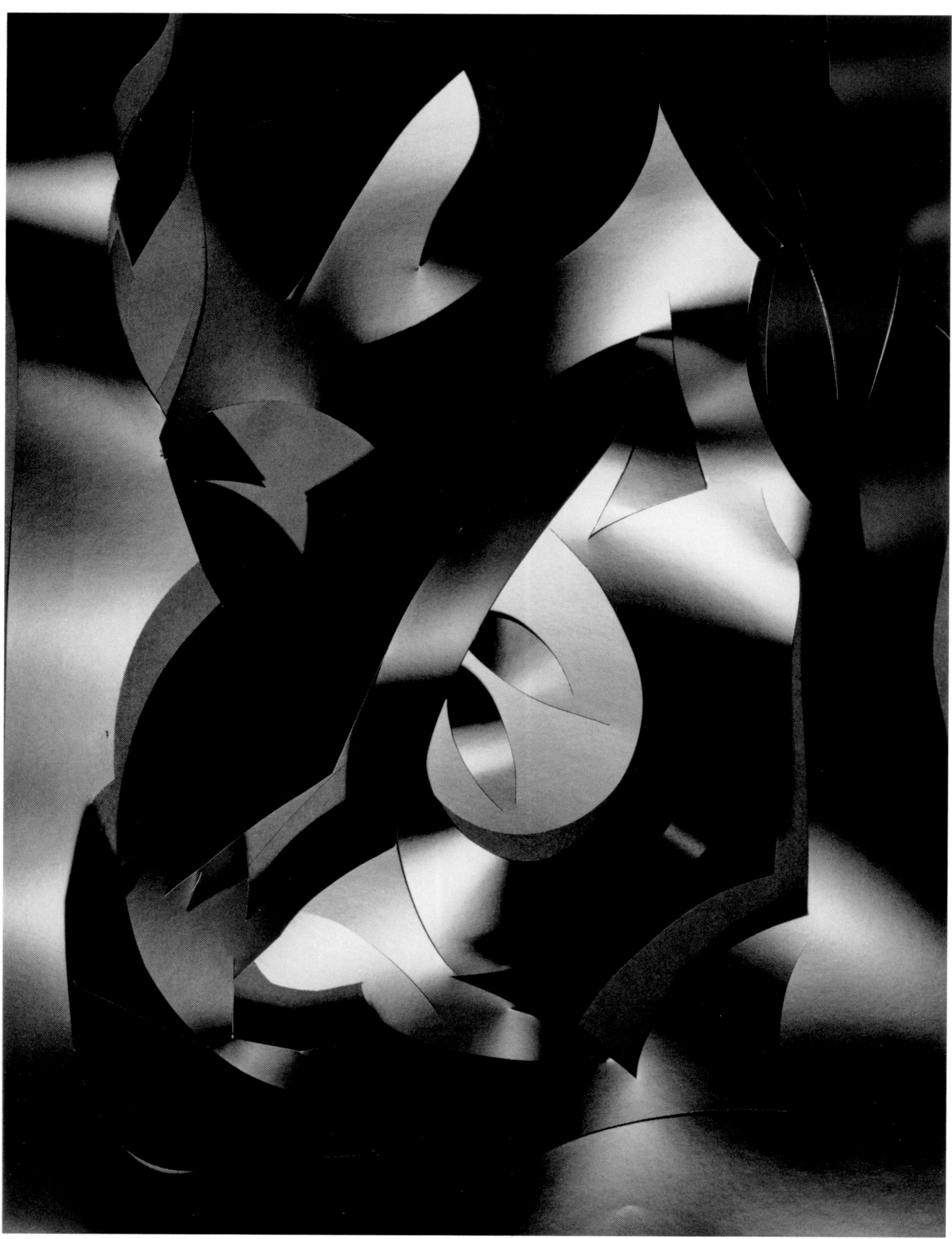

90   *Chrome Cutting,* 1972

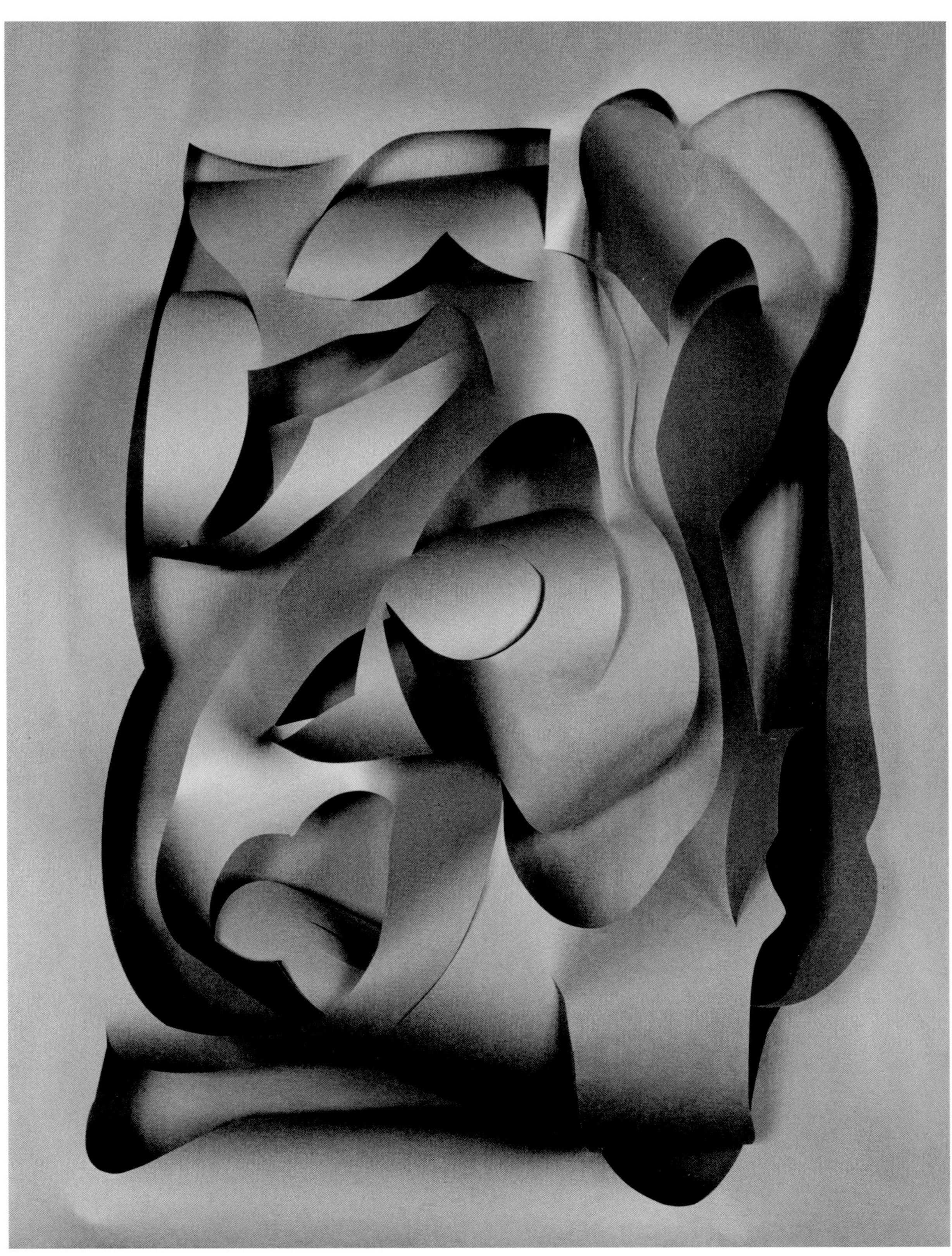

91   *Paper Cutting #3*, 1970–72

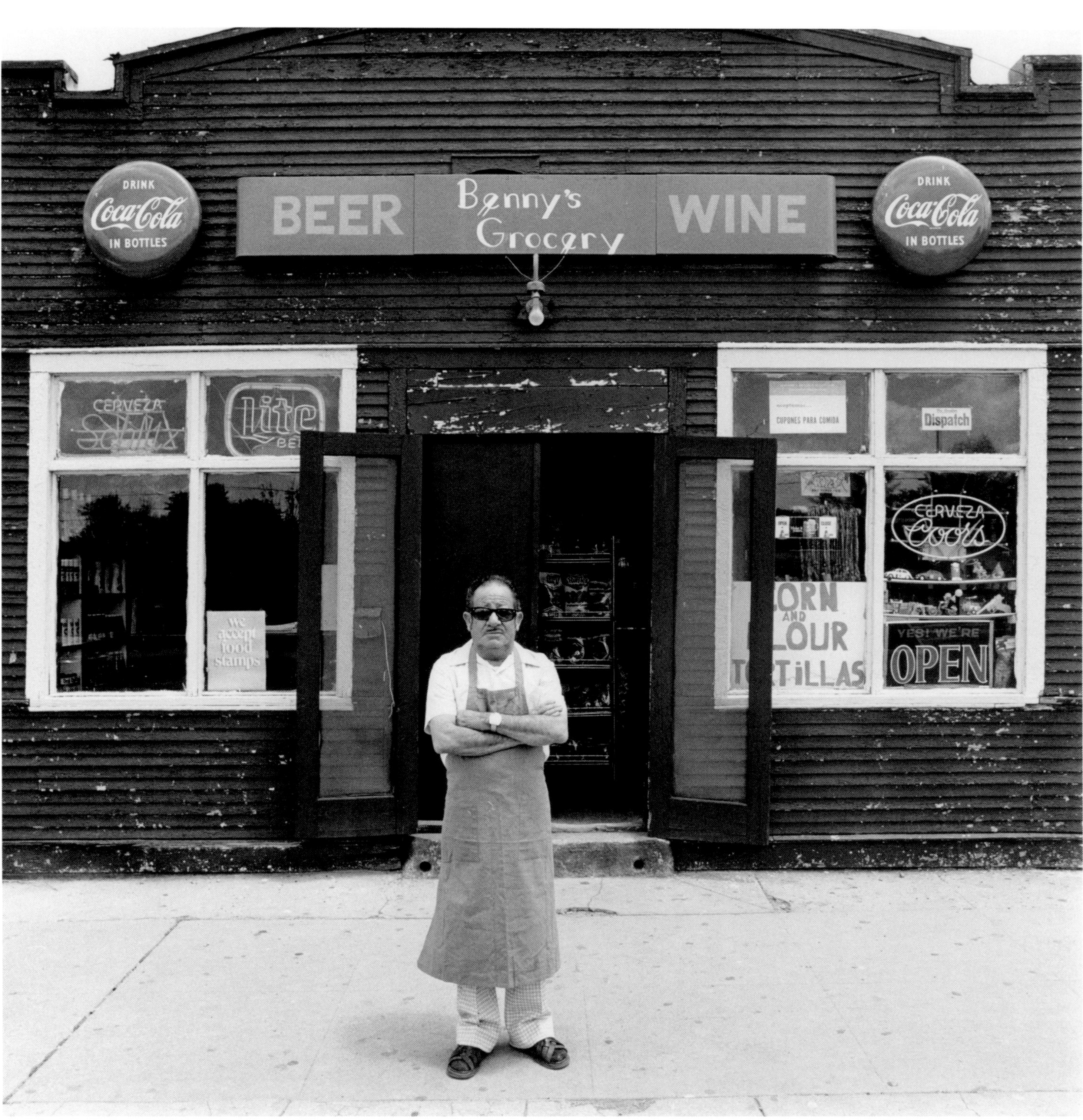

93 *Benny's Market,* 1974

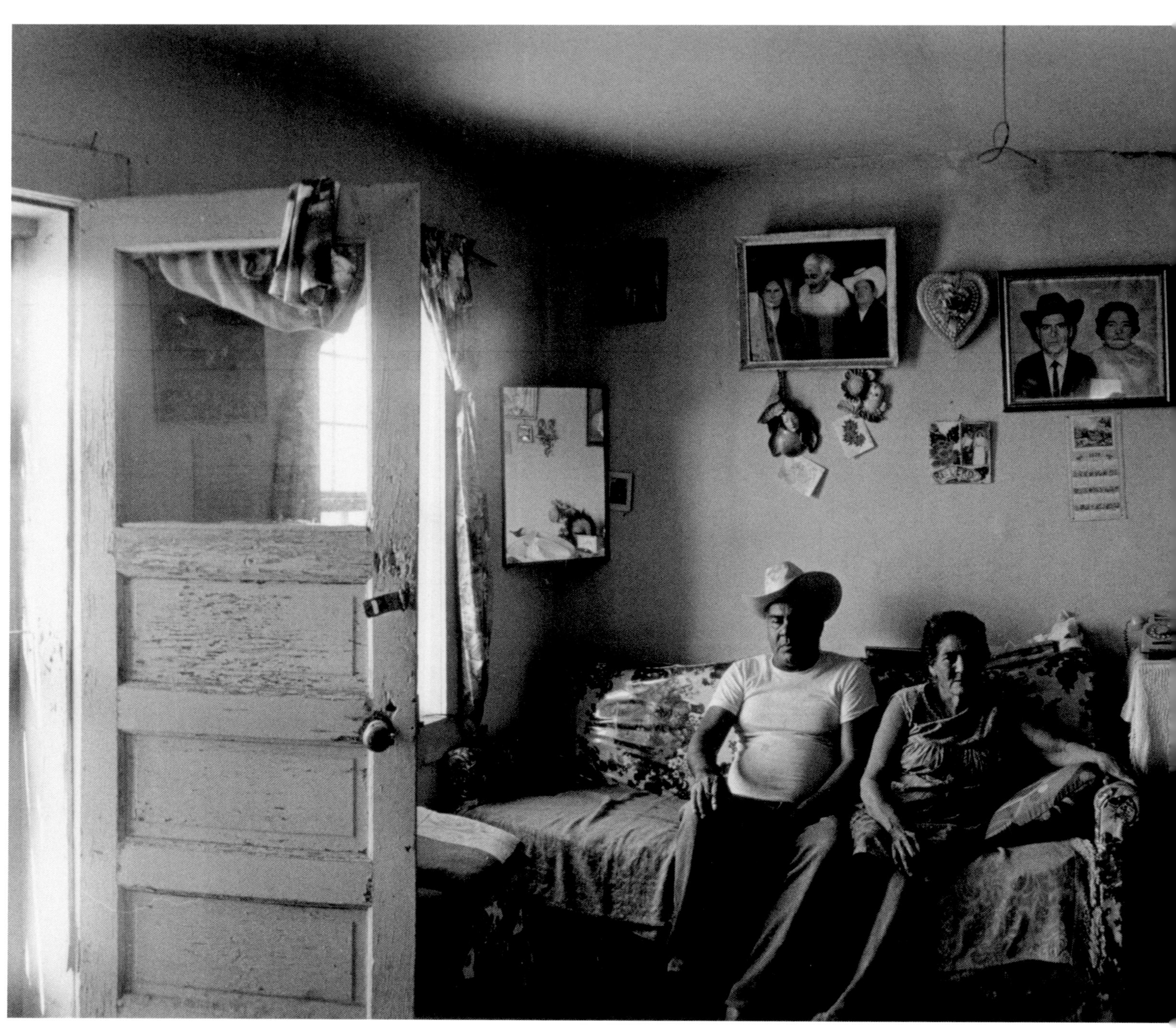

94   *4th Street Barrio, Douglas,* 1979

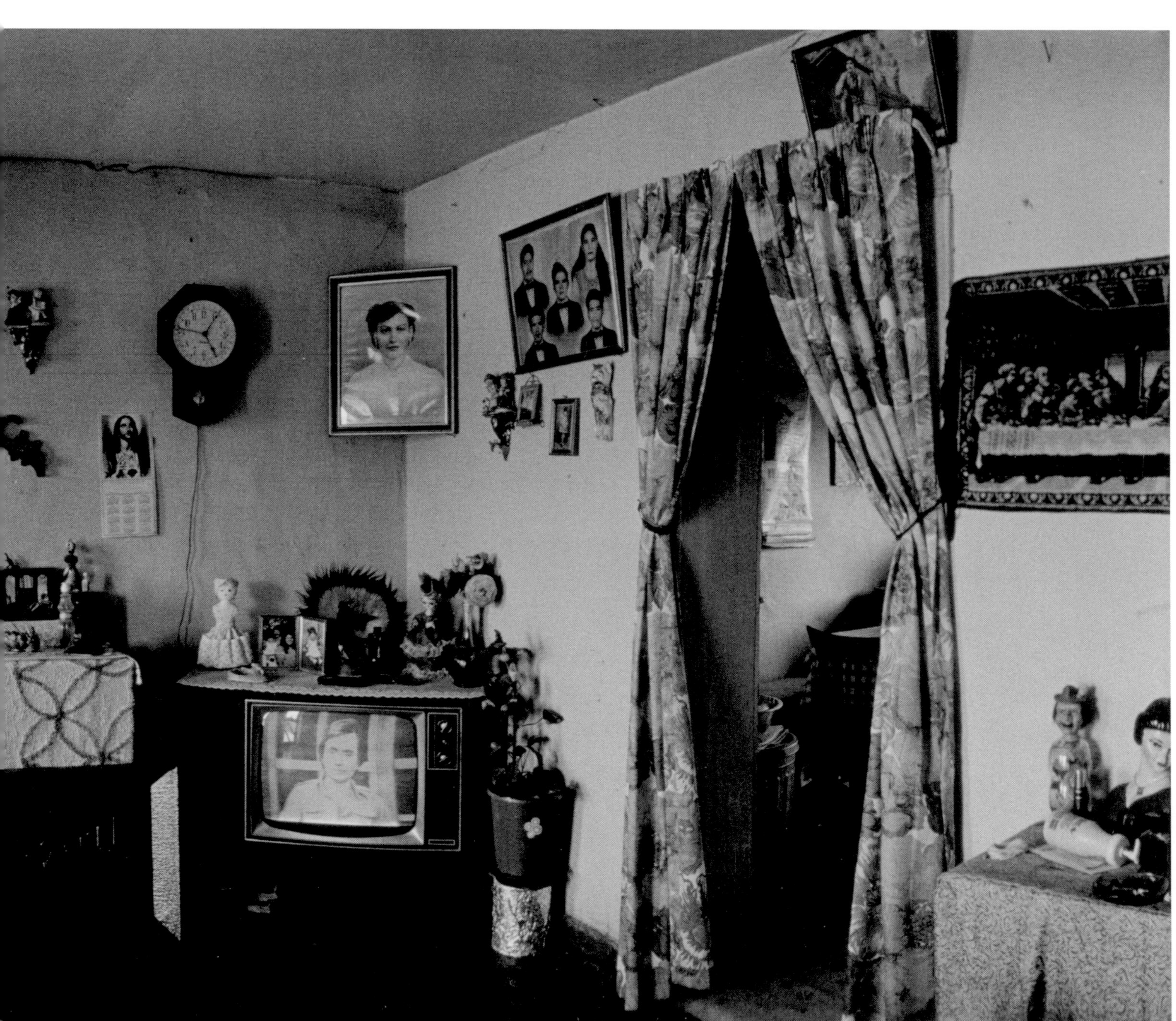

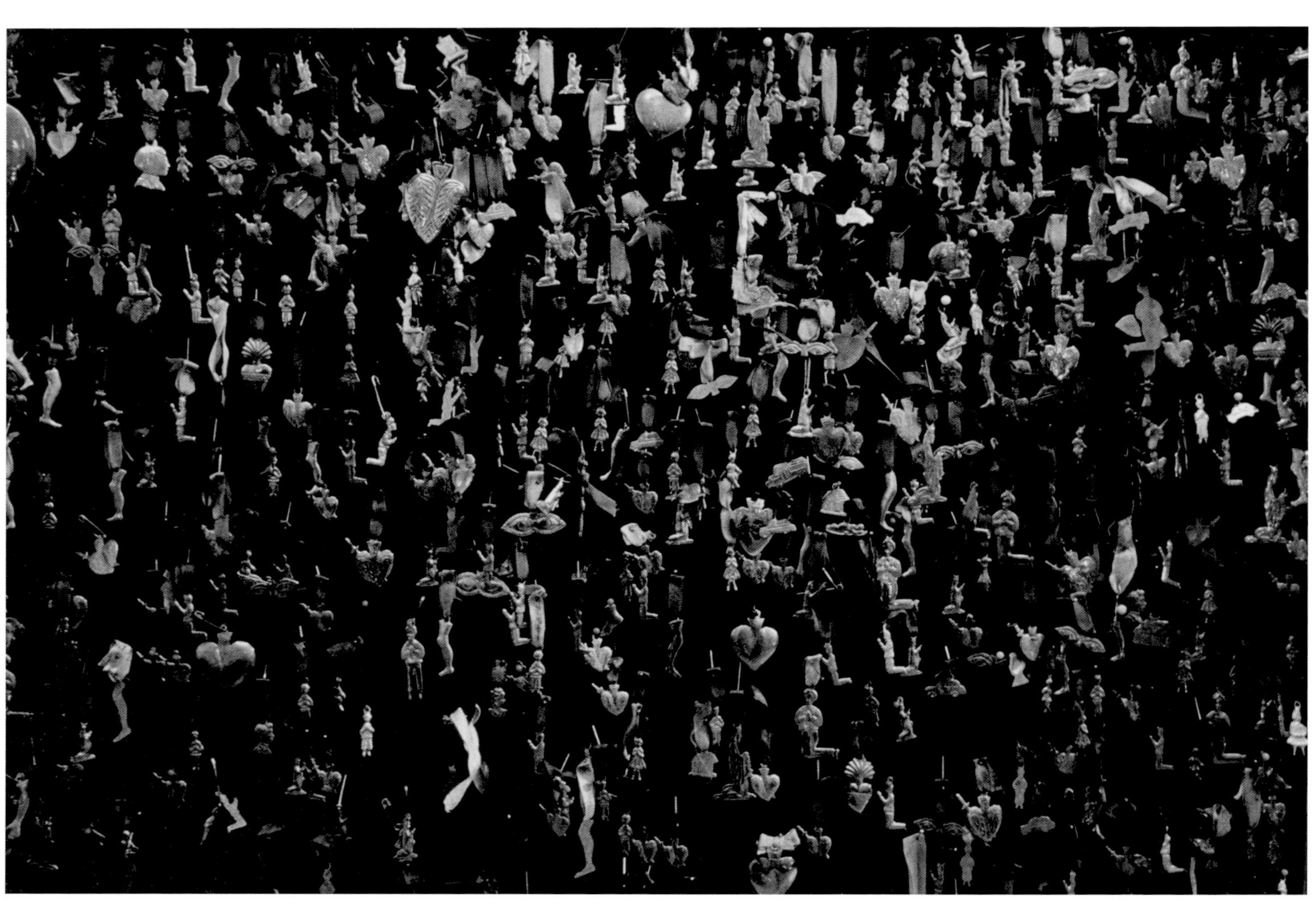

96   *Milagros, Mexico City*, 1980

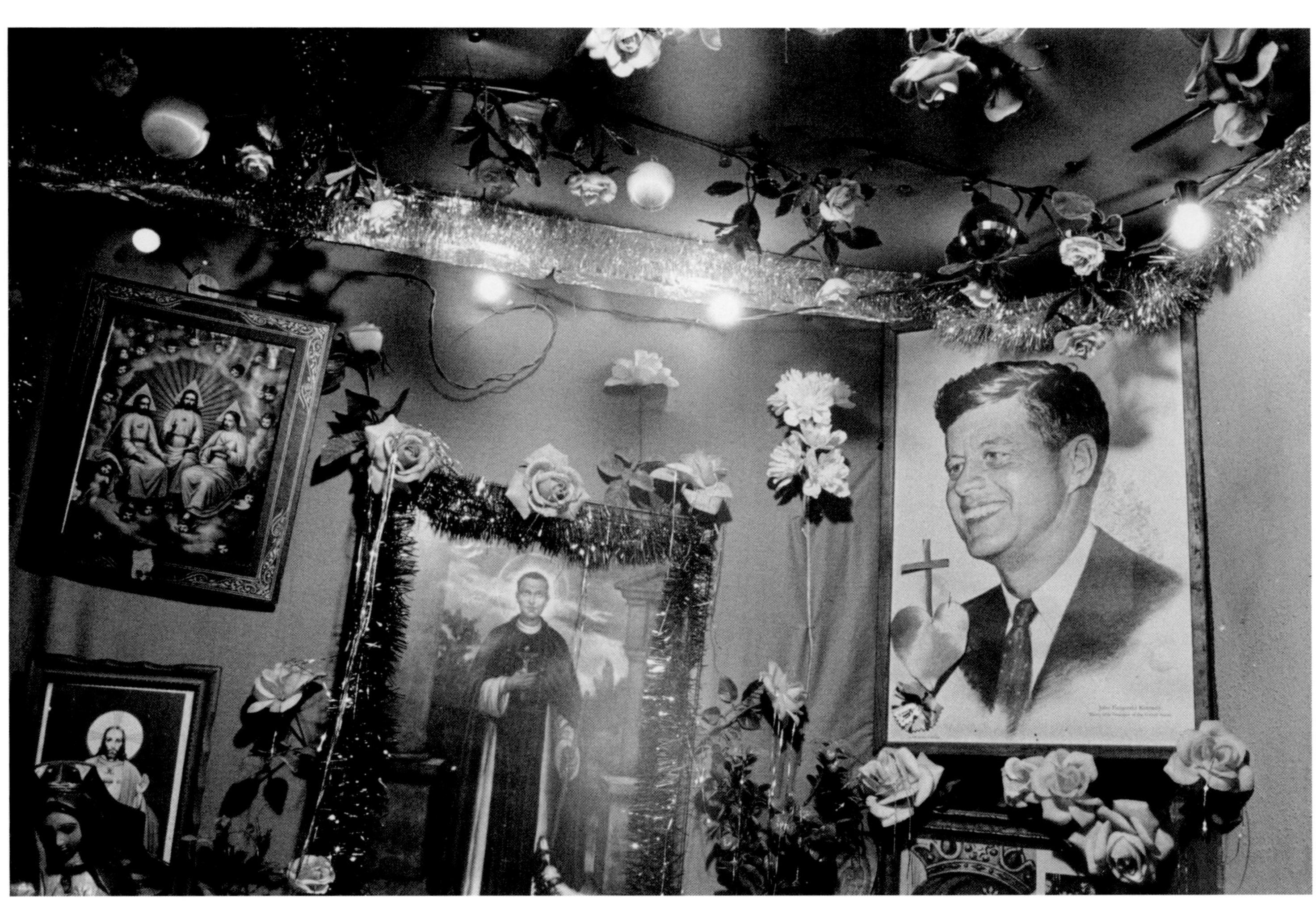

     Kennedy Cocio Altar, Tucson, 1980

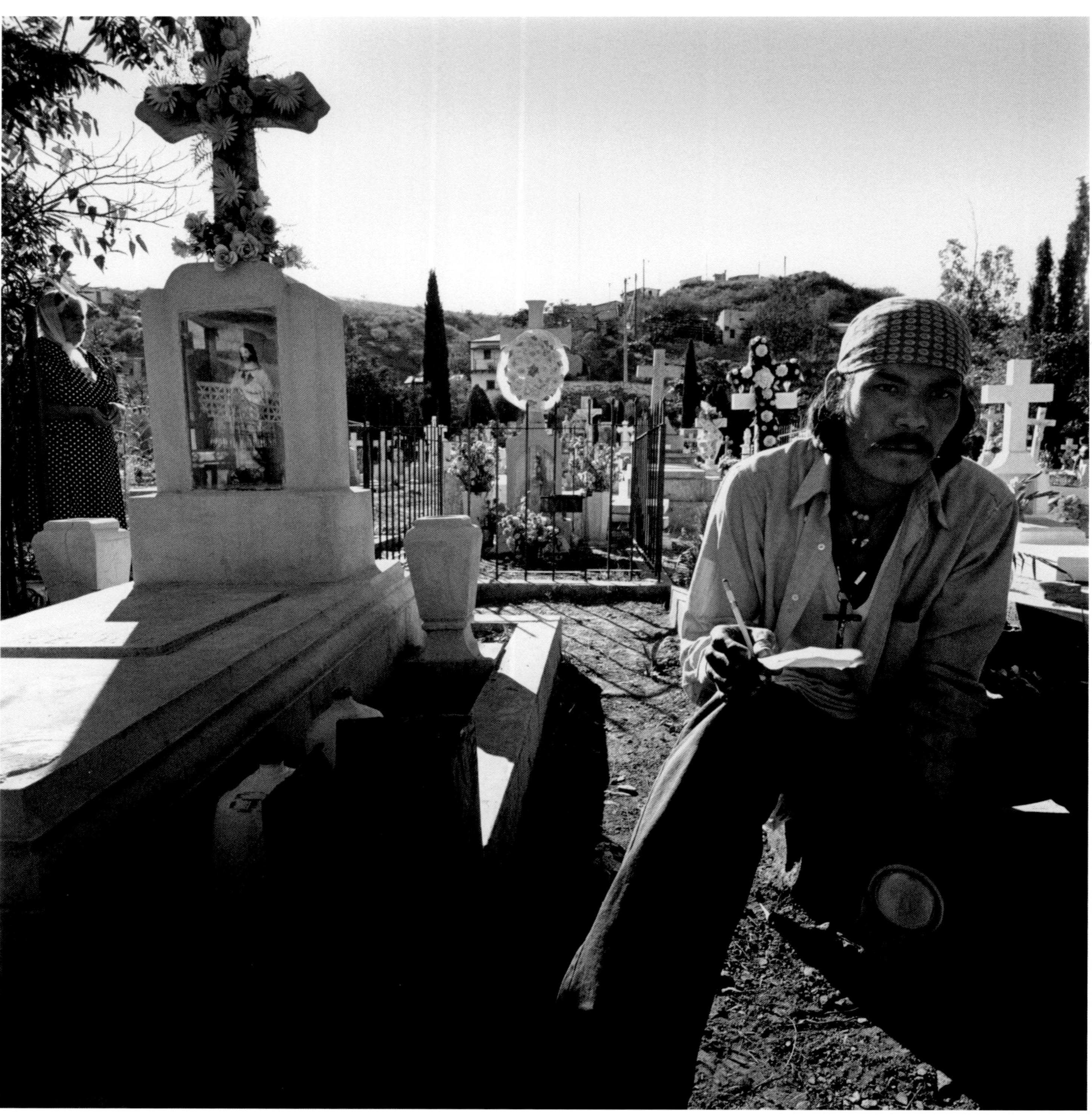

    Grave Painter, Día de los Muertos, Nogales, 1977

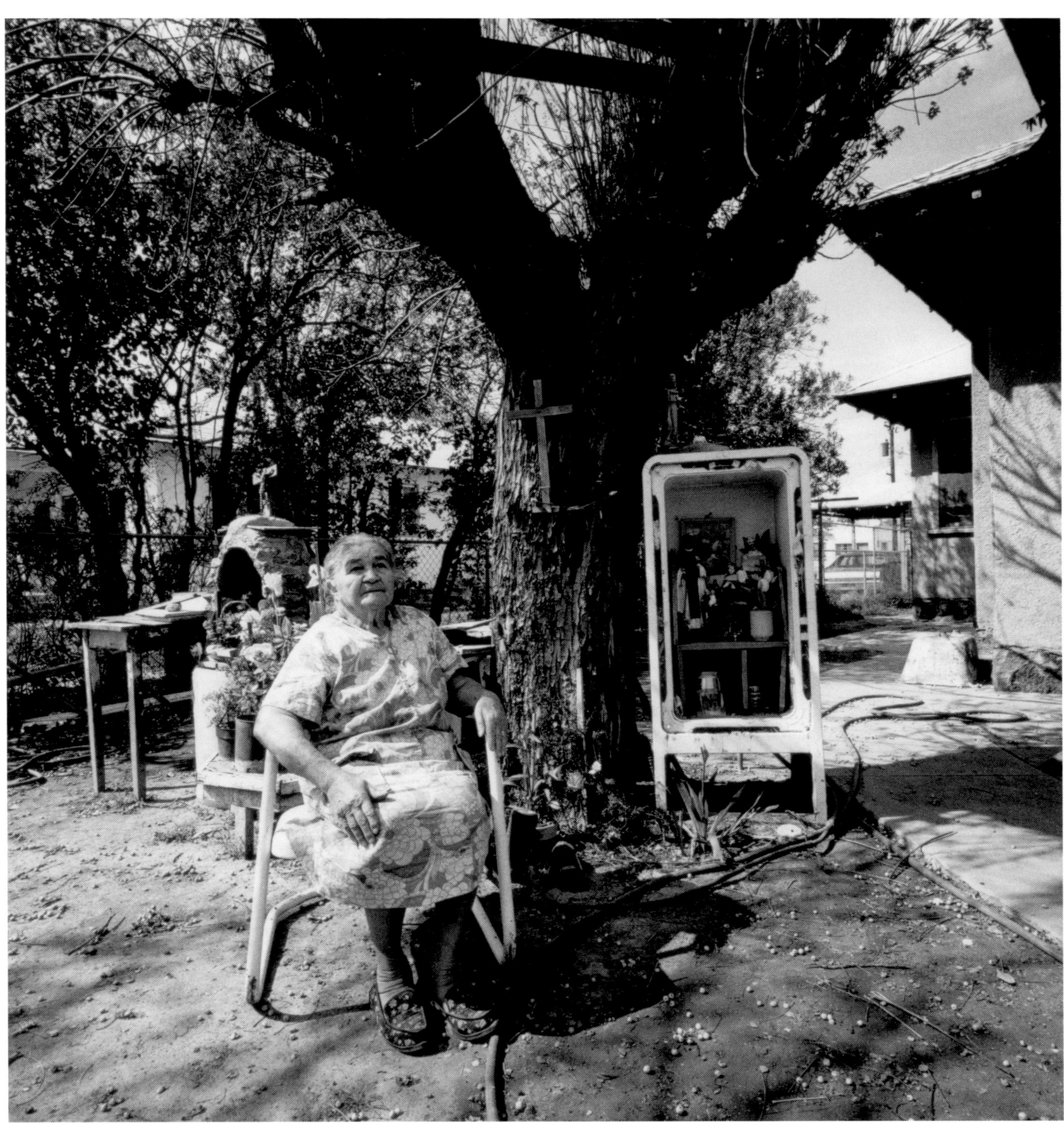

99   *Sra. Vargas, Barrio Armory Park,* 1973

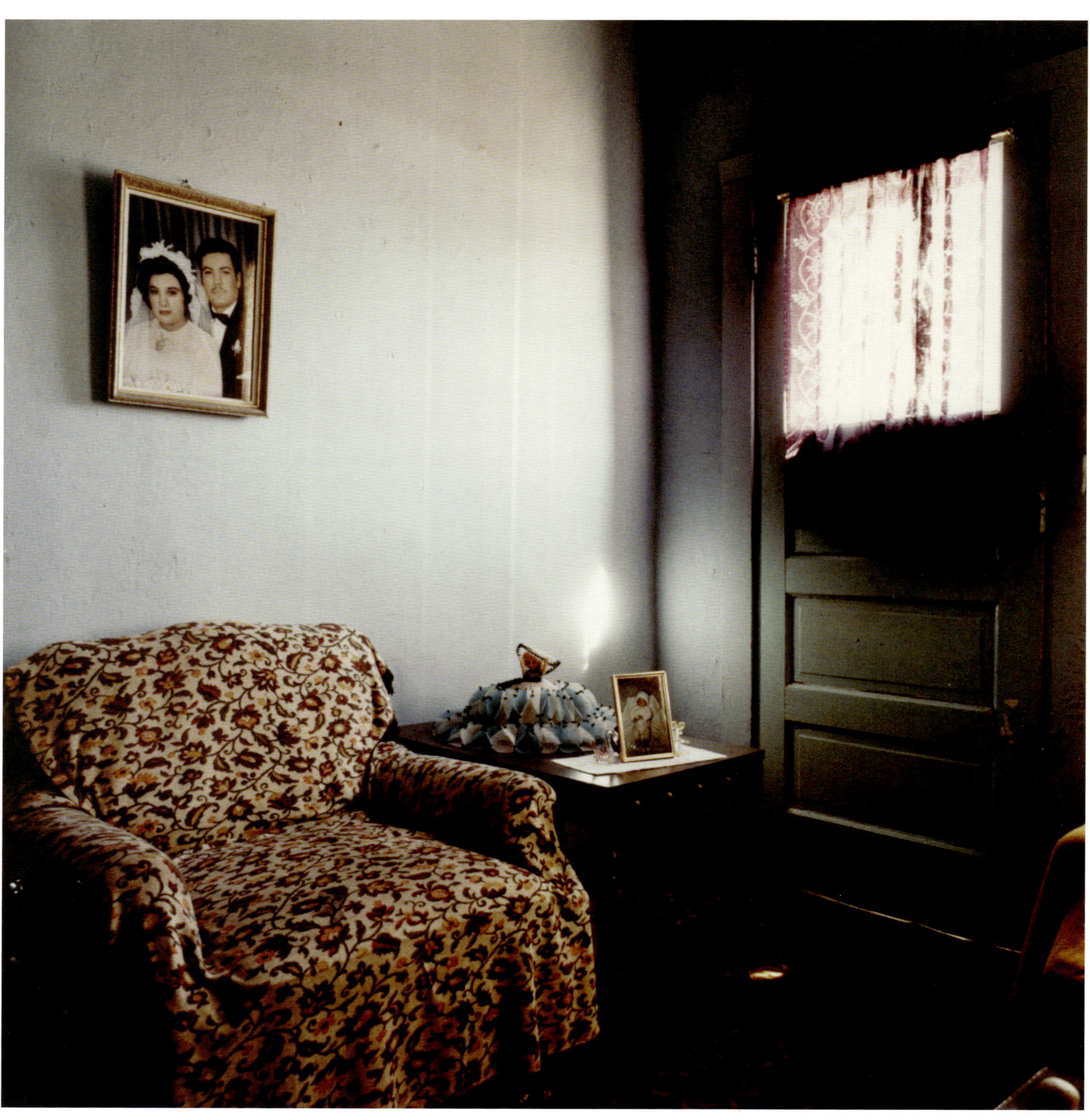

100   *Boda de Luz, Douglas, Arizona,* 1978

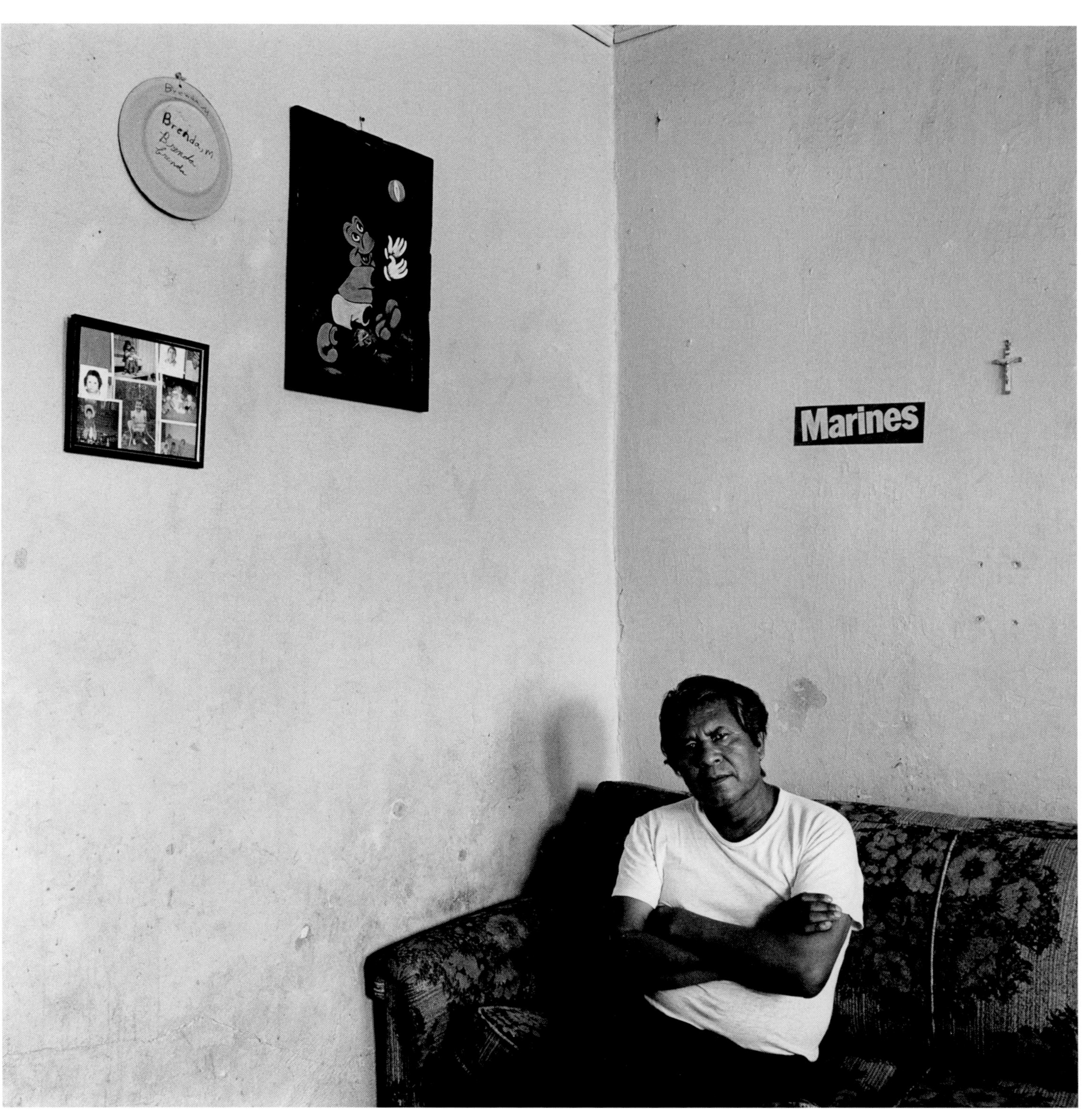

101   *Juan Mejia, Marines, Douglas, Arizona*, 1979

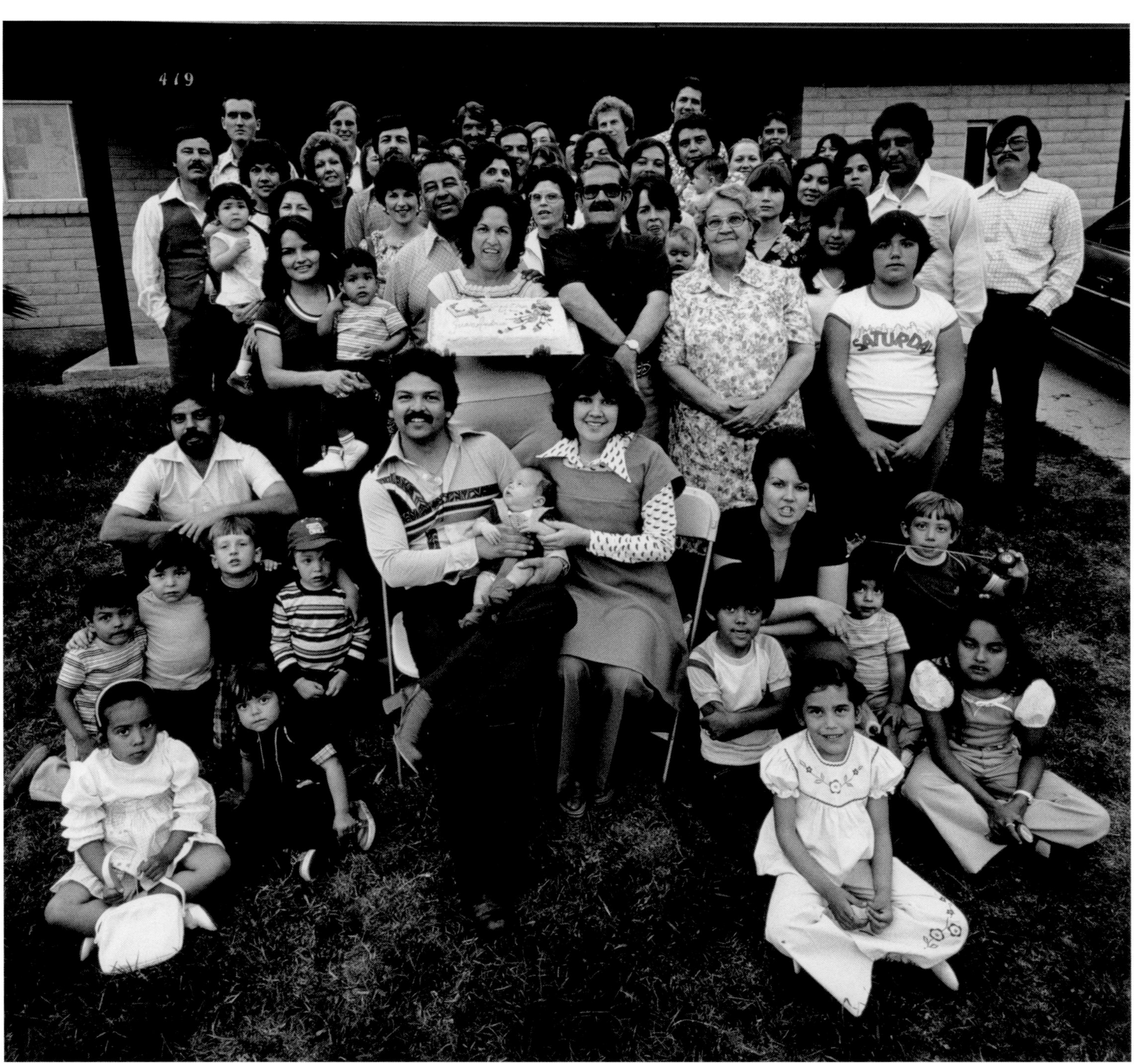

103   *Quiñonez Baptism, Tucson*, 1977

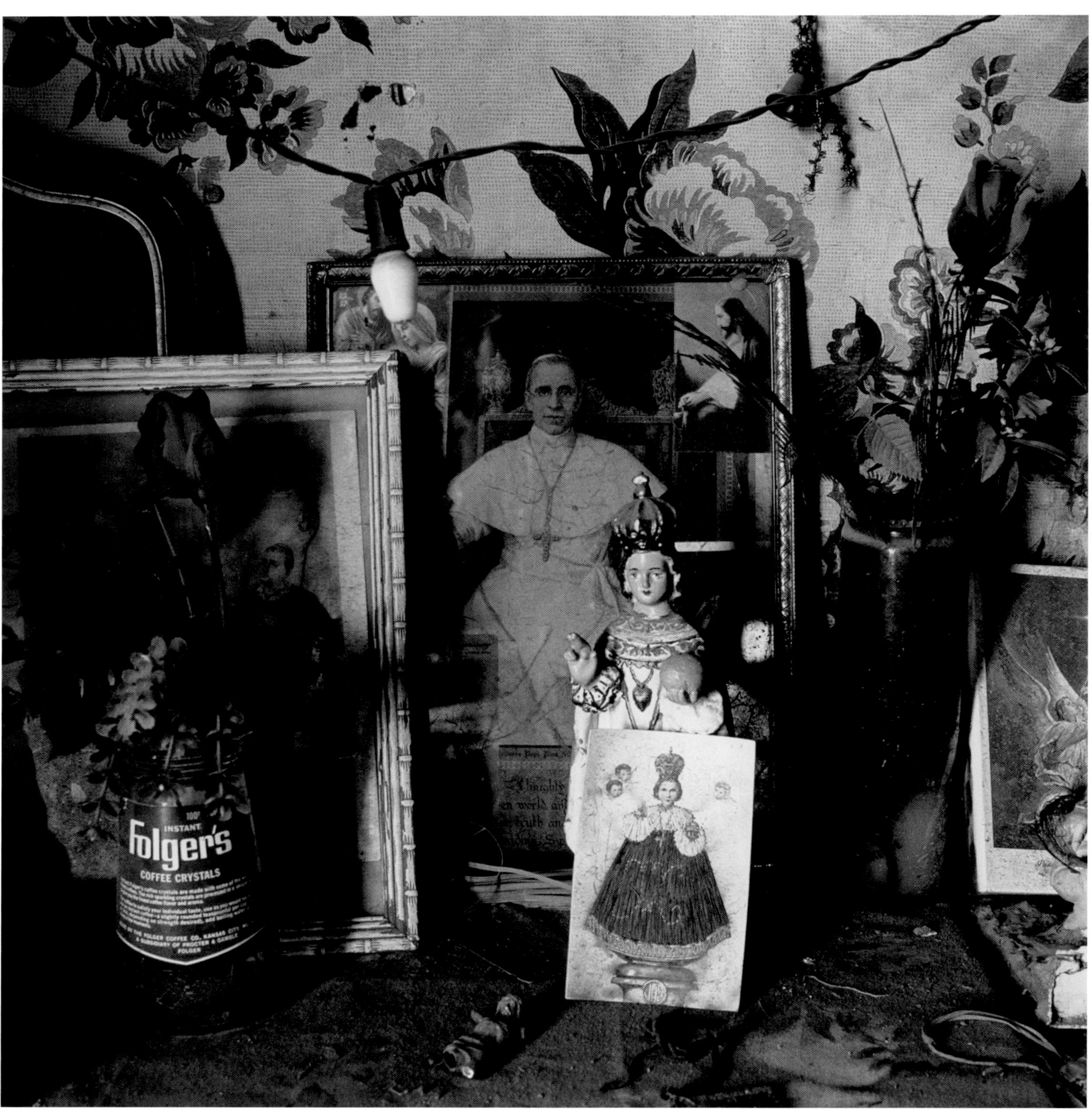

     Pope Pius XII, 1977; from the series *Benitez Suite*

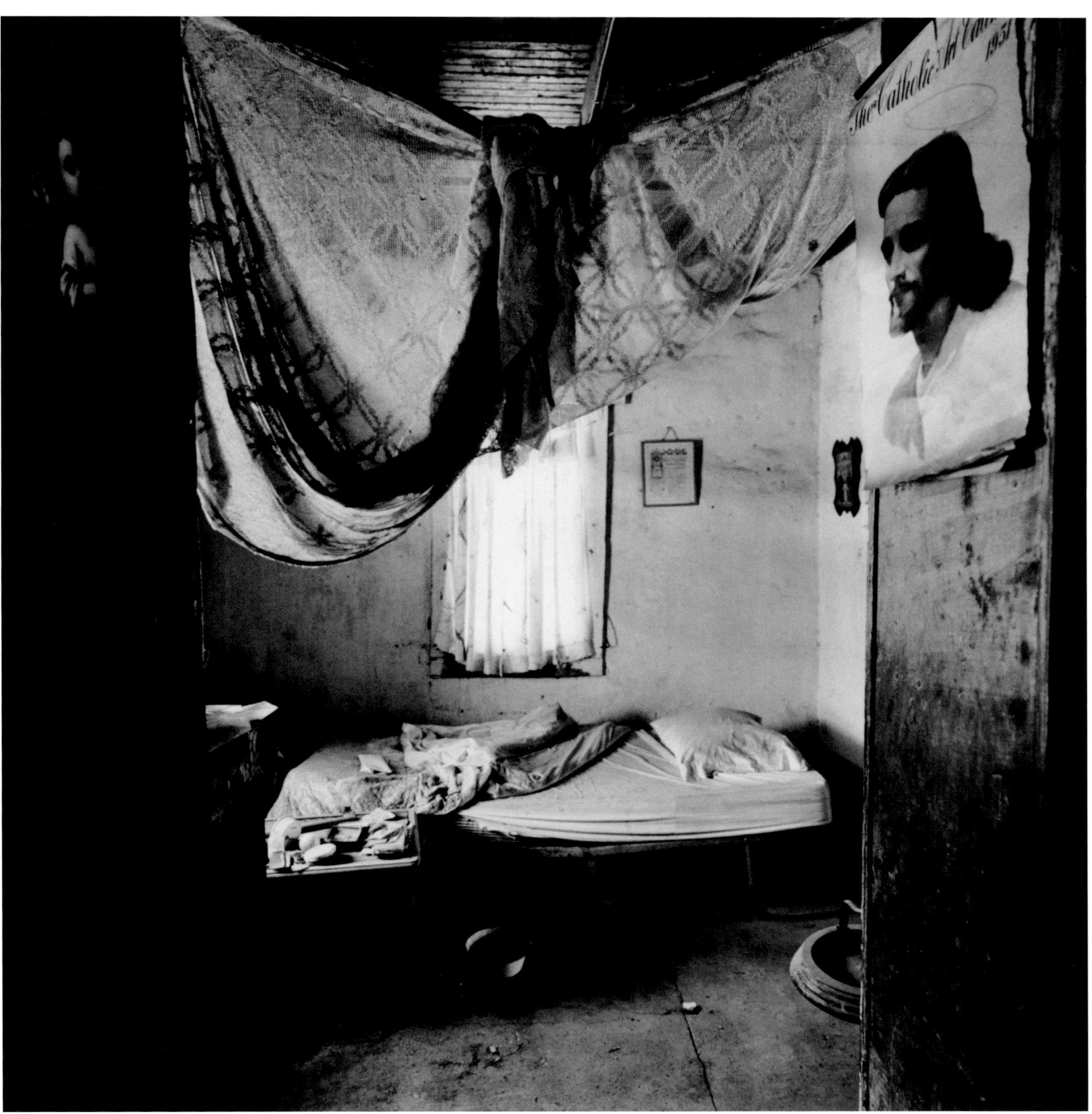

105   *Calendario,* 1977; from the series *Benitez Suite*

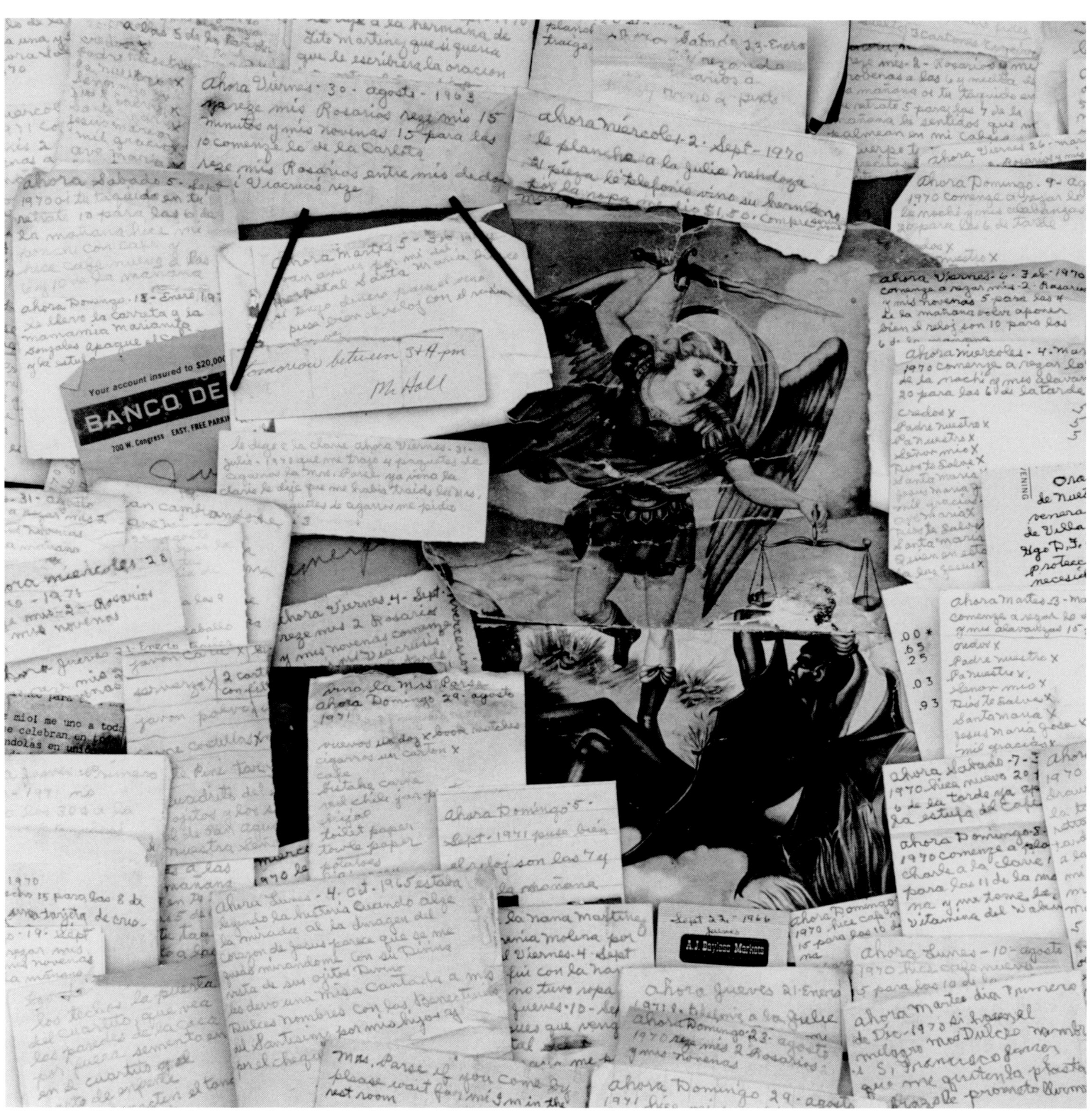

107   *Ahora*, 1977; from the series *Benitez Suite*

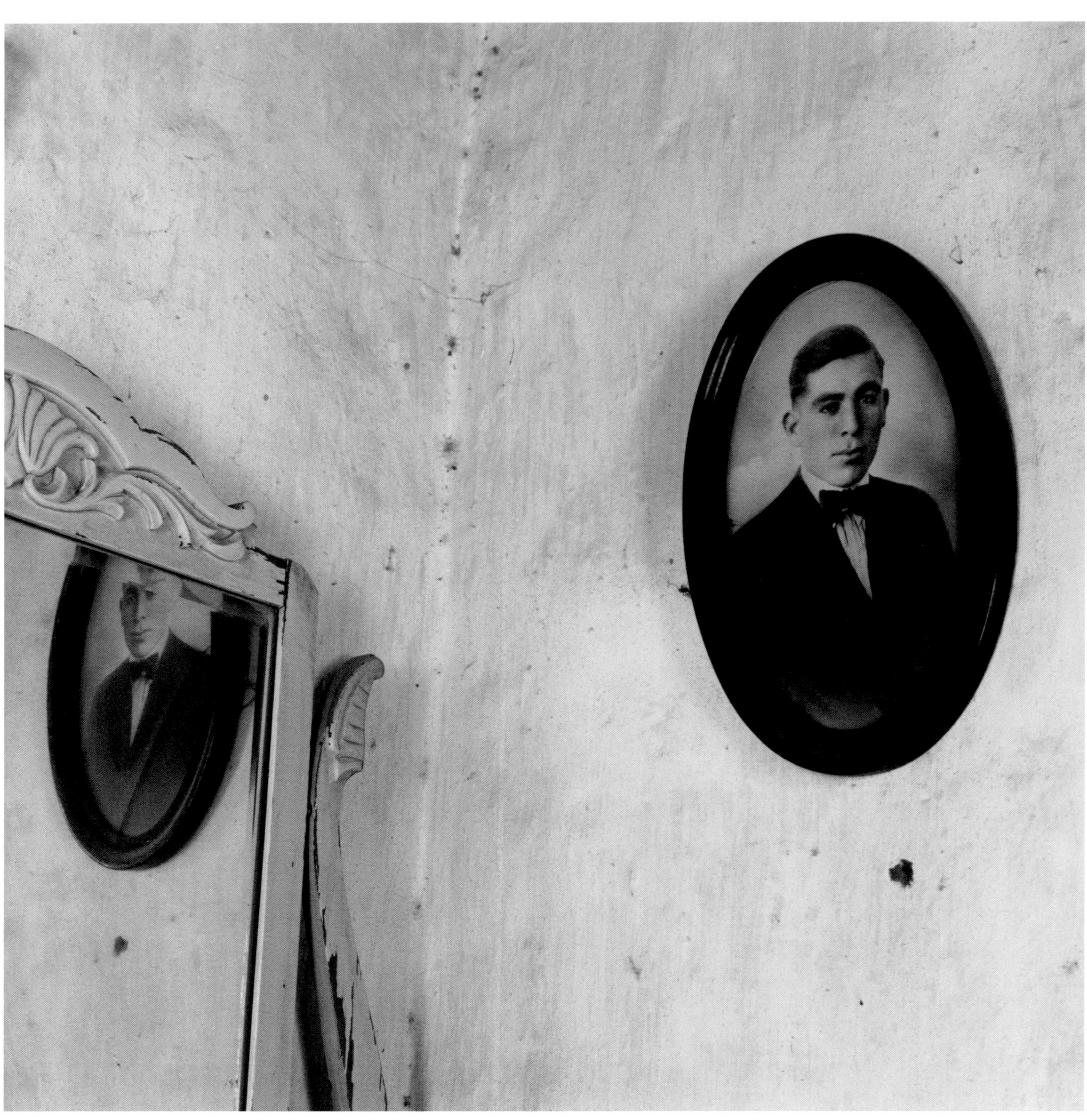

108   *Retrato,* 1977; from the series *Benitez Suite*

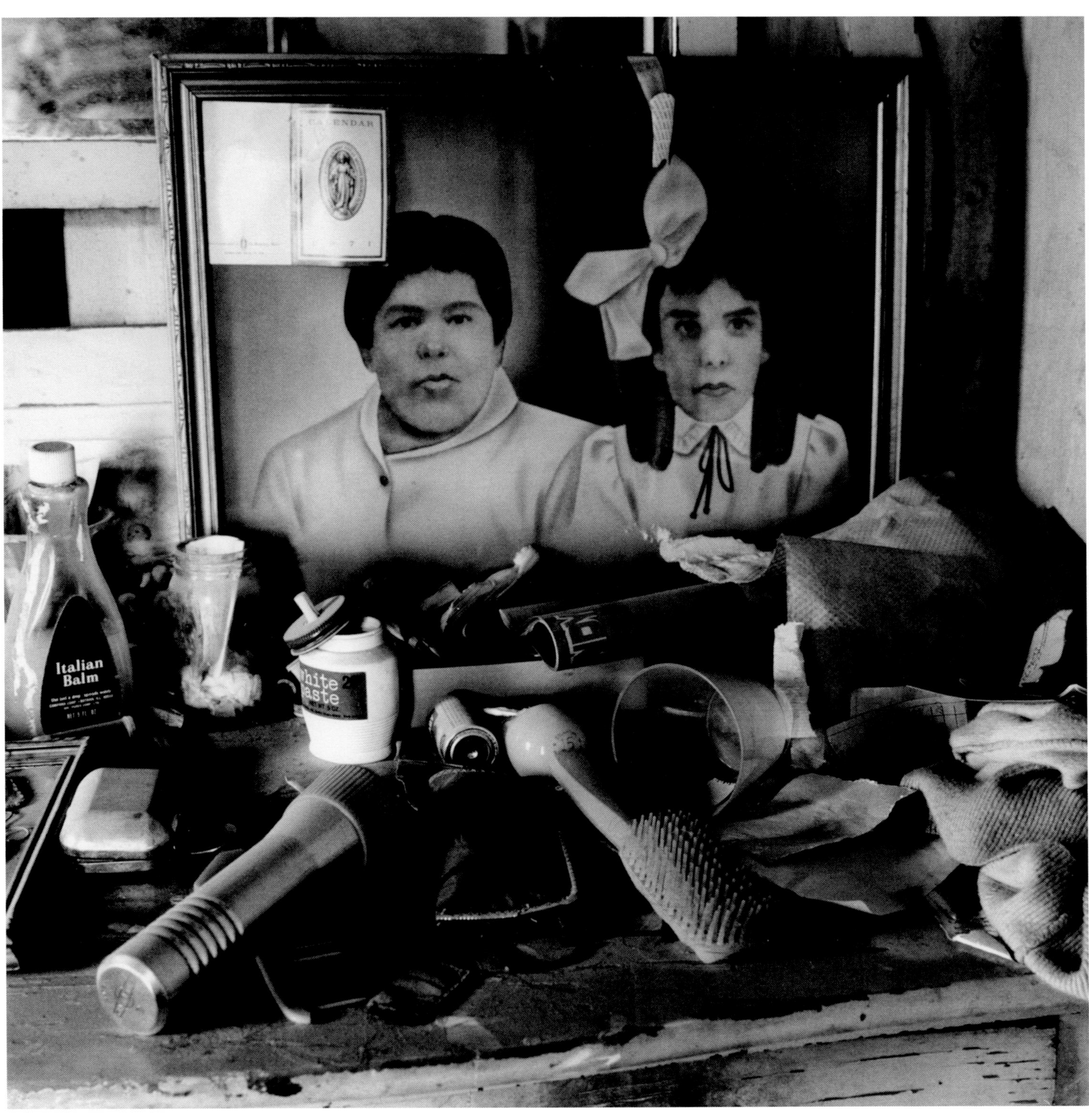

109   *Cómoda,* 1977; from the series *Benitez Suite*

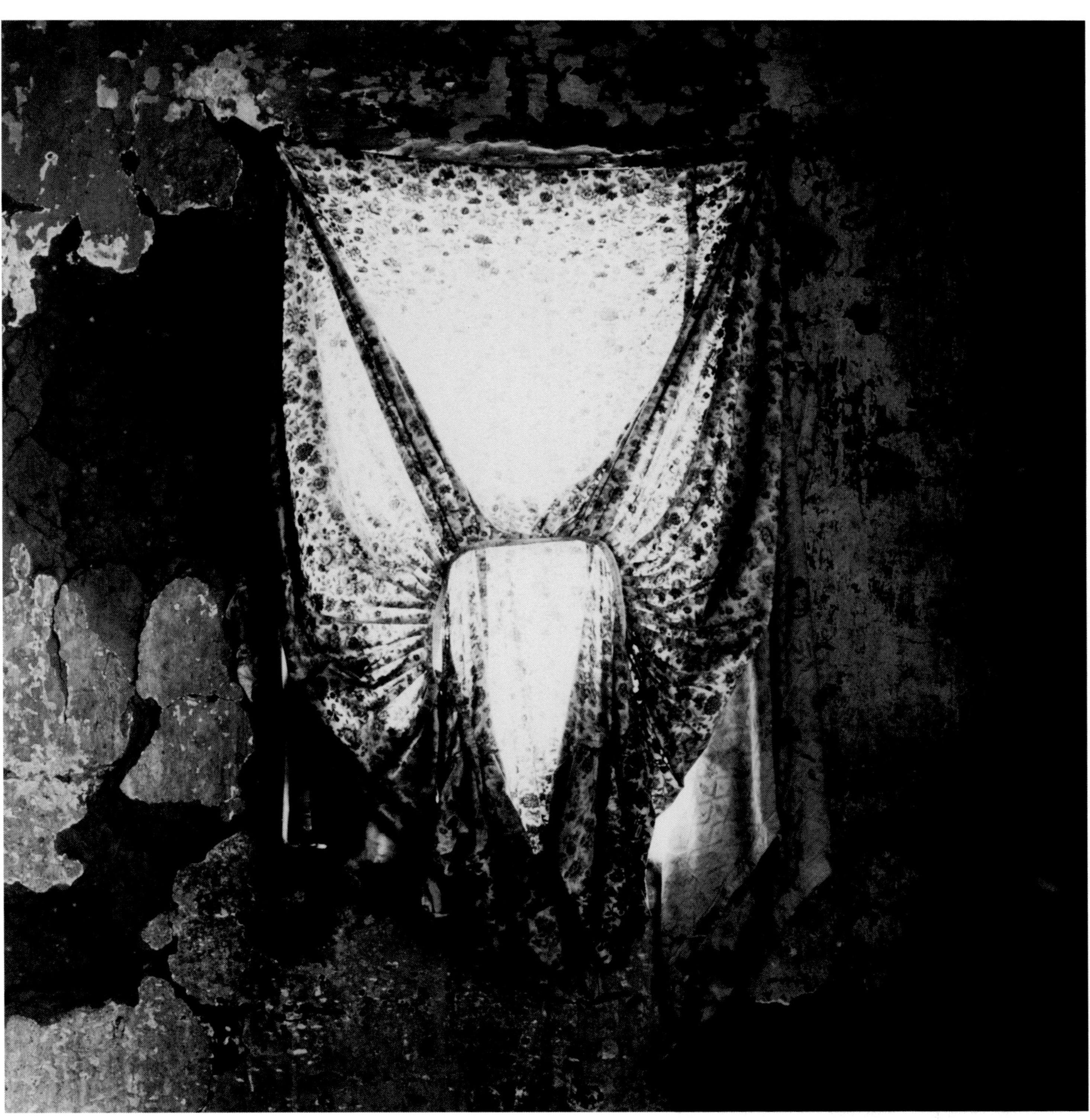

111   *Cortina de vestido*, 1977; from the series *Benitez Suite*

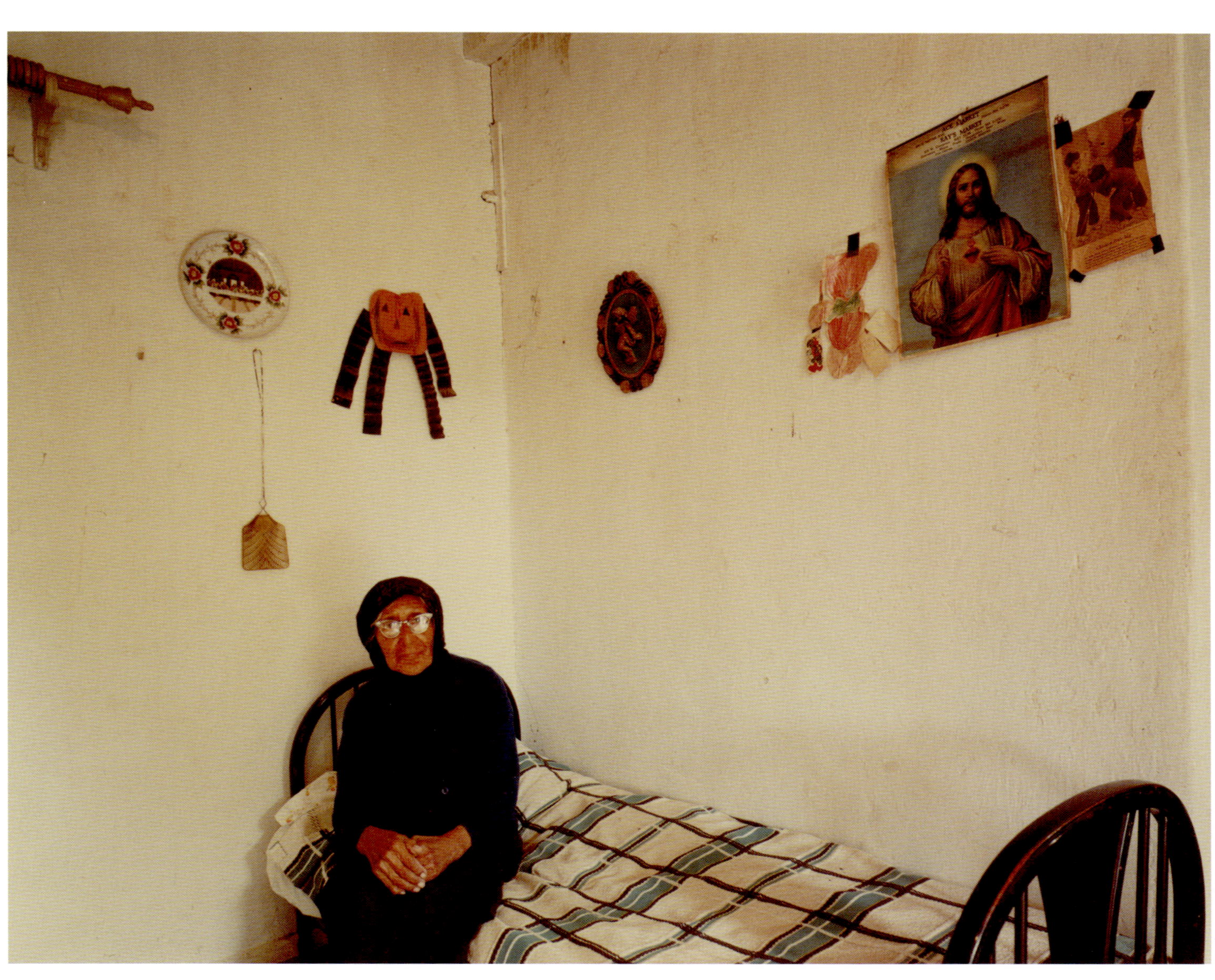

113   *Señora Espinosa, Membrillo, Tucson, Arizona*, 1978

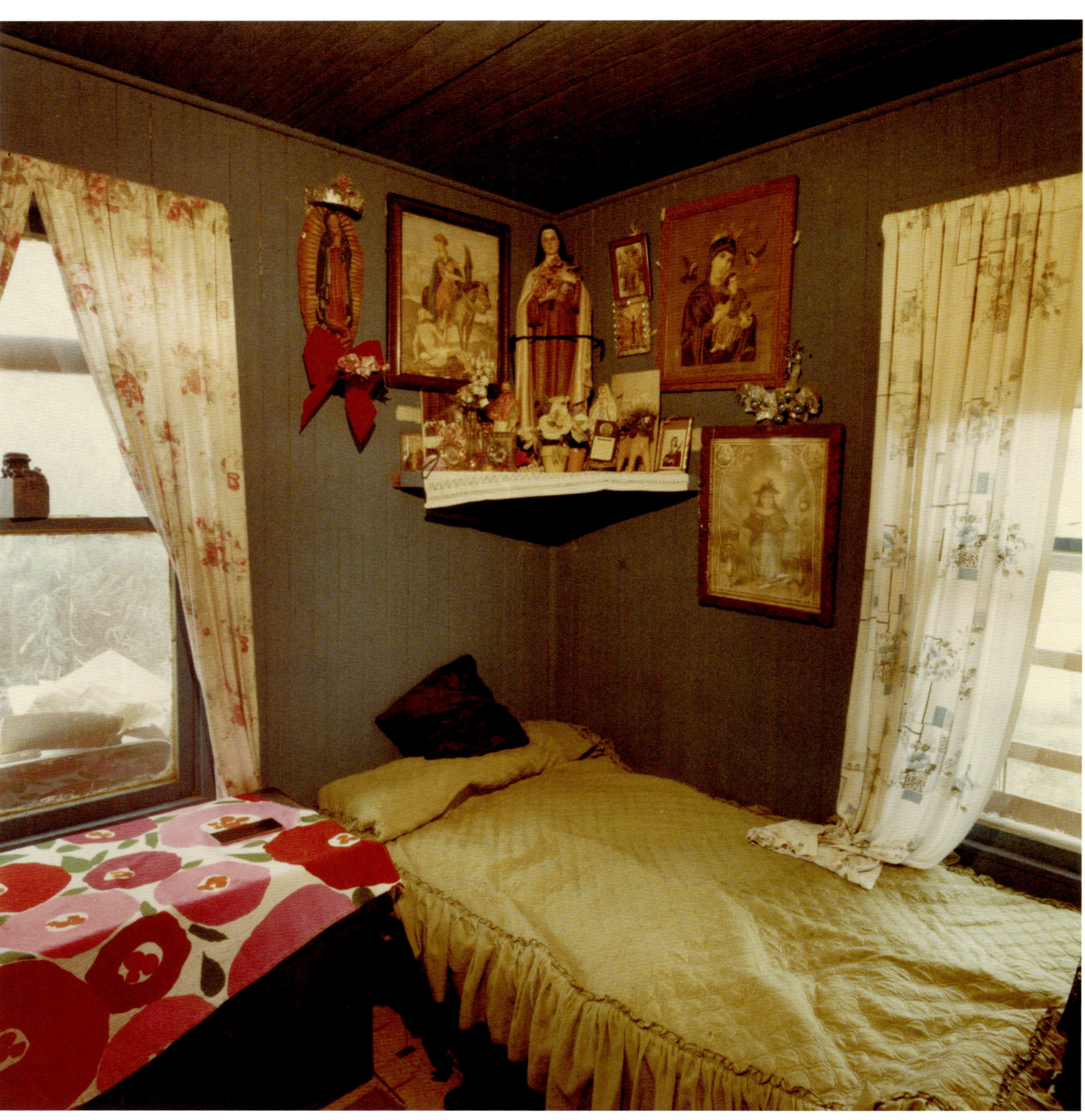

114   *Recámara de Catalina Olomos, Phoenix, Arizona, 1978*

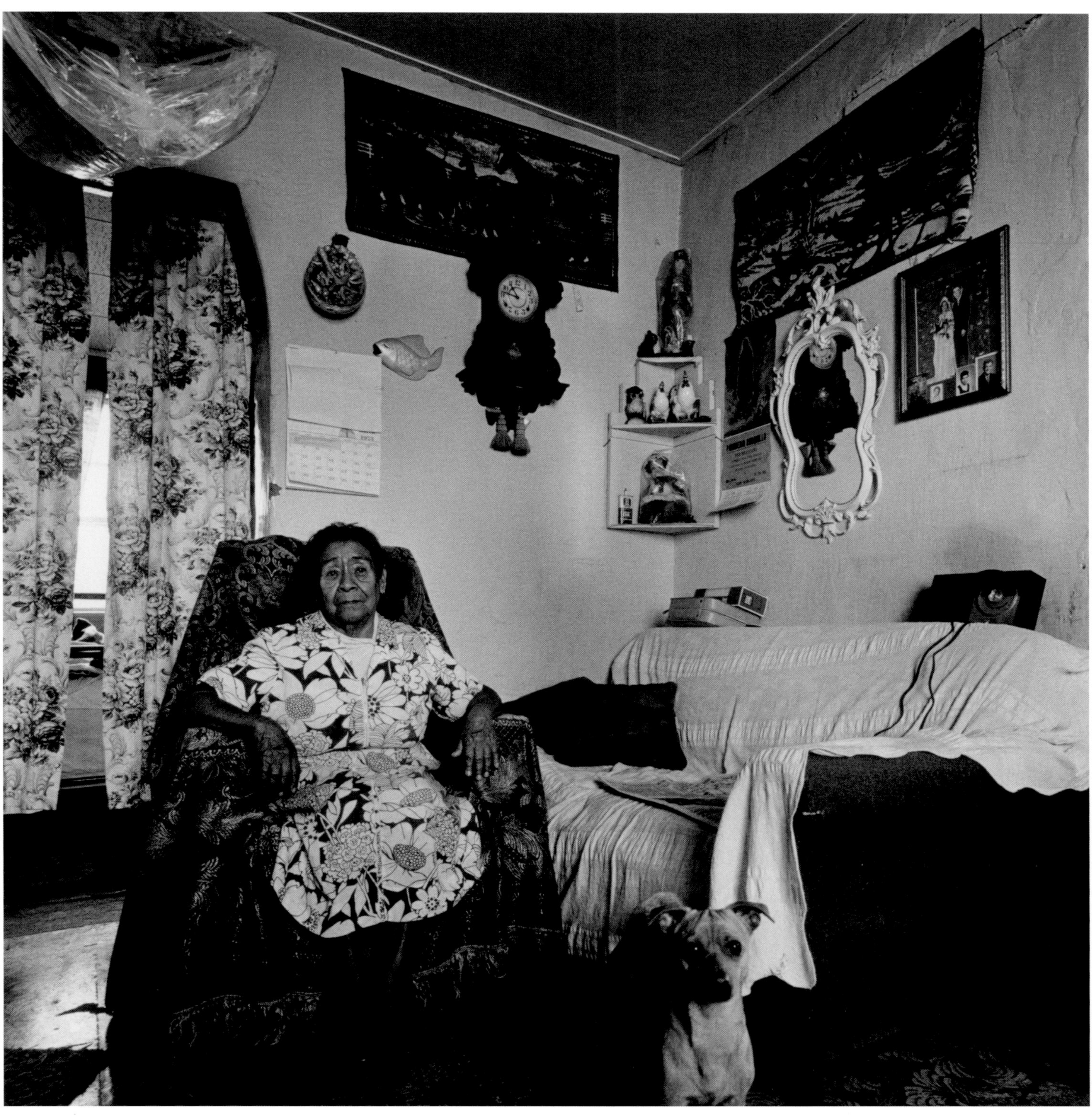

115   *Lucia Fresno,* 1973

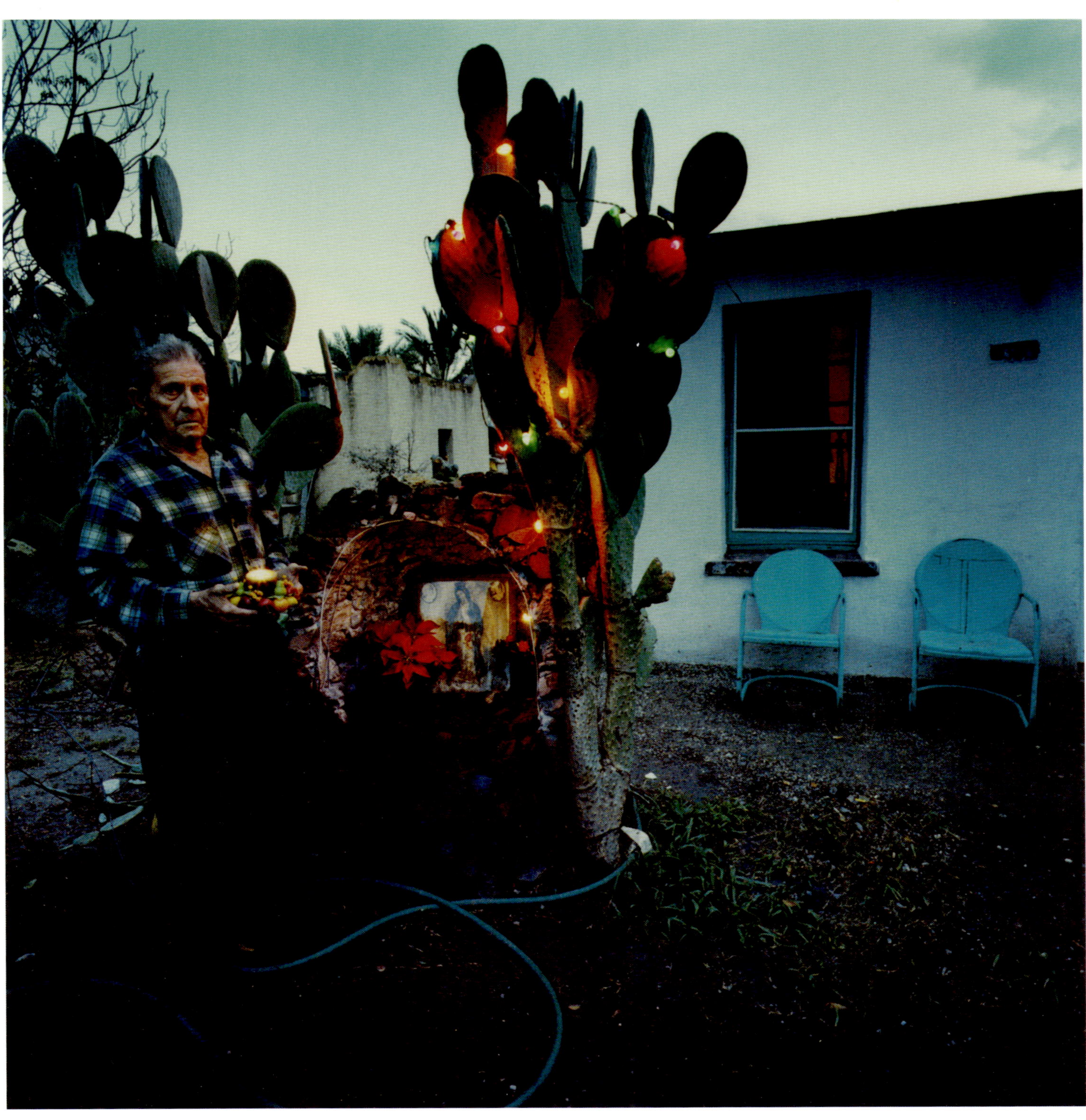

117   *Sr. Ernesto Villa, Barrio Hollywood,* 1977

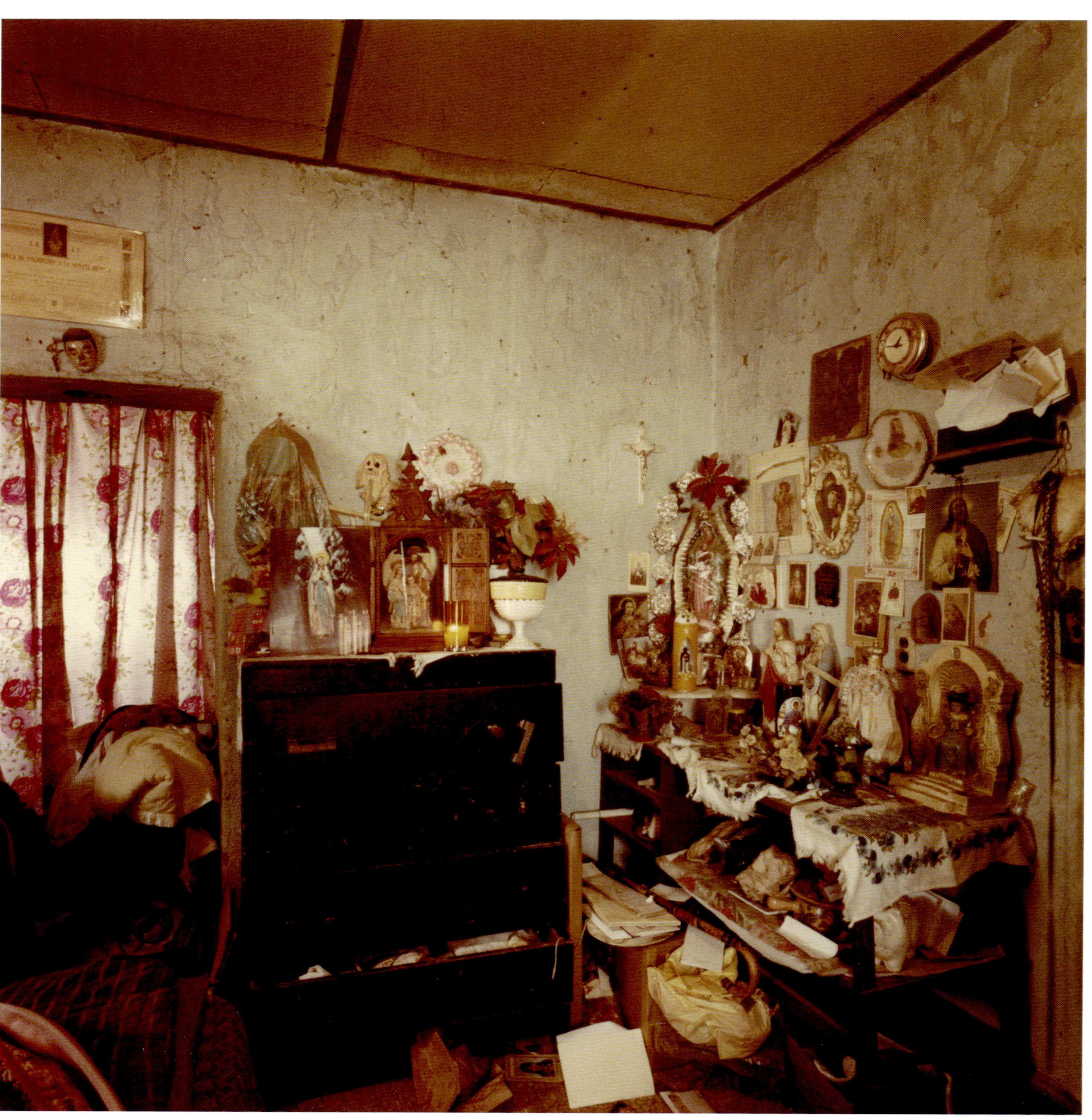

 Recámara de Blas y Pauline Flores, 1978

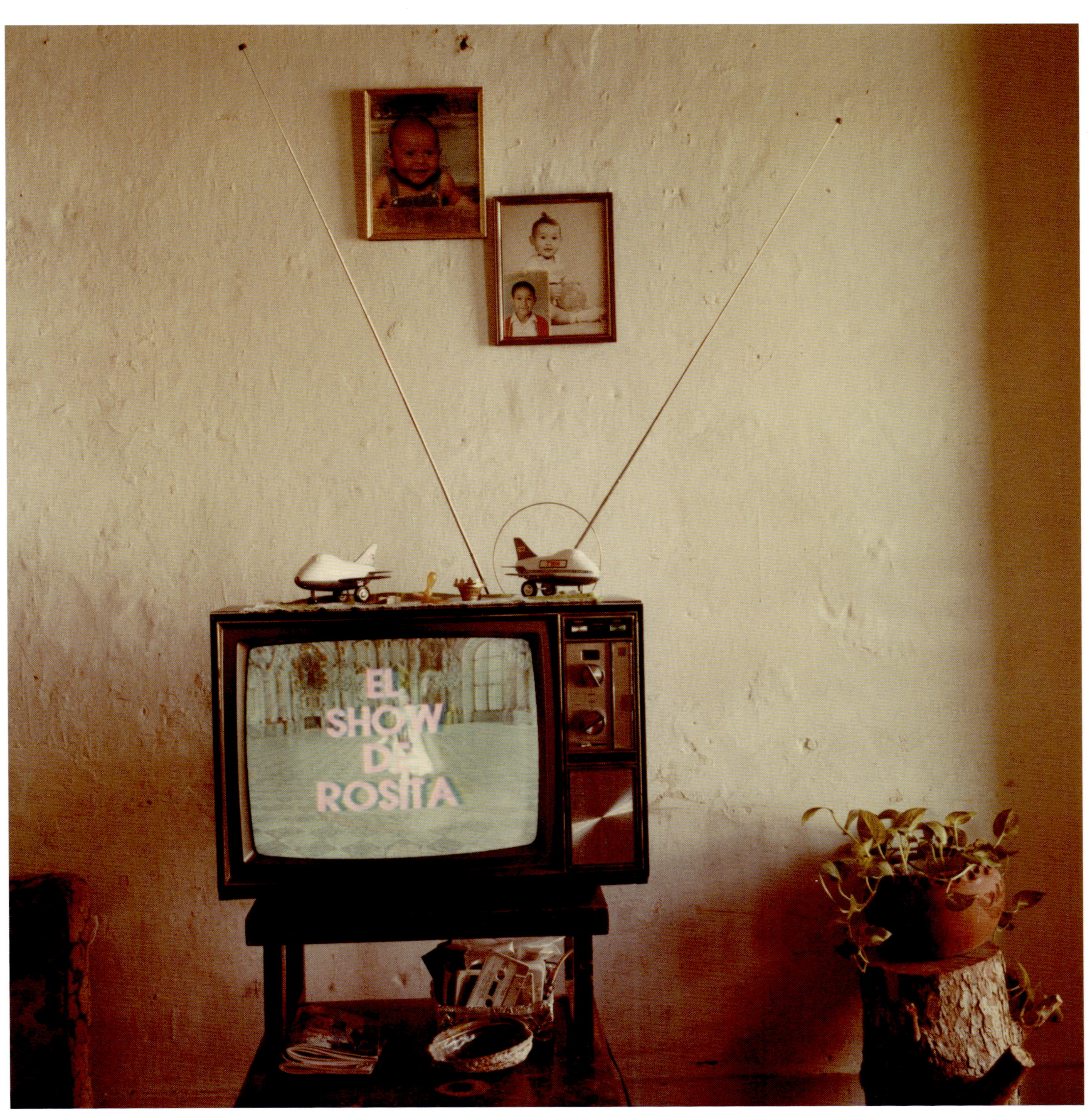

119   *El Show de Rosita, Barrio Anita*, 1978

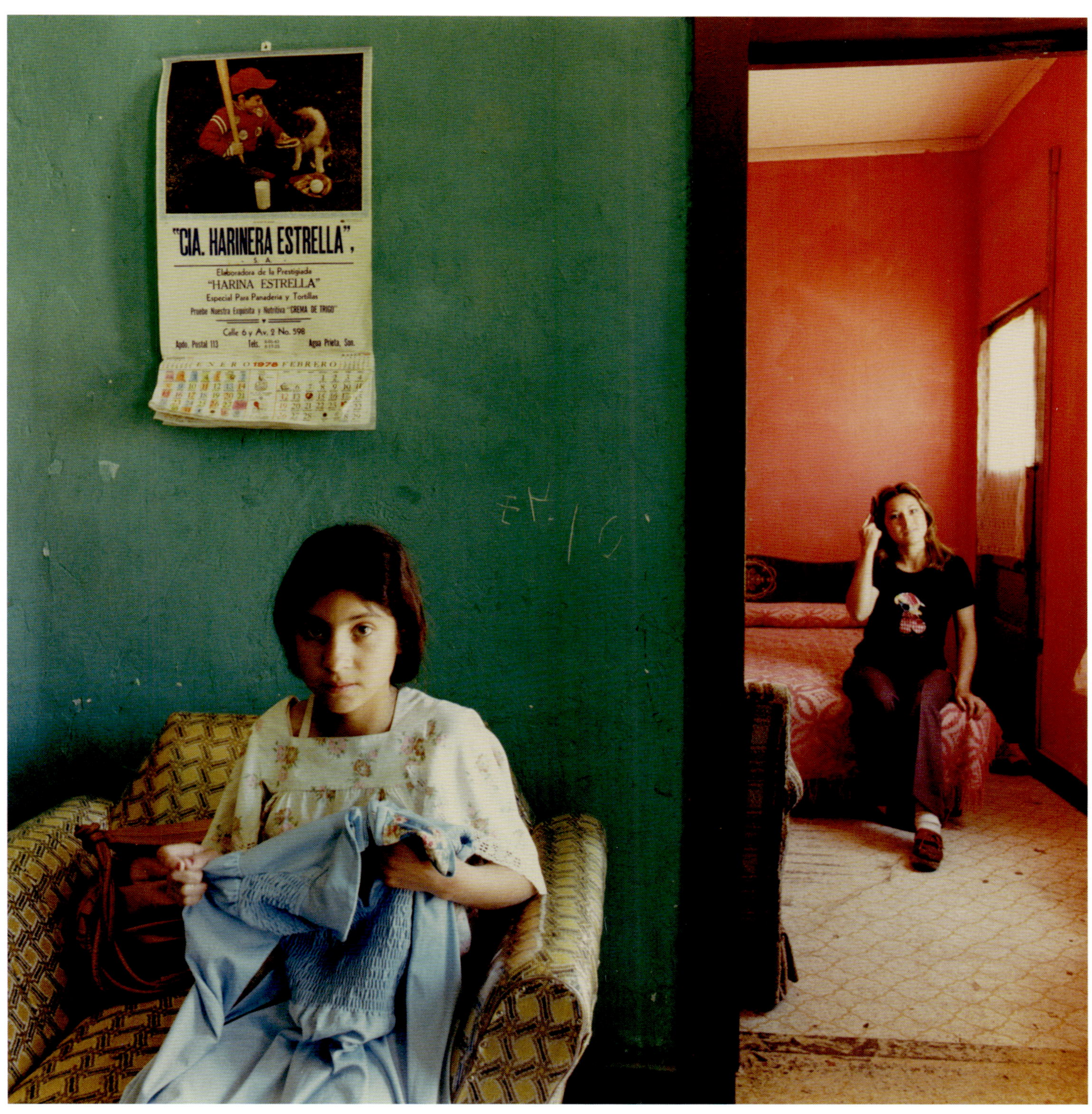

   Dos Mujeres, Douglas, Arizona, 1978

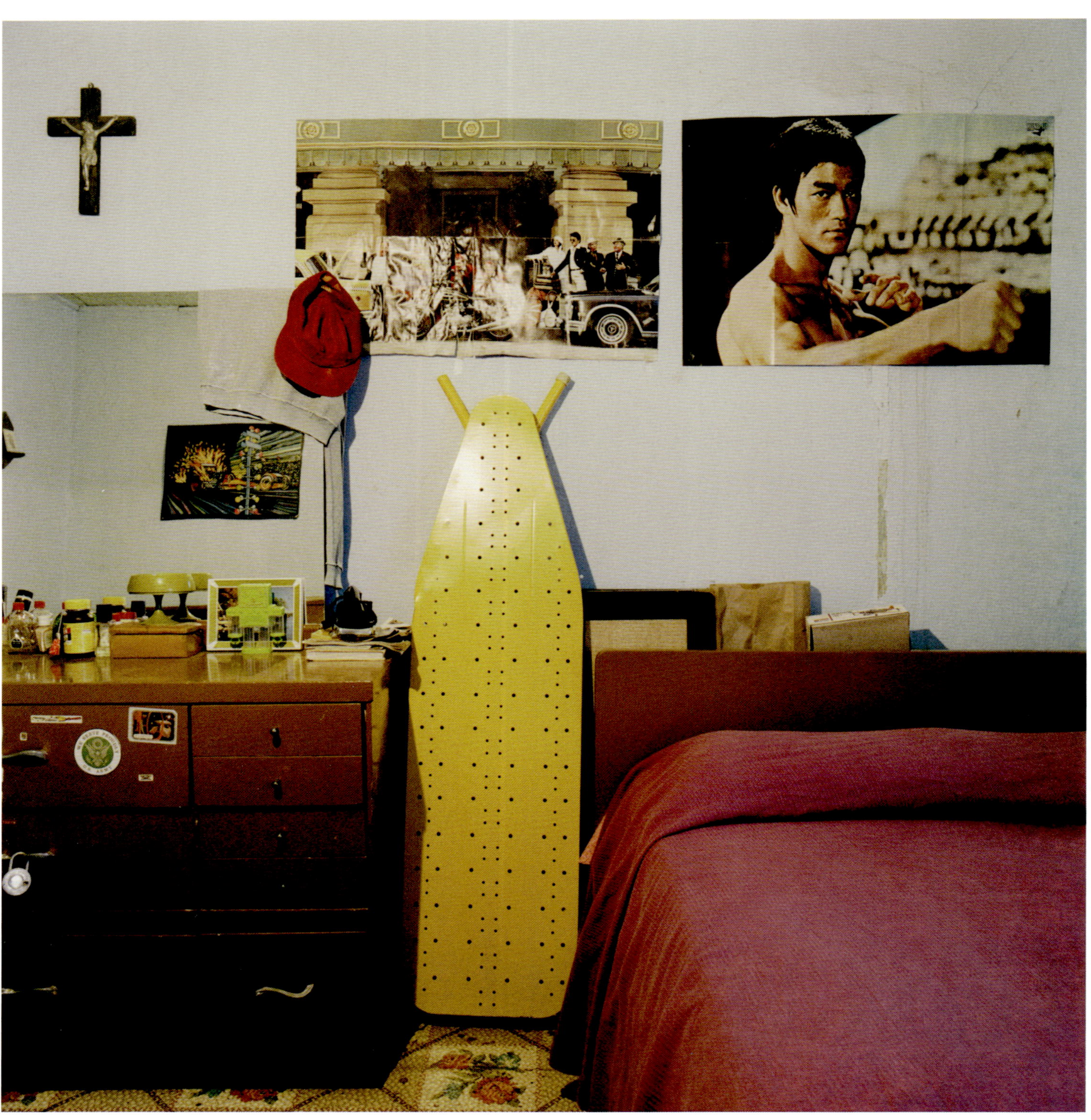

   Untitled, 1978

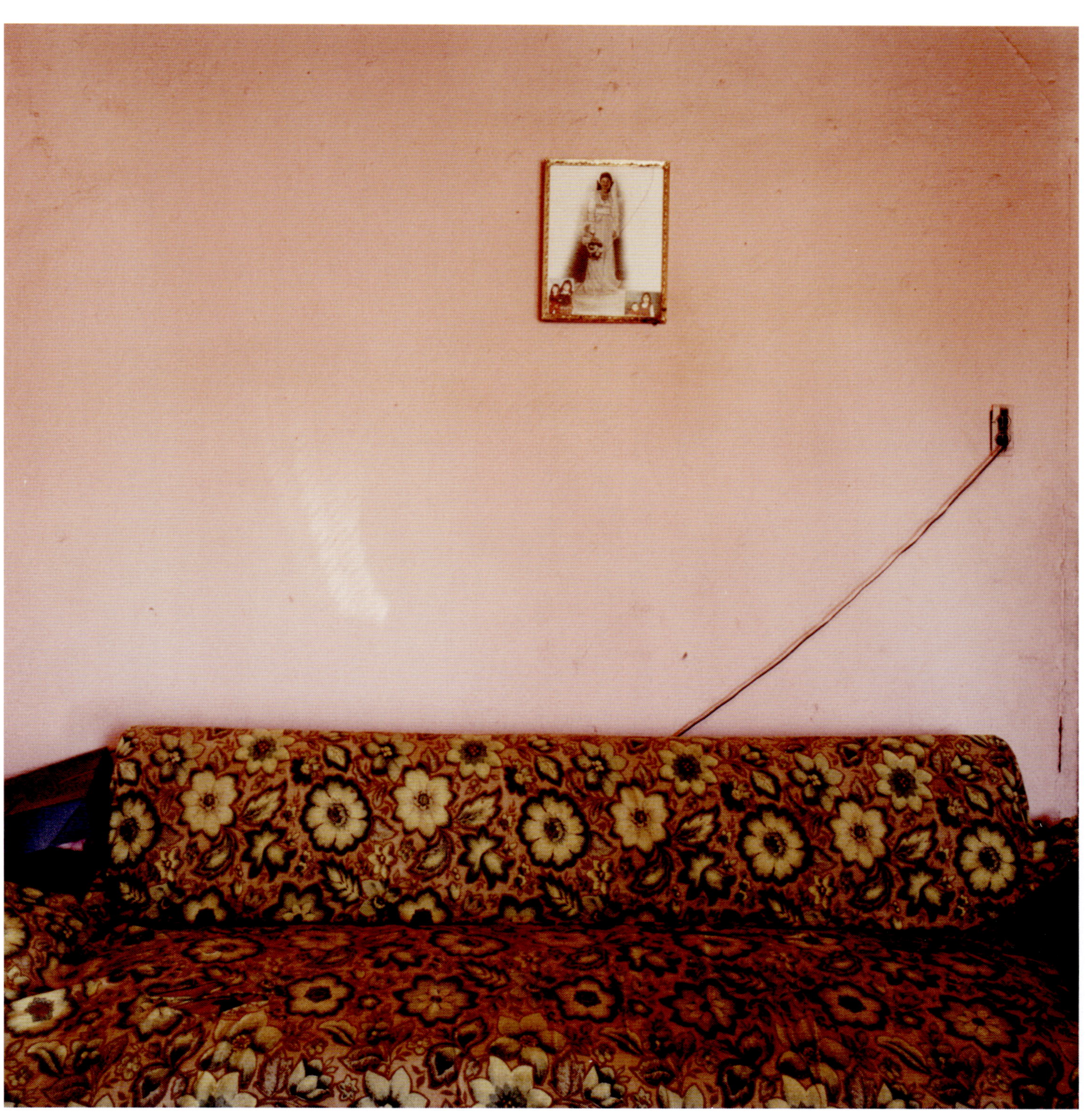

123   *Retrato de Boda Rosa*, 1978

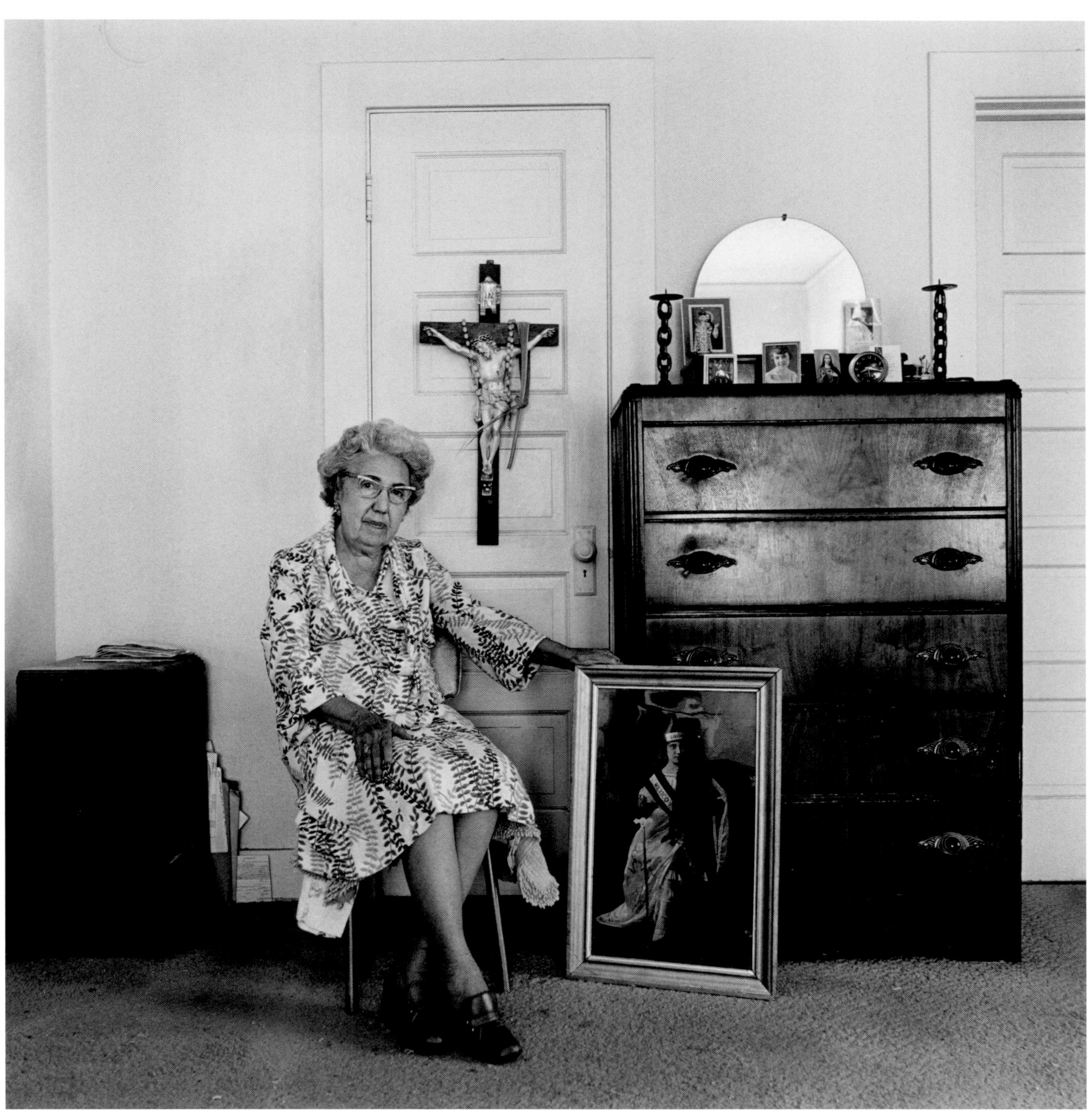

125   *María Soto Audelo, Tucson*, 1979

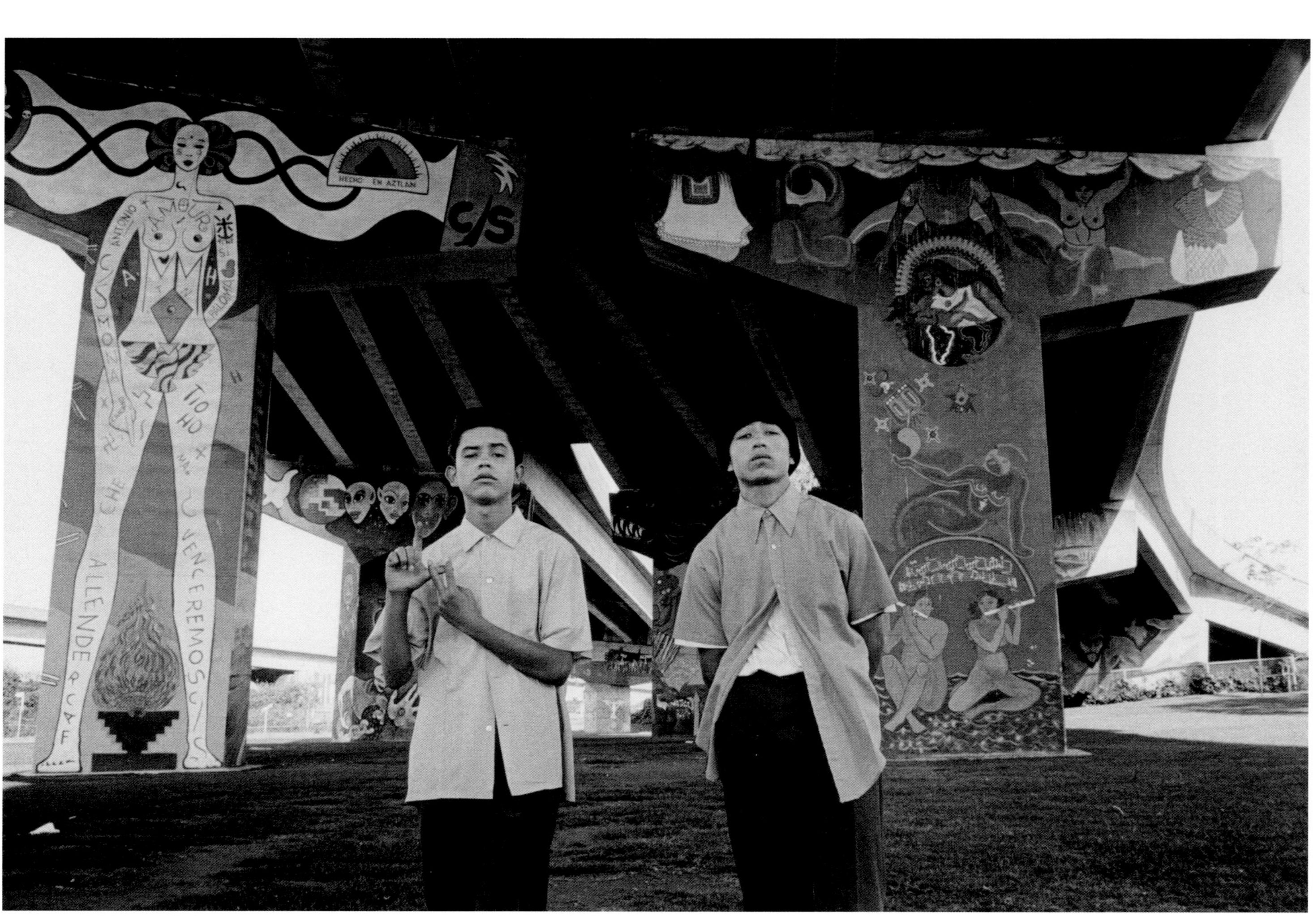

126   *Cholos, Logan Heights, San Diego,* 1980

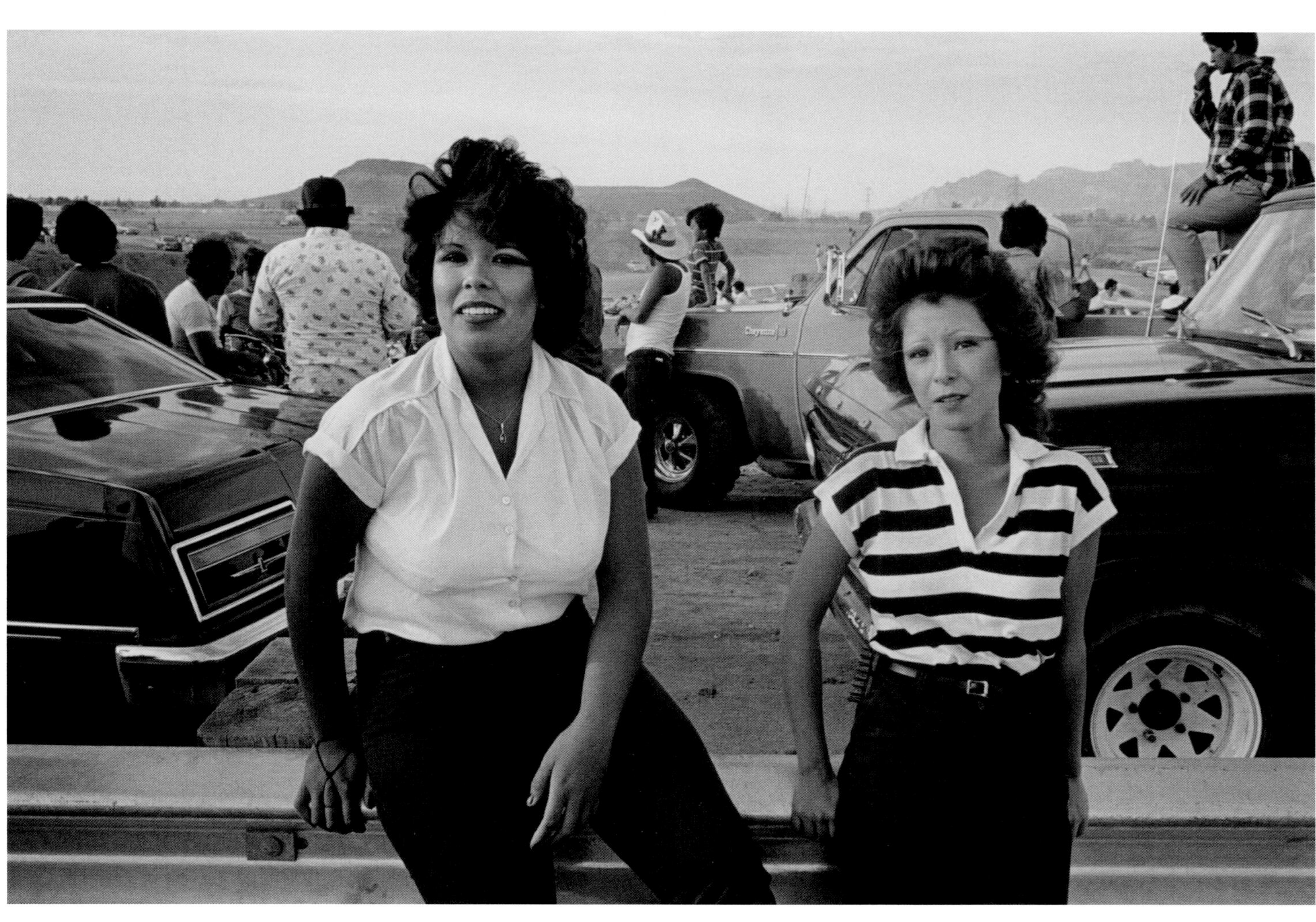

127   *Dos Cholas, Tucson, Arizona,* 1982

BREWED WITH PURE ROCKY MOUNTAIN SPRING WATER
Coors
BUDWEISER
COLD TO GO
BAR PRICES
BEER   .55
QUARTS BEER   .90
DRAFT BEER
  S. PITCHER .85
  L. PITCHER LGS
  GLASS   .35
WINE COOLER   .60
SOFT DRINKS
SIX PAC TO GO
SHRIMP 15
La Raza
La Raza

   La Raza, 1977

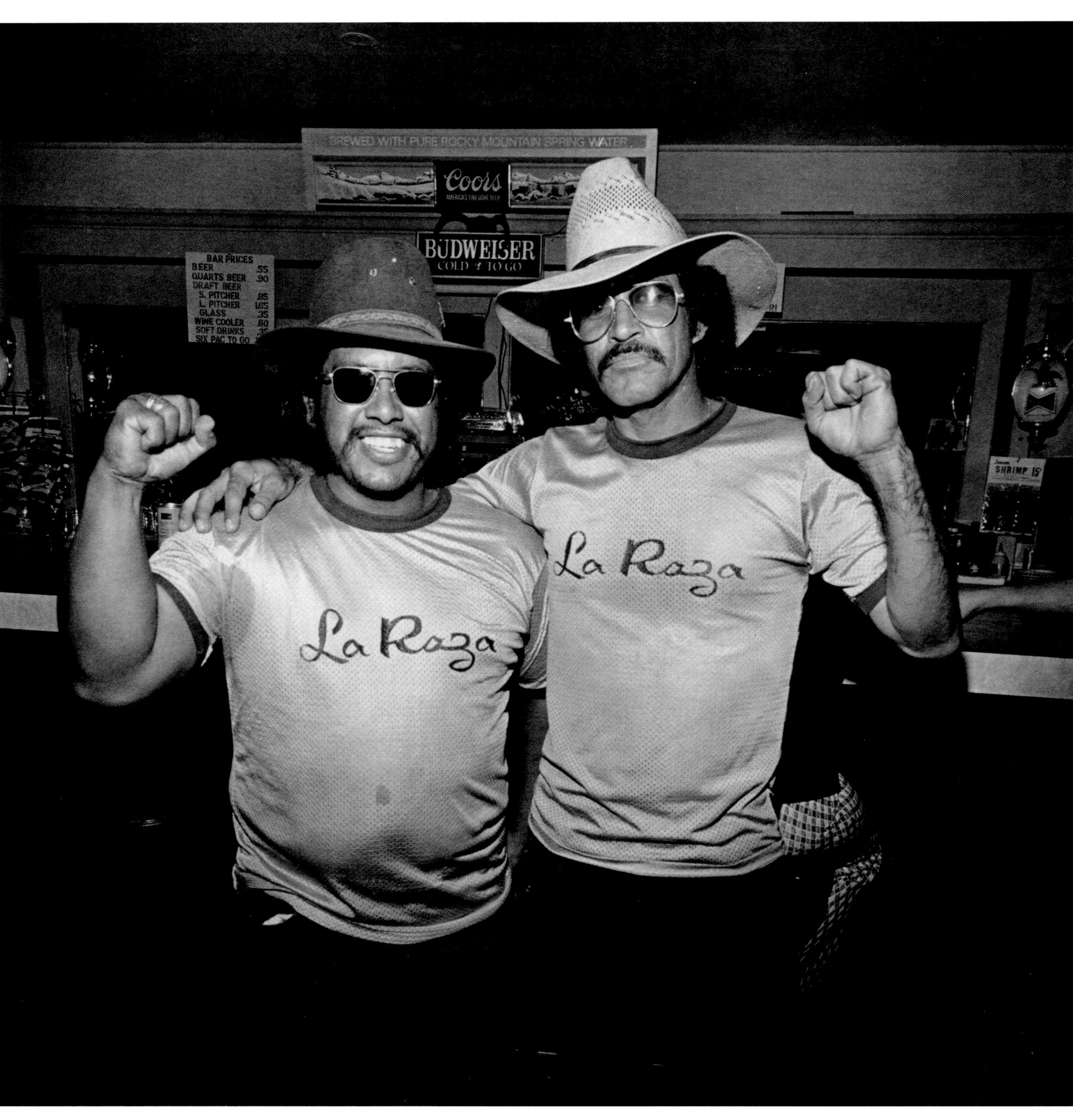

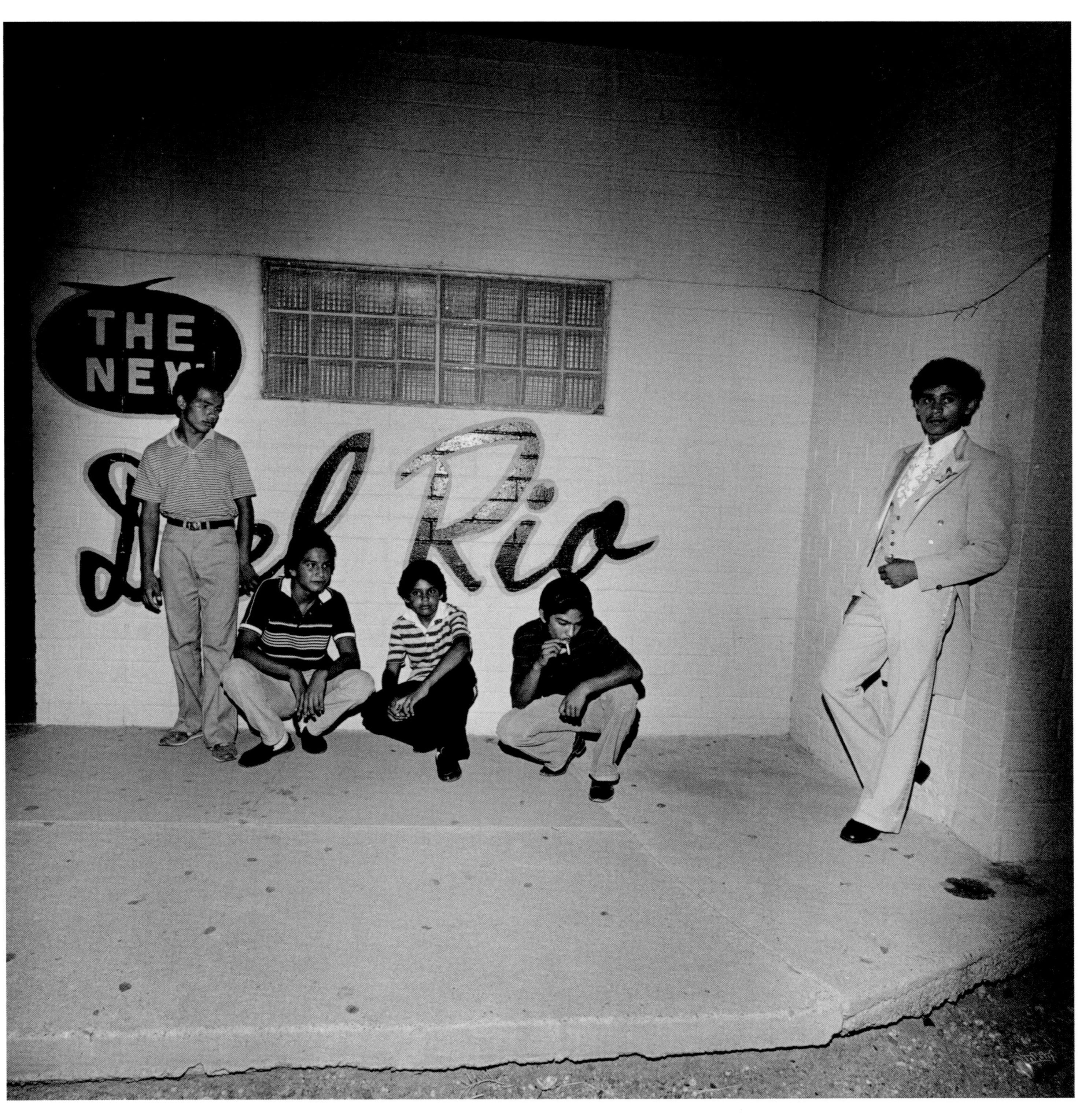

129   *Los Vatos, Del Rio Ballroom*, 1982

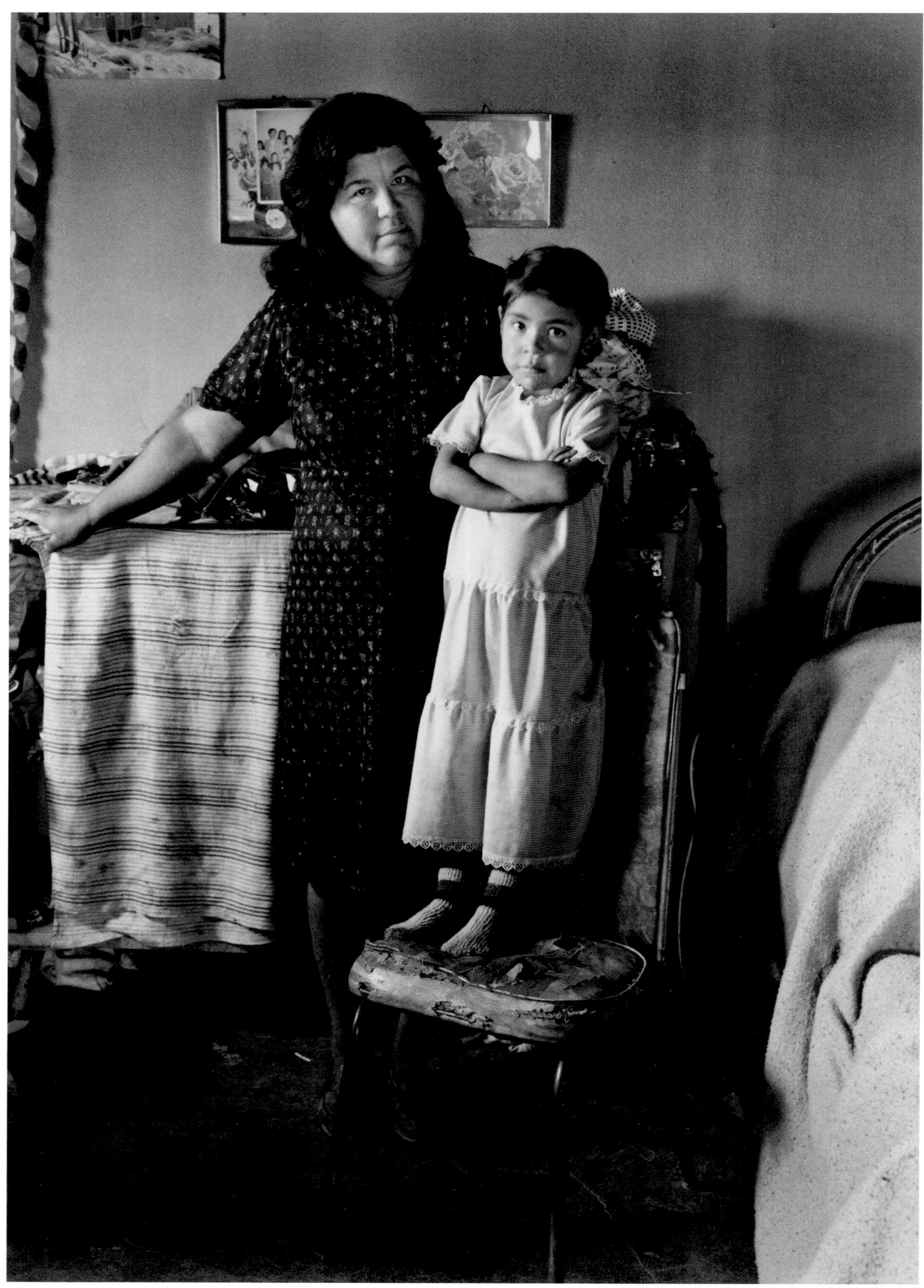

130   *Naco Portrait,* 1979

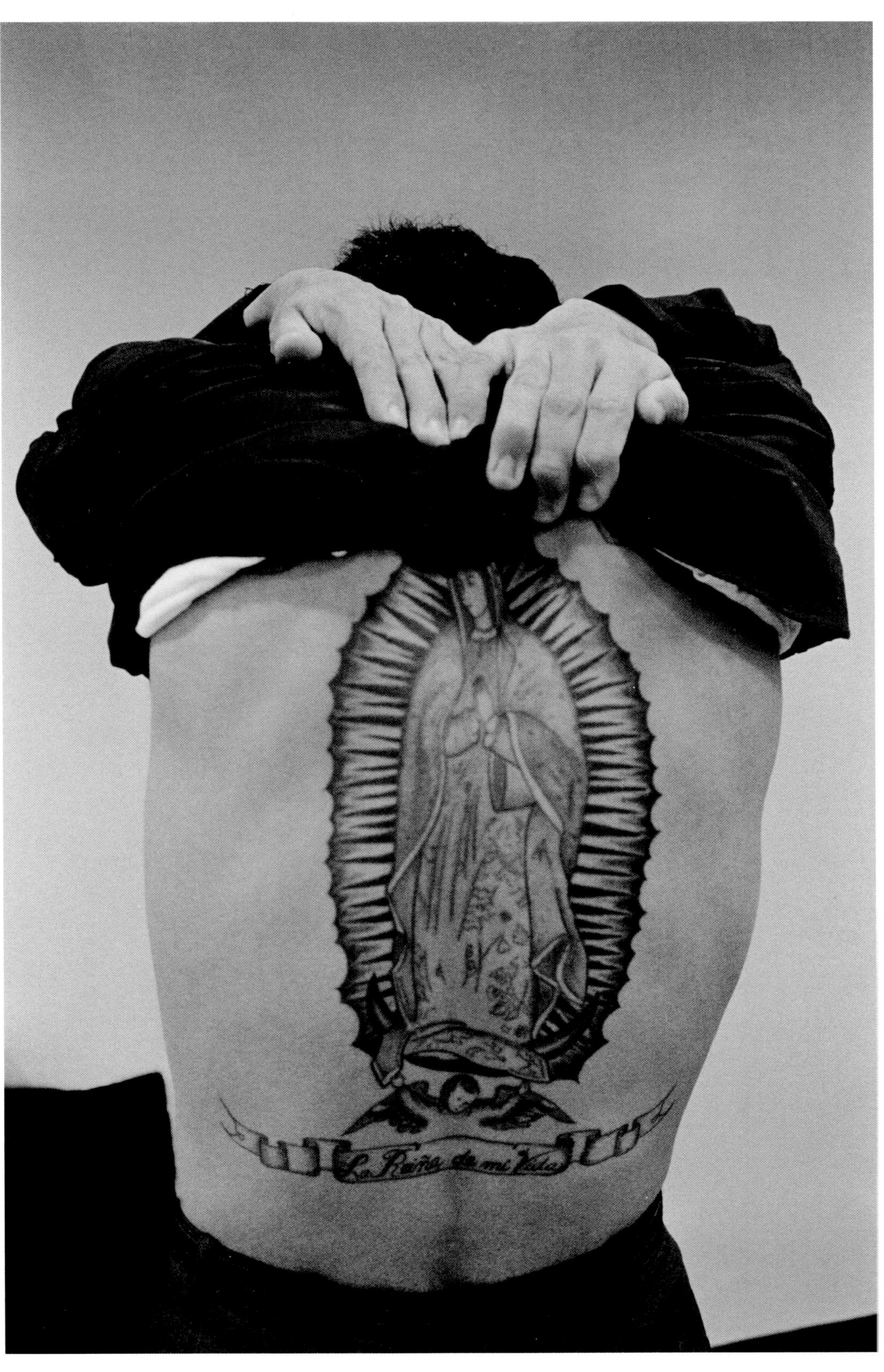

131   *La Reina de Mi Vida*, 1983

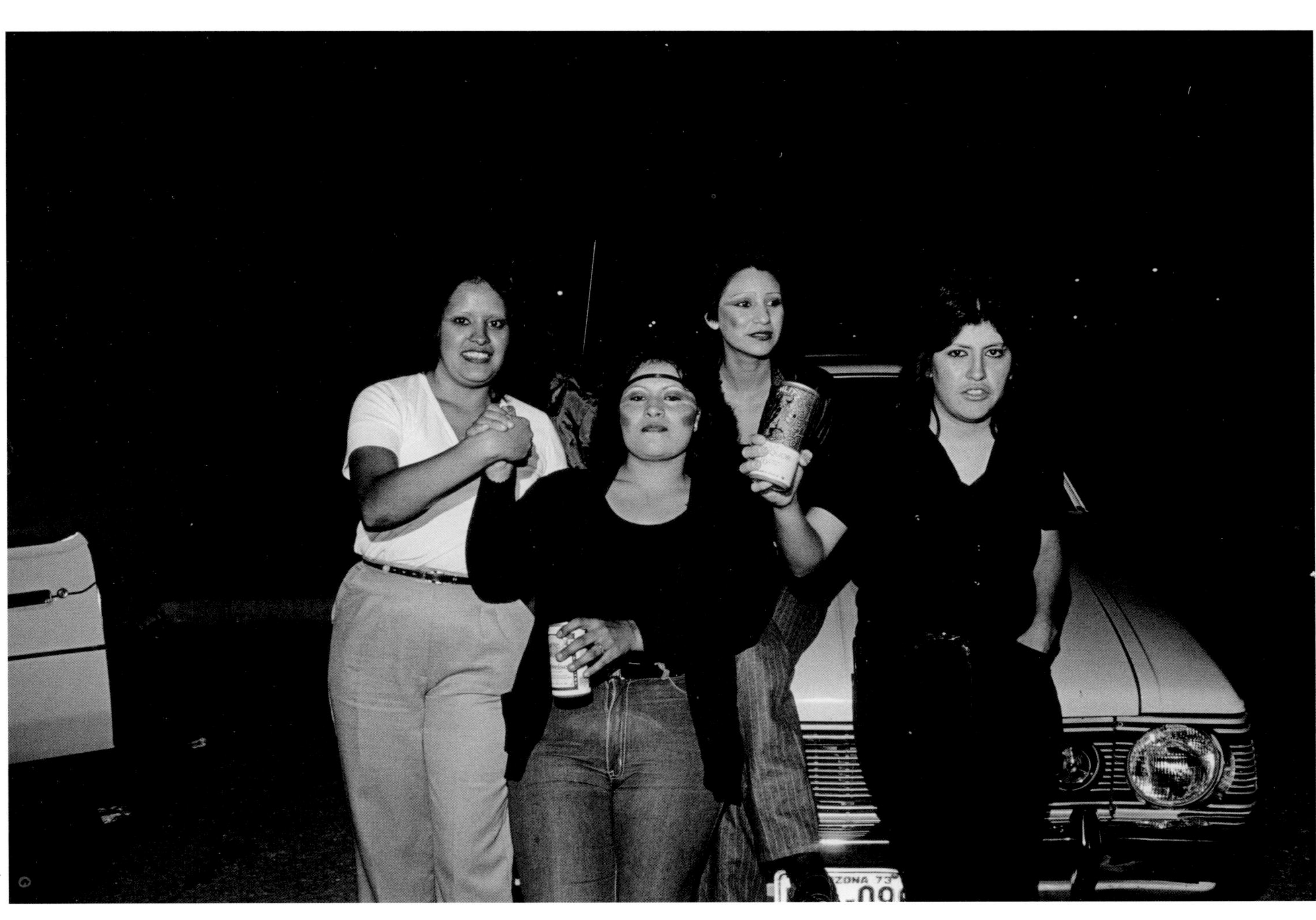

133   *Cruisin' Cholas, Tucson, Arizona*, 1984

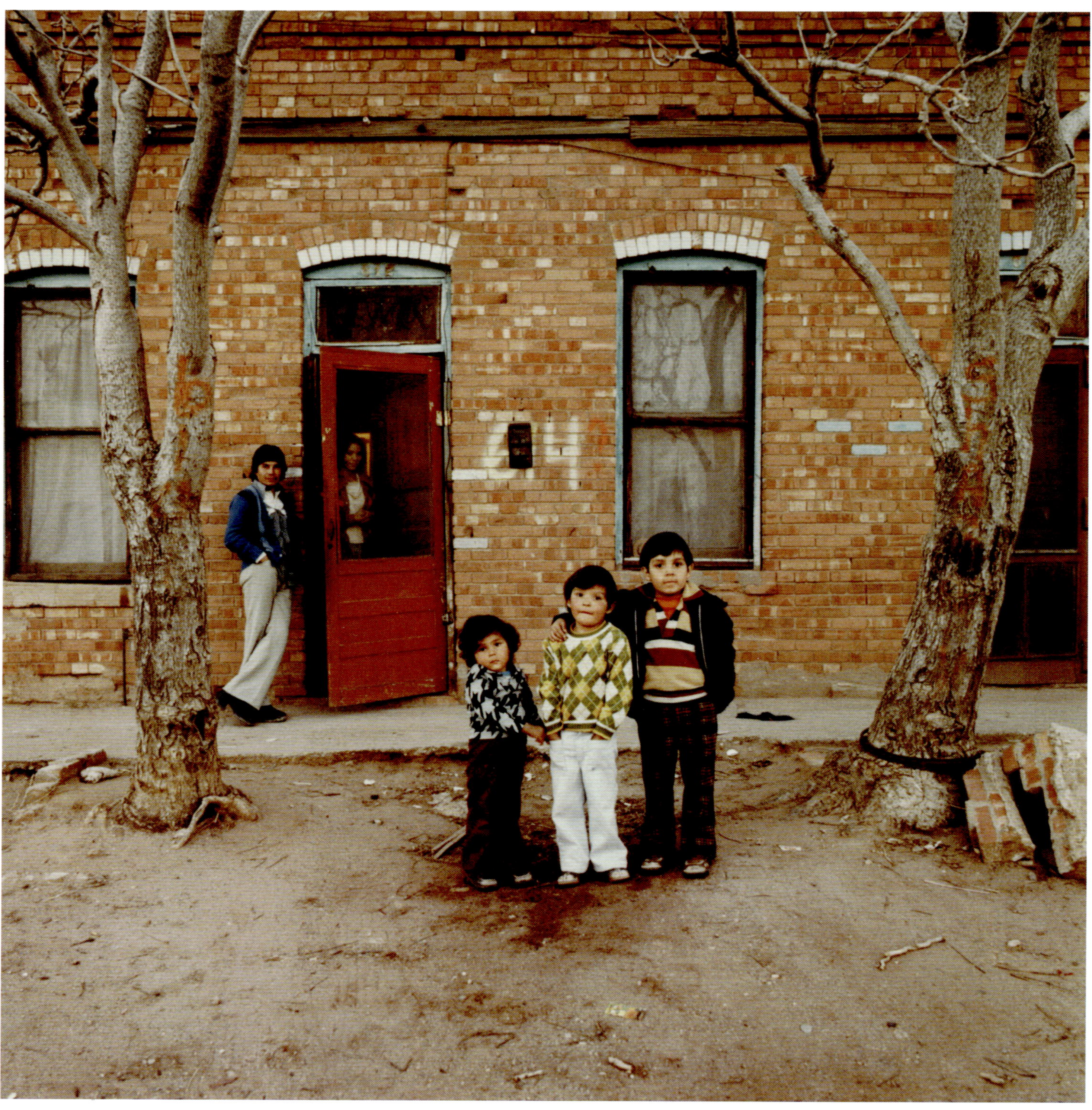

134 *Barrio Portrait, H Avenue Cuadra, Douglas, Arizona*, 1978

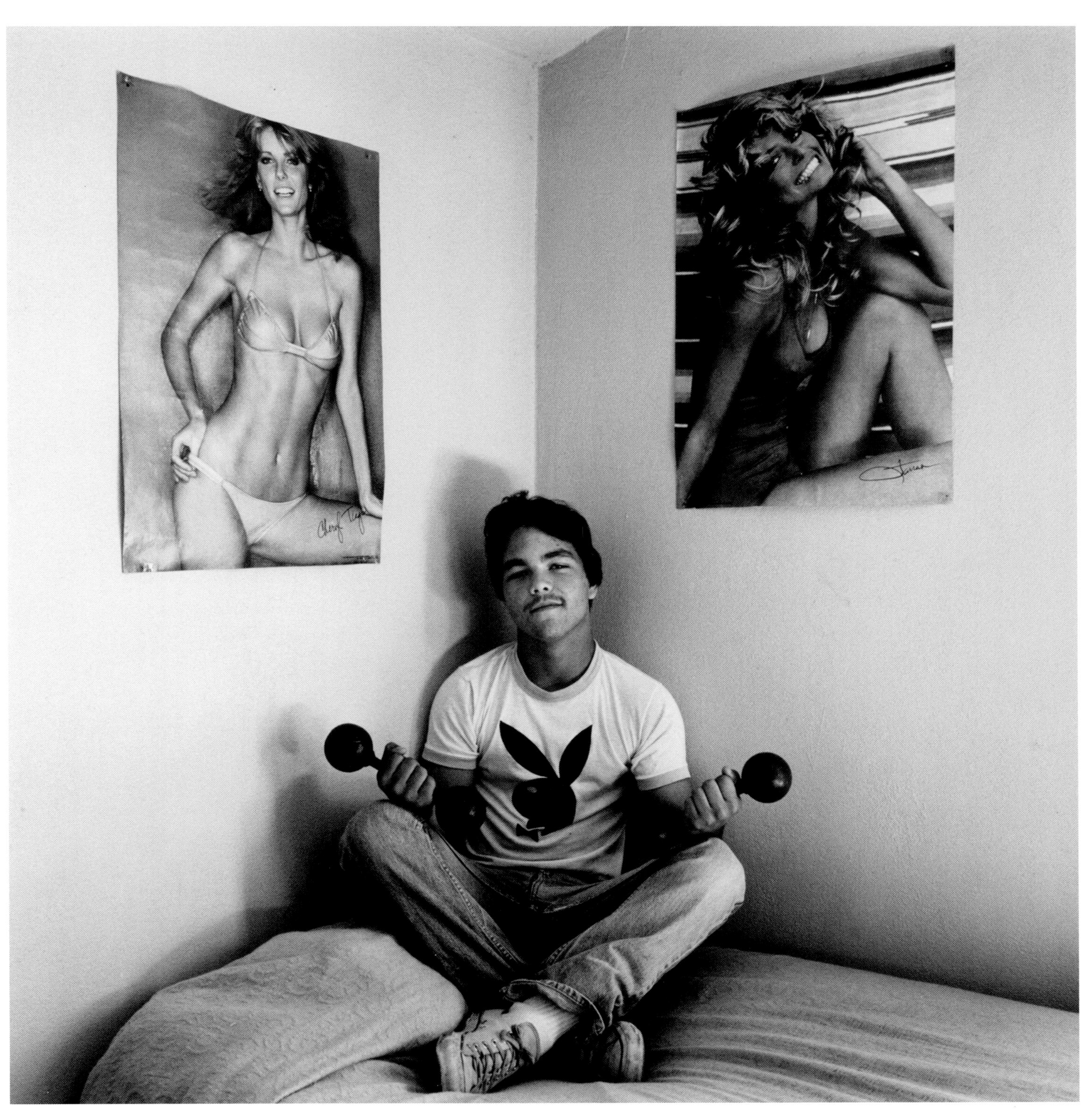

135   *Stephen Quiñonez, Douglas, Arizona,* 1979

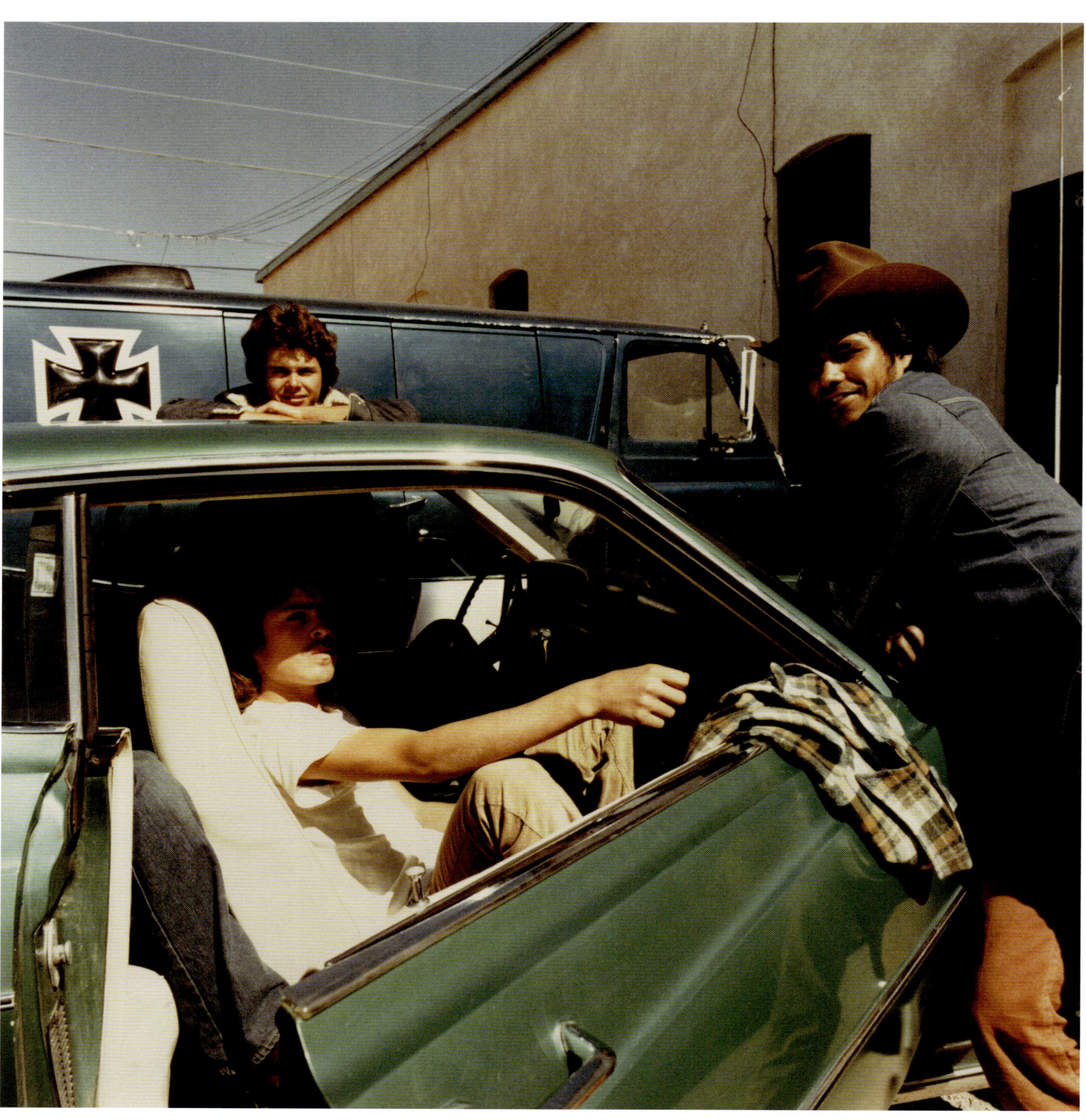

136   *Los Vatos Locos, Douglas, Arizona,* 1978

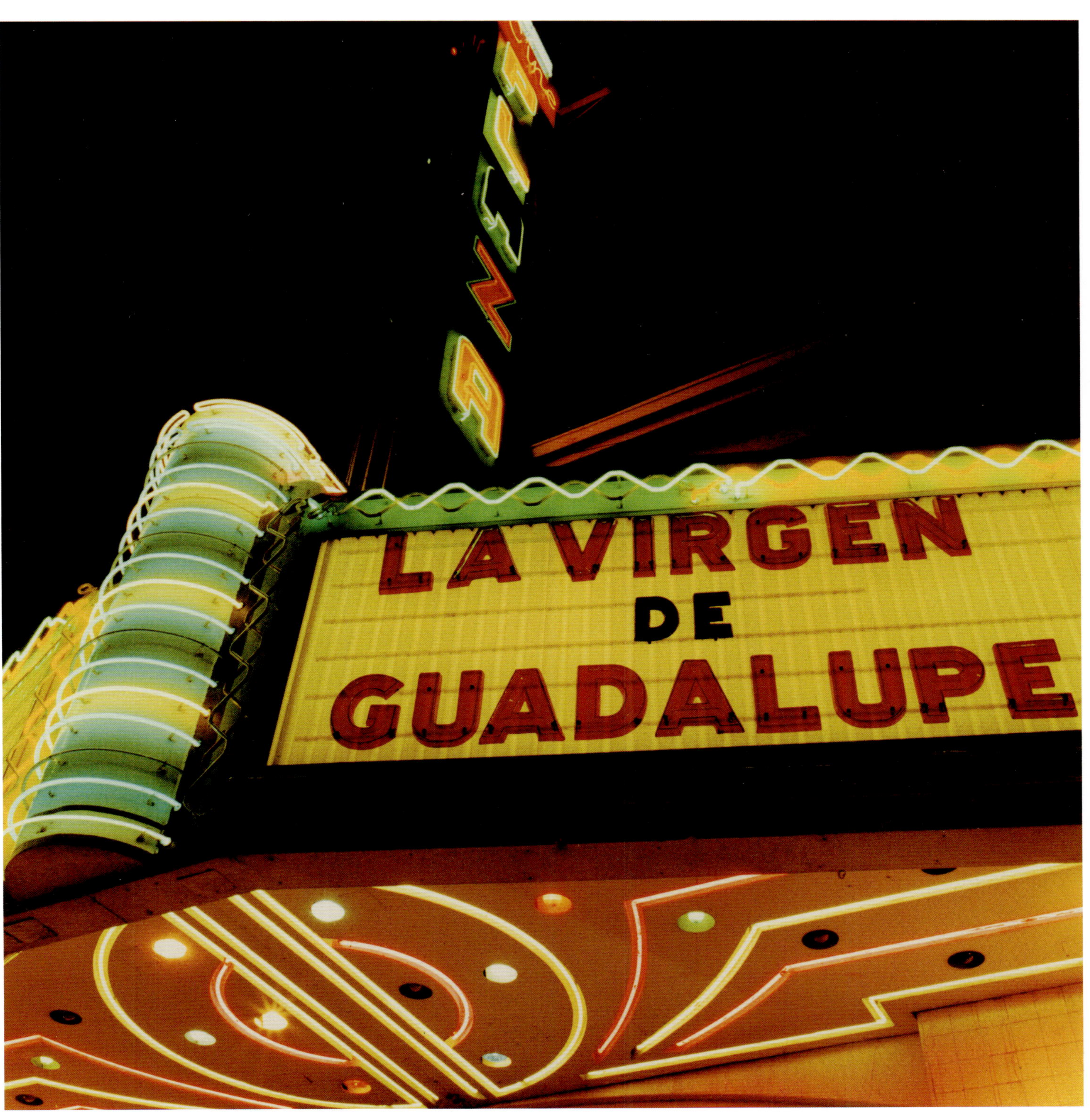

137   *Untitled*, 1979

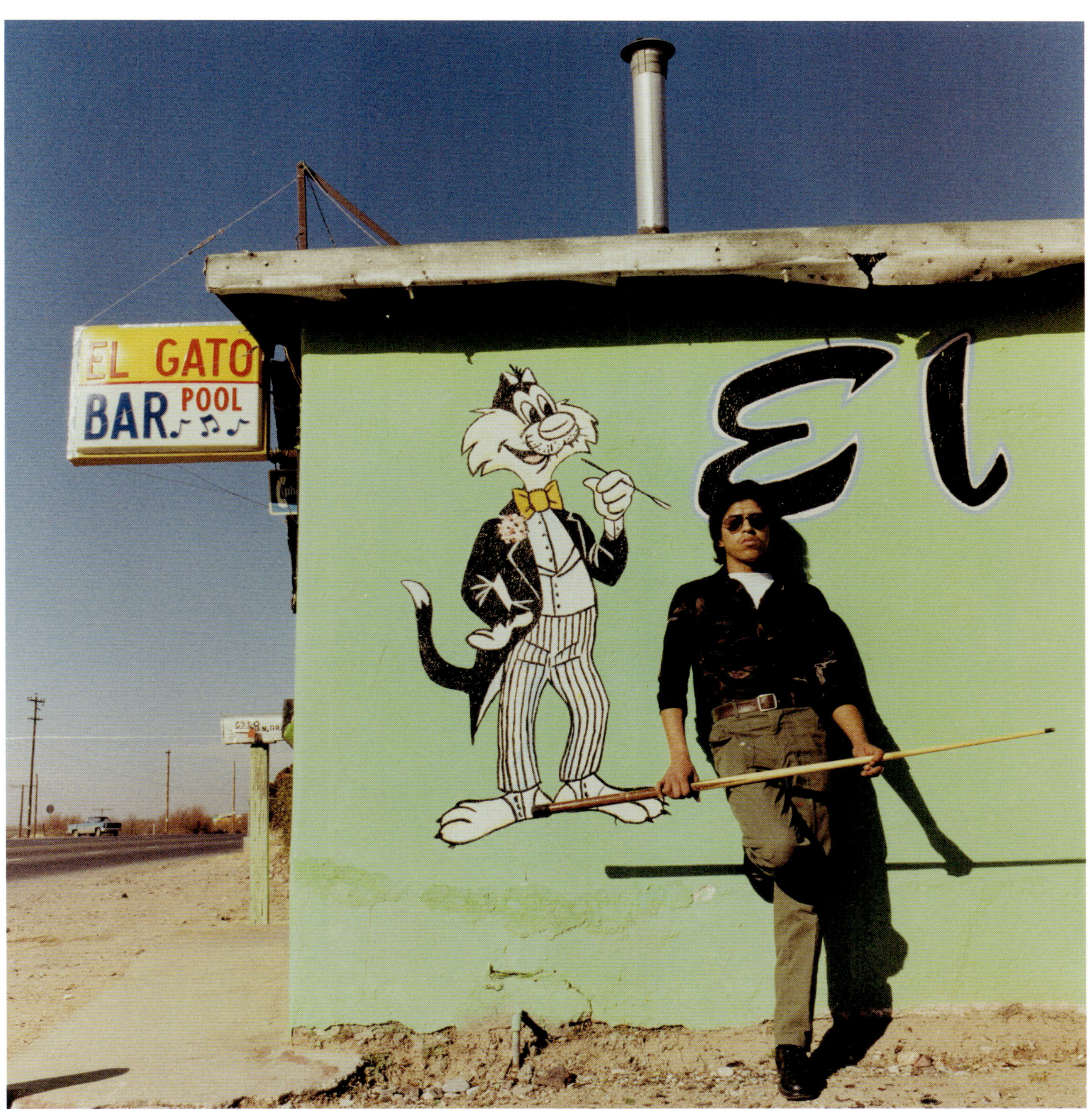

139   *El Gato, Canutillo, New Mexico*, 1979

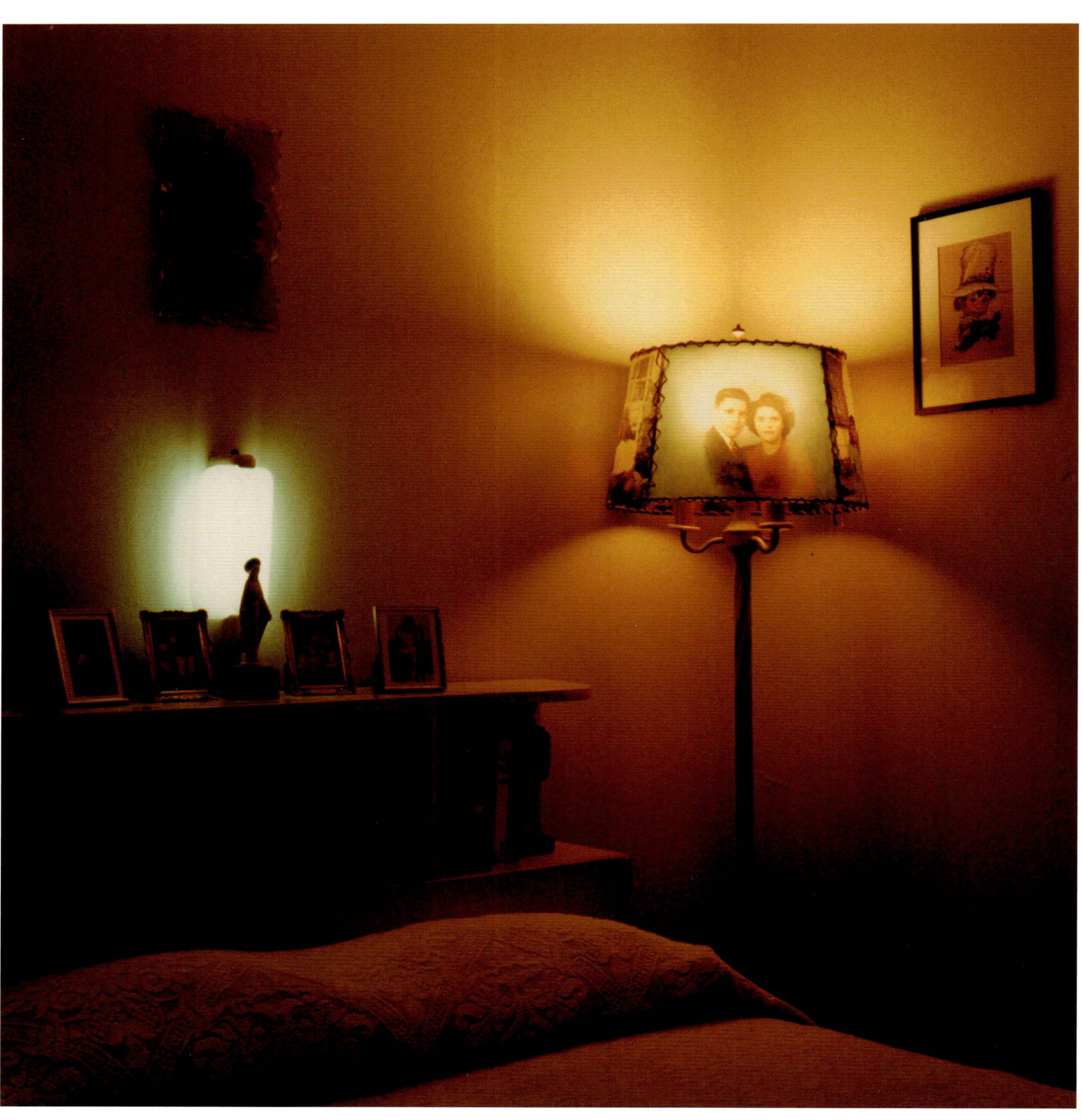

140   *Recámara de Mis Padres, Phoenix, Arizona*, 1978

LOUIS CARLOS BERNAL AND THE SNAPSHOT LENS

Rebecca Senf

In Louis Carlos Bernal's iconic image *Dos Mujeres, Douglas, Arizona* (1978, page 121), a young woman in a bedroom painted a deep orange-rose combs her hair while, in the foreground, another girl in a pine-green room, sitting on a plastic-covered armchair below a wall calendar, looks up from her mending. The interior setting, the use of color photography, and the candid poses and expressions of residents engaged in everyday domestic tasks may all remind a viewer of a snapshot or family photograph. Bernal, however, composed the photograph. Centering one of the girls within the dark-wood doorframe and highlighting each figure with lovely light that pours through windows to create gentle shadows, he presents them individually yet also in relation to one another—all within the square format of his Hasselblad camera. His careful, intentional staging of this and other pictures acknowledges the centrality of home, family, and community to his Mexican American culture.

Bernal documented his subjects—primarily families in their homes and businesses—using color film and prints, the materials associated with late-twentieth-century snapshots. Sometimes he also had them adopt informal posing. But he was making art photographs, not souvenirs, and his formal approach led to a distinct look. This fusion of relaxed poses and deliberate compositions resulted in photographs of the Chicano community in the Southwest that feel intimate and immediate, an effect underscored by his deep respect for and identification with his sitters. Through this style, he exalts the Mexican American people and places he engaged with to the status of art.

Bernal's methods contrasted with the mode of street photography that dominated the mid-twentieth century. In the 1960s and 1970s, Garry Winogrand and Lee Friedlander popularized a visual style that became known as a snapshot aesthetic. Working with handheld 35mm cameras, they created photographs that incorporate tilted horizons, haphazard and layered arrangements of figures, and dramatic diagonals—the lines of receding streets, sidewalks, and buildings. Such details emphasize the improvisational nature of street photography. In effect, Winogrand and Friedlander celebrated chance occurrences and made assets of the unintentional "errors" typical of candid, amateur snapshots. To them, the imperfect and sometimes chaotic relationships between people and their settings within the frame were exciting and dynamic. They embraced a fluid and spontaneous way of working that often involved exposing hundreds of frames and editing out scores of ineffective negatives.

Meanwhile, Bernal was known to be a selective and judicious photographer. Those who knew his working habits described his approach as "frugal," suggesting his reserve and intentionality.[1] This industriousness can be attributed to periods of his career when funds were tight, but Bernal was also in the habit of exposing only several frames in a single session and printing relatively few copies of negatives. He worked with a range of cameras, using a 4-by-5-inch camera; a 2¼-by-2¼-inch Hasselblad (with interchangeable backs for color and black-and-white film); panoramic cameras including the Widelux; and later in his career, a 35mm Leica that he often wore around his neck. But even the constant presence of the handheld Leica, designed for a looser approach, did not change his thrifty ways of making pictures.

Bernal described his work as requiring advance preparation, and he spoke in a 1982 interview of thinking, walking around, and "working things out in advance in my head before going out."[2] Those who witnessed him in action during a photographic session inside a home later described the process as quick and

1. Ben "Easy" Rider, "An Informal Chat with Louis Carlos Bernal," 1982, from Louis Carlos Bernal Archive, Center for Creative Photography, video, 16:34; Marietta Bernstorff, interview by Elizabeth Ferrer, December 29, 2021; Terry Etherton, interview by Elizabeth Ferrer, September 10, 2021.

2. Bernal, in Rider, "An Informal Chat."

economical: Bernal surveyed the situation, then swiftly captured a range of options, by, for instance, using different camera backs with color and black-and-white film, or photographing rooms in houses with and then without family members present.[3] Working in this way, he minimized the amount of time required of his subjects while giving himself the space to later evaluate the best frames from a handful of possibilities. As Bernal's contact sheets show, he typically made three or four exposures of each subject. These presented minor variations in camera placement or groupings of people. For Bernal, making pictures of the Chicano community was not about discovering and wanting to document a fleeting moment, or using the camera to haphazardly condense the world onto film, as some of his contemporaries might have. Rather, he pursued imagined images—ones he endeavored to create from the world around him, based on his deep familiarity with Chicano domestic life and cultural sensibilities.

From 1972 to 1989, Bernal was an instructor at Pima Community College in Arizona, of both the history and the technical processes of photography. His students have described how he taught comprehensively about the practice, covering topics such as composition, fieldwork, archival developing and printing techniques, darkroom maintenance, and methods of critique, including the importance of the language used to describe work and how those words are delivered.[4] He also incorporated the work of other artists and photographers, including Latinx makers such as John Valadez, Laura Aguilar, Roberto Gil de Montes, and ADÁL, in his curriculum.[5] Bernal was considered and methodical, both as a teacher and as a photographer, and he had a deep knowledge of the medium and its range of uses, its history, its contemporary practitioners, and its potential impact on his chosen photographic arena—the art world. As Elizabeth Ferrer discusses in this volume, Bernal's career followed a wave of Mexican American photographers who made pictures within the genres of social documentary or photojournalism. Instead of choosing a didactic or similarly narrow mode of working, he brought his photographs into dialogue with peers who also saw their work as art: Ansel Adams, Lola Álvarez Bravo, Manuel Álvarez Bravo, Morrie Camhi, Abigail Heyman, Graciela Iturbide, Roger Minick, Neal Slavin, W. Eugene Smith, Frederick Sommer, and Ricardo Valverde.

Bernal's hybrid style of applying formal composition to informal subjects can be understood as a thoughtful, deliberate way to create art for his Chicano community. Ferrer discusses the relationship between Bernal's work and his embrace of Chicanismo, which the artist describes in an interview after winning an award from the Southeastern Center for Contemporary Art. The move to Tucson, and what Bernal calls the "spiritual move back to the barrio," prompted him to embrace a "new attitude toward life" as someone who is Mexican American. Chicanismo, therefore, could be a way of representing pride: "The Chicano artist cannot isolate himself from the community but finds himself in the midst of his people creating art of and for the people."[6] Bernal was motivated, as Ferrer explains, by a desire to provide visibility to people without the ability to represent themselves, especially within an art context, and to picture stories that have historically faced political and cultural erasure.

In many of Bernal's works, we see family celebrations and rites of passage, and we see domestic interiors and public places of recreation. Bernal's picture of a 1978 baptism in the Quiñonez family shares a tremendous amount with a casual family snapshot: the celebrants are gathered outside, with the parents seated in the middle holding the baby (page 103). Most of the kids have been arranged

3. Marietta Bernstorff, interview by Elizabeth Ferrer, December 29, 2021.

4. Jeff Smith, interview by Elizabeth Ferrer, September 16, 2021; Chris Benson, interview by Elizabeth Ferrer, November 18, 2021.

5. Marietta Bernstorff, interview by Elizabeth Ferrer, December 29, 2021.

6. Louis Carlos Bernal, in *Awards in the Visual Arts 3* (Winston-Salem, NC: Southeastern Center for Contemporary Art, 1984), p. 16. See also Ferrer, this volume, p. 31.

to sit on either side of the lawn, and behind them stands a large group of adults (some with children in their arms), including one smiling woman holding aloft a white, frosted sheet cake. Bernal seems to have been elevated—perhaps standing on a chair or step stool—and he tightly framed the members of the party so there is just a fragment of a car and the home in the background. Not everyone looks at the camera, nor are all the people visible. The group's candid poses contribute to the photograph's spontaneous spirit.

Similarly, *Quinceañera, Phoenix, Arizona* (1981, page 17) demonstrates Bernal's particular balance of control and acceptance. The image initially looks like a candid view of two young people outside the entryway of a church. But upon closer examination, Bernal's careful choices become clear. On the left, a young man in a dark suit with tails is beautifully set against a lighter background. On the right, a young woman in an off-shoulder, white dress cinched at the waist contrasts with the deep shadow behind her; she holds a bouquet and looks at the photographer. A sculpture of a winged angel behind them fills the middle of the frame, its extended hands and the shadow they cast nearly meeting the earthly girl's bare arm. Bernal's composition is balanced, with dark and light masses of equal size dividing the picture in half. Even though the young man adjusting his shirt suggests a bit of movement, the scene has a sense of stability. Having brought the key elements of the image—shadow, light, and figures—into balance, Bernal was able to relinquish control around the perimeter and allow existing elements, such as a round stained-glass window, a pattern of roof tiles in the background, and stairs that descend into shadow, to break the frame at the picture's edges. One can almost imagine his mantra: organize the eighty percent that's important; let go of the rest.[7]

Although Bernal worked outside in public spaces, his domestic scenes are central to his legacy. These show an individual, couple, or group posed at home for the purpose of having their picture made, but Bernal's framing and composition underscore their personal environment as part of his subject. Rather than zooming in on expressions, body language, or clothing, Bernal often chose to include a large expanse of a wall above his sitters. He lavished attention on the items a person or family chose to display and how they displayed them, inviting us to linger on wall colors, artworks, floral decorations, family photos, musical instruments, religious icons, and textiles that adorn windows, couches, beds, and doorways.

In *6th Street Barrio, Douglas, Arizona* (1979, page 156), a young boy leans against an upholstered chair, the companion to a couch that stretches along a wall. The photograph presents one of Bernal's typical compositions, with the corner of the room at the center to create a strong vertical line at the back of the space. This construction produces a room that recedes in depth while maintaining a stable base; the implicit triangle references the Renaissance convention of pyramidal compositions to suggest balance, permanence, resolution, and durability. The boy looks directly at Bernal, and his figure anchors one point of a series of pyramids formed by the objects arranged in the corner of the room. Bernal's careful framing of decorative wall hangings and family photographs on an end table evokes a strong sense of the boy's environment. The picture's composition is steady and weighted, and photos hung high on the pale-yellow wall draw the viewer's eye upward to the pyramid's apex.

Bernal's 1978 portrait of Felix and Patricia Valdivezo in Leon Speer's barbershop in Lordsburg, New Mexico, is typical of his pictures made within a business (page 153). As he did when photographing in homes, Bernal stepped back

7. Elizabeth Ferrer pointed me to the concept of *rasquachismo* coined by scholar Tomás Ybarra-Frausto in 1989. *Rasquachismo* refers to a Mexican American underdog perspective that combines inventiveness and a survivalist approach as a form of empowerment and resistance, and is often used to describe repurposing, hybridization, or recontextualization in Chicano or Mexican art practices. For Bernal, it can be applied to his practice of ensuring that what is critical is precisely organized, and then allowing what's beyond his control (especially at the margins of the composition) to be what they are. This is particularly true when Bernal is working outdoors, as compared to his practice of arranging people and objects within domestic spaces.

to describe Speer's workplace. He used another favored composition for indoor space, positioning the background wall parallel to the picture plane. Like the pyramidal construction, this setup creates an organized, balanced, and easily deciphered environment in which he can present the father and daughter. The image is filled with layers of visual information, from the patterned shadows and gleaming sunlight on the tiled floor to the faces of the barber, customer, and waiting daughter, and from the repeating forms of mirrors and lights to the collection of items on a shelf just below the low, pressed-tin ceiling. Here, everyday people and an everyday place are inextricably intertwined, and equally of value for the viewer's consideration.

Bernal brought an anthropologist's eye, or perhaps that of a material historian, to his visual explorations of domestic interiors. For instance, he records one interior replete with a tree bedecked with tinsel and ornaments (page 154) and includes the holiday decorations on an ochre curtain behind the tree, framed family photographs, an image of Christ hanging on the light-teal walls, and decorations grouped on a doily on top of the television in the corner. He photographs the Christmas tree not to remember this object or celebration, but to symbolize through one living room the many others never photographed. He was creating enduring portraits of his Chicano community's culture as expressed in the environment of a family home.

Bernal worked in color and in black and white, sometimes photographing the same scene with both types of film. For instance, the variations of *Leon Speer's Barber Shop, Felix Valdivezo & Daughter Patricia, Lordsburg, New Mexico* (1978) have near-identical compositions; Bernal evidently asked everyone to hold their places while he switched film. For me, the dynamic of the image in color provides a more specific feeling of being in the space, whereas the black-and-white picture enhances formal qualities, conveying the powerful sunlight flooding in from the left and more greatly emphasizing the faces of the sitters.

His relationship to color seems significant. From the late 1960s to the 1980s, when Bernal was making pictures, fine-art photographers typically favored black-and-white images. Color was the choice for advertising and snapshots, and only a few museum-exhibited photographers, including Marie Cosindas, William Eggleston, Joel Meyerowitz, and Stephen Shore, worked primarily in color. But these attitudes were starting to change. It also seems that Bernal could more accurately and precisely describe the homes he photographed when he used color, portraying a more vivid sense of the space through his subjects' choices for walls, draperies, bed coverings, and upholstered furniture.

Working in color allowed Bernal to capture the distinct palettes of the homes in which he worked. Combinations of ruddy browns, reds, roses, ochres, greens, teals, and blues appear often. Textiles, some filtering light through windows to infuse spaces with glowing color, feature prominently. Vast expanses of painted walls, reflecting the decision to fill a home with color, create backdrops for people, collections of household furniture, and valued objects. Painted front doors are swung open, inviting in sunlight and providing a block of color that contrasts with surrounding walls. Color is not incidental in these photographs; color is essential. Could Bernal have made artworks about these places or accurately portrayed these families without recording colors as he did, in luscious detail and with such great care? Decades later, his deeply considered style still celebrates the Mexican American families he photographed. His immediacy and directness bring these photographs, and the people he featured, into an artistic dialogue.

LOUIS CARLOS BERNAL Y LA LENTE INSTANTÁNEA

Rebecca Senf

LOUIS CARLOS BERNAL Y LA LENTE INSTANTÁNEA

Rebecca Senf

En la icónica imagen de Louis Carlos Bernal *Dos Mujeres, Douglas, Arizona* (1978, página 121), una mujer joven en un dormitorio pintado de rosa anaranjado intenso se peina mientras, en el primer plano, otra chica en una habitación pintada de verde pino, se ve sentada en un sillón cubierto de plástico bajo un calendario, levantando la vista de su zurcido. La ambientación interior, el uso de fotografías a color y las poses y expresiones francas de las residentes mientras se concentran en tareas domésticas cotidianas pueden traer a la mente una instantánea o una fotografía familiar para el espectador. Sin embargo, fue compuesto por Bernal. Al posicionar a una de las chicas en el centro del marco de la puerta de madera oscura y resaltar cada figura con la luz encantadora que se cuela por las ventanas para crear sombras suaves, las presenta de manera individual pero también crea una relación entre una y otra, todo ello dentro del formato cuadrado de su cámara Hasselblad. La puesta en escena cuidadosa e intencionada de esta y otras imágenes reconoce la importancia del hogar, la familia y la comunidad en su cultura mexicano-americano.

Bernal documentó a sus sujetos —principalmente familias en sus hogares y negocios— utilizando películas e impresiones a color, materiales asociados con las instantáneas de los finales del siglo XX. A veces, también les hacía adoptar poses informales. Pero él hacía fotografías artísticas, no para el recuerdo, y su enfoque formal dio lugar a una mirada distinta. Esta fusión de poses relajadas y composiciones intencionales dio como resultado fotografías de la comunidad chicana del suroeste de Estados Unidos que parecen íntimas e inmediatas, un efecto subrayado por su profundo respeto e identificación con sus modelos. Con este estilo, eleva a la categoría de arte a las personas y los lugares mexicano-estadounidenses con los que se relacionó.

Los métodos de Bernal contrastaron con el modo de fotografía callejera que dominaba a mediados del siglo XX. En las décadas de 1960 y 1970, Garry Winogrand y Lee Friedlander popularizaron un estilo visual que se conoció como estética de la instantánea. Trabajando con cámaras de mano de 35 mm, crearon fotografías que incorporan horizontes inclinados, disposiciones de figuras al azar y en capas, así como diagonales espectaculares con líneas de calles, aceras y edificios que se alejan. Estos detalles ponen de relieve el carácter improvisado de la fotografía callejera. En efecto, Winogrand y Friedlander celebraban los sucesos fortuitos y sacaban partido a los "errores" involuntarios típicos de las instantáneas cándidas de aficionados. Para ellos, las relaciones imperfectas y a veces caóticas entre las personas y sus entornos dentro del marco eran emocionantes y dinámicas. Adoptaron una forma de trabajar fluida y espontánea que a menudo implicaba exponer cientos de fotogramas y eliminar decenas de negativos inservibles.

Mientras tanto, a Bernal se le conocía por ser un fotógrafo selectivo y juicioso. Quienes estaban familiarizados con sus hábitos de trabajo describían su enfoque como frugal, es decir, reservado e intencional.[1] Esta laboriosidad puede atribuirse a periodos de su carrera en los que los fondos eran escasos, pero Bernal también tenía la costumbre de exponer solo algunos fotogramas en una sola sesión e imprimir relativamente pocas copias de los negativos. Trabajó con diversas cámaras, a saber, una cámara de 4 por 5 pulgadas; una Hasselblad de 2¼ por 2¼ pulgadas (con respaldos intercambiables para película a color y en blanco y negro); cámaras panorámicas, incluso la Widelux; y, más adelante en su carrera, una Leica de 35 mm que a menudo llevaba colgada del cuello. Pero ni siquiera la presencia constante de la Leica de mano, diseñada para un enfoque más suelto, cambió su forma económica de hacer fotos.

Bernal describió su trabajo como algo que requiere preparación previa y, en una entrevista de 1982, habló de la necesidad de pensar, pasear y, en sus palabras, "elaborar las cosas por adelantado en mi cabeza antes de salir".[2] Quienes lo presenciaron en acción durante una sesión fotográfica en el interior de una vivienda describieron posteriormente al proceso como rápido y económico: Bernal estudiaba la situación y, después, captaba rápidamente una serie de opciones, por ejemplo, utilizando distintos respaldos de cámara con película de color y en blanco y negro o fotografiando habitaciones de casas con y sin los miembros de la familia presentes.[3] Al trabajar de este modo, minimizaba el tiempo que exigía de sus sujetos mientras que se daba a si mismo el espacio necesario para evaluar de manera posterior los mejores encuadres de entre un puñado de posibilidades. Como muestran las hojas de contacto de Bernal, normalmente hacía tres o cuatro exposiciones de cada sujeto. Estas presentaban pequeñas variaciones en la colocación de la cámara o en las agrupaciones de personas. Para Bernal, fotografiar a la comunidad chicana no consistía en descubrir y querer documentar un momento fugaz, ni en utilizar la cámara para condensar el mundo al azar en una película, como podrían haber hecho algunos de sus contemporáneos. Más bien buscaba escenas imaginarias que se esforzaba por crear a partir del mundo que le rodeaba al basarse en su profunda familiaridad con la vida doméstica y la sensibilidad cultural chicana.

De 1972 a 1989, Bernal fue profesor en Pima Community College de Arizona, tanto de la historia como de los procesos técnicos de la fotografía. Sus alumnas y alumnos han descrito cómo instruía de manera exhaustiva sobre la práctica y abarcaba temas como la composición, el trabajo de campo, las técnicas de revelado e impresión de archivos, el mantenimiento del cuarto oscuro y los métodos de crítica, al igual que la importancia del lenguaje para describir el trabajo y cómo se expresan tales palabras.[4] También incorporó a su currículo el trabajo de otros artistas y fotógrafos, entre quienes se encuentran creadores de origen latino como John Valadez, Laura Aguilar, Roberto Gil de Montes y ADÁL.[5] Bernal era considerado y metódico, tanto como profesor y como fotógrafo, y poseía un profundo conocimiento del medio y su gama de usos, su historia, los profesionales contemporáneos y su impacto potencial en el ámbito fotográfico que había elegido: el mundo del arte. Como Elizabeth Ferrer analiza en este volumen, la carrera de Bernal siguió a una oleada de fotógrafos mexicano-americanos que produjeron imágenes dentro de los géneros del documental social o el fotoperiodismo. En lugar de optar por un modo de trabajo didáctico o similarmente estrecho, puso sus fotografías en diálogo con otros compañeros quienes también veían su trabajo como arte: Ansel Adams, Lola Álvarez Bravo, Manuel Álvarez Bravo, Morrie Camhi, Abigail Heyman, Graciela Iturbide, Roger Minick, Neal Slavin, W. Eugene Smith, Frederick Sommer y Ricardo Valverde.

El estilo híbrido de Bernal de aplicar una composición formal a un tema informal puede entenderse como una forma reflexiva y deliberada de crear arte para su comunidad chicana. Ferrer analiza la relación entre la obra de Bernal y su acogida del chicanismo, que el artista describe en una entrevista tras ganar un premio del Southeastern Center for Contemporary Art. El traslado a Tucson y lo que Bernal llama el "regreso espiritual al barrio" le llevaron a adoptar una "nueva actitud ante la vida" como mexicano-americano. El chicanismo, por lo tanto, podría ser una forma de representar el orgullo: "el artista chicano no puede aislarse de la comunidad sino que se encuentra en medio de su pueblo creando arte de y para el pueblo".[6] A Bernal le motivó, como explica Ferrer, el deseo de

1. Ben "Easy" Rider, "An Informal Chat with Louis Carlos Bernal," 1982, de Louis Carlos Bernal Archive, Center for Creative Photography, vídeo, 16:34; Marietta Bernstorff, entrevista de Elizabeth Ferrer, 29 de diciembre de 2021; Terry Etherton, entrevista de Elizabeth Ferrer, 10 de septiembre de 2021.

2. Rider, "An Informal Chat".

3. Marietta Bernstorff, entrevista de Elizabeth Ferrer, 29 de diciembre de 2021.

4. Jeff Smith, entrevista de Elizabeth Ferrer, 16 de septiembre de 2021; Chris Benson, entrevista de Elizabeth Ferrer, 18 de noviembre de 2021.

5. Marietta Bernstorff, entrevista de Elizabeth Ferrer, 29 de diciembre de 2021.

6. Louis Carlos Bernal, en *Awards in the Visual Arts 3* (Winston-Salem, NC: Southeastern Center for Contemporary Art, 1984), p. 16. Véase también Ferrer, este volumen, p. 31.

dar visibilidad a las personas que no tenían la posibilidad de representarse a sí mismas —sobre todo en un contexto artístico— y de retratar historias que han sido invisibilizadas políticamente y culturalmente a lo largo de la historia.

En muchas de las obras de Bernal, vemos celebraciones familiares y ritos de iniciación, así como interiores domésticos y lugares públicos de recreo. La foto de Bernal de un bautizo celebrado por la familia Quiñonez en 1978 comparte mucho con una instantánea familiar casual: los celebrantes están reunidos fuera, mientras que la madre y el padre están sentados al centro sosteniendo al bebé (página 103). La mayoría de los niños están sentados a ambos lados del césped y, detrás de ellos, hay un grupo grande de adultos (algunos con niños en brazos), entre quienes se distingue una mujer sonriente que sostiene en alto un pastel de glaseado blanco. Bernal parece haber estado elevado —quizá de pie sobre una silla o un taburete— y encuadró de manera estrecha a los miembros de la fiesta, de modo que solo aparece una parte de un coche y la casa al fondo. No todas las personas miran a la cámara ni son visibles. Las poses cándidas del grupo contribuyen al espíritu espontáneo de la fotografía.

Del mismo modo, *Quinceañera, Phoenix, Arizona* (1981, página 17) demuestra el equilibrio particular de Bernal entre control y aceptación. En un principio, la imagen parece una vista simple de dos jóvenes a la entrada de una iglesia. Pero si se examina más de cerca, las elecciones cautelosas de Bernal quedan claras. A la izquierda, un hombre joven con traje oscuro y frac está perfectamente colocado sobre un fondo más claro. A la derecha, una mujer joven con un vestido blanco sin hombros ceñido a la cintura contrasta con la sombra profunda que hay detrás de ella; sostiene un ramo y mira al fotógrafo. Detrás de ellos, la escultura de un ángel ocupa el centro del encuadre; sus manos extendidas y la sombra que proyectan casi se encuentran con el brazo desnudo de la chica terrenal. La composición de Bernal es equilibrada, con masas oscuras y claras de igual tamaño que dividen el cuadro por la mitad. Aunque el joven que se ajusta la camisa indica un poco de movimiento, la escena tiene una sensación de estabilidad. Una vez equilibrados los elementos clave de la imagen —sombra, luz y figuras—, Bernal pudo ceder el control del perímetro y permitir que los elementos existentes, como una vidriera redonda, un patrón de tejas en el fondo y unas escaleras que descienden en la sombra, rompieran el marco en los bordes del cuadro. Uno casi puede imaginarse su mantra: "organiza el ochenta por ciento que es importante; despréndete del resto".[7]

Aunque Bernal trabajó al aire libre en espacios públicos, sus escenas domésticas forman una parte fundamental de su legado. En ellas se ve a un individuo, una pareja o un grupo posando en su casa con el fin de hacerse una foto, pero el encuadre y la composición de Bernal subrayan el entorno personal como parte de su tema. En lugar de acercarse a las expresiones, el lenguaje corporal o la ropa, Bernal a menudo optaba por incluir una gran extensión de pared por encima de sus modelos. Prestaba mucha atención a los objetos que una persona o una familia había elegido exponer y en cómo se los exponía, invitándonos a fijarnos en los colores de las paredes, las obras de arte, los adornos florales, las fotos de familia, los instrumentos musicales, los iconos religiosos y los tejidos que adornan las ventanas, los sofás, las camas y las puertas.

En *6th Street Barrio, Douglas, Arizona* (1979, página 156), un niño se apoya en una silla tapizada a tono con un sofá que se extiende a lo largo de la pared. La fotografía presenta una de las composiciones típicas de Bernal, con la esquina de la habitación en el centro para crear una línea vertical contundente en el fondo

7. Elizabeth Ferrer me señaló el concepto de *rasquachismo* acuñado por el académico Tomás Ybarra-Frausto en 1989. El rasquachismo se refiere a una perspectiva mexicoamericana marginal que combina la inventiva y un acercamiento supervivencialista como forma de empoderamiento y resistencia y, a menudo, se utiliza para describir la reutilización, hibridación o recontextualización en las prácticas artísticas chicanas o mexicanas. Para Bernal, puede aplicarse a su práctica de asegurarse de que lo que sea crítico esté organizado con precisión; y luego permitir que lo que no esté bajo su control (especialmente en los márgenes de la composición) sea lo que es. Esto es especialmente cierto cuando Bernal trabaja al aire libre, en comparación con su práctica de organizar personas y objetos en espacios domésticos.

del espacio. Esta construcción genera un cuarto que retrocede en profundidad mientras mantiene una base estable; el triángulo implícito hace referencia a la convención renacentista de las composiciones piramidales para sugerir el equilibrio, la permanencia, la resolución y la durabilidad. El niño mira directamente a Bernal y su figura funge como ancla de una serie de pirámides formadas por los objetos dispuestos en la esquina de la habitación. El encuadre cuidadoso de los tapices decorativos y las fotografías familiares sobre una mesa auxiliar evoca una idea clara del entorno del niño. La composición del cuadro es firme y equilibrada y las fotos colgadas en lo alto de la pared amarillo pálido atraen la mirada del espectador hacia el vértice de la pirámide.

El retrato que Bernal hizo en 1978 de Félix y Patricia Valdivezo en la barbería de Leon Speer en Lordsburg, Nuevo México, es típico de sus fotografías realizadas en establecimientos (página 153). Como hacía cuando fotografiaba en las casas, Bernal dio un paso atrás para describir el lugar de trabajo de Speer. Utilizó otra composición preferida para espacios interiores al colocar la pared de fondo paralela al plano del cuadro. Al igual que la construcción piramidal, este montaje crea un entorno organizado, equilibrado y fácil de descifrar en el que puede presentar al padre y a la hija. La imagen está llena de capas de información visual, desde las sombras estampadas y la luz brillante del sol en el suelo de baldosa hasta los rostros del barbero, el cliente y la hija que espera; desde las formas repetitivas de los espejos y las luces hasta la colección de artículos en una estantería justo debajo del techo bajo de hojalata prensada. Aquí, gente común y corriente y un lugar cotidiano están entrelazados de manera inextricable y son igualmente valiosos para la consideración del espectador.

Bernal aportó el ojo de un antropólogo —o quizá el de un historiador de materiales— a sus exploraciones visuales de los interiores domésticos. Por ejemplo, registra un interior con un árbol adornado con espumillón y ornamentos (página 154) e incluye adornos navideños en una cortina ocre detrás del árbol, fotografías familiares enmarcadas, una imagen de Cristo colgada en las paredes de un verde azulado claro y adornos agrupados en una blonda encima del televisor en la esquina. Retrata el árbol de Navidad no para recordar este objeto o celebración, sino para simbolizar a través de un solo salón los muchos otros nunca fotografiados. Creaba retratos perdurables de la cultura de su comunidad chicana expresada en el entorno de un hogar familiar.

Bernal trabajó a color y en blanco y negro y, a veces, fotografiaba la misma escena con ambos tipos de película. Por ejemplo, las variaciones de *Leon Speer's Barber Shop, Felix Valdivezo & Daughter Patricia, Lordsburg, New Mexico* (1978) tienen composiciones casi idénticas; Bernal evidentemente les pidió a todos que se mantuvieran en su sitio mientras cambiaba de película. Para mí, la dinámica de la imagen a color proporciona una sensación más específica de estar en el espacio, mientras que la imagen en blanco y negro realza las cualidades formales al transmitir la luz potente del sol que inunda desde la izquierda y resalta más los rostros de las personas.

Su relación con el color parece significativa. Desde finales de los sesenta hasta los ochenta, cuando Bernal hacía imágenes, los fotógrafos de bellas artes solían preferir las imágenes en blanco y negro. El color era la opción elegida para la publicidad y las instantáneas, y solo unos pocos fotógrafos expuestos en museos, como Marie Cosindas, William Eggleston, Joel Meyerowitz y Stephen Shore, se concentraban en la fotografía a color. No obstante, estas actitudes empezaron a cambiar. También parece que Bernal podía describir con mayor exactitud y precisión las casas que fotografiaba cuando utilizaba el color al retratar una sensación más vívida del espacio a través de las elecciones de sus sujetos para las paredes, las cortinas, las cubiertas de las camas y los muebles tapizados.

Trabajar a color permitió a Bernal captar las distintas paletas de las casas en las que trabajaba. A menudo aparecen combinaciones de cafés rojizos, rojos, rosas, ocres, verdes, verdes azulados y azules. Los textiles, algunos de los cuales filtran la luz a través de las ventanas para infundir a los espacios un color resplandeciente, ocupan un lugar destacado. Vastas extensiones de paredes pintadas, un reflejo de la decisión de llenar de color un hogar, crean telones de fondo para personas y colecciones de muebles domésticos y objetos valiosos. Las puertas de entrada pintadas se abren de par en par e invitan a entrar la luz del sol y proporcionan un bloque de color que contrasta con las paredes circundantes. A través de las puertas, se dejan entrever habitaciones pintadas de distintos tonos, lo que delimita el espacio y muestra cómo los propietarios desarrollaron estilos específicos para las distintas zonas de sus casas. El color no es accesorio en estas fotografías sino elemental. ¿Podría Bernal haber hecho obras sobre estos lugares o retratado con precisión a estas familias sin registrar los colores como lo hizo, con todo lujo de detalle y con tanto cuidado? Décadas más tarde, su estilo profundamente considerado sigue celebrando a las familias mexicano-estadounidenses que fotografió. Su inmediatez y franqueza llevan a estas fotografías y a sus protagonistas a un diálogo artístico.

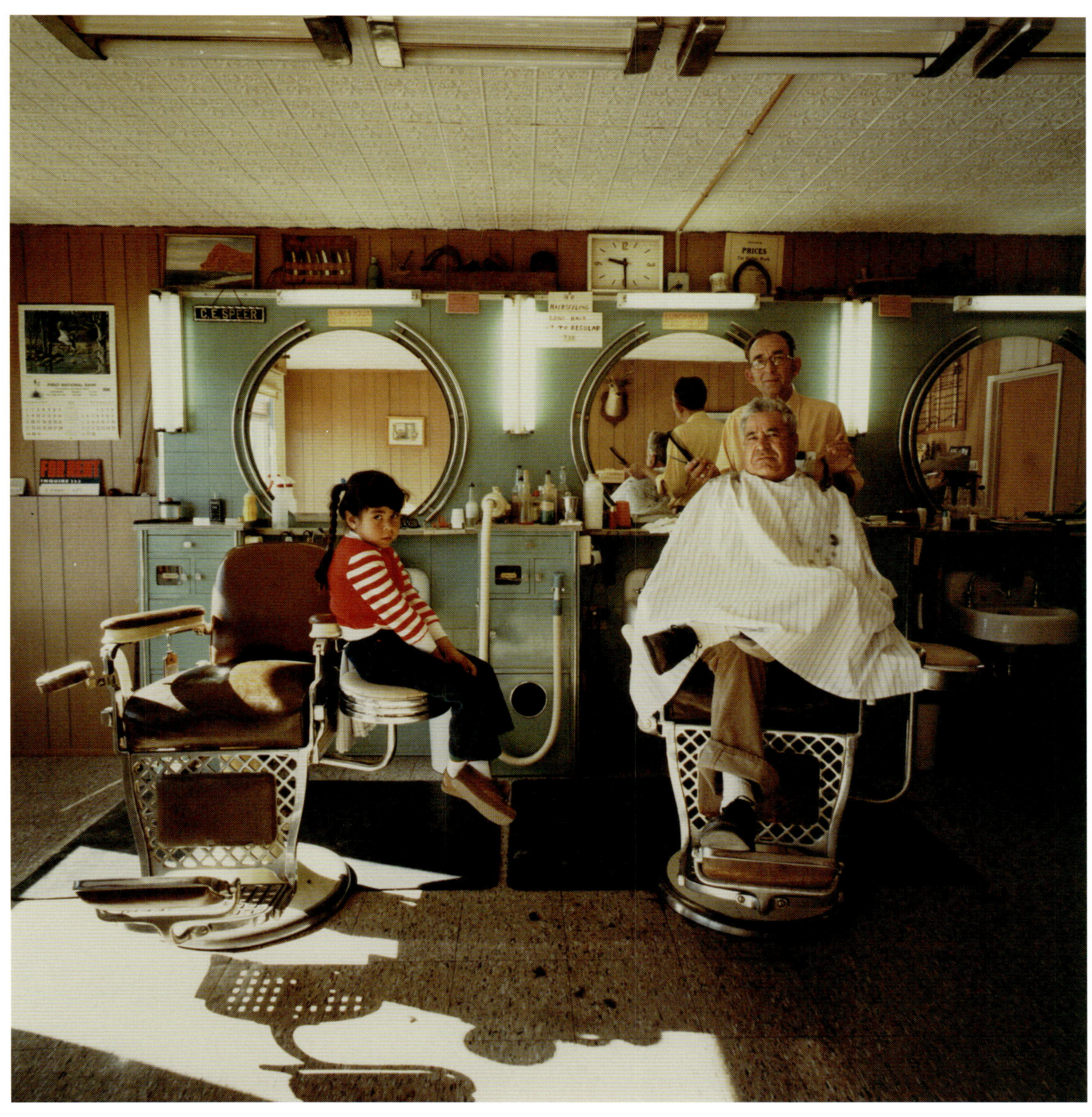

153   *Leon Speer's Barber Shop, Felix Valdivezo & Daughter Patricia, Lordsburg, New Mexico*, 1978

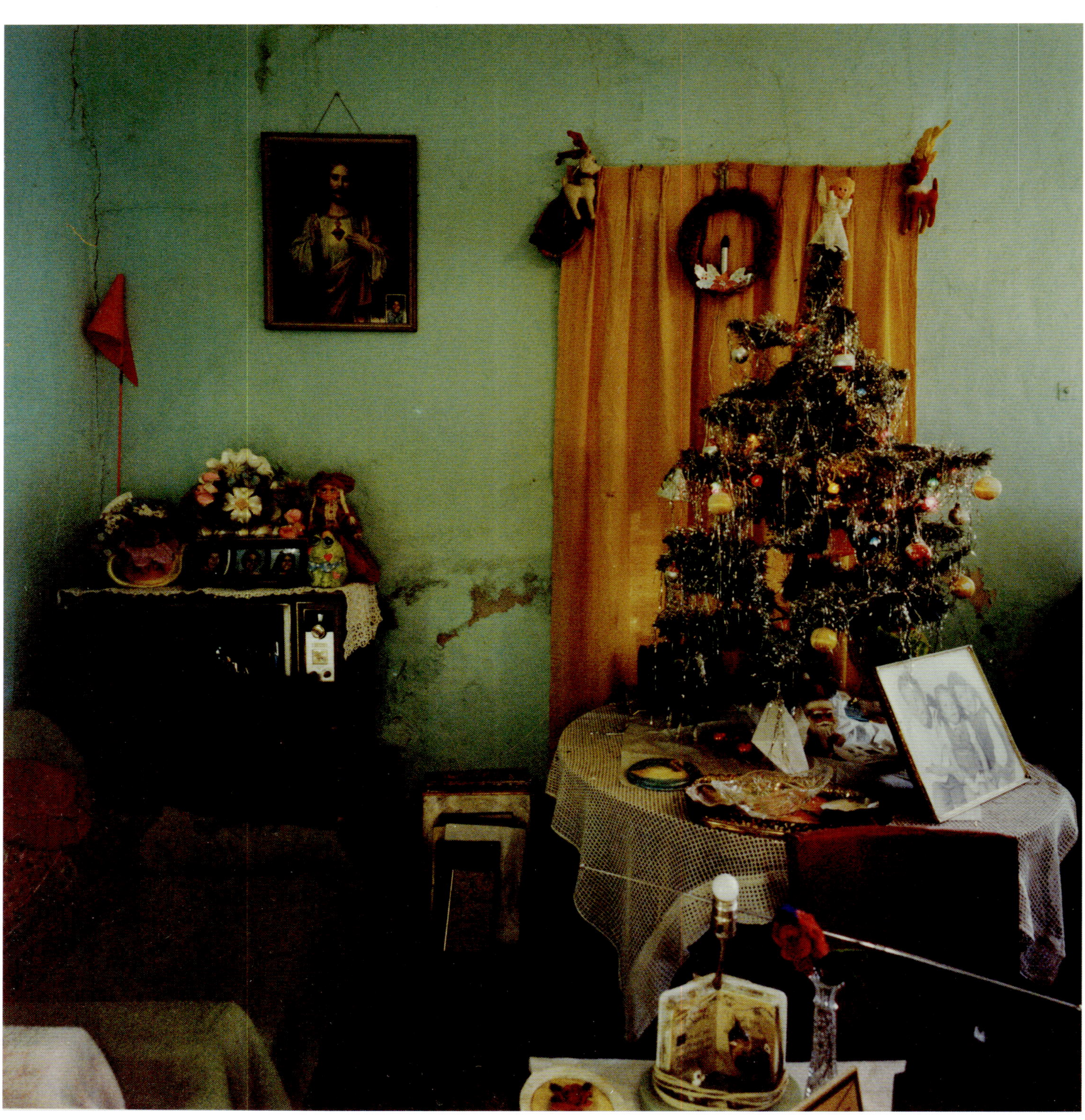

154   *Untitled,* 1978

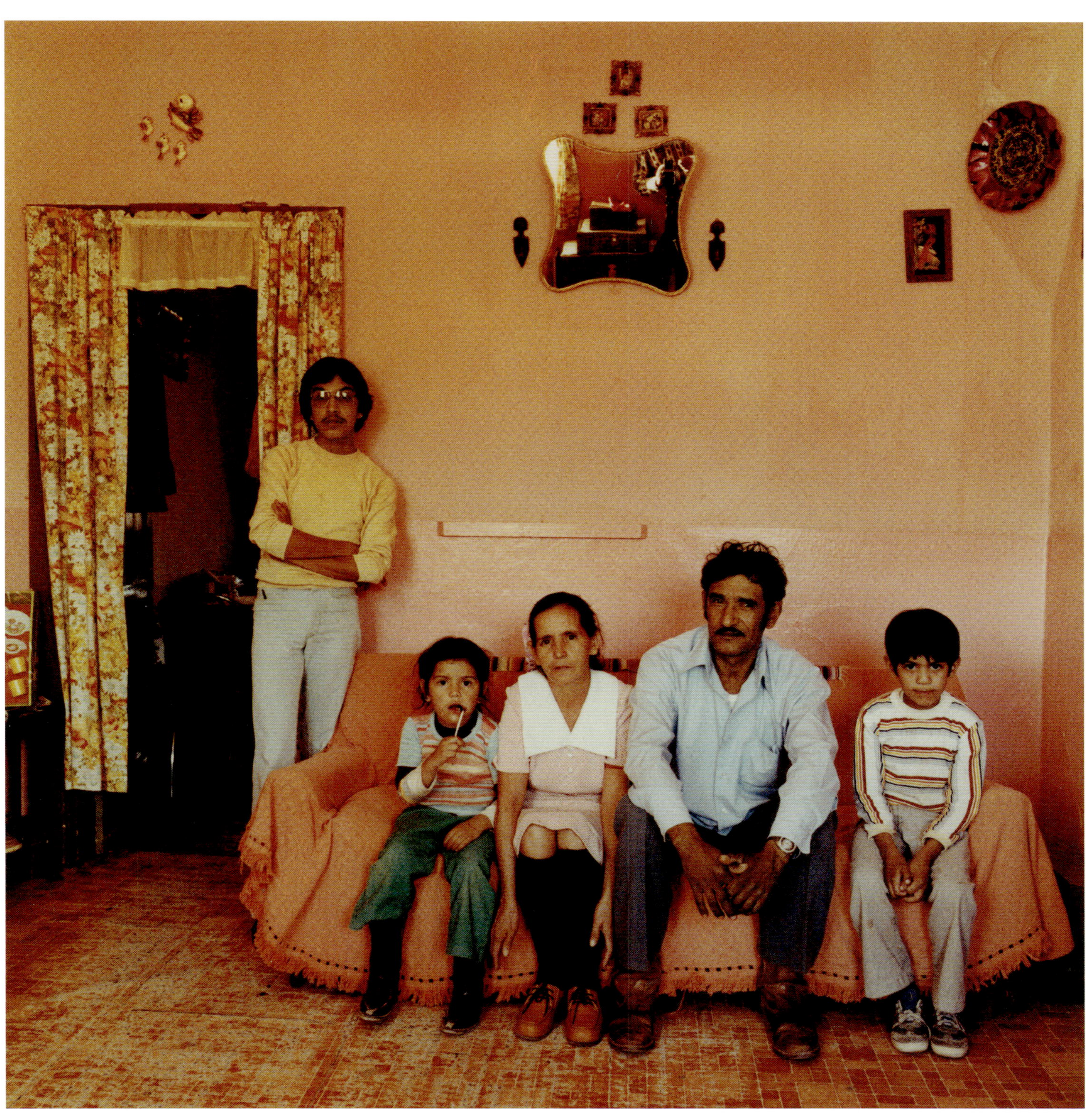

155   *New Immigrants, Douglas, Arizona,* 1980

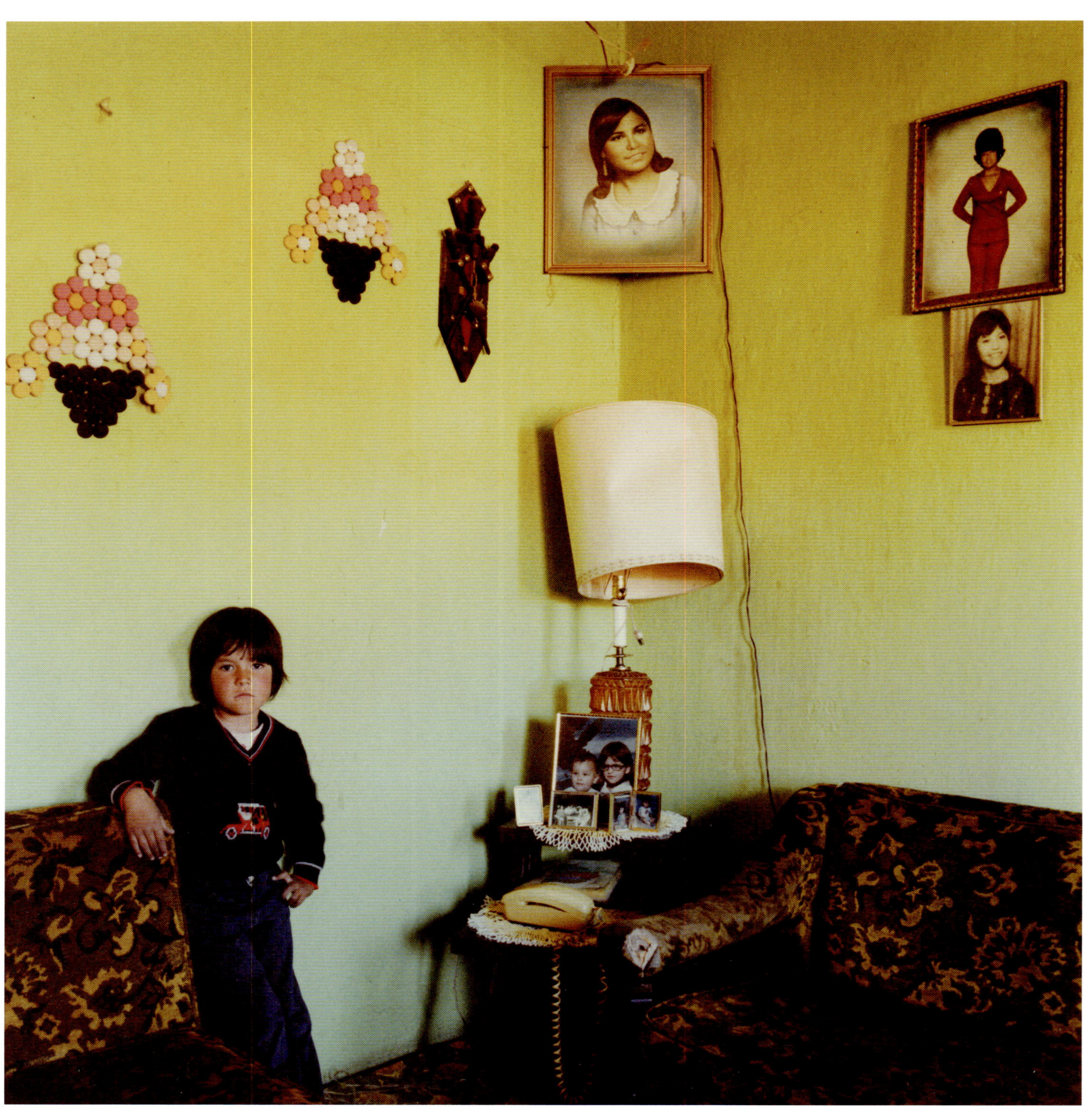

156   *6th Street Barrio, Douglas, Arizona,* 1979

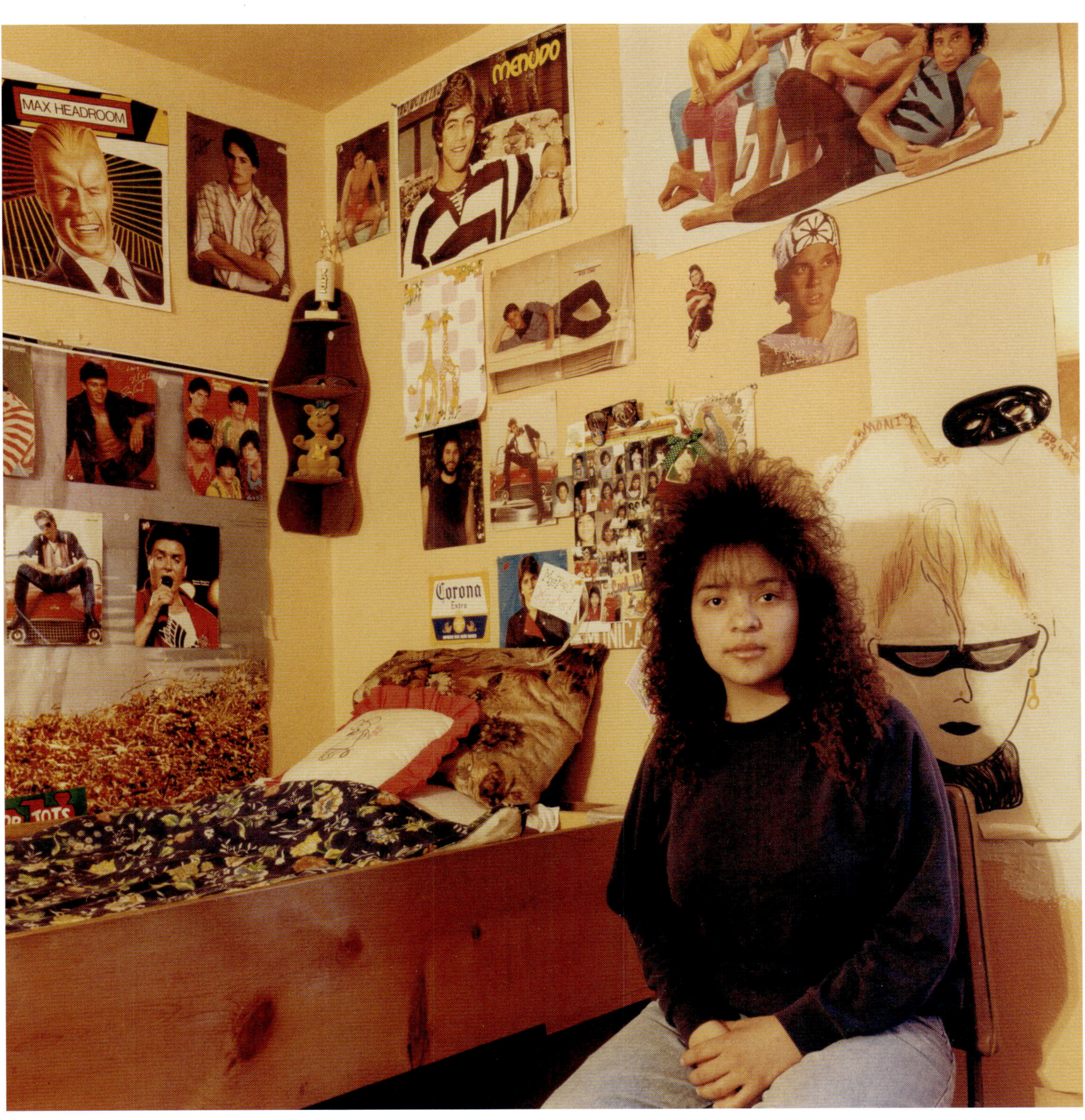

157   *Anna Quiñonez, Douglas,* 1979

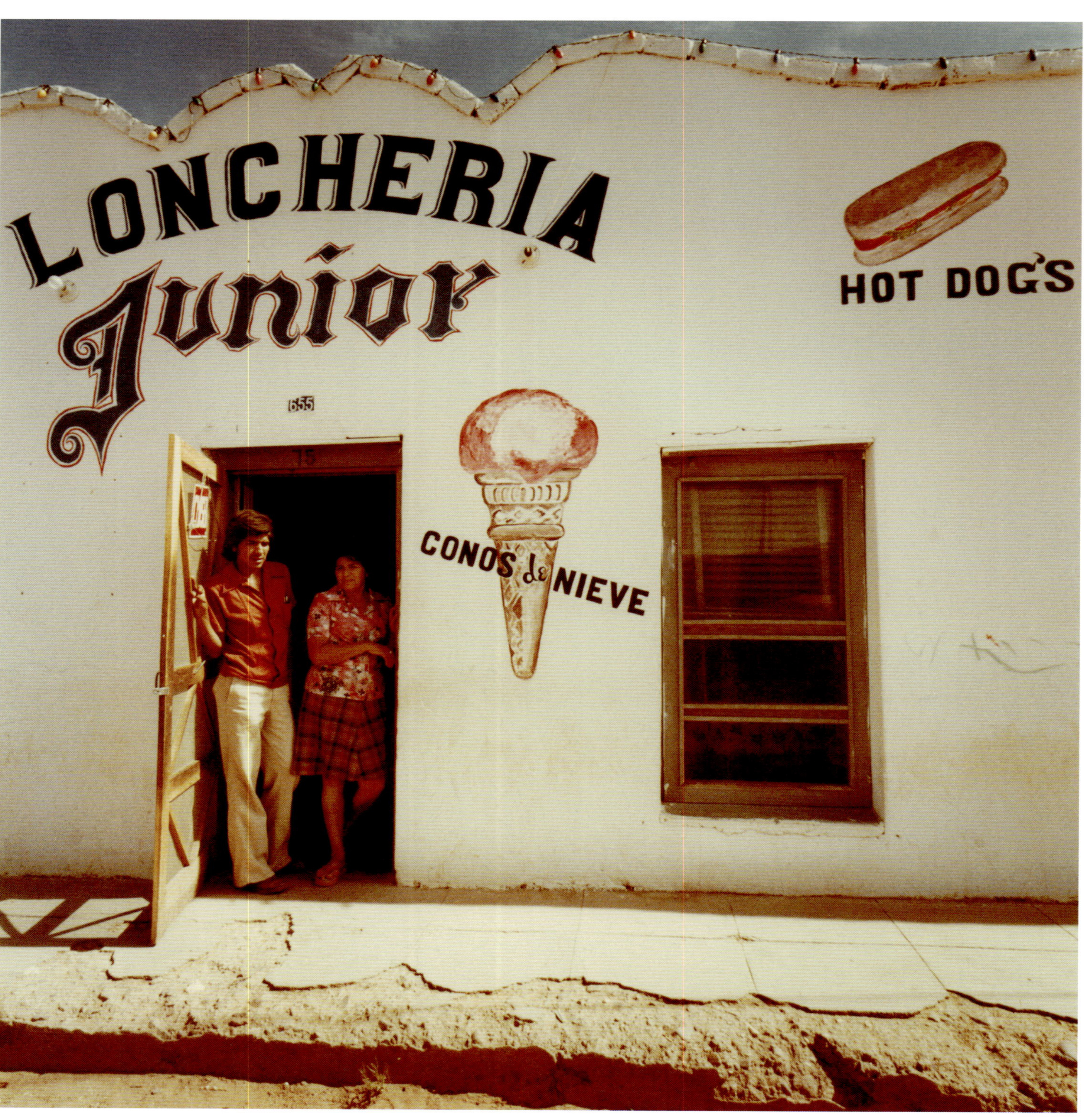

LONCHERIA
Junior
HOT DOG'S
CONOS DE NIEVE
655

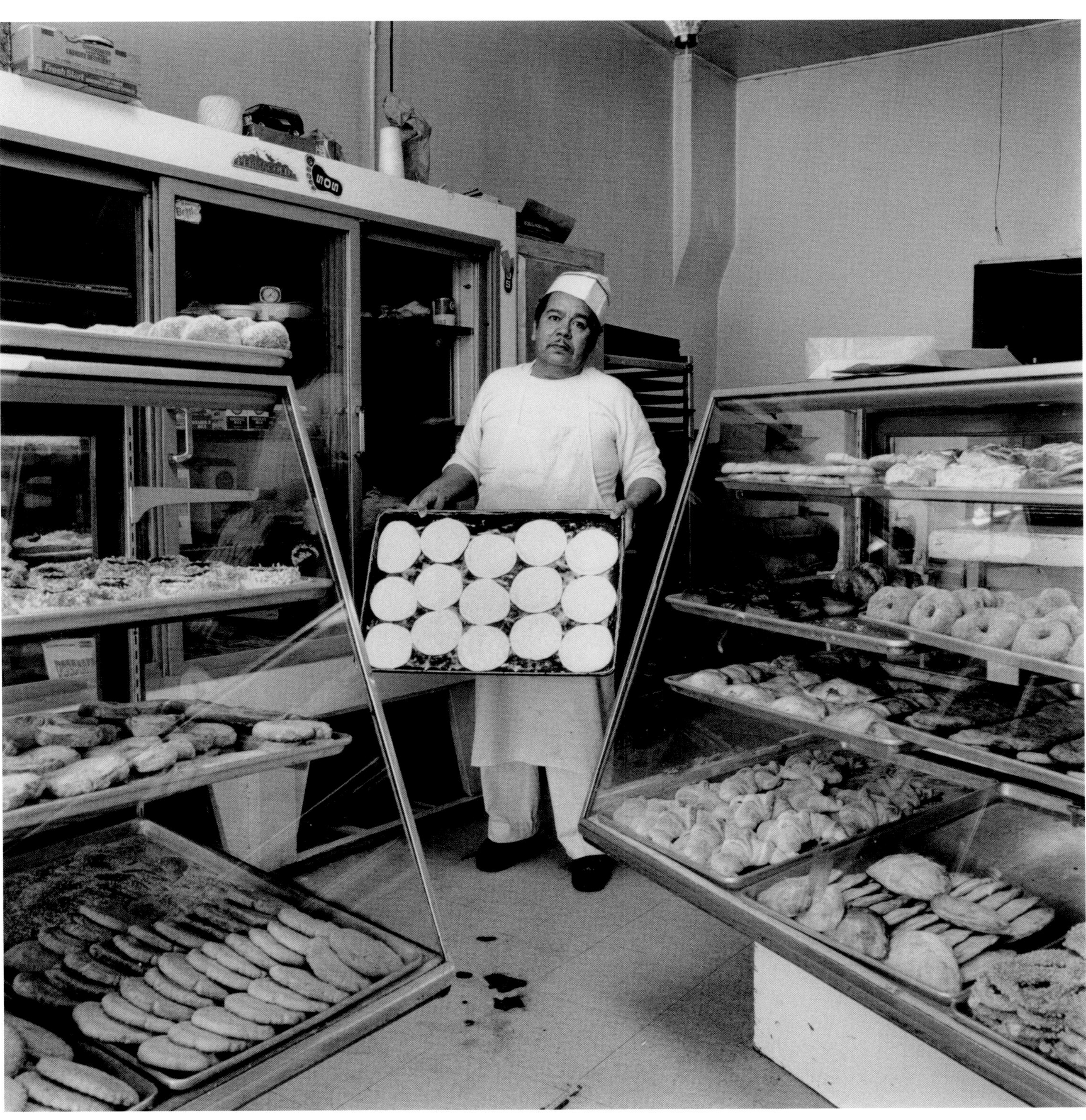

159   *José Padilla, Panadero, El Paso,* 1979

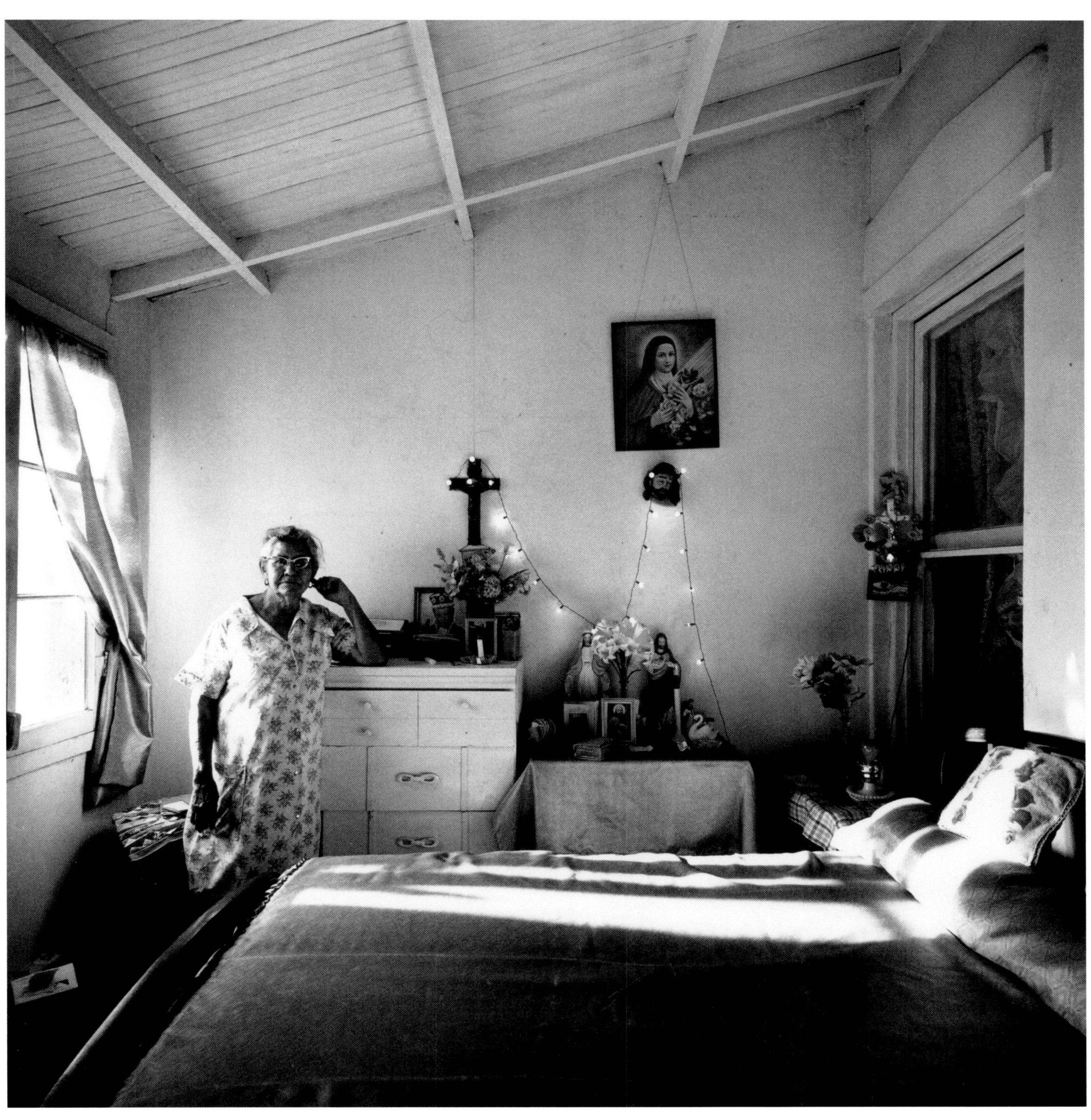

   Doña Rita Mendoza, Barrio Viejo, 1974

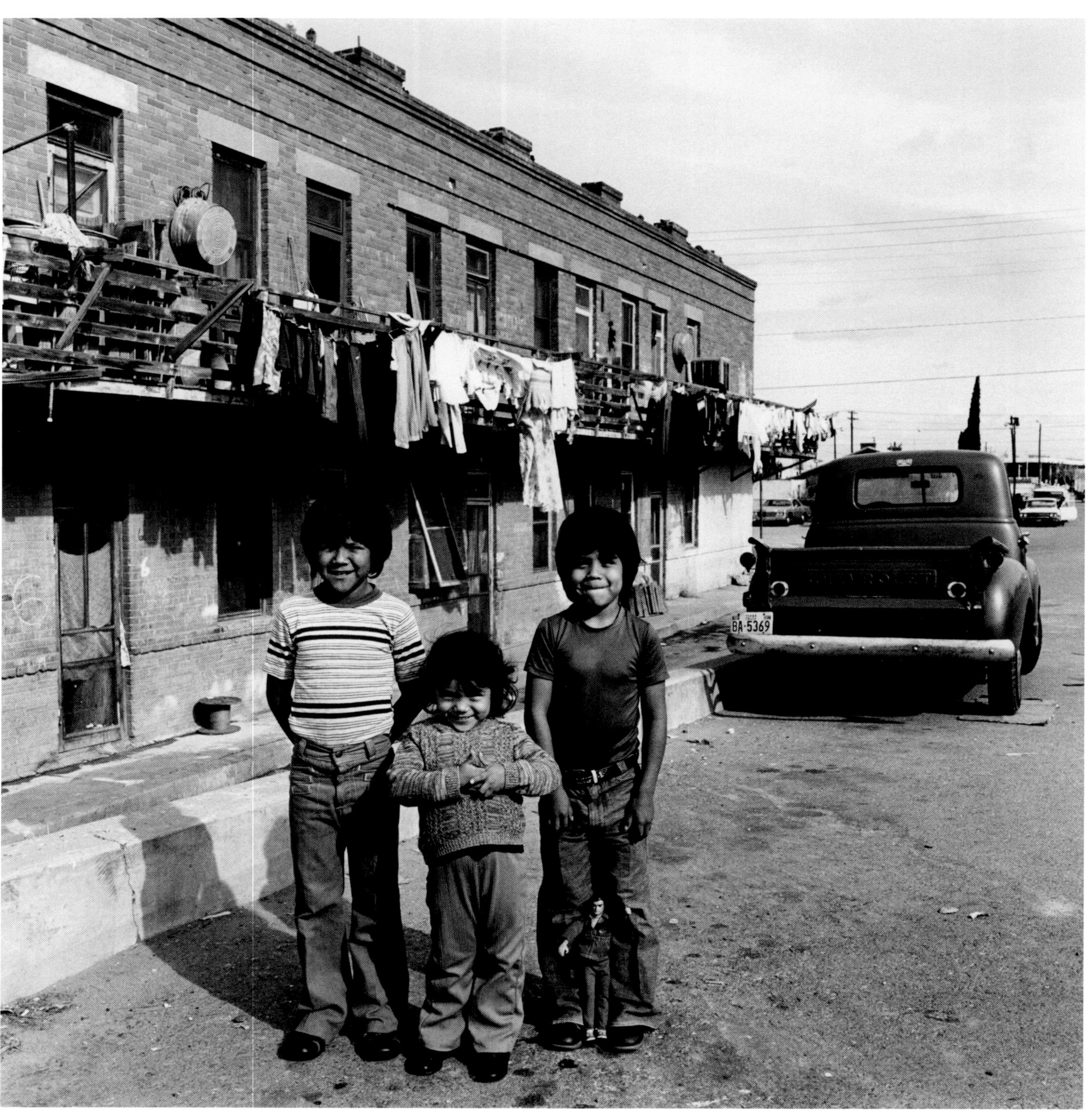

162   *Hermanos, Chihuahuita, El Paso,* 1979

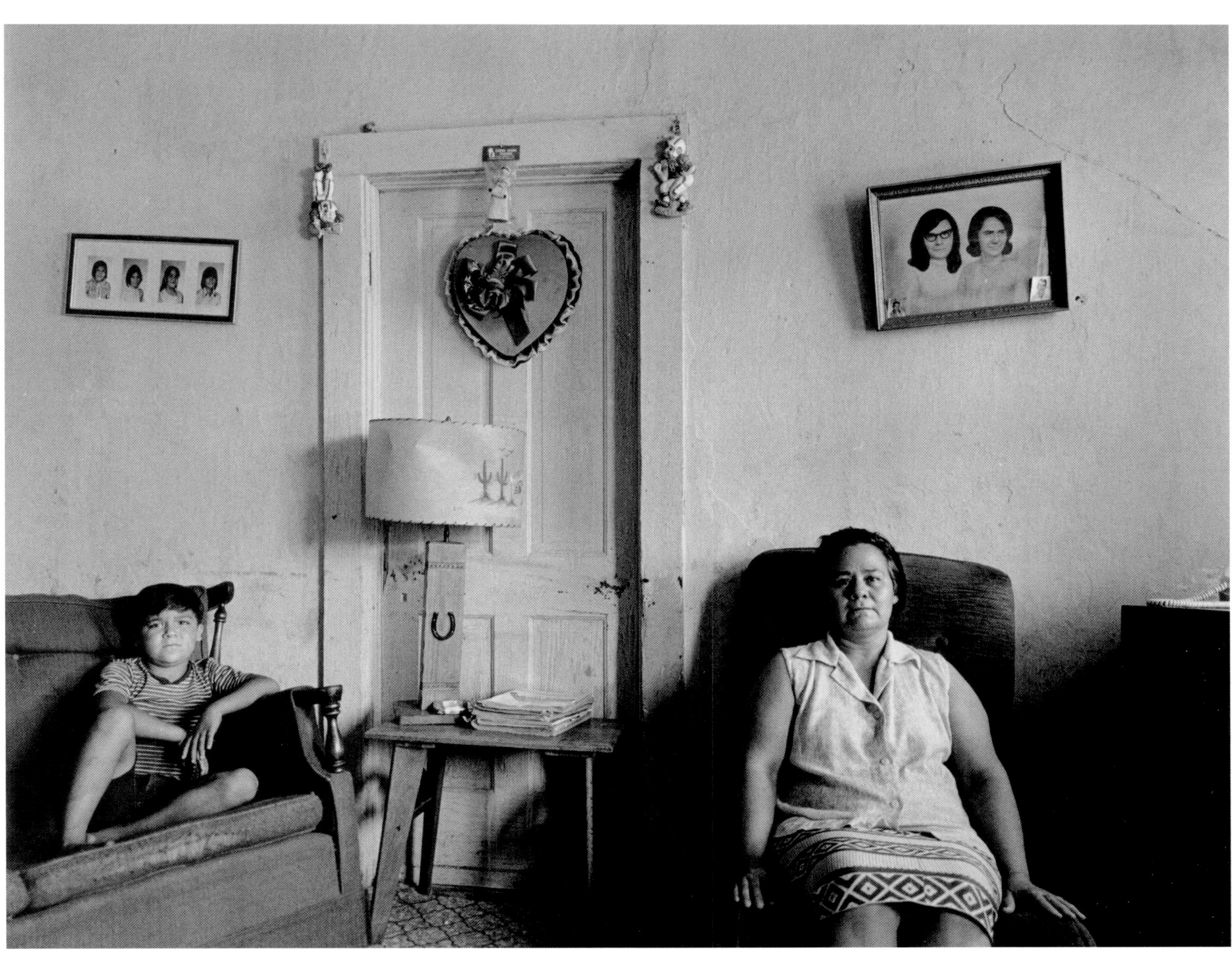

163   *Mother and Son, 6th Street Cuadra, Douglas, Arizona*, 1979

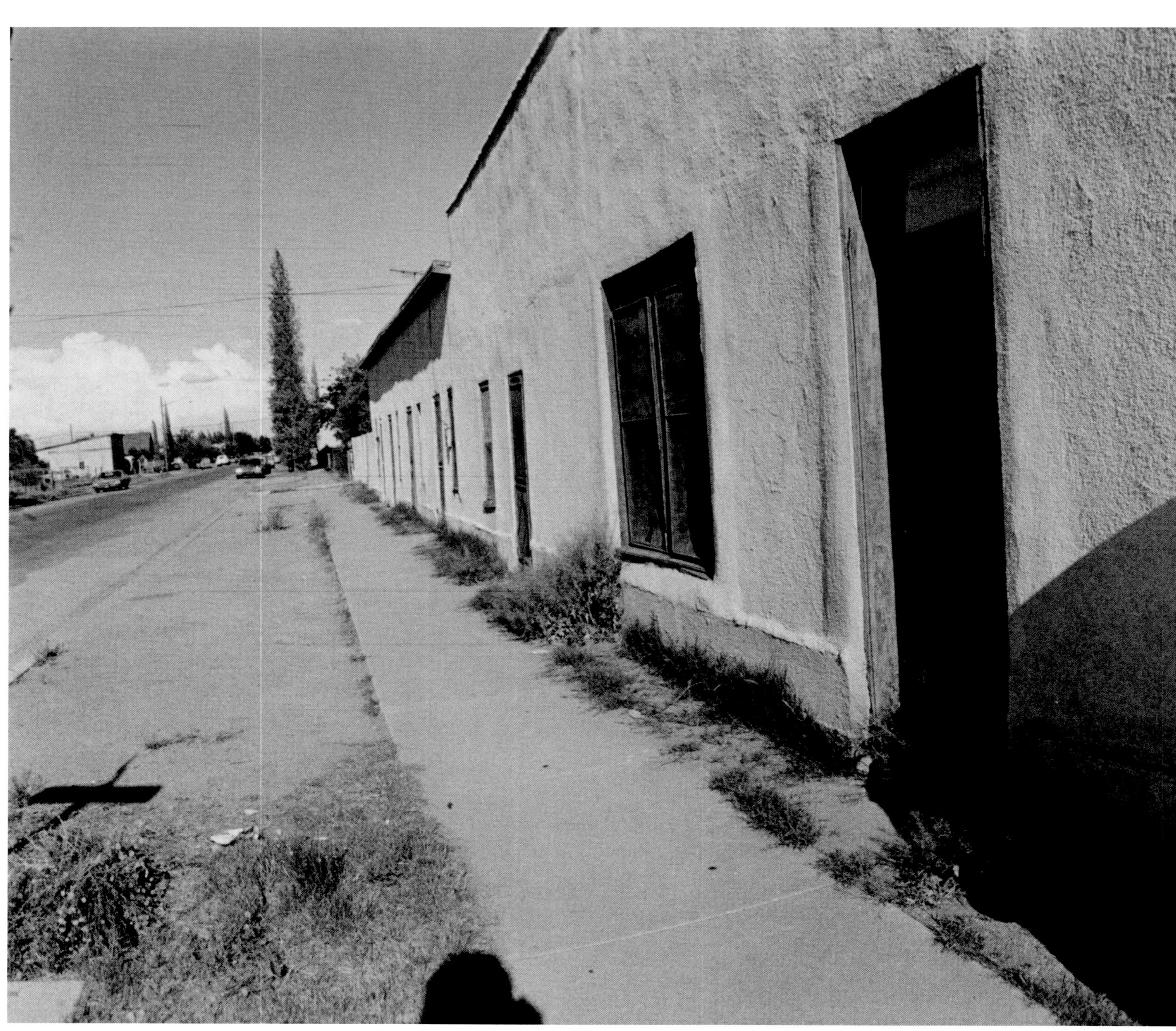

164   *4th Street Barrio, Douglas,* 1979

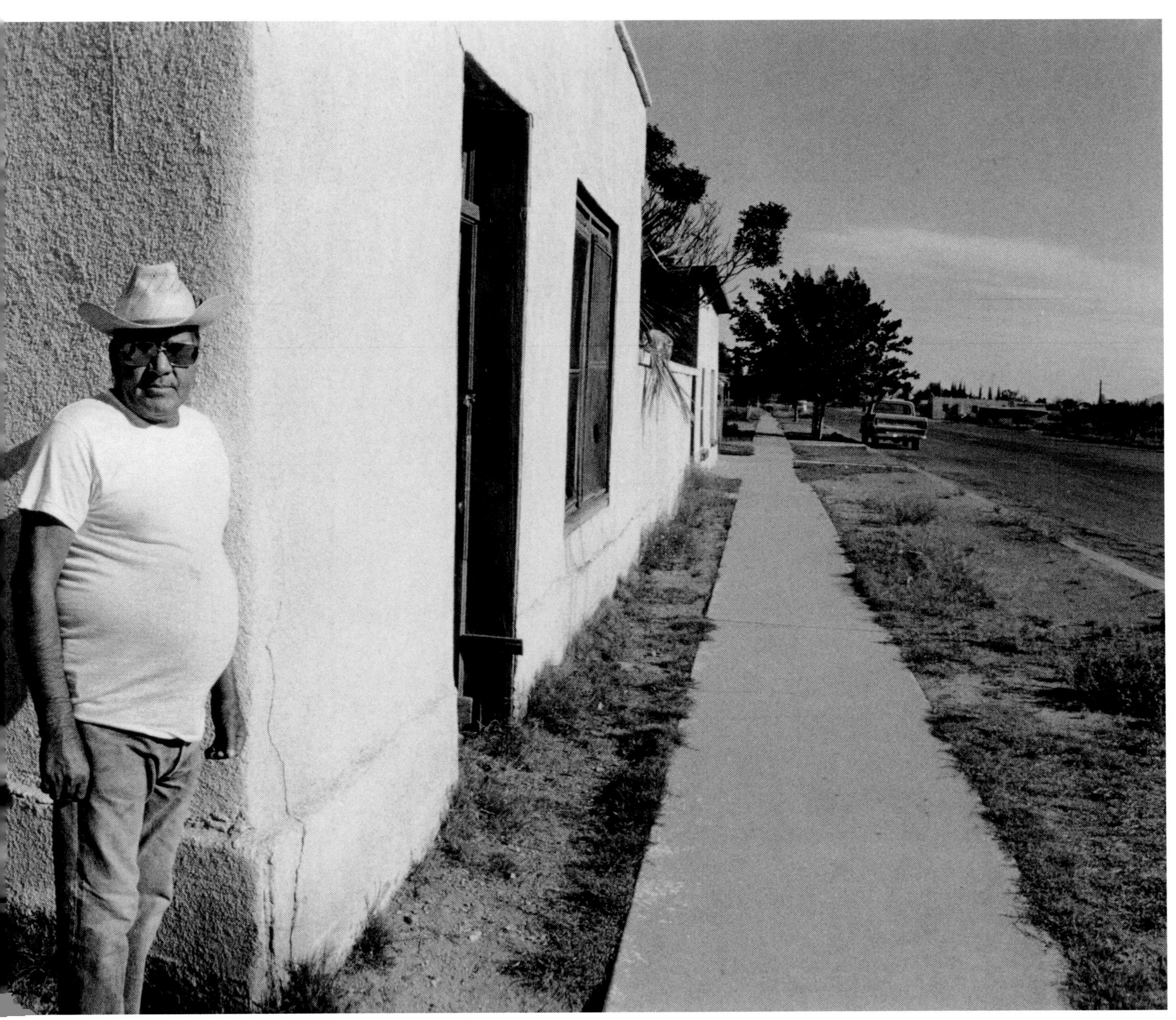

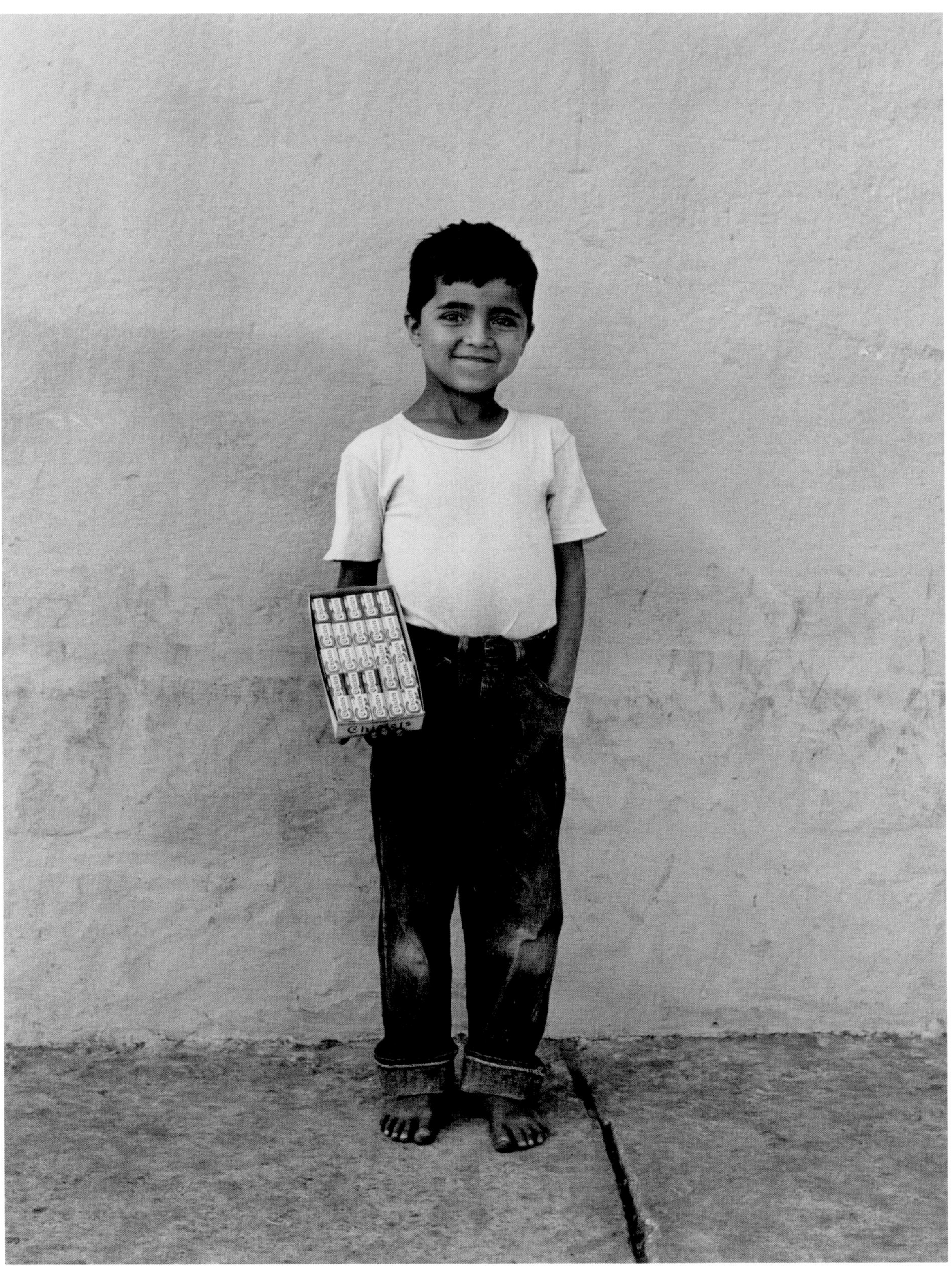

167   *Chiclets, Cuernavaca*, 1963

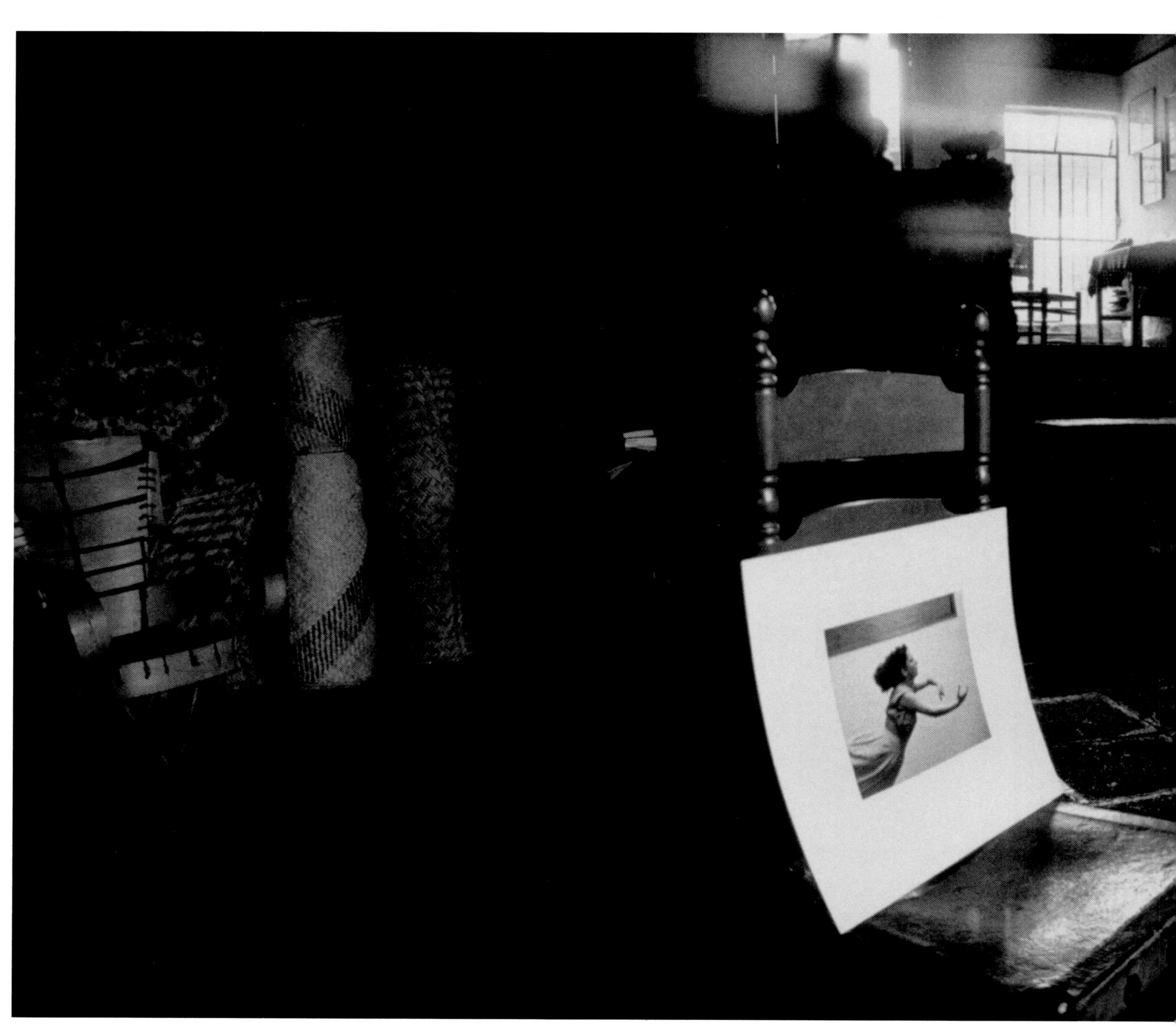

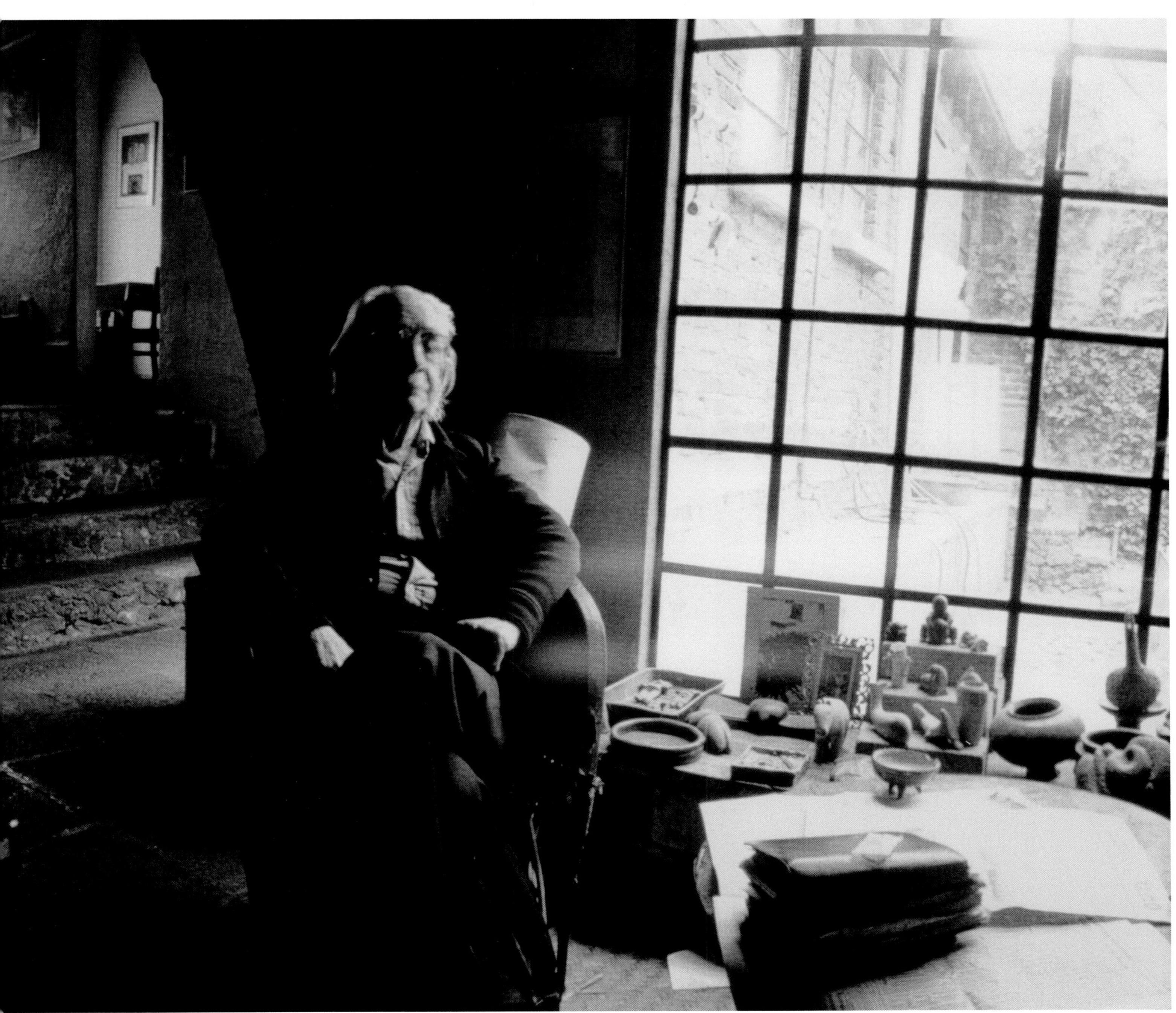

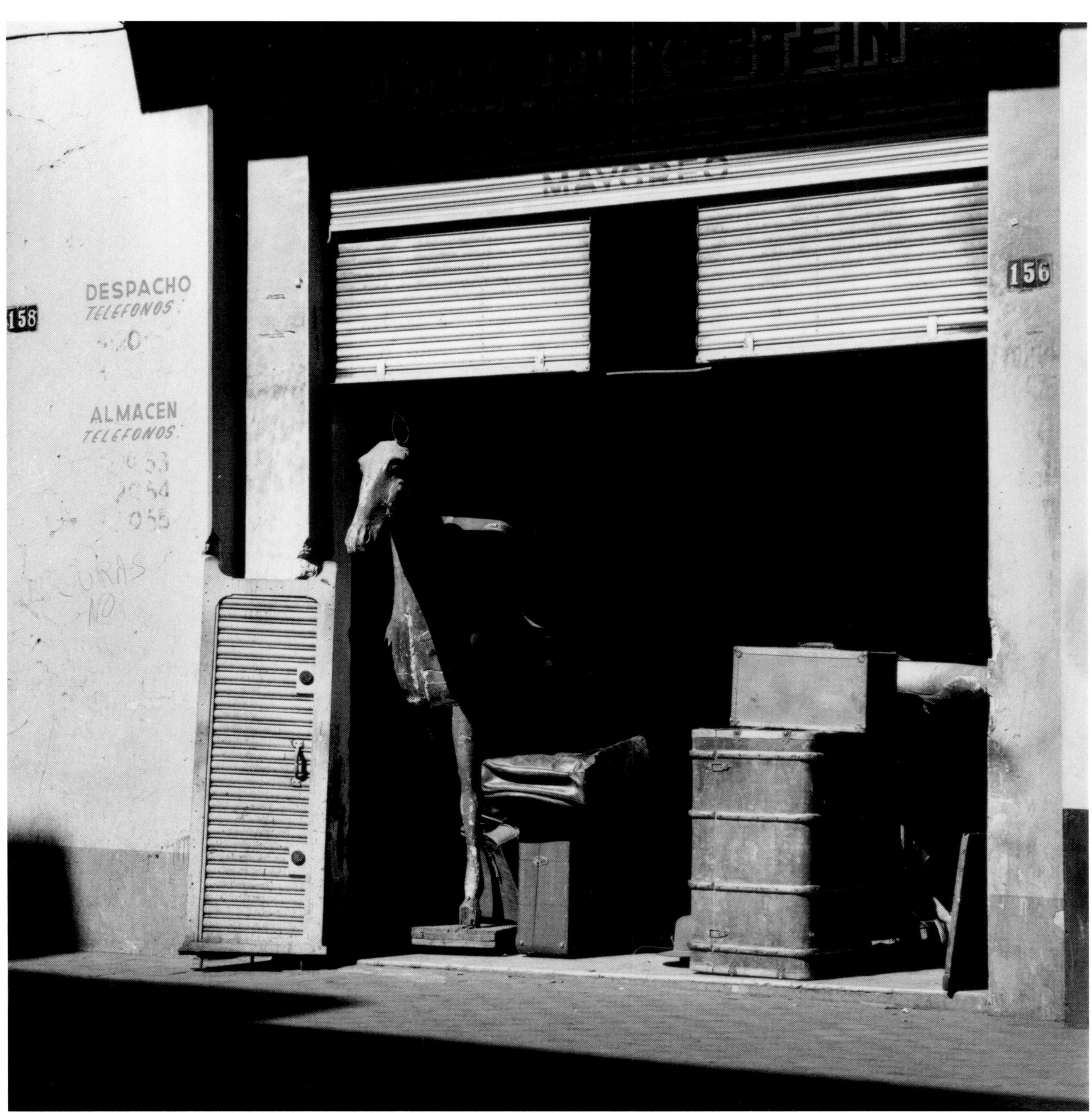

171   *Guadalajara, Mexico,* 1962

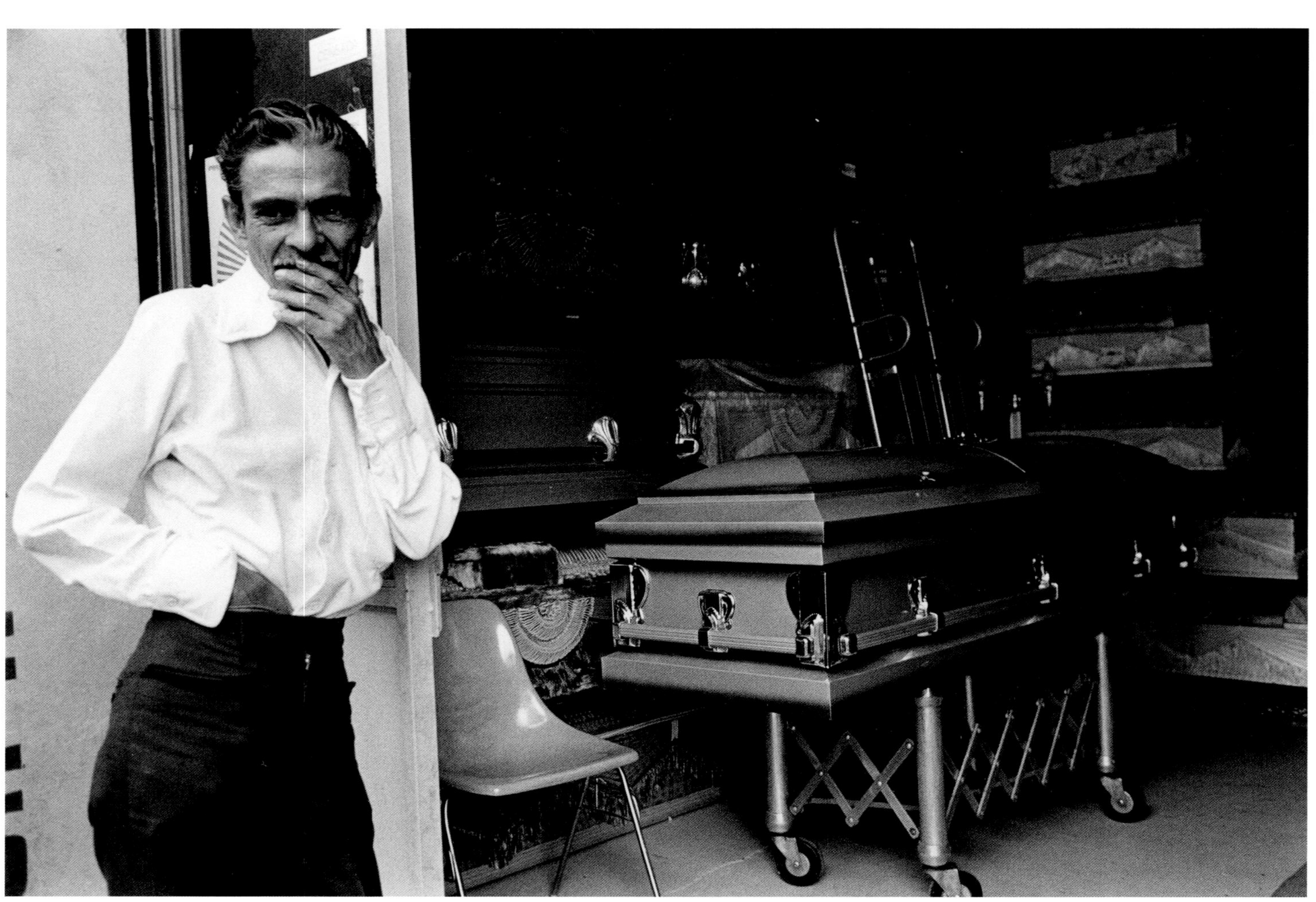

172   *La Pelona, Mexico*, 1980

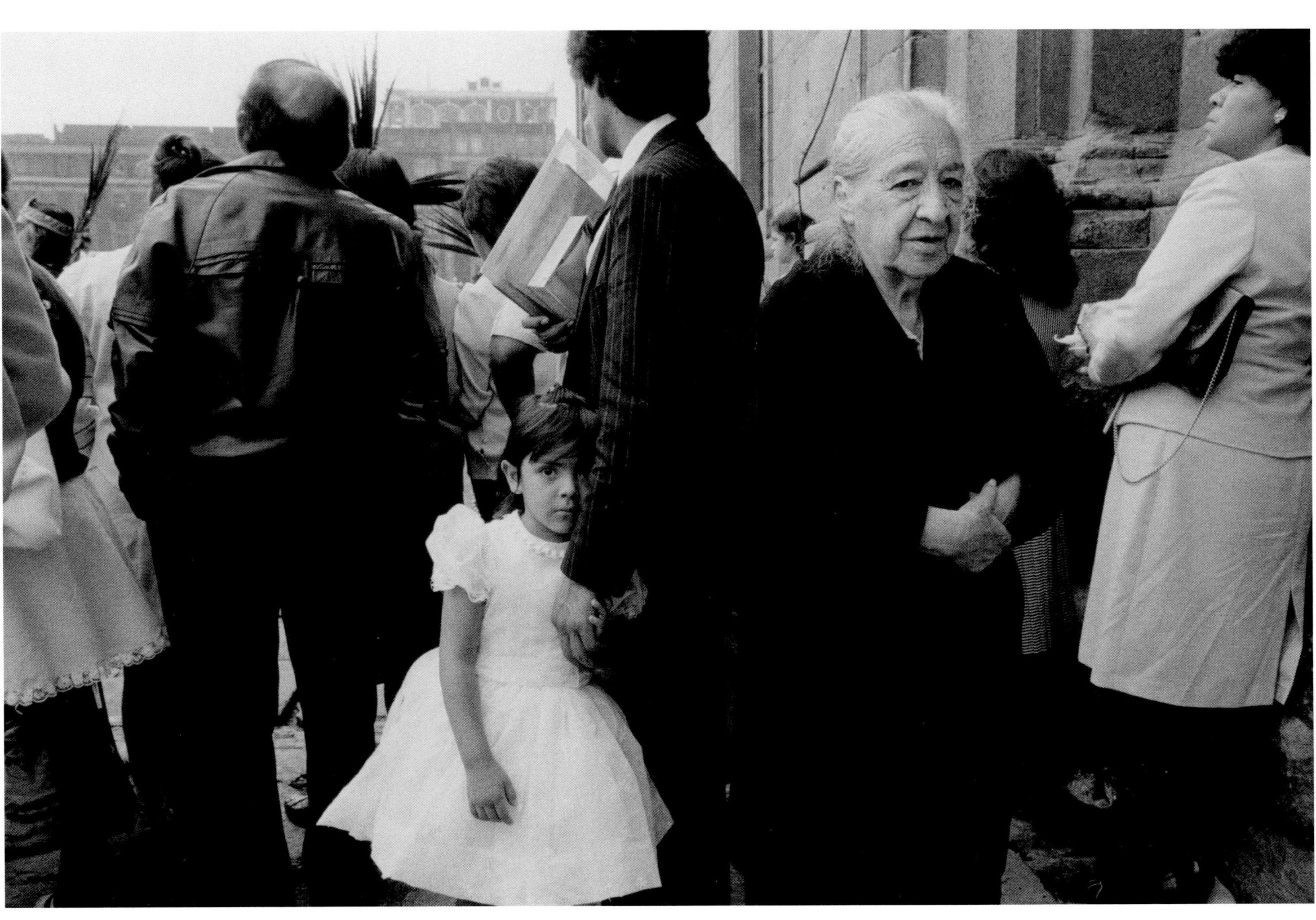

173   *Granddaughter and Grandmother, Mexico City,* 1987

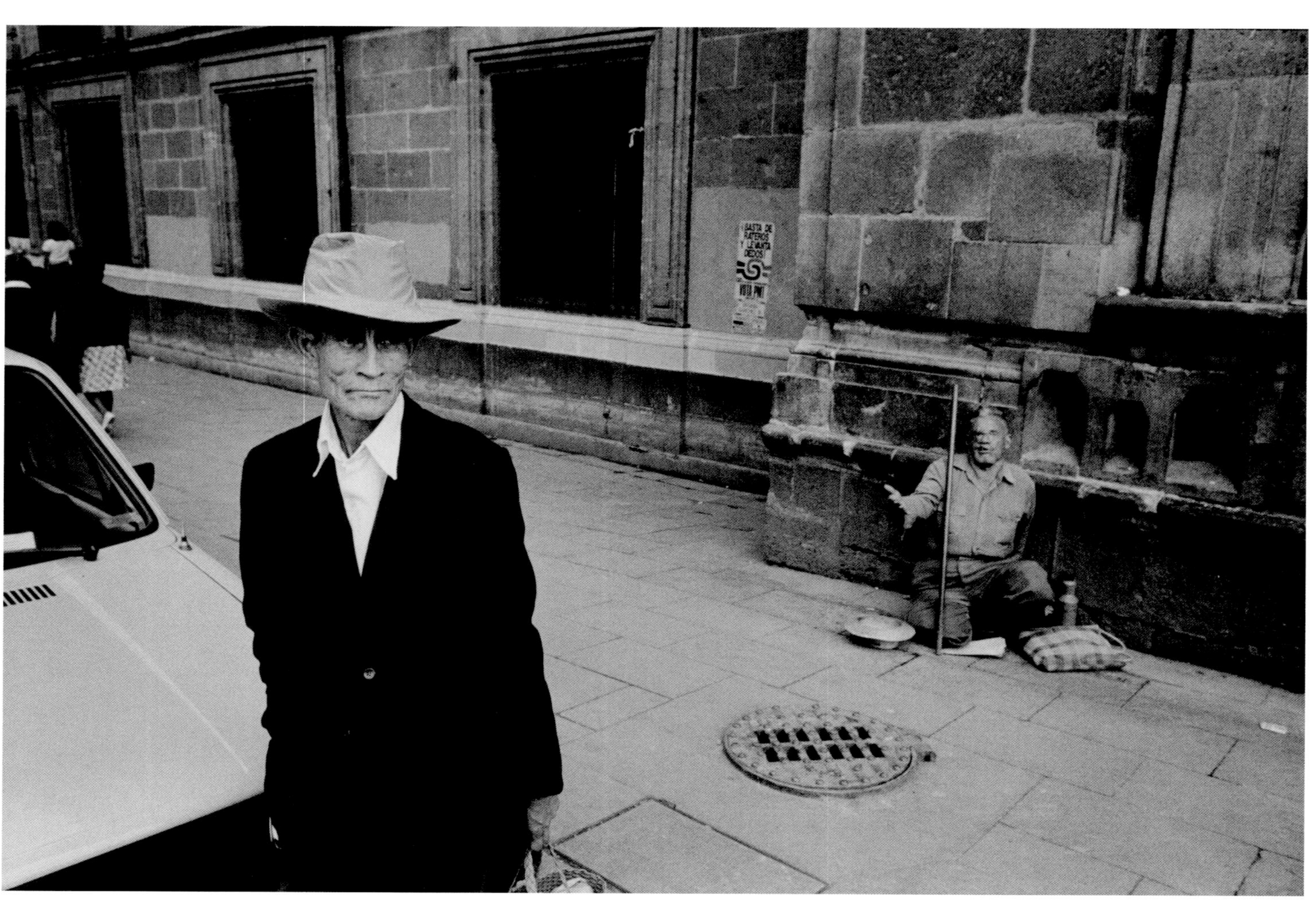

174   *El Diablo,* ca. 1985

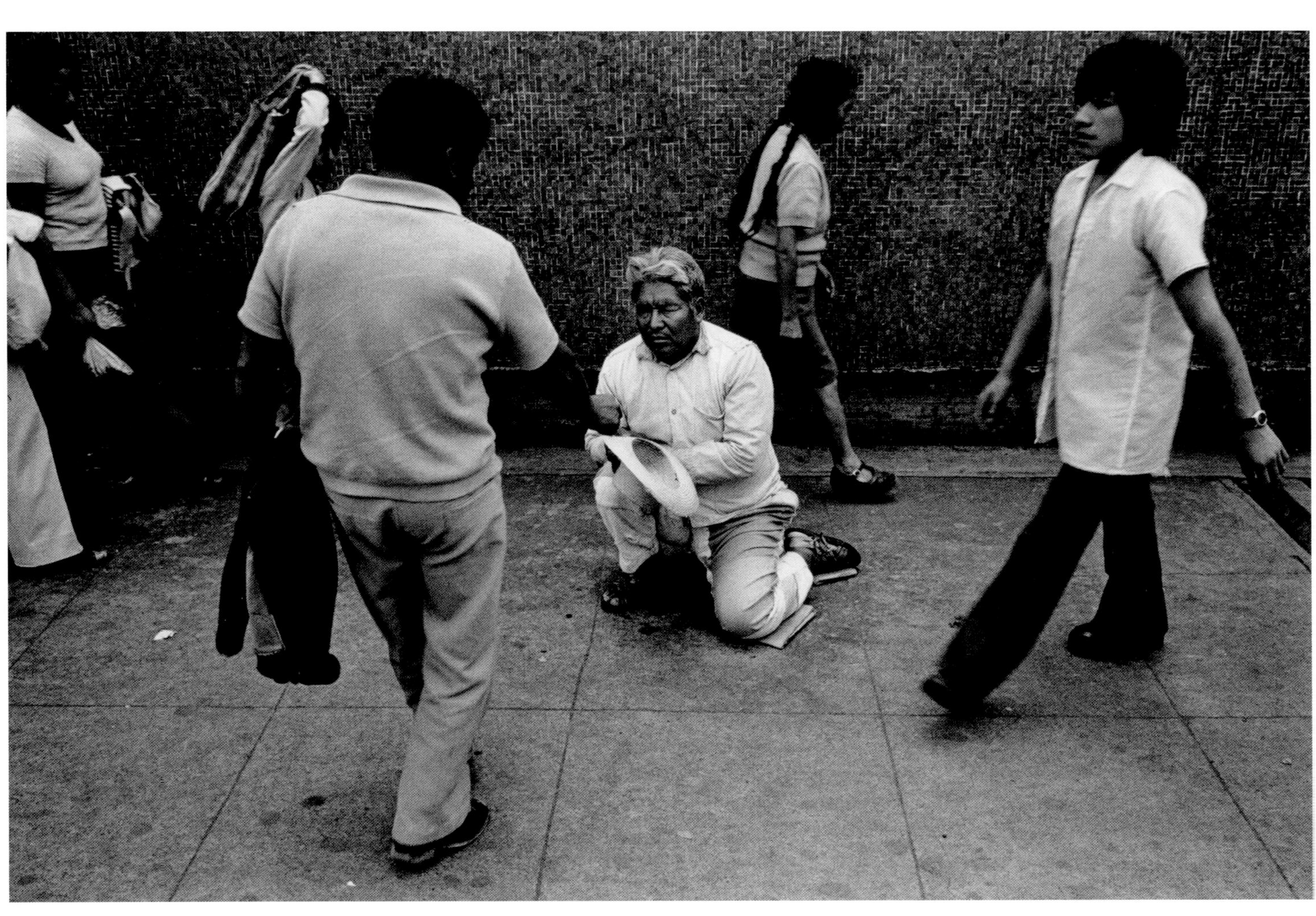

175   *Cristo de la Calle, Mexico,* 1988

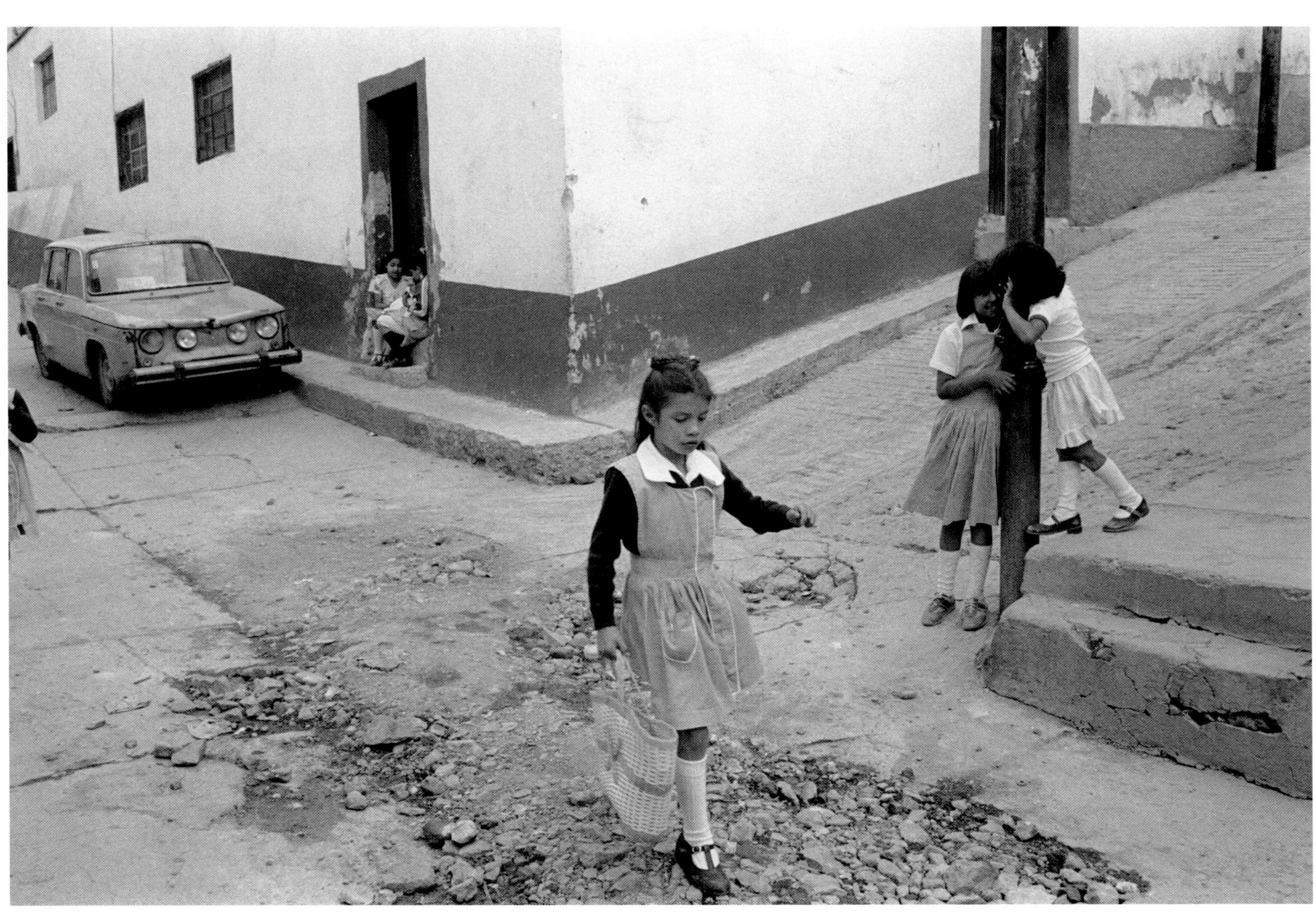

177   *Untitled (School Girls), Havana, Cuba,* 1982

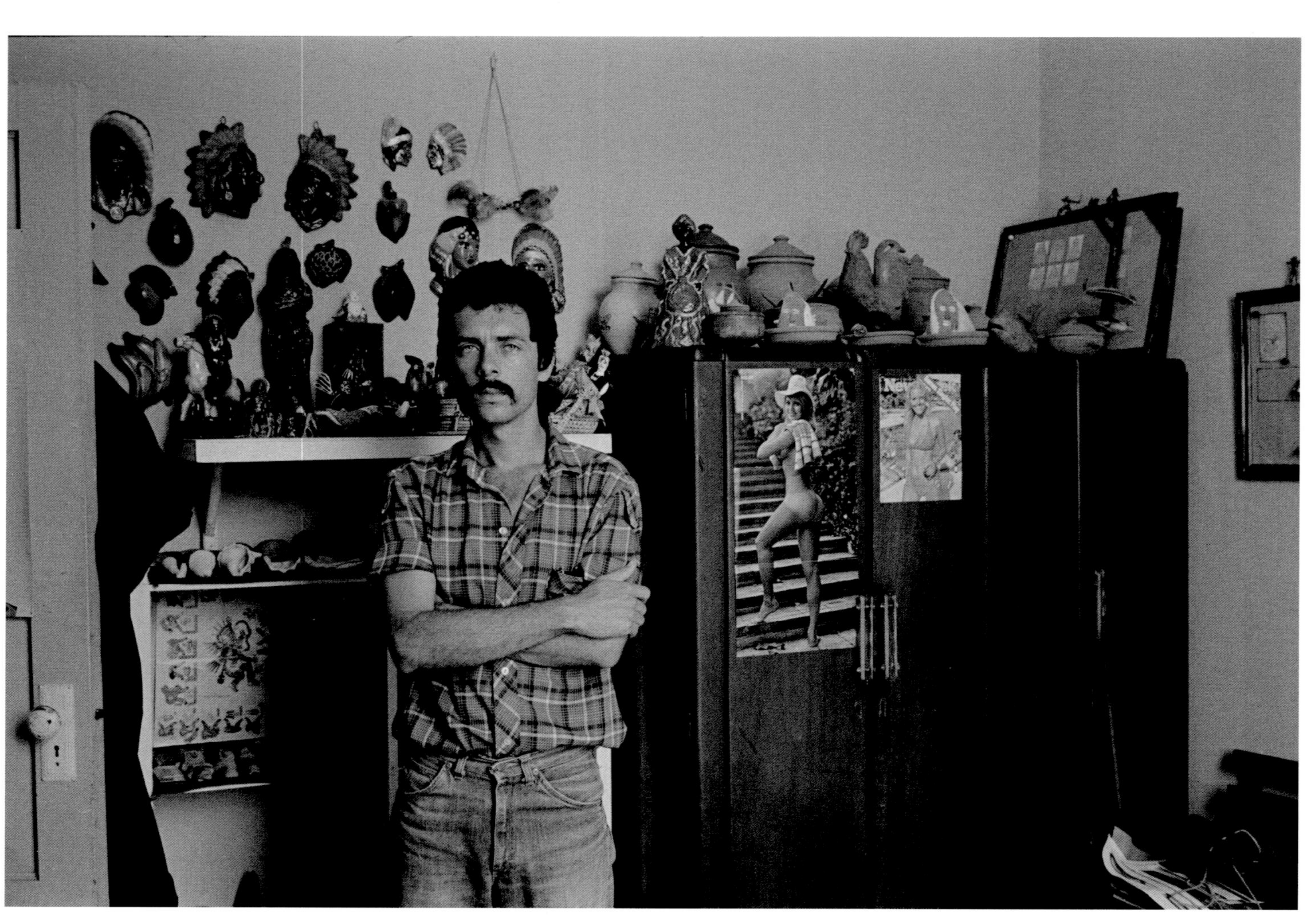

178   *Untitled (Man in interior), Havana, Cuba*, 1982

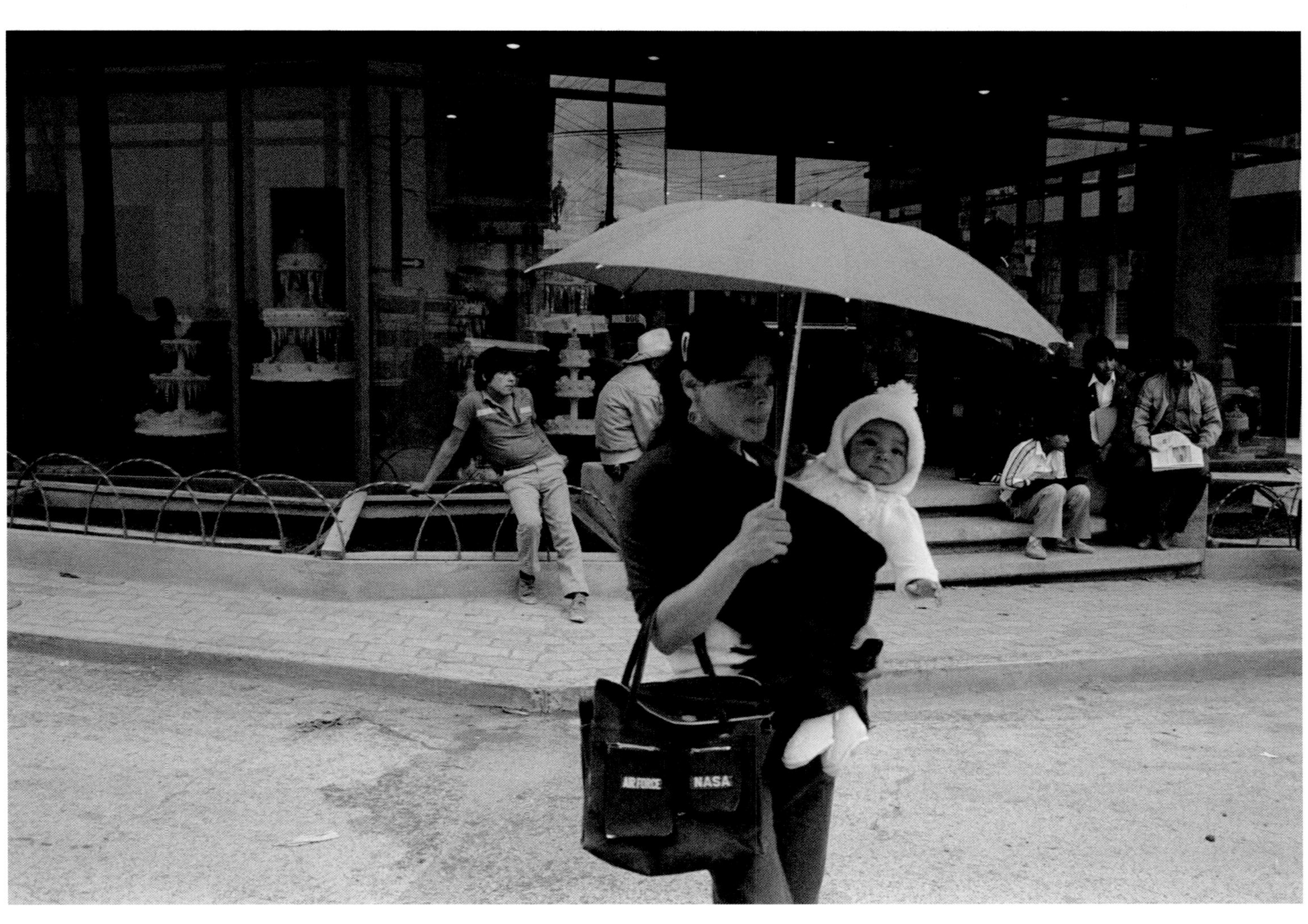

179　*Untitled (Woman with baby and umbrella), Havana, Cuba,* 1982

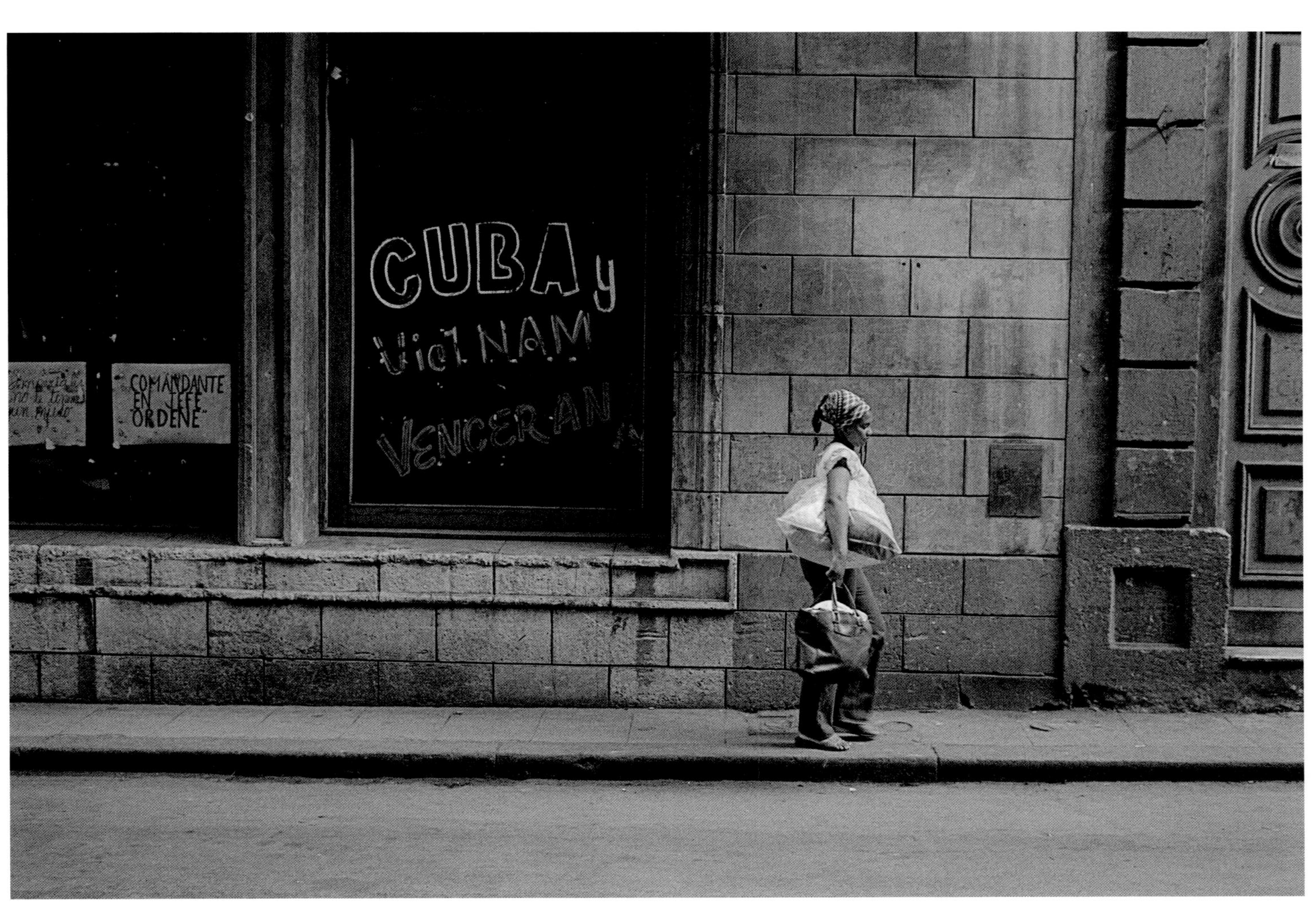

181   *Untitled (Walking Woman), Havana, Cuba,* 1982

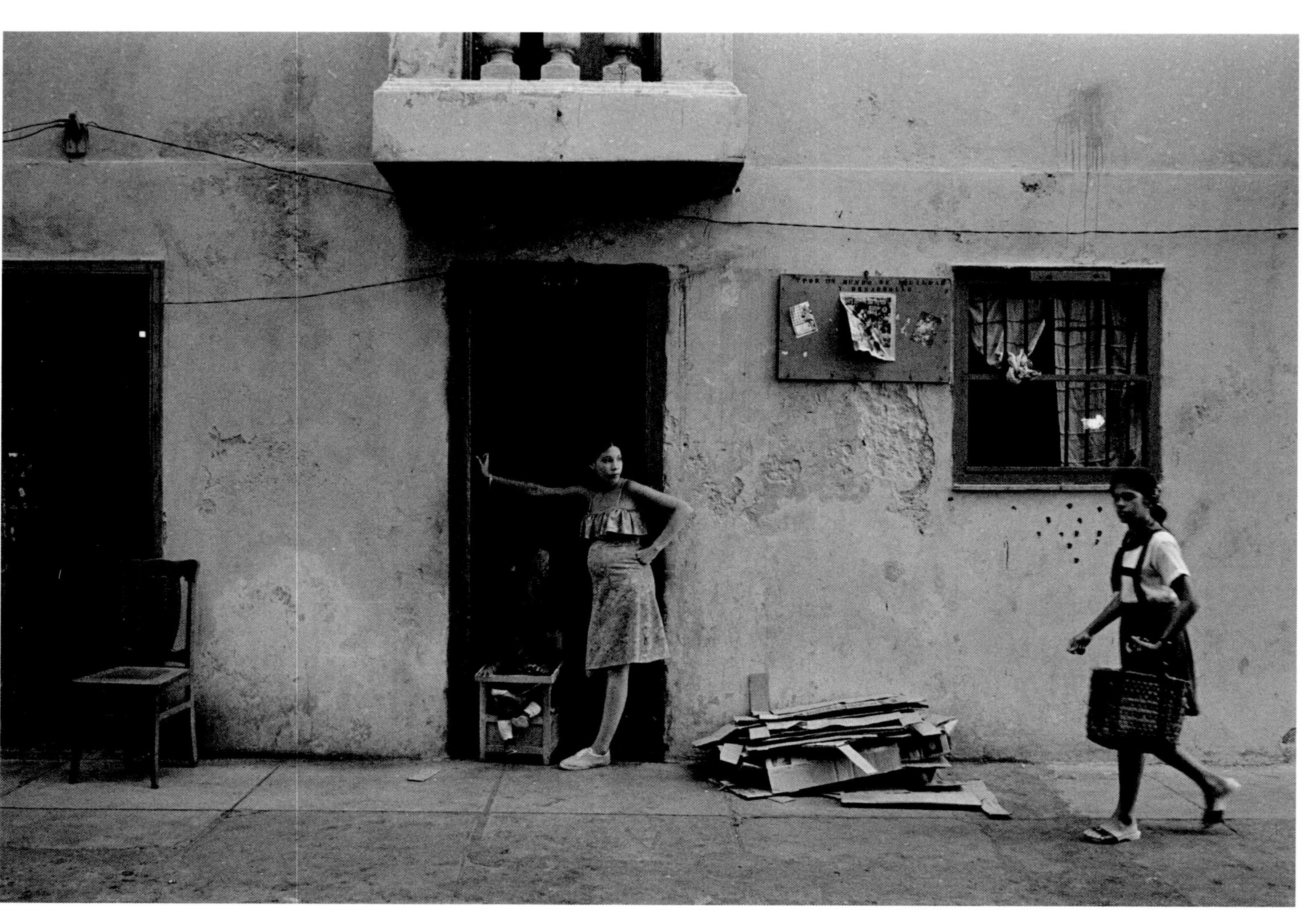

182   *Untitled (Street scene with women), Havana, Cuba*, 1982

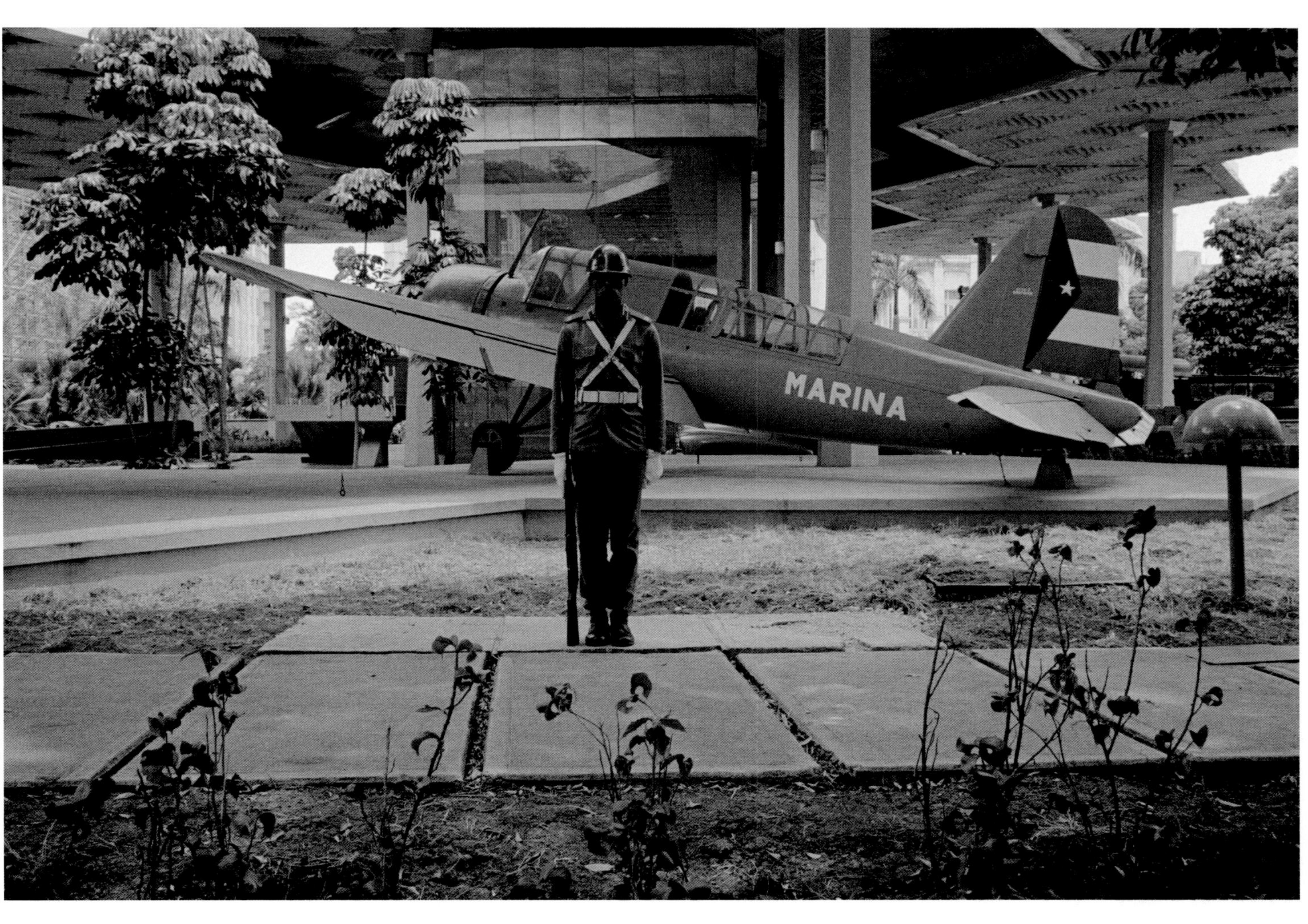

183   *Untitled (Military Guard), Havana, Cuba,* 1982

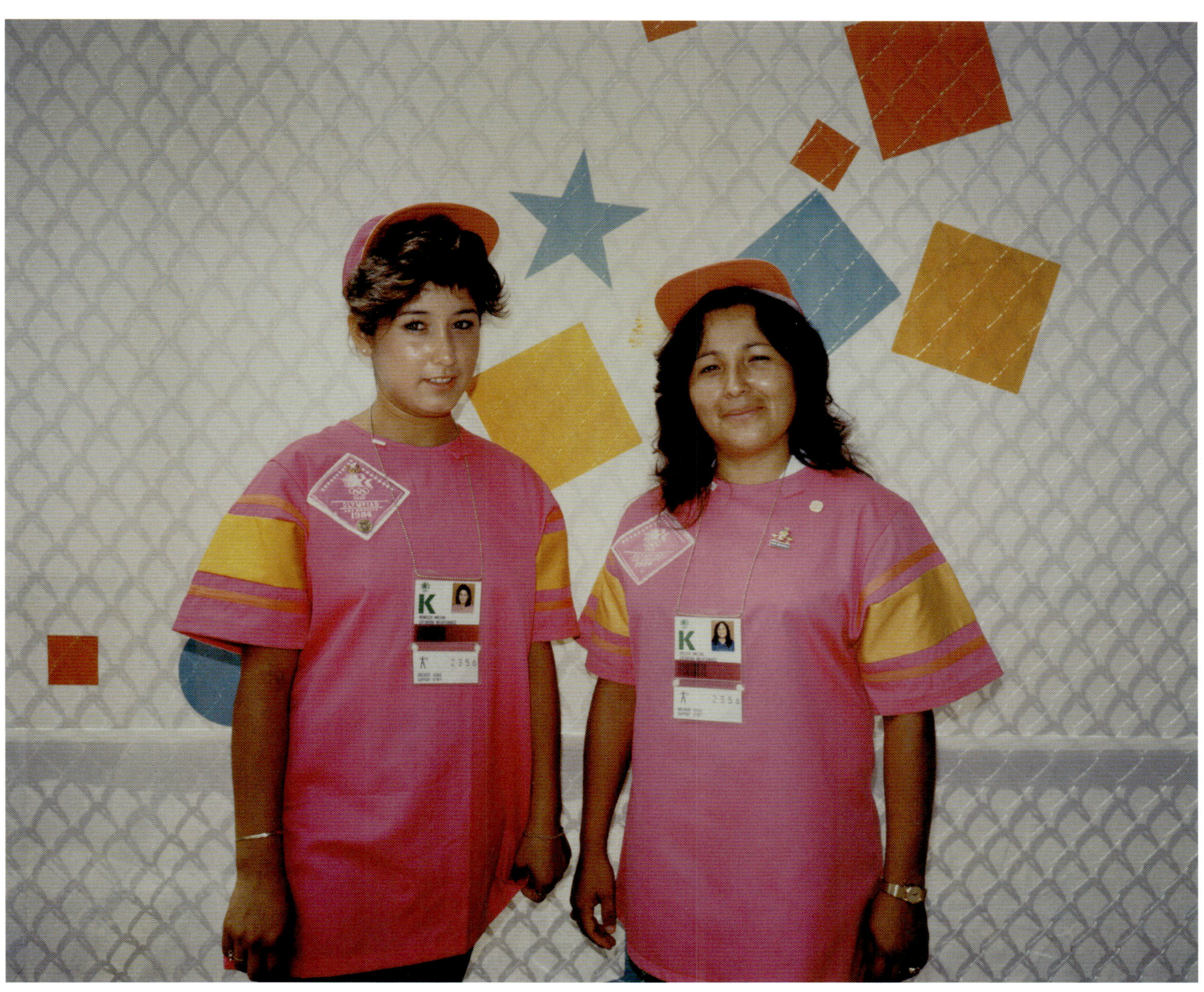

185   *Sisters, Archery, Long Beach, Los Angeles Olympics*, 1984

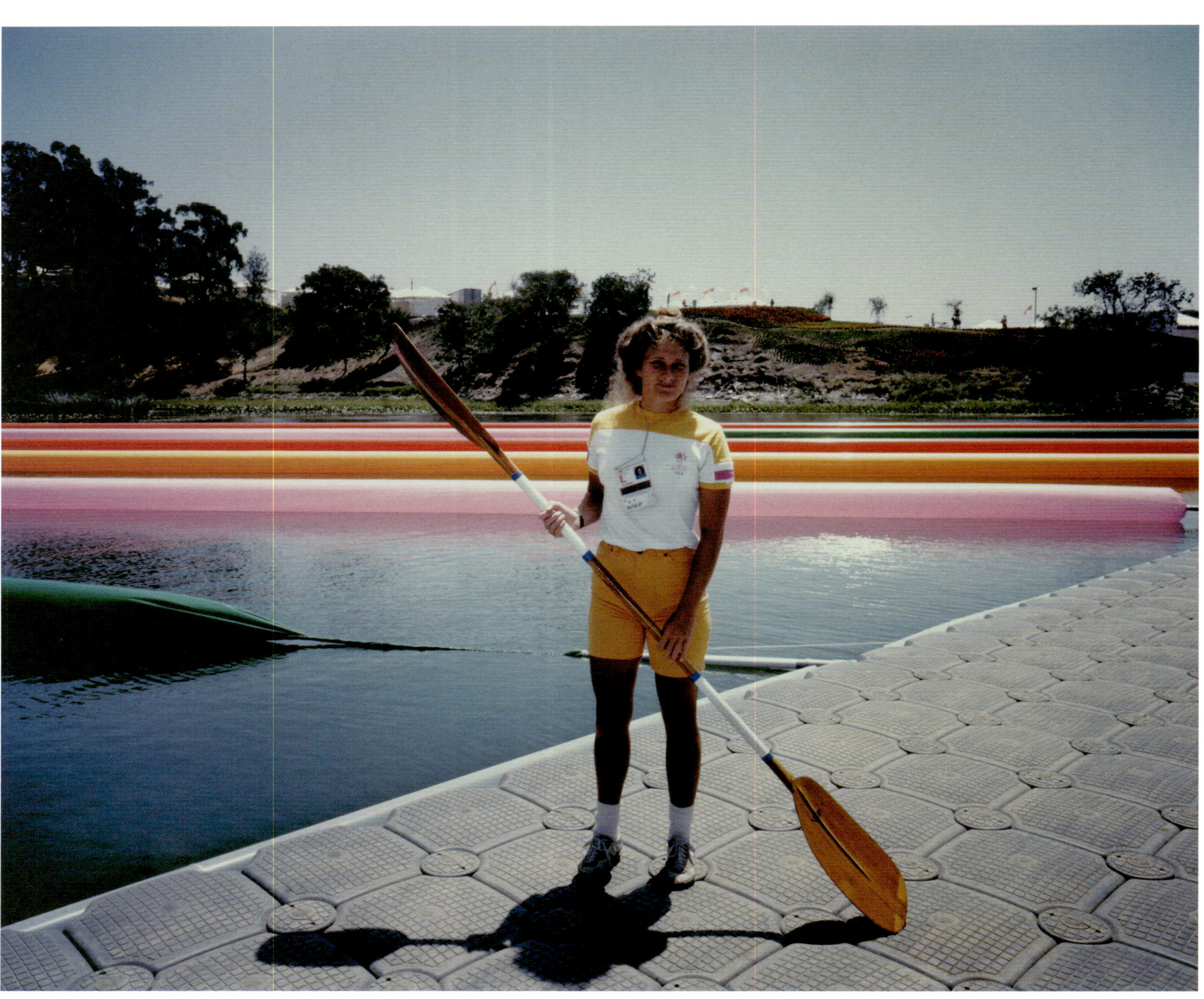

186   *Volunteers, Rowing, Lake Casitas, Los Angeles Olympics*, 1984

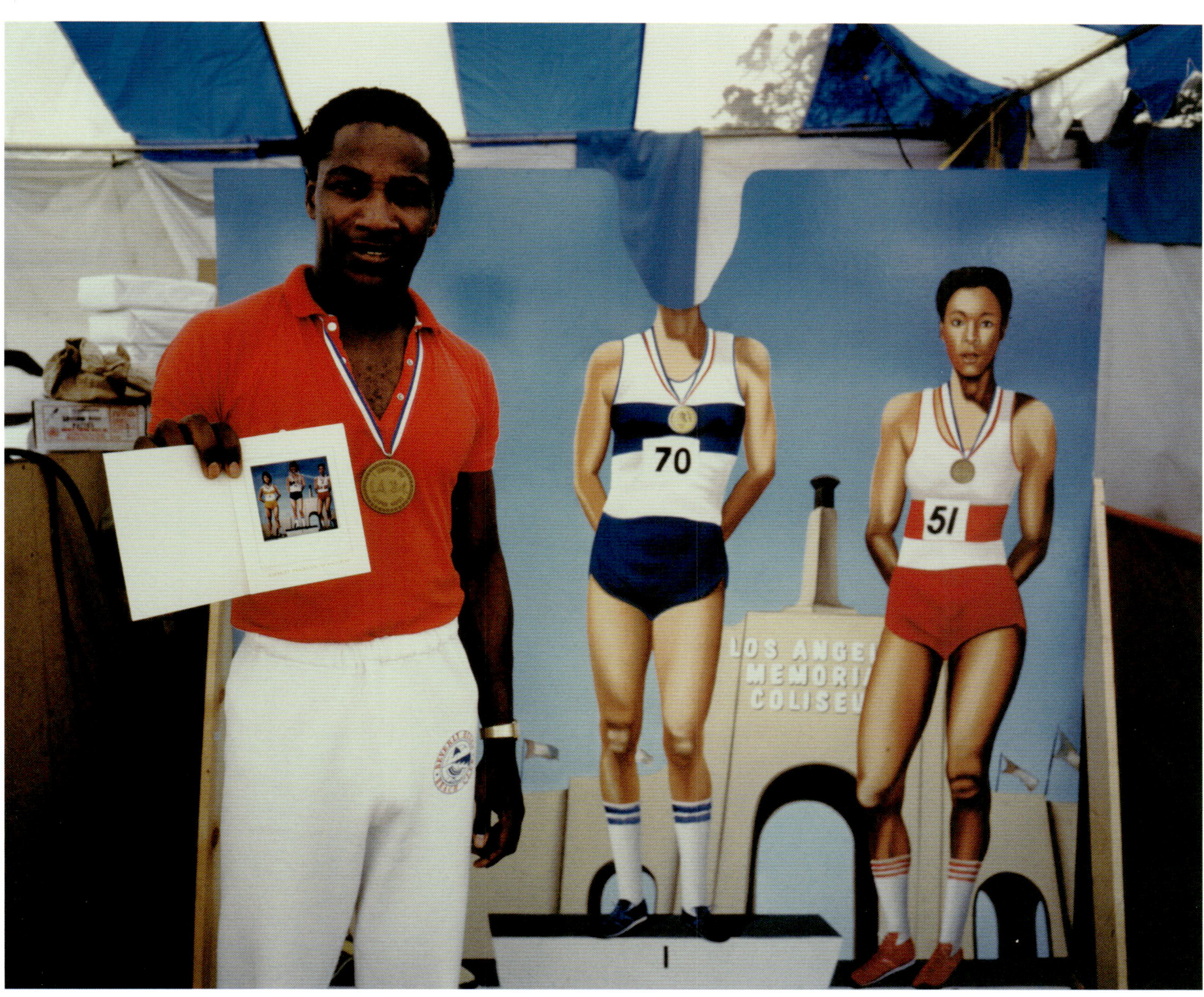

187   *Polaroid Vendor, Figueroa Street, Los Angeles Olympics*, 1984

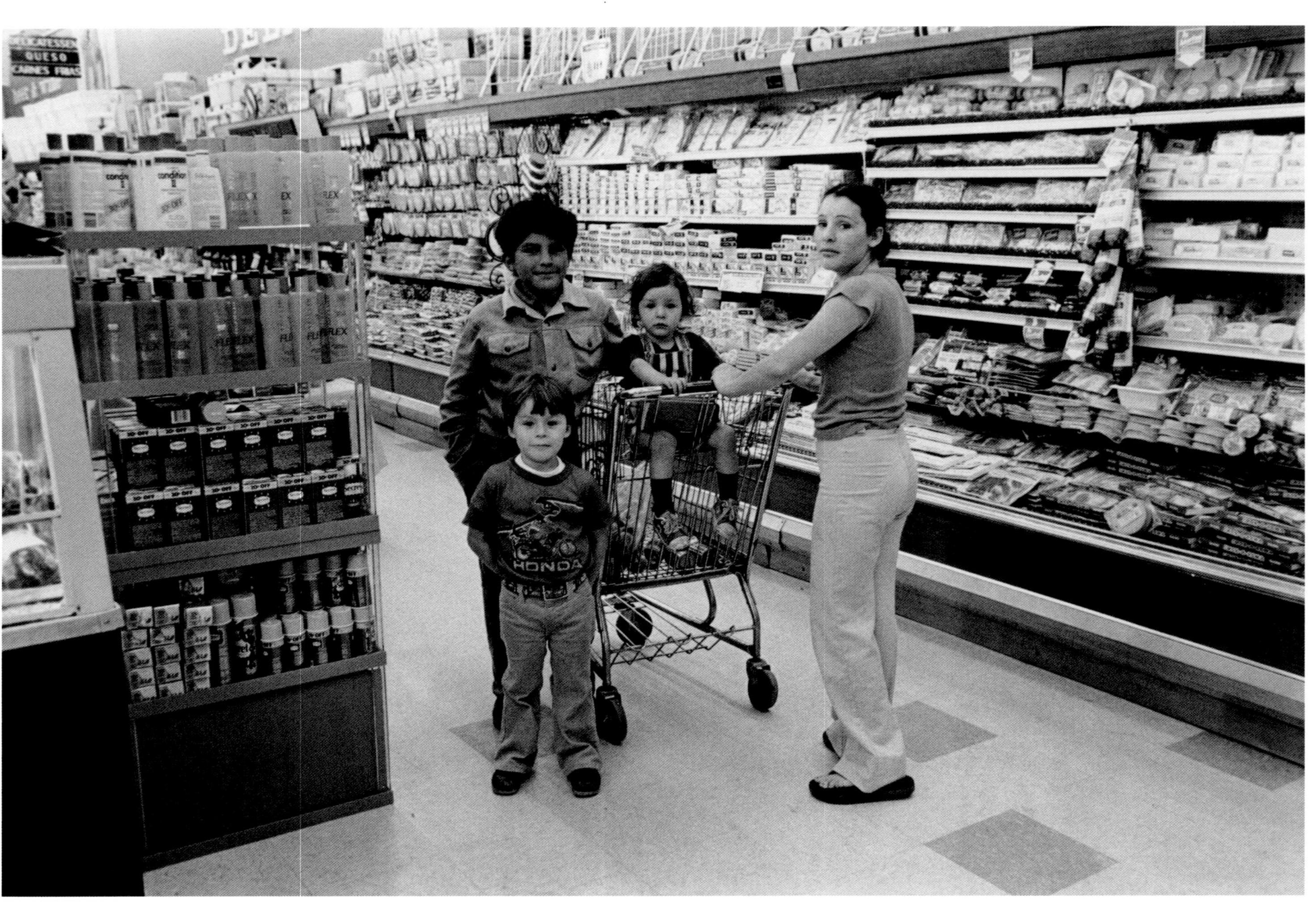

188   *Untitled (Supermarket), Los Angeles,* 1984

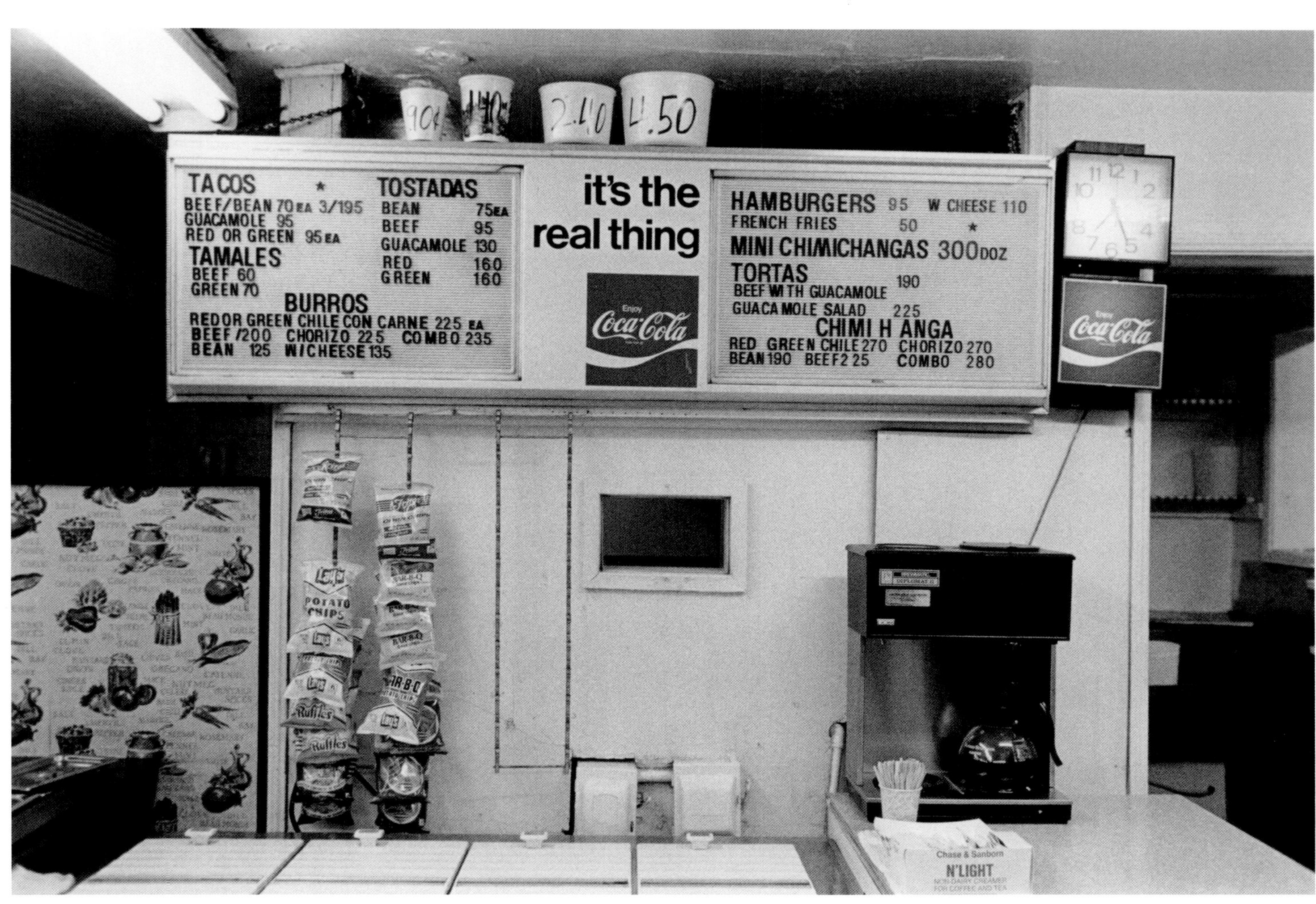

189   *Untitled (Lunch Stand), Los Angeles*, 1984

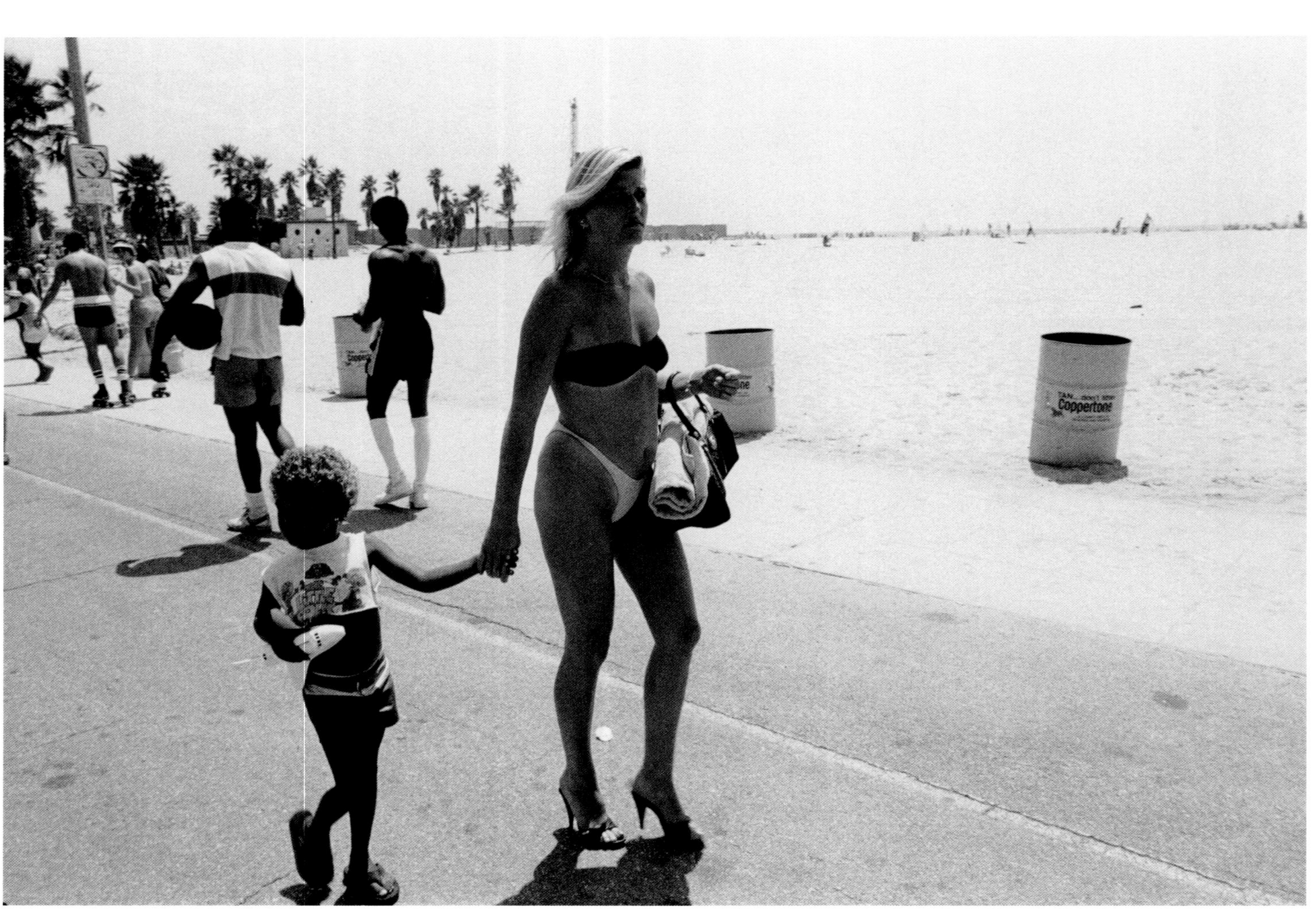

190   *Untitled (Boardwalk), Los Angeles,* 1984

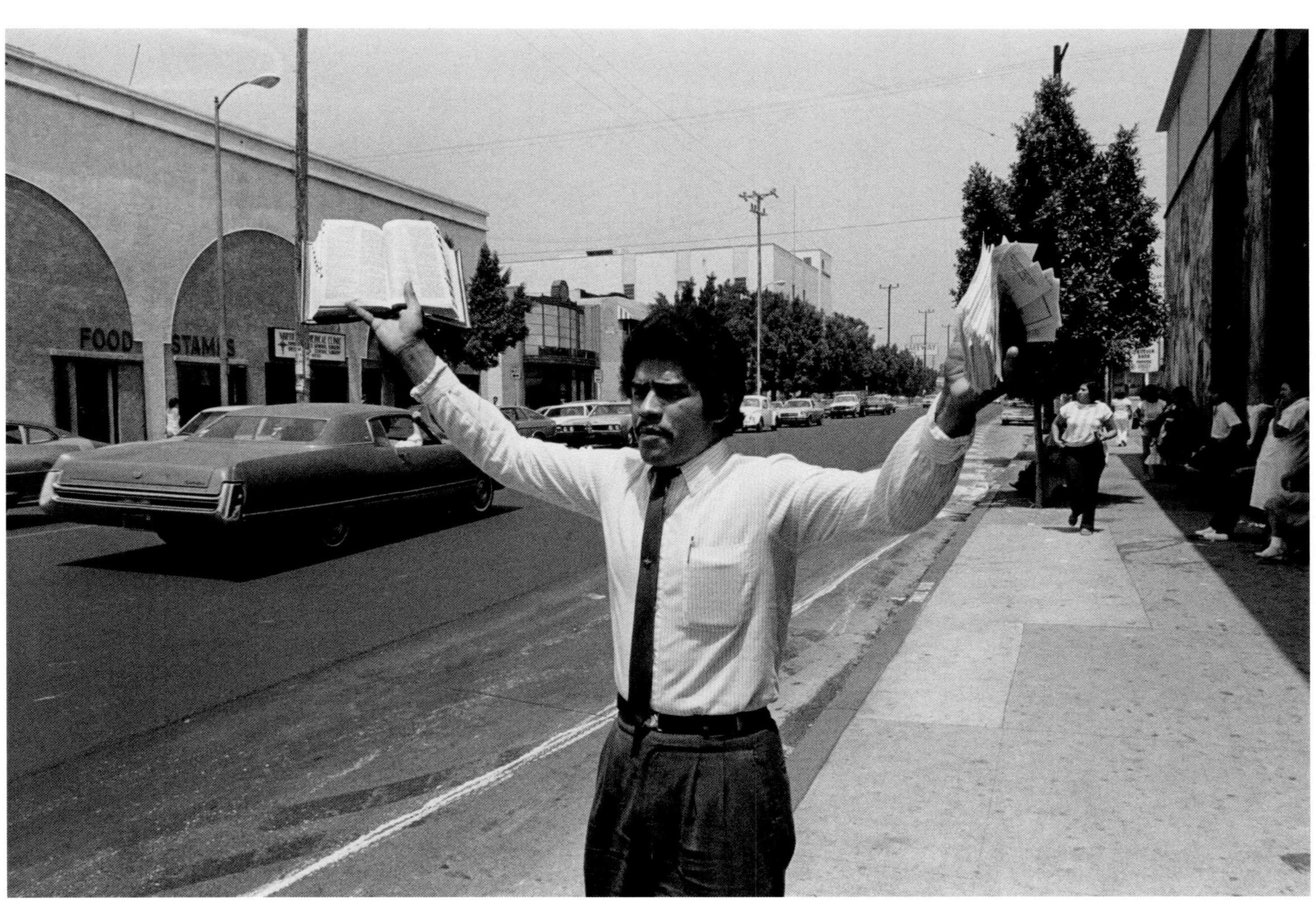

191   *Untitled (Street Preacher), Los Angeles,* 1984

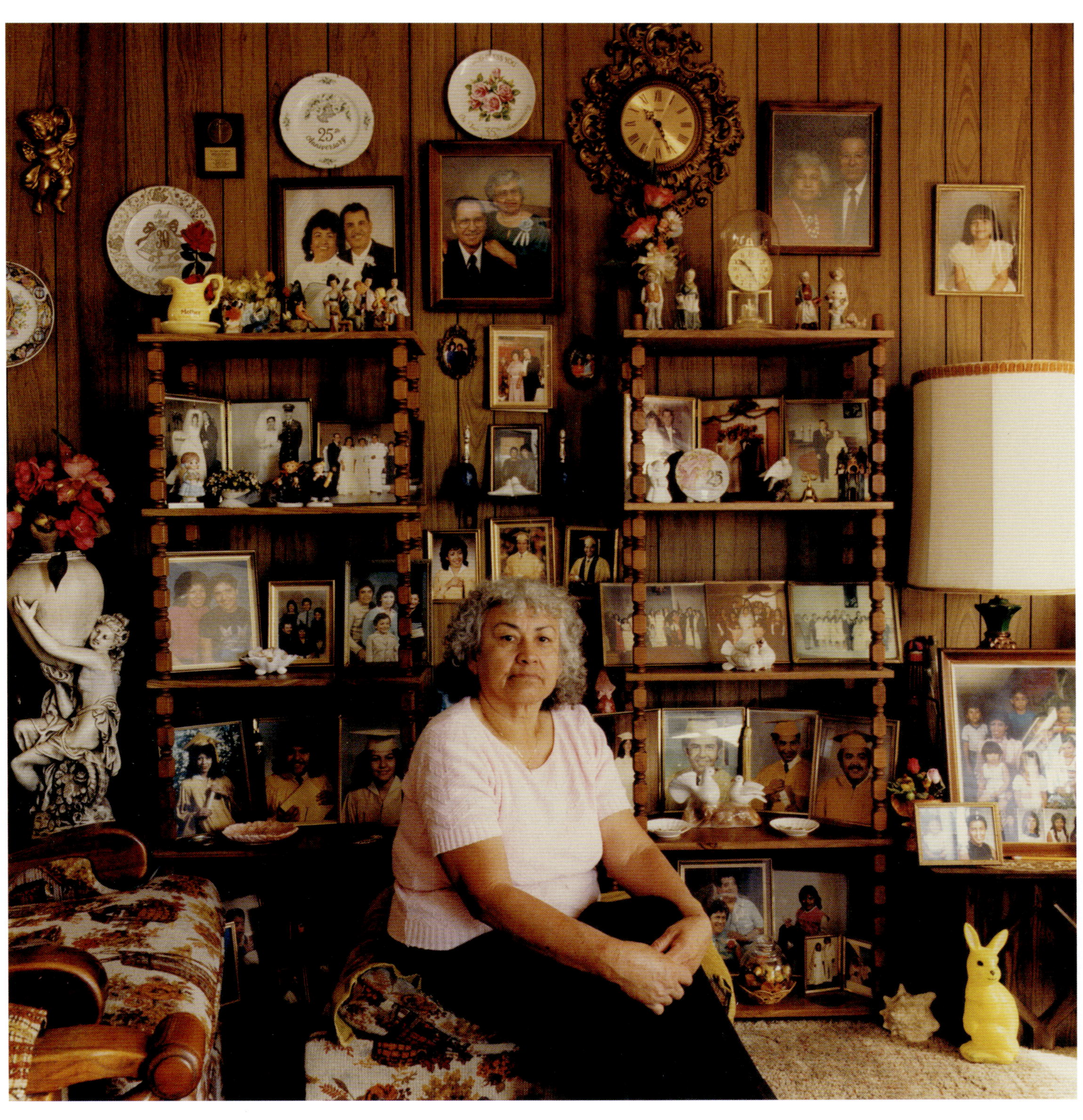

193   *Untitled*, 1988; from the series *Lubbock*

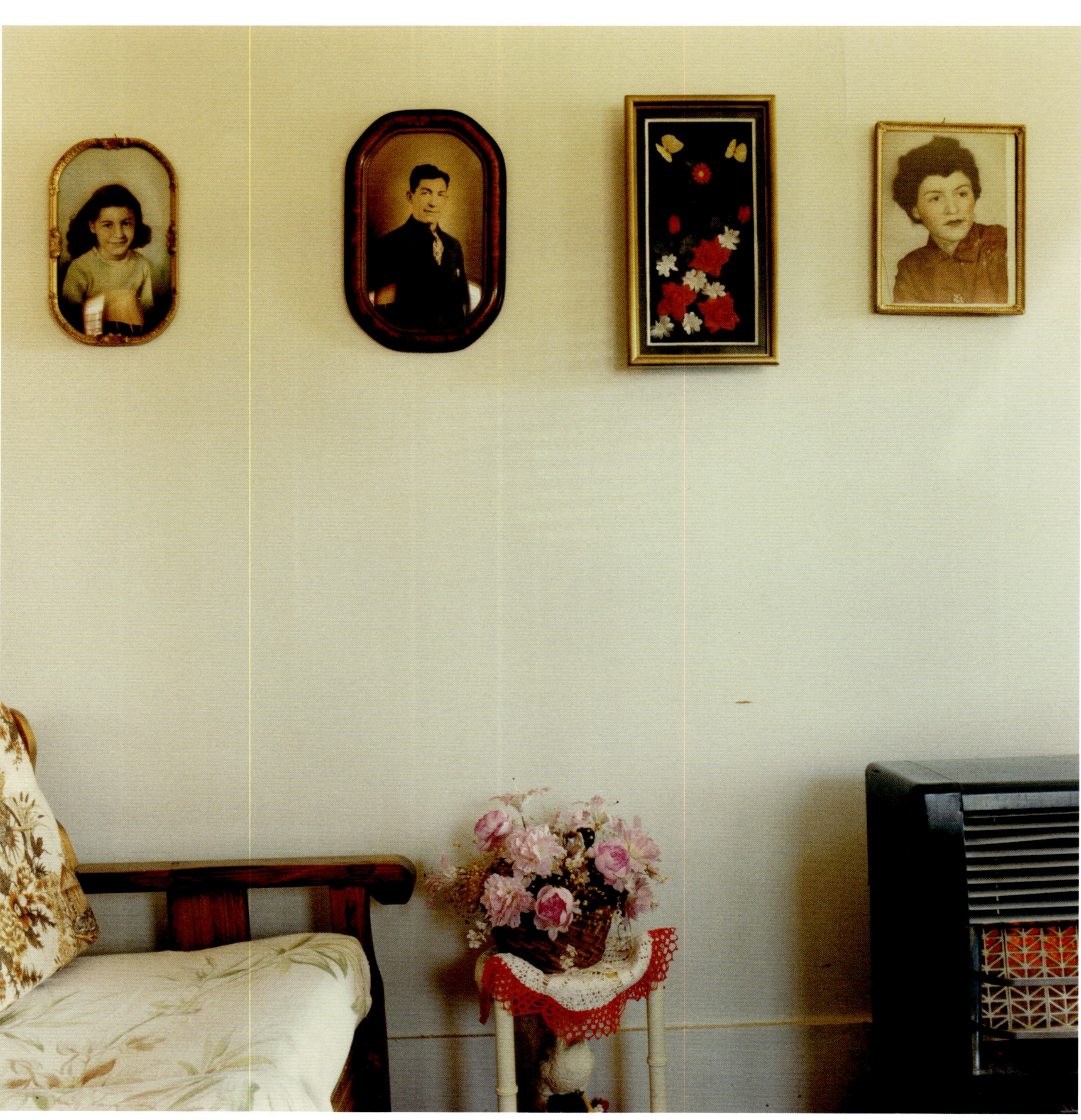

194   *Untitled*, 1988; from the series *Lubbock*

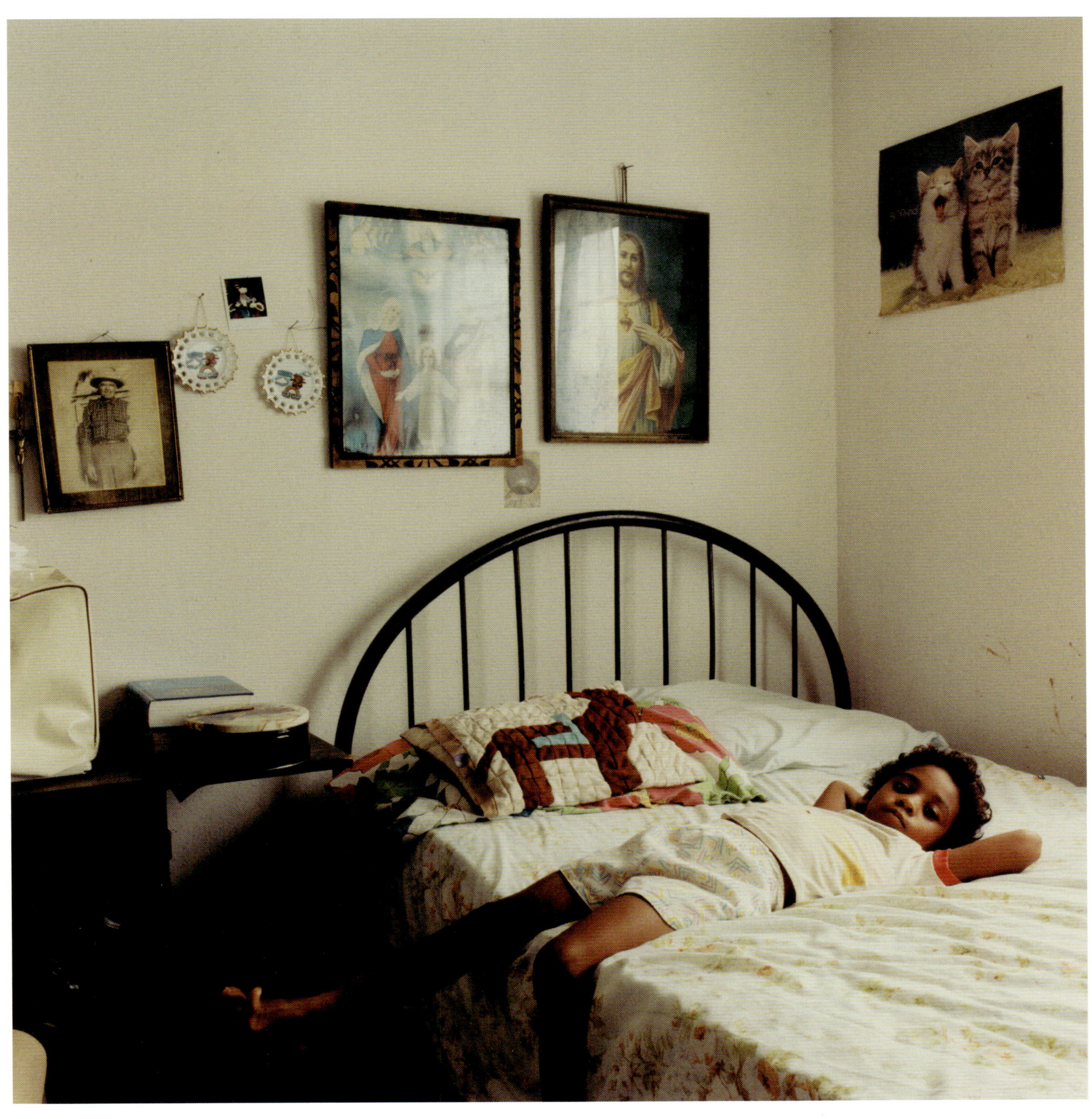

195   *Untitled*, 1988; from the series *Lubbock*

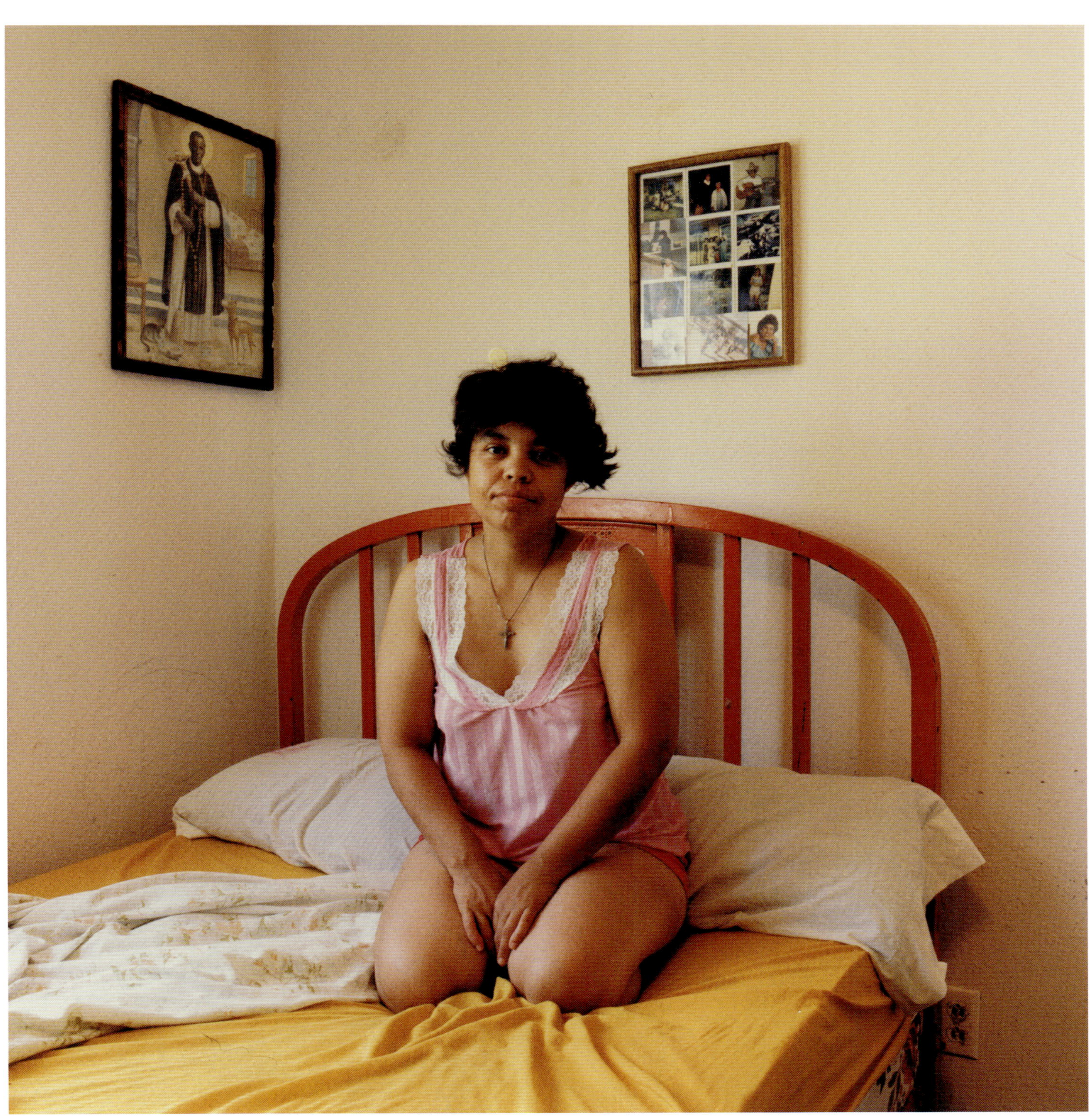

197   *Angelina*, 1988; from the series *Lubbock*

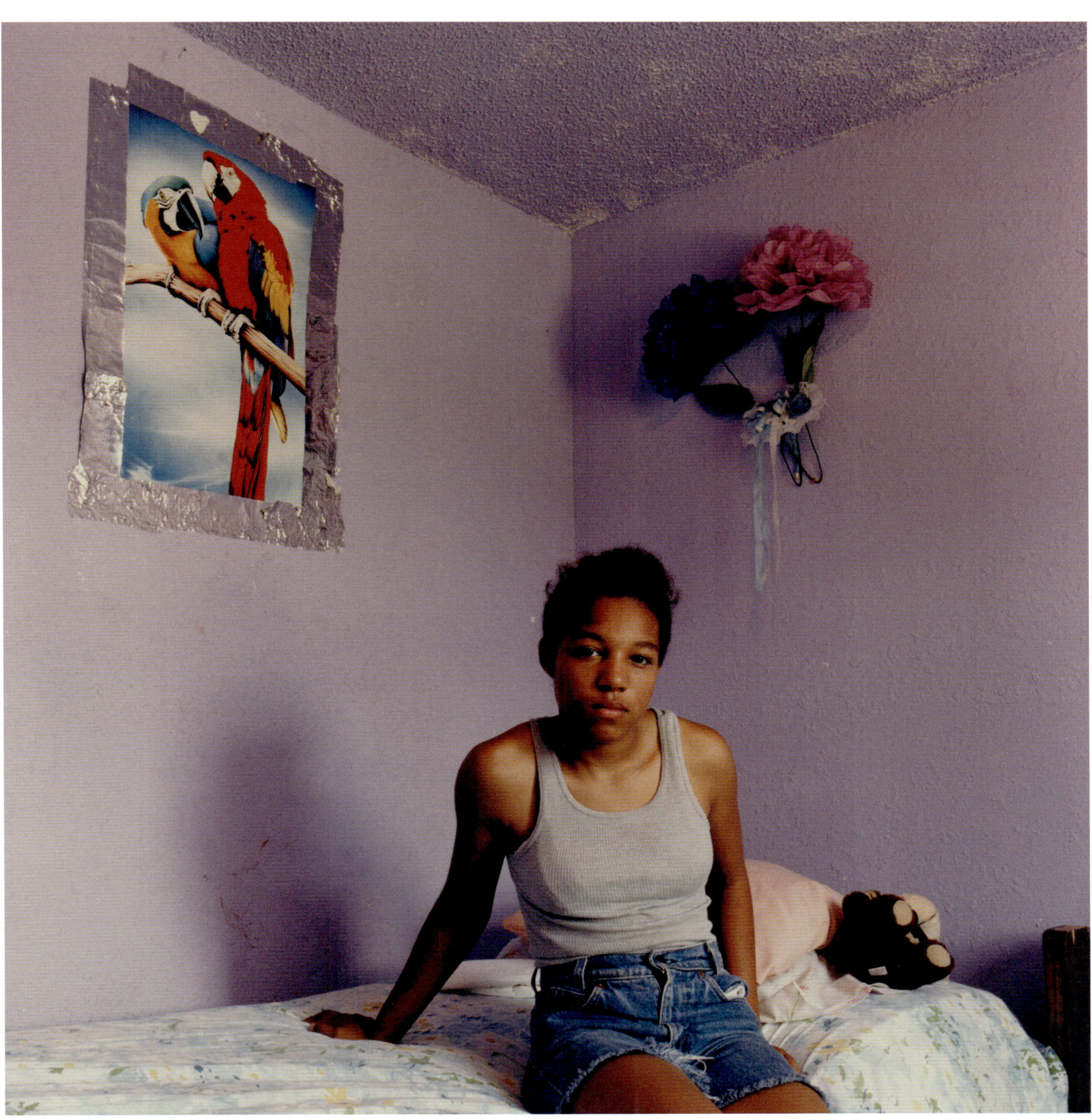

199   *Helen*, 1988; from the series *Lubbock*

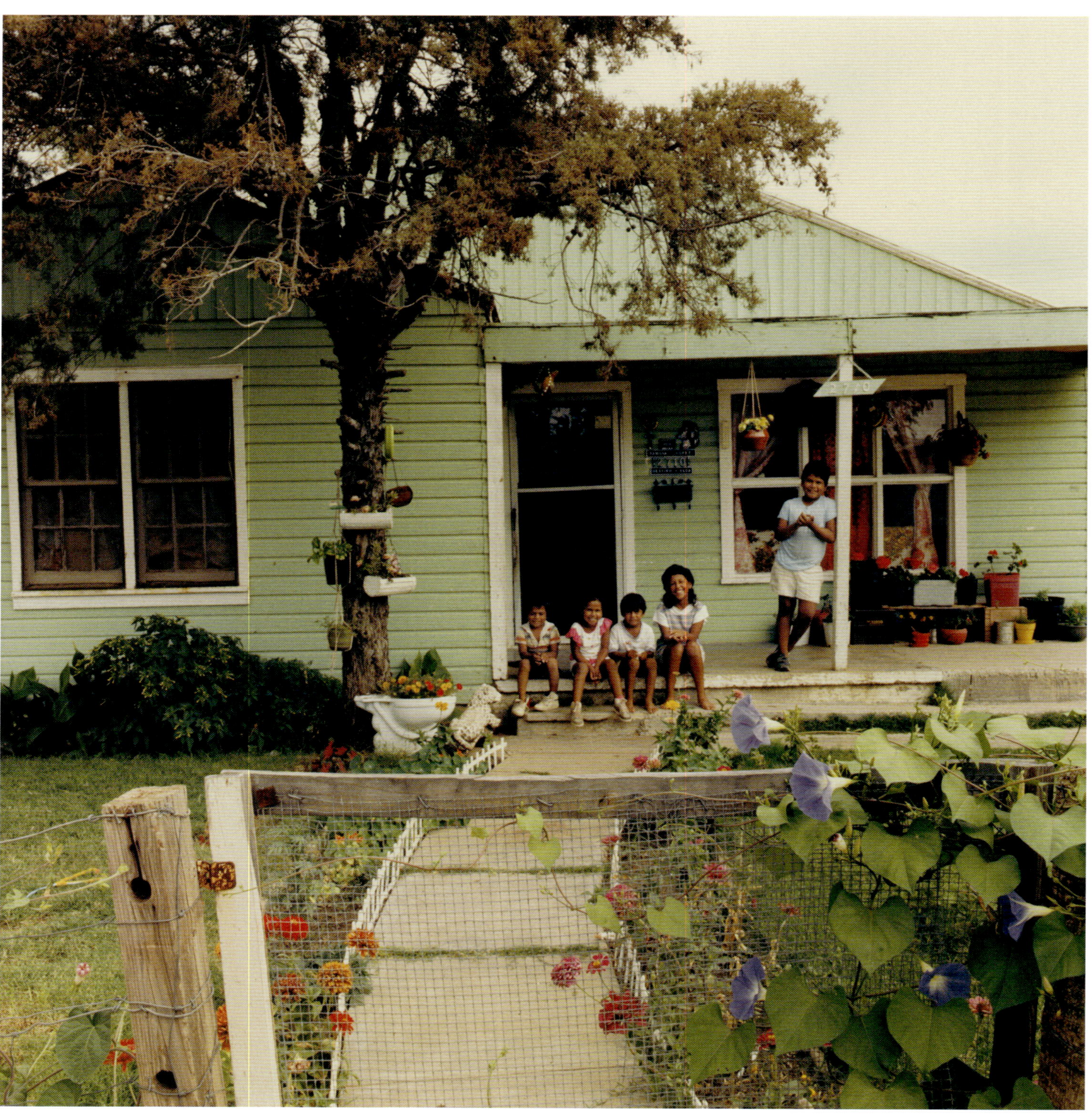

200   *Untitled*, 1988; from the series *Lubbock*

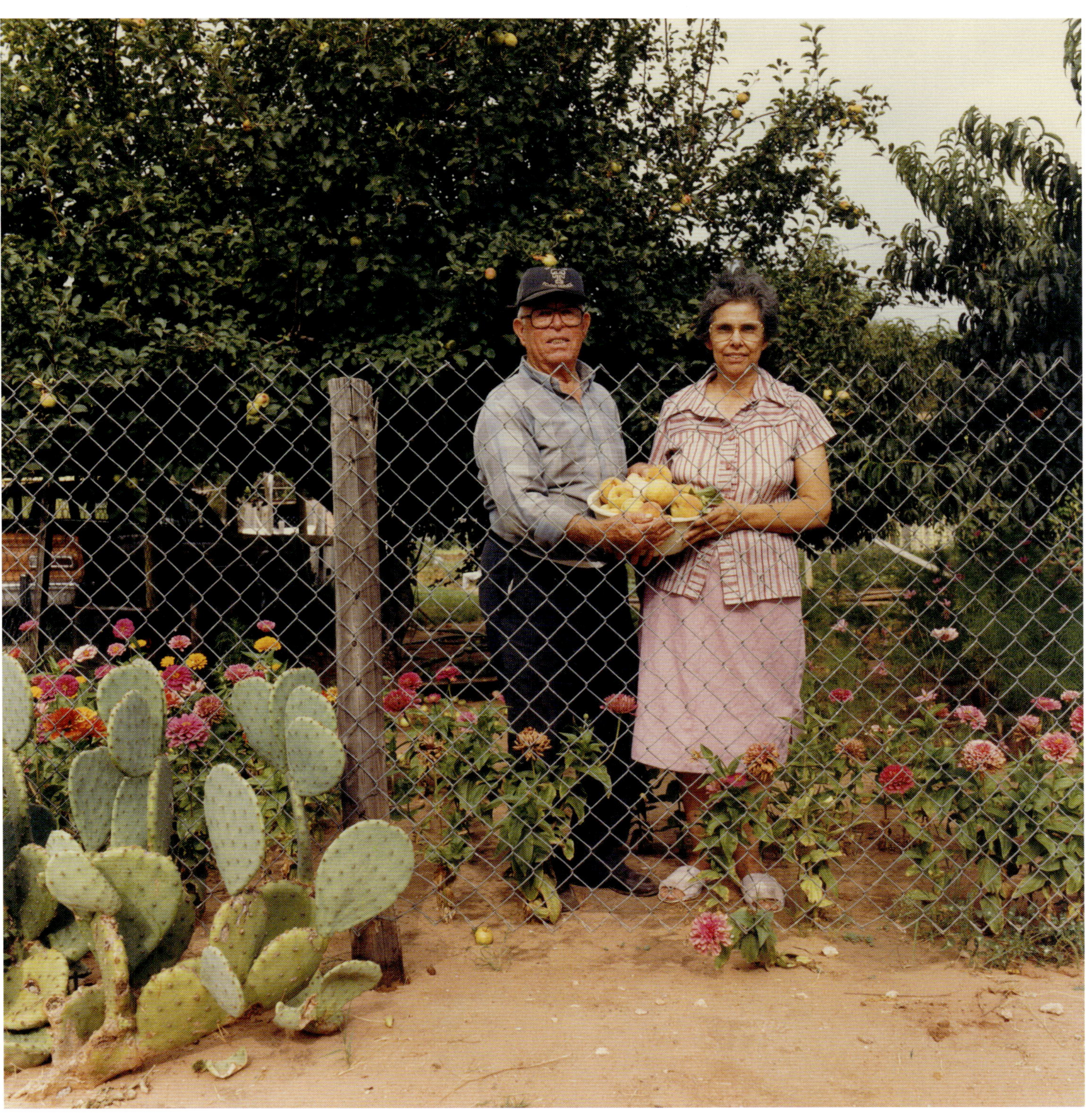

201   *Untitled*, 1987; from the series *Lubbock*

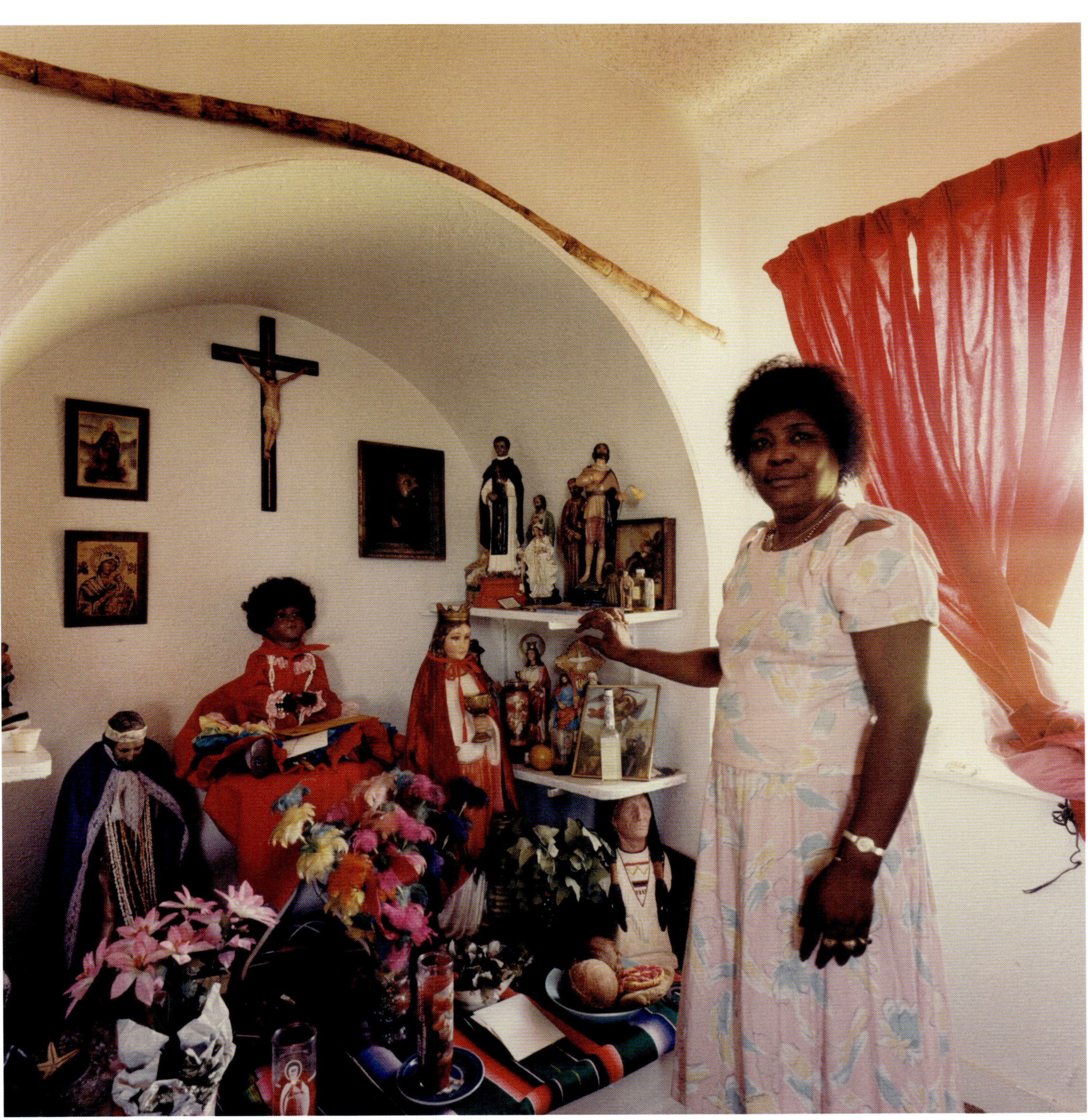

203   *Caridad Sanchez,* 1988; from the series *Lubbock*

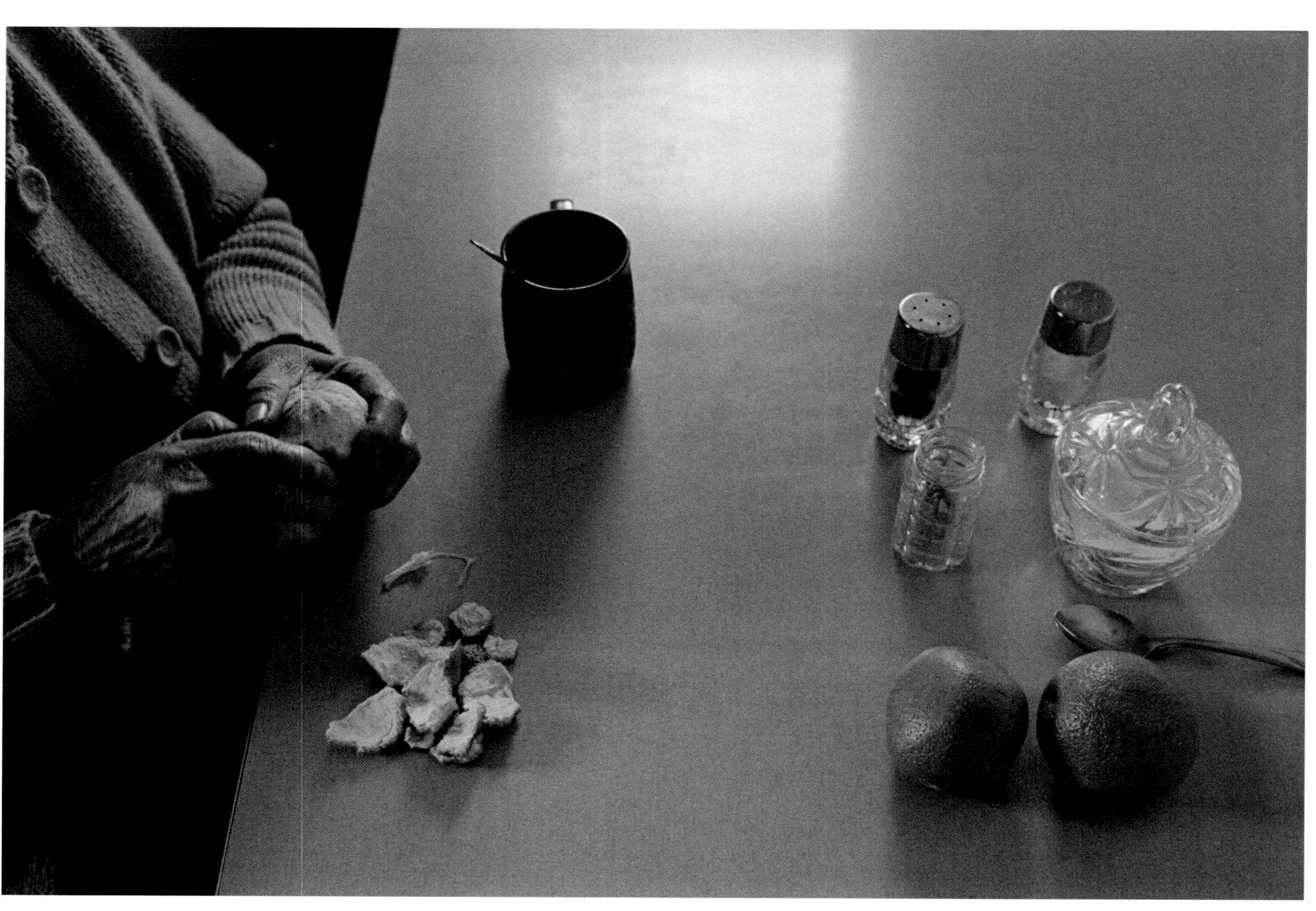

204   *Untitled (Hands on Table), Douglas,* 1989

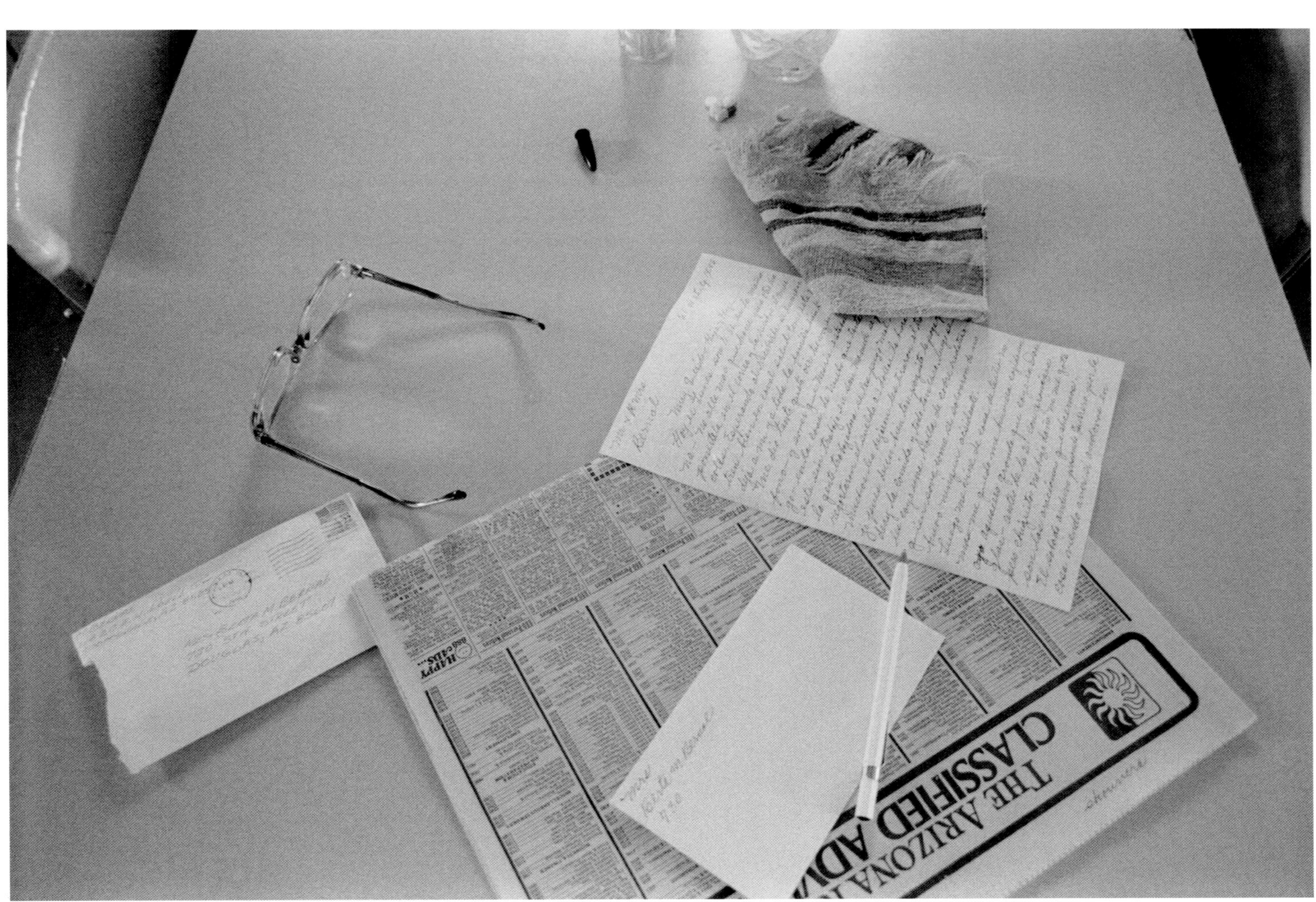

205   *Untitled (Table Top), Douglas,* 1989

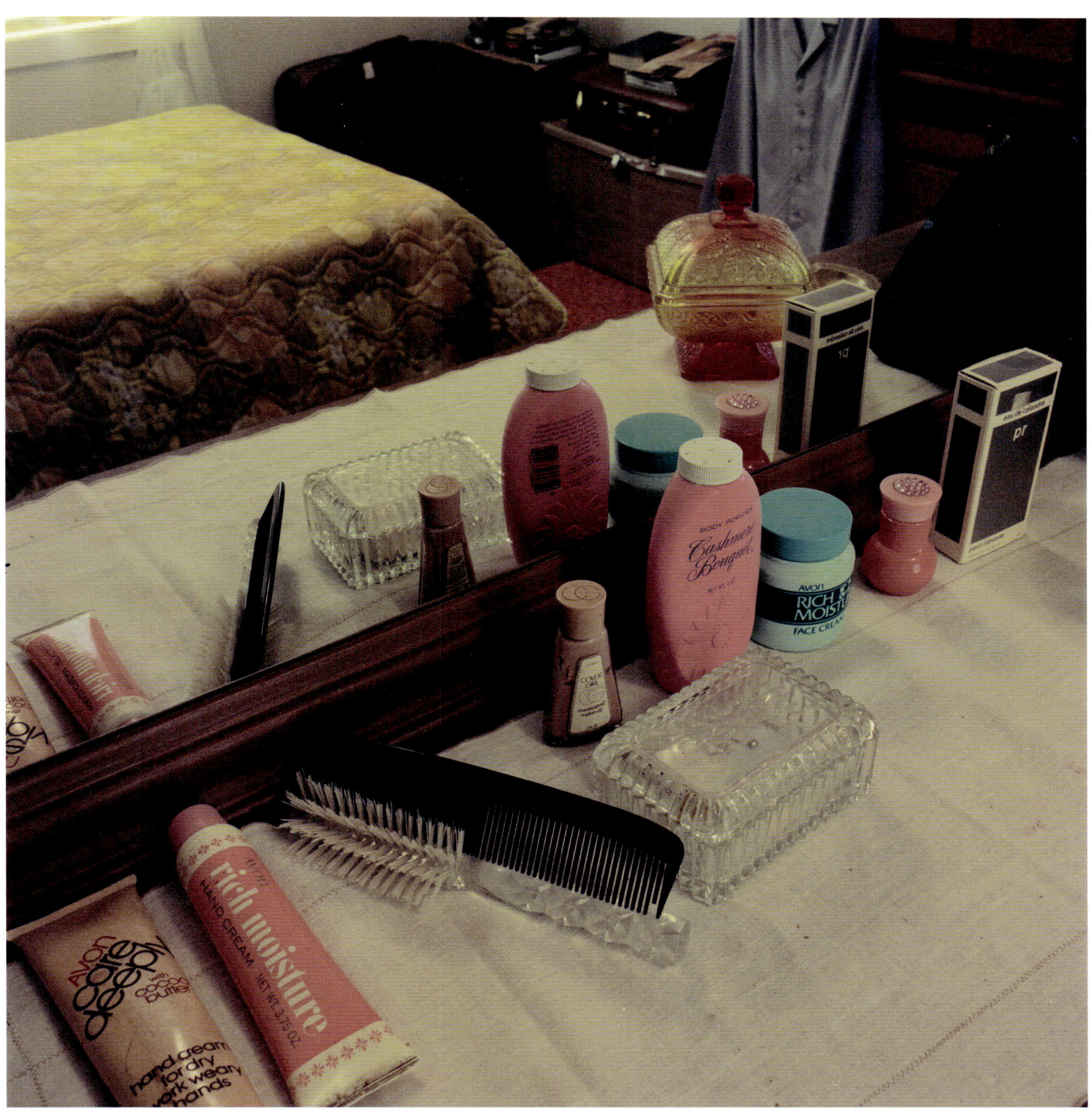

207   *Untitled (Dresser Top), Douglas, 1989*

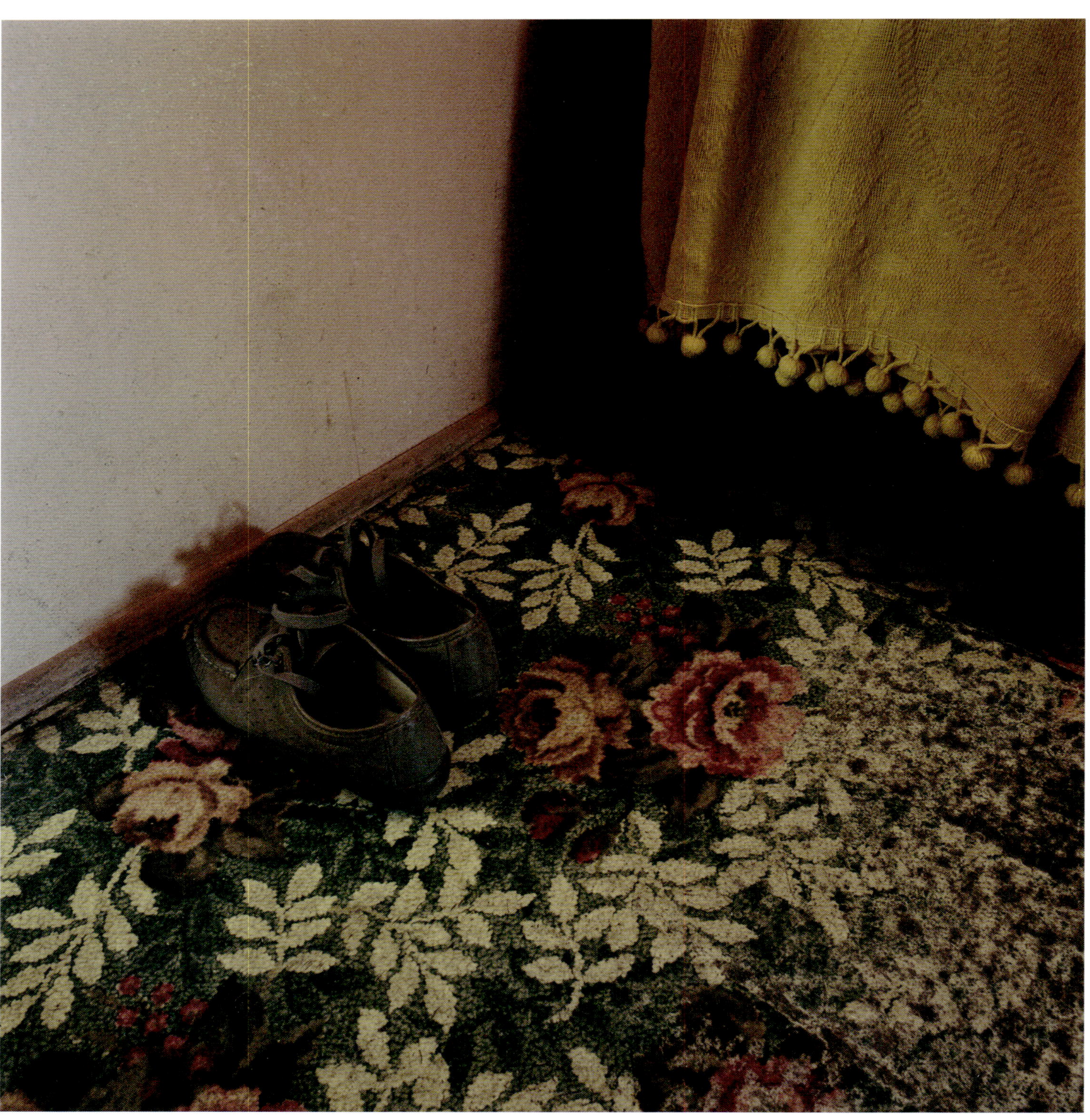

208   *Untitled (Shoes), Douglas,* 1989

1941 Louis Carlos Bernal is born August 18 in the border town of Douglas, Arizona, to Enedina de la Torre (b. 1925; d. 2004) and Carlos Molina Bernal (b. 1919; d. 1997).

1944 His brother Armando is born.

1947 When Bernal is six, the family settles into a small home less than a mile from the US–Mexico border. Bernal begins his education at Clawson Elementary School. His youngest brother, Reynaldo, or Rey, is born.

1949–53 The family moves to Phoenix for better employment and educational prospects. They purchase a home on East Virginia Avenue, which they own for decades.

Bernal and Armando enroll at St. Agnes Catholic School. By age eleven, Bernal begins to explore his interest in photography.

1956–60 Bernal is a student at St. Mary's Catholic High School. He is active in school athletics, including track, football, and swimming. He also regularly contributes photographs to the school newspaper, *The Knight*. Outside of school, he takes on some early professional photography work with local businesses. He graduates from St. Mary's in 1960.

1961 Bernal takes courses at Phoenix College. His photographs earn him praise from professors. One series entitled *The Last Half* is exhibited at the student center.

1962 A twenty-one-year-old Bernal travels to Mexico City for the first time and takes courses at Mexico City College, now known as the University of the Américas. He returns to Arizona to complete his degree, but the trip to Mexico City is one of many he makes over his lifetime as his connections to Mexican photographers and artists deepen.

1963–65 Bernal begins to exhibit his photographs. In 1963, he exhibits at the Mexican-American Cultural Galleries in Mexico City, marking his first time showing work in Mexico.

In 1964, while he is an undergraduate student majoring in Spanish at Arizona State University (ASU), Tempe, his first solo exhibition opens at the school's Memorial Union community center. He also presents work in a group exhibition at Phoenix College.

In August and September of 1965, Bernal's work is shown in a group exhibition, *Seeing Photographically*, at the George Eastman House, Rochester, New York. The exhibition features 450 photographs from college students across the country. It is organized in partnership with the Society for Photographic Education.

1966–69 Bernal earns a bachelor of arts from ASU in 1966. That same year, he marries Sandra Jean Anderson, a glass artist. They have two daughters, Lisa Marie (b. 1969) and Katrina Ann (b. 1972).

Bernal is drafted into the military in 1966. He serves as a photographer, first stationed at Fort Lewis near Tacoma, Washington, and later in Berlin.

After ending his military service, he enters the master of fine arts program in photography at ASU.

An avid cyclist, Bernal participates in races and wins various medals for his talent.

1970–72 Bernal pursues special studies with master photographer Frederick Sommer, who is based in Prescott, Arizona, and teaches at Prescott College.

In 1972, he graduates with his MFA. He moves to Tucson to launch the photography program at the growing Pima Community College.

1973 Bernal makes his first photographs in Tucson's barrios.

1974–76 In 1974, Bernal is recognized by Time, Inc. with a Time Life Yearbook Discovery Award, given to fifty outstanding young photographers around the world. He receives the same honor five years later.

Bernal is awarded a five-hundred-dollar grant from the Arizona Commission on the Arts and Humanities to photograph "the unique aspects of Mexican-American culture." He spends much of his time in Barrio Hollywood in Tucson.

He also works on his series *An American Fairy Tale*, which satirizes President Richard Nixon. These photographs are exhibited in 1975 at Limner Gallery, Scottsdale, Arizona, in the solo exhibition *An American Fairy Tale: Portrait of a Well-Known Personality*.

1977–79 Bernal produces the series *Benitez Suite* in 1977.

That same year, photographer Morrie Camhi invites Bernal to participate in a major project to photograph Chicanx life and culture, *Espejo: Reflections of the Mexican American*. The project is organized by Camhi and sponsored by the Mexican American Legal Defense and Educational Fund (MALDEF). Bernal receives a grant from MALDEF to participate. *Espejo* also features work by Camhi, Abigail Heyman, Roger Minick, and Neal Slavin. The exhibition is shown at the Oakland Museum of California and later travels to the Chicago Center for Contemporary Photography (now known as the Museum of Contemporary Photography) and Mount St. Mary's College Fine Arts Gallery in Los Angeles.

In 1977, Bernal also contributes work to *Ancient Roots/New Visions*, one of the first nationally touring exhibitions of Latinx art. It features the work of some eighty artists, including Ana Mendieta, Lorenzo Homar, and Patssi Valdez. The exhibition is curated by Marc Zuver, and it originates at the Tucson Museum of Art before traveling to nine other cities, including Washington, DC, Albuquerque, Los Angeles, Chicago, and Syracuse, New York.

In May 1978, Bernal exhibits photographs as part of the Primer Coloquio Latinoamericano de Fotografía in Mexico City, organized by the Consejo Mexicano de Fotografía, the Instituto de Bellas Artes, and the Secretaría de Educación Pública.

In 1979, Bernal exhibits work in *La Familia*, a group show organized by the Bronx-based nonprofit En Foco. The exhibition opens in September at El Museo del Barrio and features the work of seven photographers.

Bernal also continues to regularly exhibit his photographs in group and solo shows at the Galería de la Raza, San Francisco; Los Angeles Contemporary Exhibitions (LACE); Heard Museum, Phoenix; Santa Barbara Museum of Art, California; and Center for Creative Photography (CCP), Tucson.

1980–82 Bernal increasingly draws recognition for his work. He receives a grant from the National Endowment for the Arts, a photography grant from the Polaroid Corporation, the Still Life Photo award from *American Photography* magazine, and the Virginia McCormick Scully Literary Award.

In April 1981, Bernal is invited as a special lecturer and guest panelist to the Segundo Coloquio Latinoamericano de Fotografía, hosted by the Consejo Mexicano de Fotografía and La Casa de la Fotografía in Mexico City. He delivers a talk on photography as a reflection of social structures and teaches a workshop on the zone system.

In September 1981, Bernal's work is featured in the group exhibition *Five Photographers: Contemporary Views of Mexican and Mexican-American Culture* at the Mandeville Art Gallery at University of California, San Diego.

He begins to participate in lectures and panels on his work across the Southwest and West, at the University of Arizona, Arizona State University, Eastern Washington University, and Self Help Graphics & Art in East Los Angeles, among others.

1983 Bernal serves as an instructor at a Friends of Photography workshop, The Photograph as Document, in Carmel, California. Other faculty members include Burk Uzzle, Danny Lyon, Morrie Camhi, and Mary Ellen Mark.

Bernal provides photographs for a book by Patricia Preciado Martin, *Images and Conversations: Mexican Americans Recall a Southwestern Past*, published by the University of Arizona Press.

In June, Bernal exhibits work in a group show titled *La Gran Pasión* at the New Museum in New York. The show is organized by En Foco and features the work of thirty artists, including Bernal's good friend Ricardo Valverde.

Bernal exhibits work in *Con Cariño: Photos of Another America* at the University of Erlangen–Nuremberg, West Germany. The first-ever exhibition of Chicanx photography shown abroad, it is organized by the Aztlán Cultural Center in Oakland, California, which is unable to secure a single US venue for the project.

1984 Bernal is one of ten photographers selected by the Los Angeles Olympic Organizing Committee to interpret the 1984 Olympic Games. His series, focusing on the labor behind the spectacle of the Games, is exhibited in *10 Photographers: Olympic Images* at the Museum of Contemporary Art, Los Angeles. Other photographers include Jo Ann Callis and Robert C. Buitrón.

In November, Bernal participates as a guest in the Tercer Coloquio Latinoamericano de Fotografía in Havana. He teaches another workshop on the zone system.

Bernal receives an Award in the Visual Arts from the Southeastern Center for Contemporary Art in Winston-Salem, North Carolina. He participates in a group exhibition, *Awards in the Visual Arts 3*, which opens at the San Antonio Museum of Art. The show also travels to the Loch Haven Art Center, Orlando, Florida, and Cranbrook Academy of Art Museum, Bloomfield Hills, Michigan.

1985 In March, Bernal's work is exhibited in a group show entitled *Facets of the Collection: Excerpts from Espejo: Reflections of the Mexican American* at the San Francisco Museum of Modern Art.

A solo show, *Louis Carlos Bernal*, opens at the California Museum of Photography in Riverside. A second solo show, *Images from the 1984 Olympics*, opens at CCP.

Bernal and Sandra Anderson divorce. Bernal and his partner Marietta Bernstorff later move into a house in the Barrio El Hoyo in Tucson.

1986 Bernal exhibits in *State of the State: An Exhibition of Arizona Photography* at the Arizona State Capitol Museum, Phoenix.

1987–88 Bernal participates in a National Endowment for the Arts Visual Projects panel in Washington, DC. He receives a grant from the Tucson Pima Arts Council, now the Arts Foundation for Tucson and Southern Arizona.

In 1987, Texas Tech University commissions Bernal to work on his *Lubbock* series. The photographs are exhibited in 1988 at the Museum of Texas Tech University as *Espiritu Mejicano: Lubbock*. The series is also exhibited at Etherton Gallery, Tucson.

Bernal takes his final trip to Mexico in 1988. He travels with his partner Marietta Bernstorff and good friend Armando Cristeto.

1989 Bernal exhibits work in a group show, titled *La imagen antes y después de la cámara*, at La Agencia, a gallery in Mexico City operated by artist Adolfo Patiño. The show is organized as part of the 150 Años de la Fotografía en México festival held across the city, which features exhibitions, events, and panels, sponsored by the Consejo Nacional para la Cultura y las Artes (Conaculta), and a slate of parallel events and exhibitions at commercial galleries and nonprofit cultural spaces.

On October 24, Bernal is left in a coma after being struck by a car in Tucson while bicycling to work.

1990 Bernal's work is exhibited in *The Decade Show: Frameworks of Identity in the 1980s*, an influential exhibition featuring works by ninety-four artists, including Jean-Michel Basquiat, Barbara Kruger, James Luna, Adrian Piper, and Lorna Simpson. It is a collaboration between three institutions in New York: the New Museum, Museum of Contemporary Hispanic Art, and Studio Museum in Harlem.

Bernal's work is included in the landmark exhibition *Chicano Art: Resistance and Affirmation* (*CARA*). It originates at the University of California at Los Angeles's Wight Gallery and travels for nearly three years to museums in ten cities. It includes the work of 180 Chicanx artists and is considered a major milestone in Chicanx art history.

1991 The Louis Carlos Bernal Fund is established through the Pima Community College Foundation to support Bernal's medical expenses. Numerous college faculty and staff contribute to the fund.

1992 Bernal's work is featured in *Chicanismo*, a group exhibition organized by the George Eastman House, Rochester, New York.

In March, a solo exhibition, *Louis Carlos Bernal*, opens at CCP. The organization also hosts a closing reception and a photographic print auction to benefit the Louis Carlos Bernal Fund. Prints donated by dozens of prominent photographers, including Manuel Álvarez Bravo, Graciela Iturbide, Morrie Camhi, Sally Mann, Pedro Meyer, Judy Dater, Danny Lyon, and Robert C. Buitrón, are auctioned to raise funds.

1993 Louis Carlos Bernal dies at the age of fifty-two on August 18, his birthday, in the Barrio El Hoyo home he shared with Marietta Bernstorff. He is buried at St. Francis Catholic Cemetery in Phoenix.

1996 Bernal's photographs are included in the largest exhibition of Latinx photography ever mounted, *American Voices: Latino Photographers in the United States*, organized by FotoFest in Houston and curated by fellow photographers Kathy Vargas, Robert C. Buitrón, Charles Biasiny-Rivera, and Ricardo Viera. The following year, the exhibition travels to the Smithsonian Institution in Washington, DC, where it is exhibited at the S. Dillon Ripley Center.

2002 Curated by Ann Simmons-Myers, a solo exhibition of Bernal's work, titled *Barrios*, opens at Pima Community College in the newly dedicated Louis Carlos Bernal Gallery. It features more than eighty images across his career. Friends and colleagues Simmons-Myers, James Enyeart, Luis Jiménez, Patricia Preciado Martin, and Leslie Marmon Silko contribute essays to the exhibition catalog.

2014 The Center for Creative Photography acquires the Louis Carlos Bernal Archive, a donation made by his daughters Lisa Bernal Brethour and Katrina Bernal. The collection includes photographic prints, negatives, and contact sheets, as well as correspondence, publications, video recordings, and other materials.

2016 *Louis Carlos Bernal: Arizona Unseen, Color Photographs 1978–1988*, curated by Ann Simmons-Myers, opens at the Louis Carlos Bernal Gallery at Pima Community College. The exhibition features previously unseen color photographs.

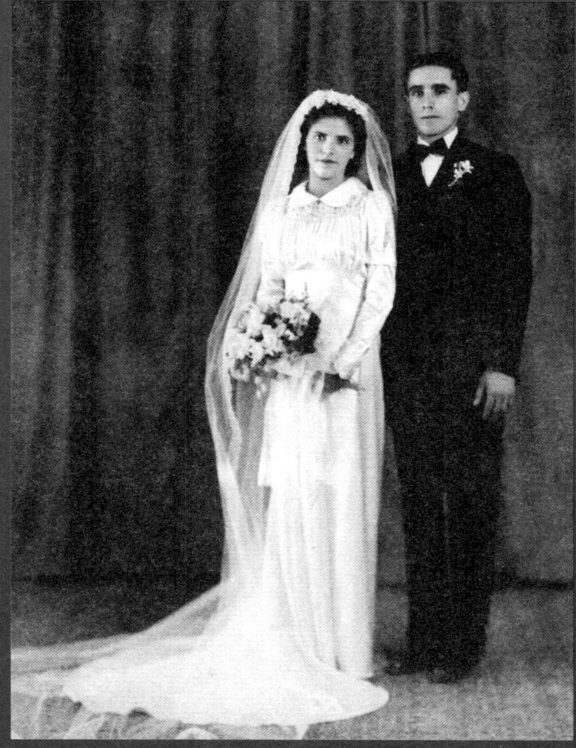

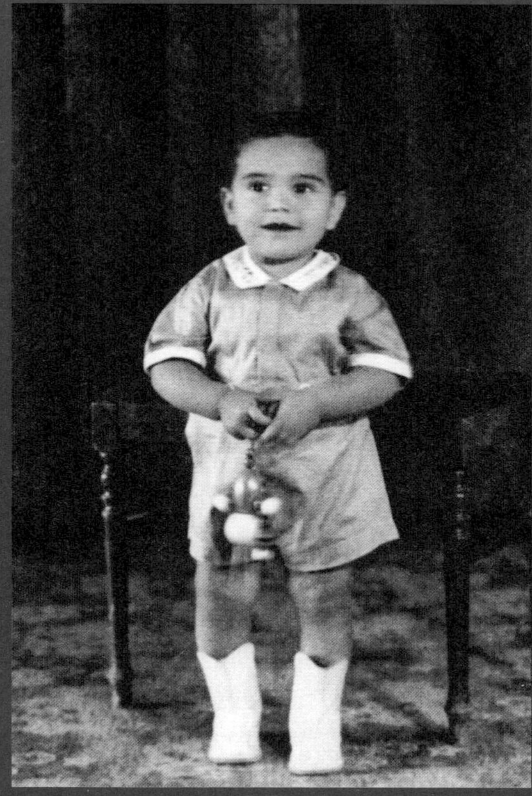

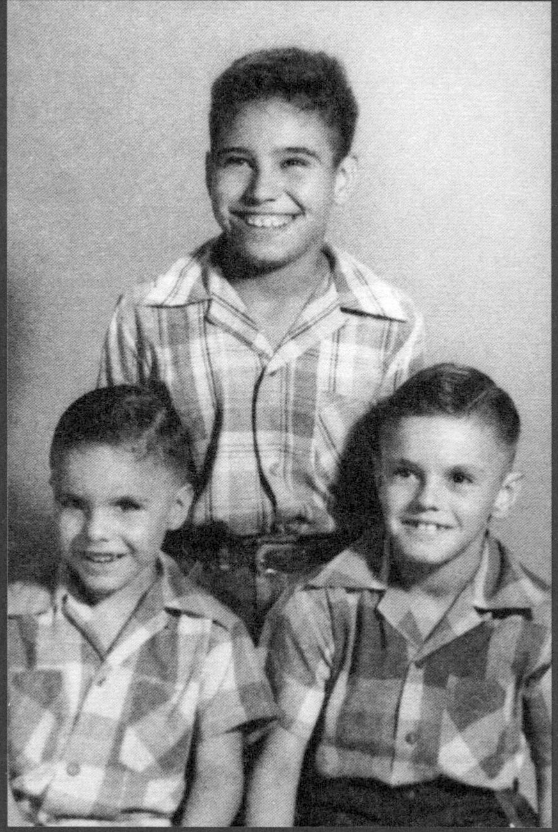

EN
1. Bernal's parents, Enedina and Carlos, 1940
2. Bernal at nineteen months, ca. 1943
3. Bernal (center) at ten years old, ca. 1951

ES
1. Los padres de Bernal, Enedina y Carlos, 1940
2. Bernal a los diecinueve meses, ca. 1943
3. Bernal (centro) a los diez años, ca. 1951

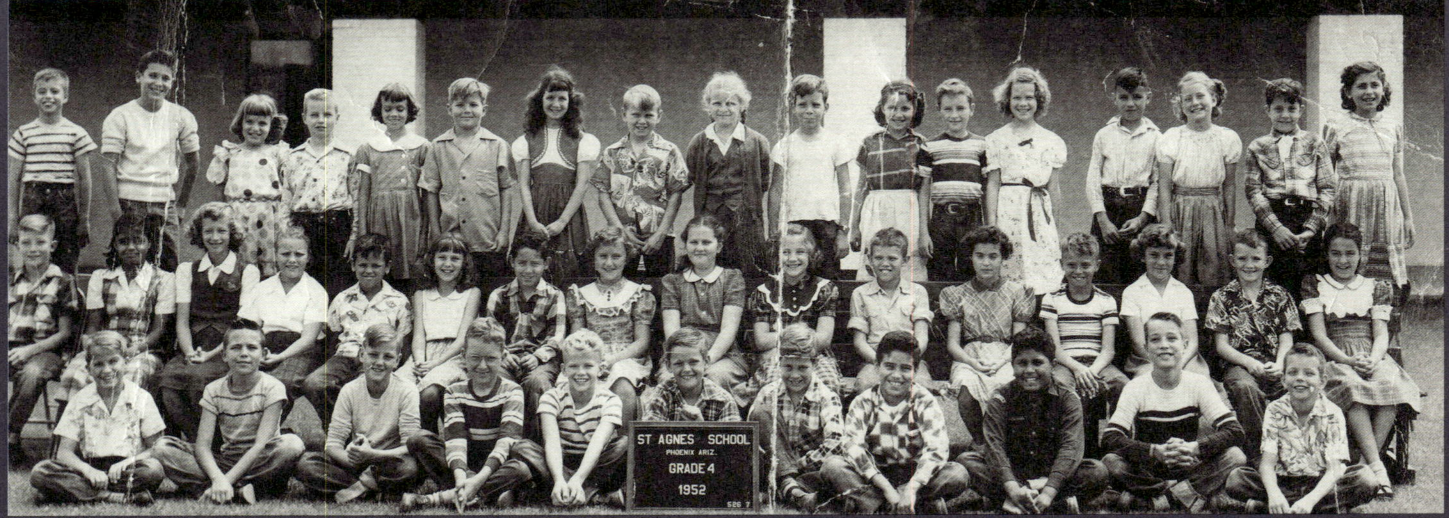

4

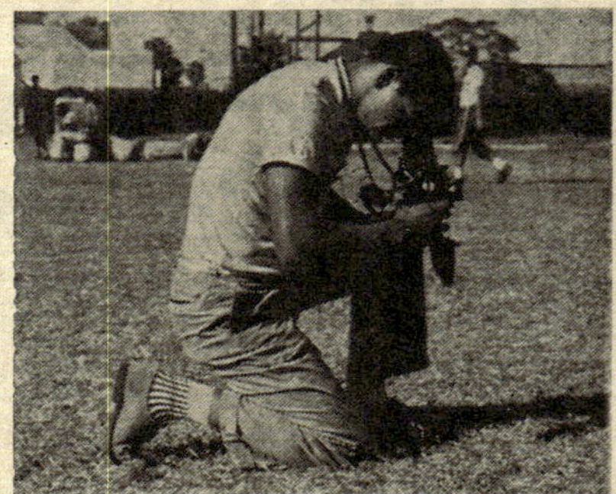

THE KNIGHT   Friday, October 24, 1958

"Click-Clock"
'Watch the Birdie' says Louie, S.M.'s Photographer

Who is it that is seen at all football and basketball games and most other school activities? Why it's shutterbug Louie Bernal, known to most students as just plain "Louie".

Since he was eleven, Louie has been interested in photography. His love of his hobby has since snowballed into a $400 investment.

Louie's conception of photography is: Photography is a language. A photographer wants to interpret things as he sees them, and show these sights to others. Aside from being a hobby, it is a duty and an obligation to the school. According to Bernal's opinion, a good photographer should be able to take a variety of pictures and not just one certain type.

Apart from photographic work done on the Annual, Louie has done some professional work with with real estate, babies, and Wing's restaurant. However, his main ambition is becoming a fashion photographer.

When asked whether he enoys photography, Louie replied, "Do I? My camera is my ticket to see things and go places I normally am not able to.

Doing almost anything for a picture, Louie Bernal, '60 kneels to get a good angle shot.

5

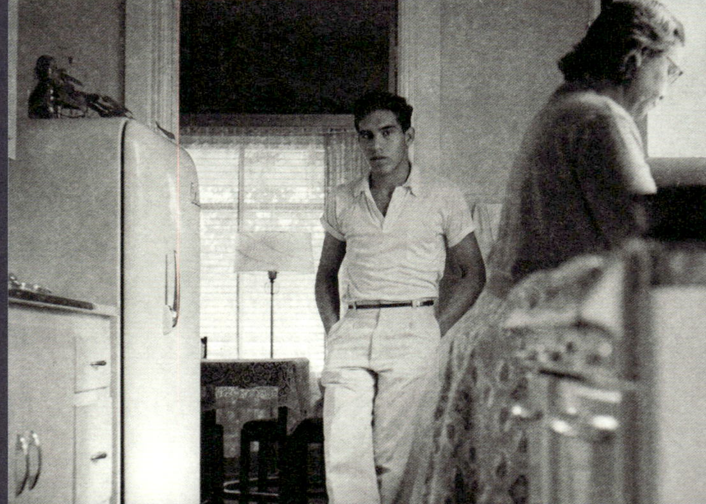

6

EN
4. St. Agnes School Grade 4, Phoenix, Arizona, 1952. Bernal is in the front row, fourth from right.
5. Clipping from St. Mary's newspaper, *The Knight*, with photograph of Bernal, 1958. The caption reads: "Doing almost anything for a picture, Louie Bernal, '60, kneels to get a good angle shot."
6. Bernal as a teenager, in the kitchen with his mother, Phoenix, Arizona, late 1950s

ES
4. La escuela de St. Agnes Cuarto grado, Phoenix, AZ, 1952. Bernal esta en la primera fila, cuarto de la derecha.
5. Recorte del diario de St. Mary's, *The Knight*, con fotografía de Bernal, 1958. Pie de foto dice: "Haciendo casi lo que sea para una foto, Louie Bernal, '60, se agacha para conseguir un buen ángulo para la toma".
6. Bernal de adolescente en la cocina con su madre, Phoenix, Arizona, finales de los 1950s

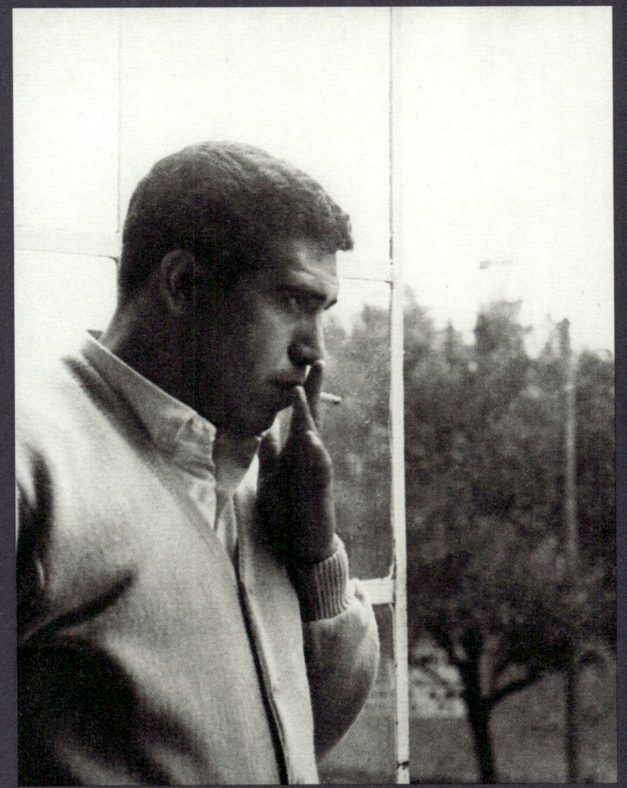

7

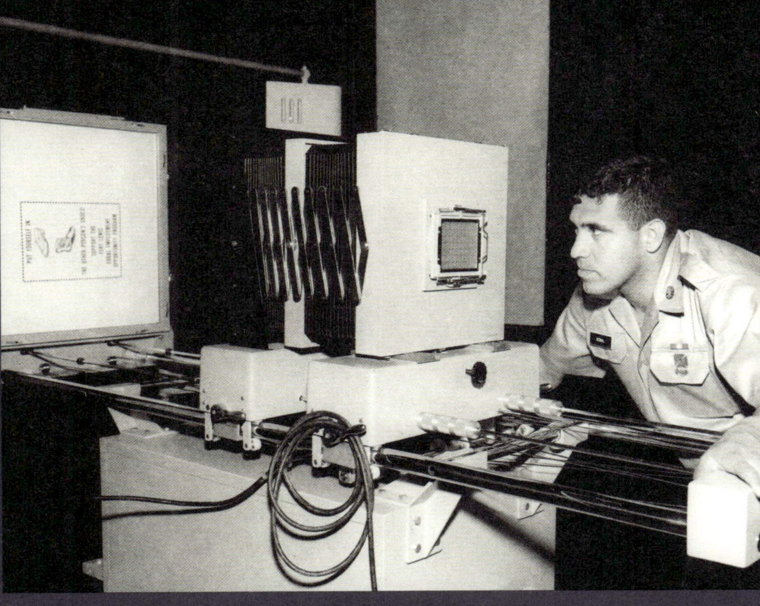

8

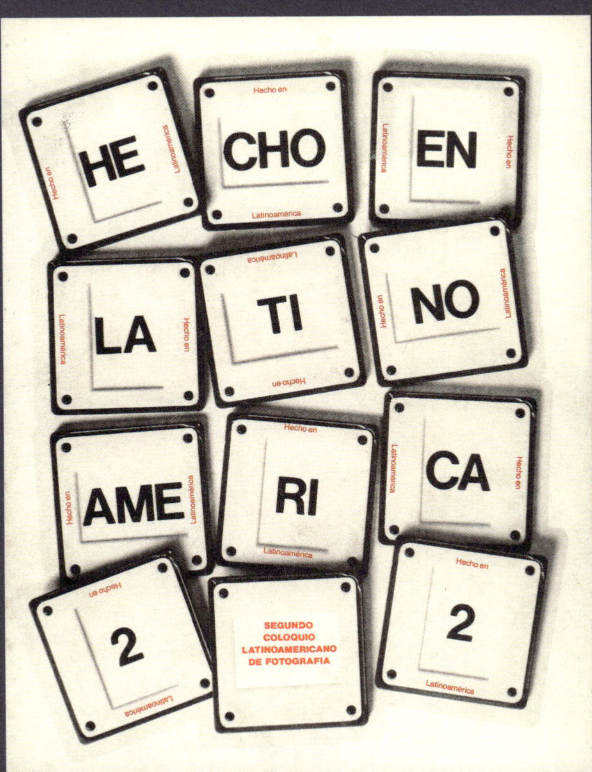

9

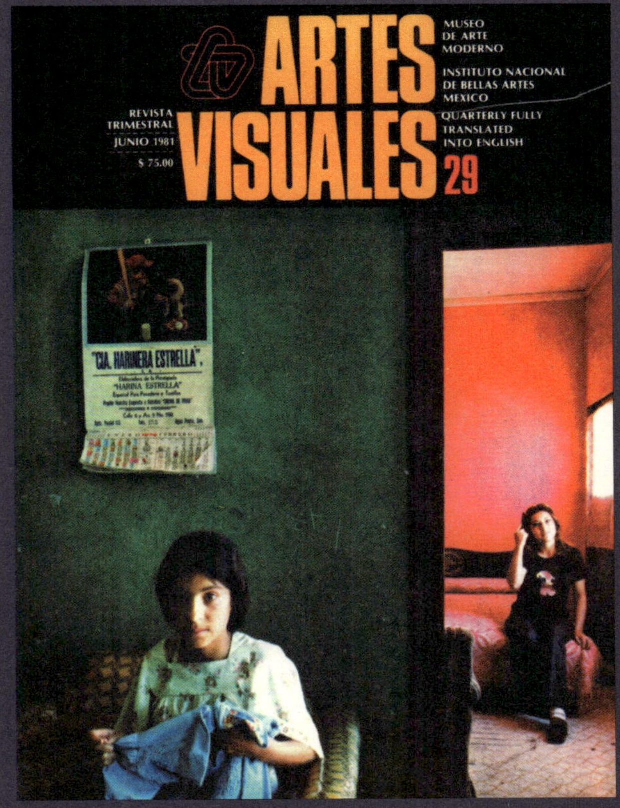

10

EN

7. Bernal in his twenties, ca. 1960s
8. Bernal at the photography facility at Fort Lewis, Washington, May 22, 1967
9. Cover of *Hecho en latinoamérica 2* (Made in Latin America), 1981
10. Cover of the quarterly review *Artes Visuales* (Mexico City), Carla Stellweg, ed., issue 29, June 1981, with photograph by Bernal

ES

7. Bernal a los veinte, ca. 1960s
8. Bernal en la instalación de fotografía en Fort Lewis, Washington, 22 de mayo, 1967
9. Portada de *Hecho en latinoamérica 2*, 1981
10. Portada de la revista trimestral *Artes Visuales* (Ciudad de México), Carla Stellweg, ed., número 29, junio 1981, con fotografía por Bernal

Diario testimonial de un coloquio*

Katya Mandoki

Lunes 20 de abril

Se inaugura la exposición del fotógrafo español Rafael Navarro en el Instituto Cultural Hispano Mexicano, obra lírica de impecable factura hecha en parejas de contactos de formato grande que conforman enunciados sugerentes.

Martes 21 de abril

Se inician simultáneamente —en diversos puntos de la ciudad— seis talleres preparación de portafolios personal, la fotografía y el mimeógrafo, fotoperiodismo, trabajando con cámara de formato grande, lectura de la imagen fotográfica y sistema de zonas.

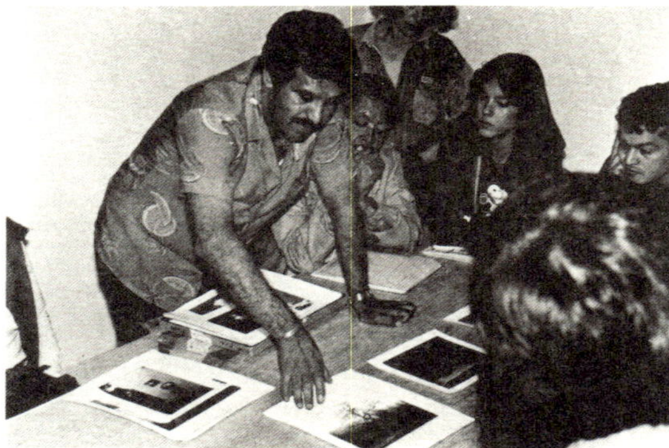

Louis Carlos Bernal en su taller "Sistema de zonas"

* Publicado originalmente en *uno más uno* el 3 de mayo de 1981

11

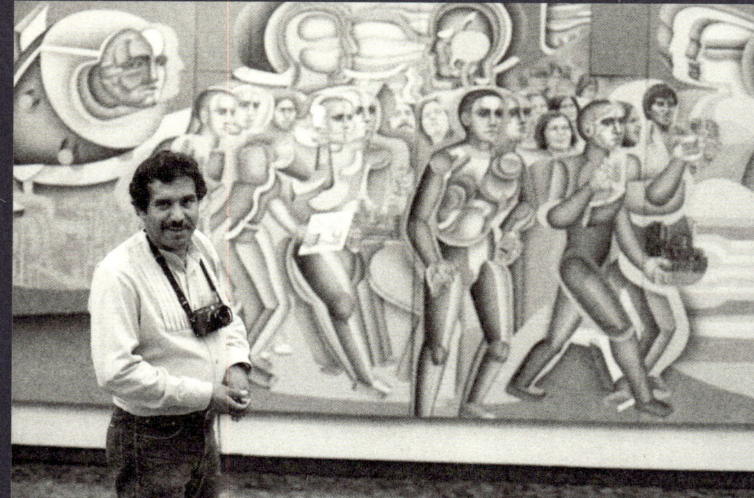

12

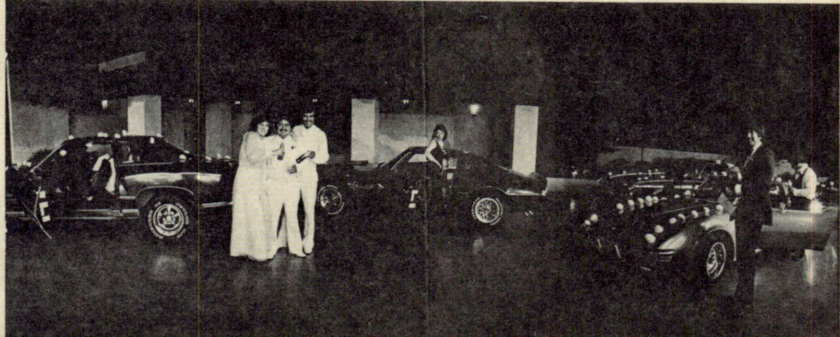

13

1941 Louis Carlos Bernal nace el 18 de agosto en la ciudad fronteriza de Douglas, Arizona, hijo de Enedina de la Torre (nacida en 1925 y fallecida en 2004) y Carlos Molina Bernal (nacido en 1919 y fallecido en 1997).

1944 Nace su hermano Armando.

1947 Cuando Bernal tiene seis años, la familia se instala en una pequeña casa a menos de dos kilómetros de la frontera entre Estados Unidos y México. Bernal comienza su educación en la Clawson Elementary School. Nace su hermano menor, Reynaldo, también conocido como Rey.

1949–53 La familia se traslada a Phoenix en busca de mejores perspectivas laborales y educativas. Compran una casa en East Virginia Avenue, de la que son propietarios por varias décadas.

Bernal y Armando se matriculan en St. Agnes Catholic School. A los once años, Bernal empieza a explorar su interés por la fotografía.

1956–60 Bernal estudia en St. Mary's Catholic High School. Participa activamente en deportes escolares como atletismo, fútbol americano y natación. También contribuye fotografías regularmente al periódico escolar *The Knight*. Fuera de la escuela, realiza algunos primeros trabajos de fotografía profesional con empresas locales. Se gradúa de St. Mary's en 1960.

1961 Bernal toma cursos en el Phoenix College. Sus fotografías le consiguen los elogios del profesorado. Una serie titulada *The Last Half* (La última mitad) se expone en el centro de estudiantes.

1962 Bernal, de veintiún años, viaja por primera vez a la Ciudad de México y cursa estudios en el Mexico City College, lo que hoy se conoce como la Universidad de las Américas. Regresa a Arizona para terminar su licenciatura, pero el viaje a la Ciudad de México es uno de los muchos que realiza a lo largo de su vida a medida que se profundizan sus conexiones con fotógrafos y artistas mexicanos.

1963–65 Bernal comienza a exponer sus fotografías. En 1963, expone en las Galerías Culturales México-Americanas de la Ciudad de México; es la primera vez que muestra su obra en México.

En 1964, mientras estudia para su bachillerato con una especialización en español en Arizona State University (ASU), en Tempe, se inaugura su primera exposición individual en el centro comunitario Memorial Union en la universidad. También presenta su obra en una exposición colectiva en el Phoenix College.

En agosto y septiembre de 1965, la obra de Bernal se muestra en una exposición colectiva, *Seeing Photographically*, en la George Eastman House, en Rochester, Nueva York. La exposición presenta 450 fotografías de estudiantes universitarios de todo el país. Se organiza en colaboración con la Society for Photographic Education.

1966–69 Bernal obtiene la licenciatura en artes de ASU en 1966. Ese mismo año, se casa con Sandra Jean Anderson, artista del vidrio. Tienen dos hijas, Lisa Marie (nacida en 1969) y Katrina Ann (nacida en 1972).

En 1966, el ejército recluta a Bernal. Sirve como fotógrafo, primero destinado en Fort Lewis, cerca de Tacoma, Washington y, después, en Berlín.

Tras finalizar su servicio militar, ingresa en el programa de Máster en Bellas Artes en la disciplina de fotografía en ASU.

Bernal, ávido ciclista, participa en carreras y gana varias medallas por su talento.

1970–72 Bernal se dedica a estudios especiales con el maestro de la fotografía Frederick Sommer, quien está radicado en Prescott, Arizona, y es profesor en Prescott College.

En 1972, se gradúa del máster en Bellas Artes. Se traslada a Tucson para poner en marcha el programa de fotografía del creciente Pima Community College.

1973 Bernal toma sus primeras fotos en los barrios de Tucson.

1974–76 En 1974, Bernal recibe el reconocimiento de Time, Inc. con el premio Time Life Yearbook Discovery Award, concedido a cincuenta fotógrafas y fotógrafos jóvenes destacados de todo el mundo. Recibe el mismo honor cinco años después.

Bernal recibe una subvención de quinientos dólares de la Arizona Commission on the Arts and Humanities para fotografiar "los aspectos únicos de la cultura mexicano-estadounidense." Pasa gran parte de su tiempo en el Barrio Hollywood de Tucson.

También trabaja en su serie *An American Fairy Tale* (Un cuento de hadas americano) que satiriza al presidente Richard Nixon. Estas fotografías se exhiben en 1975 en la Limner Gallery, en Scottsdale, Arizona, en la exposición individual *An American Fairy Tale: Portrait of a Well-Known Personality* (Un cuento de hadas americano: Retrato de un personaje conocido).

1977–79 Bernal produce la serie *Benítez Suite* en 1977.

Ese mismo año, el fotógrafo Morrie Camhi invita a Bernal a participar en un gran proyecto para fotografiar la vida y cultura de la comunidad chicana, *Espejo: Reflections of the Mexican American*. El proyecto está organizado por Camhi y patrocinado por el Mexican American Legal Defense and Educational (MALDEF). Bernal recibe una subvención de MALDEF para su participación. *Espejo* también presenta obras de Camhi, Abigail Heyman, Roger Minick y Neal Slavin. La exposición se exhibe en el Oakland Museum of California y después viaja al Chicago Center for Contemporary Photography y la Mount St. Mary's College Fine Arts Gallery en Los Ángeles.

En 1977, Bernal también contribuye con obras a *Ancient Roots/New Visions* (Raíces antiguas/Nuevas visiones), una de las primeras exposiciones itinerantes nacionales de arte latino. Presenta obras de unos ochenta artistas, entre ellos Ana Mendieta, Lorenzo Homar y Patssi Valdez. La exposición está comisariada por Marc Zuver y tiene su origen en el Tucson Museum of Art antes de viajar a otras nueve ciudades, entre ellas Washington, DC, Albuquerque, Los Ángeles, Chicago y Syracuse, Nueva York.

En mayo de 1978, Bernal expone fotografías en el marco del Primer Coloquio Latinoamericano de Fotografía en la Ciudad de México, organizado por el Consejo Mexicano de Fotografía, el Instituto de Bellas Artes y la Secretaría de Educación Pública.

En 1979, Bernal expone en *La Familia*, una muestra colectiva organizada por la organización sin ánimo de lucro En Foco, con sede en el Bronx, Nueva York. La exposición se inaugura en septiembre en el Museo del Barrio de Nueva York y presenta la obra de siete fotógrafos.

Bernal también sigue exponiendo sus fotografías en muestras colectivas e individuales en la Galería de la Raza, San Francisco; Los Angeles Contemporary Exhibitions (LACE); el Heard Museum en Phoenix; y el Santa Barbara Museum of Art; y el Center for Creative Photography, Tucson.

1980–82 Bernal obtiene cada vez más reconocimiento por su trabajo. Recibe una beca de National Endowment for the Arts, una beca de fotografía de la Polaroid Corporation, el premio Still Life Photo de la revista *American Photography* y el premio literario Virginia McCormick Scully.

En abril de 1981, Bernal recibe una invitación como ponente especial y panelista invitado al Segundo Coloquio Latinoamericano de Fotografía, auspiciado por el Consejo Mexicano de Fotografía y La Casa de la Fotografía de la Ciudad de México. Imparte una charla sobre la fotografía como reflejo de las estructuras sociales e imparte un taller sobre el sistema de zonas.

En septiembre de 1981, la obra de Bernal se presenta en la exposición colectiva *Five Photographers: Contemporary Views of Mexican and Mexican-American Culture* en la Mandeville Art Gallery de University of California, San Diego.

Comienza a participar en conferencias y mesas redondas sobre su obra por todo el Suroeste y el Oeste de los Estados Unidos, en la Universidad de Arizona, Arizona State University, Eastern Washington University y Self Help Graphics & Art en East Los Ángeles, entre otras.

1983 Bernal ejerce de instructor en Friends of Photography en Carmel, California, La fotografía como documento. Otros miembros del profesorado son Burk Uzzle, Danny Lyon, Morrie Camhi y Mary Ellen Mark.

Bernal aporta fotografías para un libro de Patricia Preciado Martin, *Images and Conversations: Mexican Americans Recall a Southwestern Past* (Imágenes y conversaciones: Mexicano-americanos recuerdan un pasado del Sudoeste), publicado por University of Arizona Press.

En junio, Bernal expone en una exposición colectiva titulada *La Gran Pasión* en el New Museum de Nueva York. La muestra está organizada por En Foco y cuenta con la obra de treinta artistas, entre quienes se encuentra el buen amigo de Bernal, Ricardo Valverde.

Bernal también participa en la exposición *Con Cariño: Photos of Another America* (Con cariño: Fotos de otra América) en la Universidad de Erlangen-Nuremberg, Alemania Occidental. Esta primera exposición de fotografía chicana en el extranjero está organizada por el Centro Cultural Aztlán de Oakland, California, que no ha podido conseguir ni una sola sede en Estados Unidos para el proyecto.

1984 Bernal es uno de los diez fotógrafos seleccionados por el Los Angeles Olympic Organizing Committee (el Comité Organizador de los Juegos Olímpicos de Los Ángeles) para interpretar los Juegos Olímpicos de 1984. Su serie, centrada en el trabajo que hay detrás del espectáculo de los Juegos, se expone en *10 Photographers: Olympic Images* en el Museum of Contemporary Art de Los Ángeles. Otros fotógrafos incluidos son Jo Ann Callis y Robert C. Buitrón.

En noviembre, Bernal participa como invitado en el Tercer Coloquio Latinoamericano de Fotografía de La Habana. Imparte otro taller sobre el sistema de zonas.

Bernal recibe un premio en Artes Visuales del Southeastern Center for Contemporary Art de Winston-Salem, Carolina del Norte. Participa en una exposición colectiva llamada *Awards in the Visual Arts 3* que se inaugura en el San Antonio Museum of Art. La muestra viaja también al Loch Haven Art Center en Orlando, Florida, y al Cranbrook Academy of Art Museum en Bloomfield Hills, Michigan.

1985 En marzo, la obra de Bernal se expone en una muestra colectiva titulada *Facets of the Collection: Excerpts from Espejo: Reflections of the Mexican American* en el San Francisco Museum of Modern Art.

Se inaugura una exposición individual, *Louis Carlos Bernal*, en el California Museum of Photography en Riverside. Una segunda exposición individual, *Images from the 1984 Olympics* se inaugura en el CCP.

Bernal y Sandra Anderson se divorcian. Bernal y su compañera Marietta Bernstorff se mudan más tarde a una casa en el Barrio El Hoyo de Tucson.

1986 Bernal expone en *State of the State: An Exhibition of Arizona Photograph* en el Arizona State Capitol Museum en Phoenix.

1987–88 Bernal participa en un panel del jurado de proyectos de arte visual del National Endowment for the Arts (el Fondo Nacional de las Artes) en Washington, DC. Recibe una beca del Tucson Pima Arts Council, ahora conocido como el Arts Foundation for Tucson y Southern Arizona.

En 1987, Texas Tech University encarga a Bernal su serie *Lubbock*. Las fotografías se exponen en 1988 en el Museum of Texas Tech como *Espíritu Mejicano: Lubbock*. La serie también se expone en la Etherton Gallery en Tucson.

Bernal realiza su último viaje a México en 1988. Viaja con su compañera Marietta Bernstorff y su buen amigo Armando Cristeto.

1989 Bernal expone en una exposición colectiva titulada *La imagen antes y después de la cámara*, en La Agencia, una galería en la Ciudad de México dirigida por el artista Adolfo Patiño. La muestra se organiza en el marco del festival 150 Años de la Fotografía en México, que se celebra en toda la ciudad con exposiciones, eventos y paneles, patrocinados por el Consejo Nacional para la Cultura y las Artes y una serie de eventos y exposiciones paralelas en galerías comerciales y espacios culturales sin ánimo de lucro.

El 24 de octubre, Bernal queda en coma después de que un coche lo atropelle en Tucson mientras se dirigía al trabajo en bicicleta.

1990 La obra de Bernal se expone en *The Decade Show: Frameworks of Identity in the 1980s*, una influyente exposición con obras de noventa y cuatro artistas, entre ellos Jean-Michel Basquiat, Barbara Kruger, James Luna, Adrian Piper y Lorna Simpson. Se trata de una colaboración entre tres instituciones de Nueva York: el New Museum, el Museum of Contemporary Hispanic Art, y el Studio Museum in Harlem.

La obra de Bernal está incluida en la exposición hita, *Chicano Art: Resistance and Affirmation (CARA)*. Se origina en la University of California at Los Angeles Wight Gallery y viaja durante casi tres años por museos de diez ciudades. Esta conformada por la obra de 180 artistas chicanas y chicanos y se considera un hito importante en la historia del arte de esta cultura.

1991 El Fondo Louis Carlos Bernal se establece a través de la Pima Community College Foundation para apoyar los gastos médicos de Bernal. Varias personas de la facultad y el personal de la universidad contribuyen al fondo.

1992 La obra de Bernal es el sujeto de *Chicanismo*, una exposición colectiva organizada por la George Eastman House de Rochester, Nueva York.

En marzo, se inaugura en el CCP una exposición individual, *Louis Carlos Bernal*. La organización también organiza una recepción de clausura y una subasta de obras fotográficas a beneficio del Fondo Louis Carlos Bernal. Para recaudar fondos, se subastan fotografías donadas por decenas de fotógrafas y fotógrafos como Manuel Álvarez Bravo, Graciela Iturbide, Morrie Camhi, Sally Mann, Pedro Meyer, Judy Dater, Danny Lyon y Robert C. Buitrón.

1993 Louis Carlos Bernal muere a los cincuenta y dos años, el 18 de agosto, el día de su cumpleaños, en la casa del Barrio El Hoyo que compartía con su compañera Marietta Bernstorff. Está enterrado en el cementerio católico de San Francisco de Phoenix.

1996 Las fotografías de Bernal forman parte de la mayor exposición de fotografía latina jamás montada, *American Voices: Latino Photographers in the United States*, organizada por FotoFest en Houston y comisariada por los también fotógrafos Kathy Vargas, Robert C. Buitrón, Charles Biasiny-Rivera y Ricardo Viera. Al año siguiente, la exposición viaja a la Smithsonian Institution en Washington, DC, donde se exhibe en el S. Dillon Ripley Center.

2002 Curada por Ann Simmons-Myers, se inaugura en el Pima Community College una exposición individual de la obra de Bernal titulada *Barrios* en la recién inaugurada Louis Carlos Bernal Art Gallery. Presenta más de ochenta imágenes de toda su carrera. Los amigos y colegas Simmons-Myers, James Enyeart, Luis Jiménez, Patricia Preciado Martin y Leslie Marmon Silko contribuyen ensayos al catálogo de la exposición.

2014 El Centro para la Fotografía Creativa adquiere el archivo de Louis Carlos Bernal, una donación realizada por sus hijas Lisa Bernal Brethour y Katrina Bernal. La colección incluye impresiones fotográficas, negativos y hojas de contacto, así como correspondencia, publicaciones, grabaciones de vídeo y otros materiales.

2016 *Louis Carlos Bernal: Arizona Unseen, Color Photographs 1978–1988* (Louis Carlos Bernal: Arizona invisible, Fotografías de color 1978–1988), comisariada por Ann Simmons-Myers, se inaugura en Louis Carlos Bernal Art Gallery del Pima Community College. La exposición presenta fotografías en color inéditas.

1er Coloquio Nacional de Fotografía. Hidalgo: Gobierno Estado de Hidalgo; Mexico City: Instituto Nacional de Bellas Artes and Consejo Mexicano de Fotografía, 1984.

Acuña, Rodolfo. *Occupied America: A History of Chicanos*. New York: HarperCollins, 1987.

Alinder, James G., ed. *Light Years: The Friends of Photography 1967–1987 (Untitled 43)*. Carmel, CA: Friends of Photography, 1987.

Alurista [pseud.]. "El plan espiritual de Aztlán." *El Grito del Norte* 2, no. 9 (July 6, 1969): p. 5.

Anaya, Rudolfo A., Francisco A. Lomelí, and Enrique R. Lamadrid. *Aztlán: Essays on the Chicano Homeland*, rev. ed. Albuquerque: University of New Mexico Press, 2017.

The Art of Frederick Sommer: Photography, Drawing, Collage. Prescott, AZ: Frederick and Frances Sommer Foundation, 2005.

Awards in the Visual Arts 3. Winston-Salem, NC: Southeastern Center for Contemporary Art, 1984.

Bernal, Louis Carlos, Morrie Camhi, Abigail Heyman, Roger Minick, and Neal Slavin. *Espejo: Reflections of the Mexican American*. Oakland, CA: Oakland Museum, 1978.

Bernal, Louis Carlos. "Benitez Suite." In *Chicanismo: Photographs by Louis Carlos Bernal*. Rochester, NY: International Museum of Photography at George Eastman House, 1992.

Cásares, Oscar. "Louis Carlos Bernal: Barrios." *Aperture* 245: "Latinx" (Winter 2021): pp. 66–71.

Center for Creative Photography. *Exhibiting Photography. Twenty Years at the Center for Creative Photography*. Tucson: Center for Creative Photography, University of Arizona, 1996.

Corkovic, Laura M. *Indigenes Erbe im Internet: Zur Identitätspolitik der Chicano-Fotografie im digitalen Zeitalter*. Bielefeld, Germany: Transcript Verlag, 2017.

Ferrer, Elizabeth. "First Encounters: Latino Artists at the Colloquiums of Latin American Photography." Paper presented at the Latino Art Now Conference, University of Illinois, Chicago, April 9, 2016.

—. *Latinx Photography in the United States: A Visual History*. Seattle: University of Washington Press, 2020.

Flor y Canto IV and V: An Anthology of Chicano Literature from the Festivals Held in Albuquerque, New Mexico, 1977 and Tempe, Arizona, 1978. Albuquerque: Pajarito Publications, 1980.

Foster, David William. "Barrios & the Visibility of Enduring Lives: Louis Carlos Bernal." In *Picturing the Barrio: Ten Chicano Photographers (Latinx and Latin American Profiles)*, pp. 59–72. Pittsburgh: University of Pittsburgh Press, 2017.

Goldman, Shifra M. "The Iconography of Chicano Self-Determination: Race, Ethnicity, and Class." Special issue, *Art Journal: Depictions of the Dispossessed* 49, no. 2 (Summer 1990): pp. 167–73.

Gomez-Novy, Juan, and Stefanos Polyzoides. "A Tale of Two Cities: The Failed Urban Renewal of Downtown Tucson in the Twentieth Century." *Journal of the Southwest* 45, no. 1/2 (2003): pp. 87–119.

Grace, Ruthann. "Don Pedro Pellón: Tucson's Pioneer Actor and Activist." *Journal of Arizona History* 57, no. 2 (2016): pp. 153–96.

Griswold del Castillo, Richard, Teresa McKenna, and Yvonne Yarbro-Bejarano, eds. *Chicano Art: Resistance and Affirmation, 1965–1985*. Los Angeles: Wight Art Gallery, University of California Los Angeles, 1991.

Gunckel, Colin. "The Chicano/a Photographic: Art as Social Practice in the Chicano Movement." *American Quarterly* 67, no. 2 (June 2015): pp. 377–412.

Hecho en Latinoamérica: Segundo Coloquio Latinoamericano de Fotografía. Mexico City: Consejo Mexicano de Fotografía, 1981.

Herzberg, Julia P. "Re-membering Identity: Vision of Connections." In *The Decade Show: Frameworks of Identity in the 1980s*, pp. 37–59. New York: Museum of Contemporary Hispanic Art, The New Museum, The Studio Museum in Harlem, 1990.

hooks, bell. "In Our Glory: Photography and Black Life." In *Art on My Mind: Visual Politics*, pp. 54–64. New York: New Press, 1995.

Johnstone, Mark. "Observations in a Social Environment." *Artweek* 16, no. 30 (May 28, 1985): p. 12.

Kay, Jane. "Home Is Disappearing," in "Tucson's Barrio's: A Report from the Inside." *Arizona Daily Star*, July 16, 1978.

"Luis [*sic*] Bernal, Espejos del Alma." *Latina*, February 1986, pp. 52–53.

"Louis Bernal." *Arizona Illustrated* segment. Aired January 24, 1990, on KUAT-TV, 29:34.

Louis Carlos Bernal Archive, 1953–1993. Center for Creative Photography, University of Arizona, Tucson. AG 182.

Martin, Patricia Preciado, and Louis Carlos Bernal. *Images and Conversations: Mexican Americans Recall a Southwestern Past*. Tucson: University of Arizona Press, 1983.

Mesa-Bains, Amalia. "Domesticana: The Sensibility of Chicana Rasquache." *Aztlán: A Journal of Chicano Studies* 24, no. 2 (Fall 1999): pp. 157–67.

"Mexicans Who Had Led Strikes Sign Contract with a Goldwater." *New York Times*, February 4, 1979.

Ortiz Monasterio, Pablo. "Close to the Boom." *VIST*, October 5, 2021, https://vistprojects.com/en/close-to-the-boom/.

Ortiz-Torres, Rubén. "De cómo el color migro al sur desde Aztlán en busca de una águila devorando a una serpiente en una penca de maguey." *Luna Córnea* 34 (2013): pp. 397–401.

—. "¡El Pachuco Actual Se Nueva A Morir!" In *Mex/L.A.: "Mexican" Modernism(s) in Los Angeles, 1930–1985*, p. 31. Berlin: Hatje Cantz and Long Beach, CA: Museum of Latin American Art, 2011.

Otero, Lydia R. *In the Shadows of the Freeway: Growing Up Brown & Queer*. Tucson: Planet Earth Press, 2019.

Pitts, Terrence. *Contemporary Photography in Mexico: 9 Photographers*. Tucson: Center for Creative Photography, University of Arizona, 1978.

Preciado Regan, Margaret. "Douglas Revisited." *Tucson Weekly*, November 24, 2016.

Radding, Cynthia. *Wandering Peoples: Colonialism, Ethnic Spaces, and Ecological Frontiers in Northwestern Mexico, 1700–1850*. Durham, NC: Duke University Press, 1997.

Rider, Ben "Easy." "An Informal Chat with Louis Carlos Bernal," 1982, from Louis Carlos Bernal Archive, Center for Creative Photography, video, 1:03:34.

Rigat, Leticia. "Los Coloquios Latinoamericanos de Fotografía y la reconfiguración de las prácticas fotográficas." *Dixit* no.32, 2020. EPUB.

Rios, Josh. "Race to the Periphery." *Dilettante Army*, n.d., https://dilettantearmy.com/articles/race-to-the-periphery.

Rule, Amy, and Nancy Solomon, eds. *Original Sources. Art and Archives at the Center for Creative Photography*. Tucson: Center for Creative Photography, University of Arizona, 2002.

Simmons-Myers, Ann, and Louis Carlos Bernal. *Louis Carlos Bernal: Barrios*. Tucson: Pima Community College, in association with University of Arizona Library, 2002.

Solis Gomez, Antonio, "The Inception of a Cycle, Part II, A Conversation with Patricia Preciado Martin, Author of *Images and Conversations* with Photographs by Luis [*sic*] Carlos Bernal." *La Bloga,* February 10, 2018, https://labloga.blogspot.com/2018/02/the-inception-of-cycle-part-ii.html.

Tarsiers, Paul. "Politics and Photographs: Second Latin American Colloquium on Photography." *Aperture*, Spring 1982, pp. 2–7.

10 Photographers, Olympic Images. Los Angeles: Los Angeles Center for Photographic Studies, 1984.

Troy, Timothy. "Louis Carlos Bernal." In *Original Sources: Art and Archives at the Center for Creative Photography*, pp. 53–55. Edited by Amy Rule and Nancy Solomon. Tucson: Center for Creative Photography, University of Arizona, 2002.

Tubis, Roberta. "Photographer Seeks to Promote Hispanic Arts." *El Independiente* (Tucson), October 30, 1981.

"Tucson's Barrio's: A Report from the Inside," *Arizona Daily Star*, July 16, 1978, http://www.barriostories.org/wp-content/uploads/2015/11/Tucson-Barrios-Section-ADS-1978.pdf.

Vento, Arnoldo Carlos."The *Flor y Canto* and *Canto al Pueblo* Festivals." In *Mestizo: The History, Culture and Politics of the Chicano and Mexican*, pp. 237–42. Lanham, MD: University Press of America, 1997.

Ybarra-Frausto, Tomás. "Rasquachismo: A Chicano Sensibility." In *Chicano Aesthetics: Rasquachismo*, pp. 5–8. Phoenix: Movimiento Artístico del Rio Salado, 1989.

Zuver, Marc, et al. *Raíces Antiguas/Visiones Nuevas: Ancient Roots/New Visions*. Tucson: Tucson Museum of Art, 1977.

EXHIBITION CHECKLIST / LISTA DE EXPOSICIÓN

P. 171
Guadalajara, Mexico, 1962
Gelatin-silver print / Impresión en gelatina de plata
6 × 6 in. (15.2 × 15.2 cm)
2022.05.87

P. 167
Chiclets, Cuernavaca, 1963
Gelatin-silver print / Impresión en gelatina de plata
11 ⅝ × 9 in. (29.5 × 22.9 cm)
2015.36.1

P. 48; fig. 5
American Landscape, 1970
Film positive over photomechanical print / Película positiva sobre Impresión fotomecánica
5 ¾ × 7 ¼ in. (14.6 × 18.4 cm)
2022.05.84

P. 87
Untitled (Lisa Bernal), 1970
Gelatin-silver print / Impresión en gelatina de plata
6 ½ × 6 ½ in. (16.5 × 16.5 cm)
2022.05.78

P. 88
Untitled, 1970
Film positive over silvered mat board / Película positive sobre cartulina de enmarcar plateado
9 × 6 ¾ in. (22.9 × 17.1 cm)
2022.05.85

P. 89
Untitled, 1970
Film positive over silvered mat board / Película positive sobre cartulina de enmarcar plateado
9 × 7 ¼ in. (22.9 × 18.4 cm)
2022.05.86

P. 48; fig. 4
Untitled, ca. 1970
Grid of film positives / Cuadrícula de positivas de película
12 ¼ × 9 in. (31.1 × 22.9 cm)
2023.03.01

P. 91
Paper Cutting #3, 1970–72
Gelatin-silver print / Impresión en gelatina de plata
11 × 8 ½ in. (27.9 × 21.6 cm)
2022.05.81

—

Untitled, 1970–72
(Not illustrated in this publication / No esta ilustrada en esta publicación)
Gelatin-silver print / Impresión en gelatina de plata
6 ½ × 4 in. (16.5 × 10.2 cm)
2022.05.79

P. 90
Chrome Cutting, 1972
Gelatin-silver print / Impresión en gelatina de plata
10 ¾ × 8 ½ in. (27.3 × 21.6 cm)
2022.05.82

P. 86
Untitled (Katrina Bernal), 1972
Gelatin-silver print / Impresión en gelatina de plata
7 ⅛ × 7 ⅛ in. (18.1 × 18.1 cm)
2022.05.77

P. 115
Lucia Fresno, 1973
Gelatin-silver print / Impresión en gelatina de plata
9 × 9 in. (22.9 × 22.8 cm)
2023.03.02

P. 99
Sra. Vargas, Barrio Armory Park, 1973
Gelatin-silver print / Impresión en gelatina de plata
7 × 7 in. (17.8 × 17.8 cm)
2022.05.89

P. 93
Benny's Market, 1974
Gelatin-silver print / Impresión en gelatina de plata
9 × 9 in. (22.9 × 22.9 cm)
2022.05.75

P. 161
Doña Rita Mendoza, Barrio Viejo, 1974
Gelatin-silver print / Impresión en gelatina de plata
8 ½ × 8 ¾ in. (21.6 × 22.2 cm)
2022.05.80

P. 81
I'm Not a Crook, 1974; from the series *An American Fairy Tale*
Gelatin-silver print / Impresión en gelatina de plata
6 ¾ × 6 ¾ in. (17.1 × 17.1 cm)
2022.05.08

P. 77
Mexican Escapade, 1974; from the series *An American Fairy Tale*
Gelatin-silver print / Impresión en gelatina de plata
8 × 6 ¾ in. (20.3 × 17.1 cm)
2022.05.01

P. 83
Old Clothes, New Faces, 1974; from the series *An American Fairy Tale*
Gelatin-silver print / Impresión en gelatina de plata
7 × 7 in. (17.8 × 17.8 cm)
2022.05.05

P. 85
Sticking Together, 1974; from the series *An American Fairy Tale*
Gelatin-silver print / Impresión en gelatina de plata
6 ¾ × 7 in. (17.1 × 17.8 cm)
2022.05.03

P. 80
Tide, Handiwipes, and Richard Millhouse, 1974; from the series *An American Fairy Tale*
Gelatin-silver print / Impresión en gelatina de plata
7 × 7 in. (17.8 × 17.8 cm)
2022.05.06

P. 84
White House, Blue Skies, 1974; from the series *An American Fairy Tale*
Gelatin-silver print / Impresión en gelatina de plata
7 × 7 in. (17.8 × 17.8 cm)
2022.05.04

P. 79
A Lot of Bull, 1975; from the series *An American Fairy Tale*
Gelatin-silver print / Impresión en gelatina de plata
7 × 7 in. (17.8 × 17.8 cm)
2022.05.07

P. 78
Untitled (Browns Boarding House), 1975; from the series *An American Fairy Tale*
Gelatin-silver print / Impresión en gelatina de plata
6 ¾ × 7 in. (17.1 × 17.8 cm)
2022.05.02
—
Barrio Children, Sunday Morning, Douglas, Arizona, 1977
(Not illustrated in this publication / No esta ilustrada en esta publicación)
Gelatin-silver print / Impresión en gelatina de plata
9 × 8 ¹⁵/₁₆ in. (22.9 × 22.7 cm)
2023.03.03

P. 98
Grave Painter, Día de los Muertos, Nogales, 1977
Gelatin-silver print / Impresión en gelatina de plata
9 × 8 ¹⁵/₁₆ in. (22.9 × 22.7 cm)
97.46.16

P. 128
La Raza, 1977
Gelatin-silver print / Impresión en gelatina de plata
9 × 9 in. (22.9 × 22.9 cm)
2022.05.23

P. 117
Sr. Ernesto Villa, Barrio Hollywood, 1977
Chromogenic print / Copia cromogénica
9 × 9 in. (22.9 × 22.9 cm)
97.46.35

P. 103
Quiñonez Baptism, Tucson, 1977
Gelatin-silver print / Impresión en gelatina de plata
8 ¼ × 9 in. (21 × 22.9 cm)
2022.05.36

P. 107
Ahora, 1977; from the series *Benitez Suite*
Gelatin-silver print / Impresión en gelatina de plata
9 × 9 in. (22.9 × 22.9 cm)
79.87.7

P. 105
Calendario, 1977; from the series *Benitez Suite*
Gelatin-silver print / Impresión en gelatina de plata
9 × 9 in. (22.9 × 22.9 cm)
79.87.5

P. 109
Cómoda, 1977; from the series *Benitez Suite*
Gelatin-silver print / Impresión en gelatina de plata
9 × 9 in. (22.9 × 22.9 cm)
79.87.3

P. 24
Corazón de Jesús, 1977; from the series *Benitez Suite*
Gelatin-silver print / Impresión en gelatina de plata
9 × 8 ¾ in. (22.9 × 22.2 cm)
79.87.1

P. 111
Cortina de vestido, 1977; from the series *Benitez Suite*
Gelatin-silver print / Impresión en gelatina de plata
9 ¹/₁₆ × 9 ¹/₁₆ in. (23 × 23 cm)
79.87.4

P. 104
Pope Pius XII, 1977; from the series *Benitez Suite*
Gelatin-silver print / Impresión en gelatina de plata
9 ¹/₁₆ × 9 ¹/₁₆ in. (23 × 23 cm)
79.87.2

P. 108
Retrato, 1977; from the series *Benitez Suite*
Gelatin-silver print / Impresión en gelatina de plata
9 × 9 in. (22.9 × 22.9 cm)
2022.05.71

P. 11
Albert y Lynn Morales, Silver City, New Mexico, 1978
Chromogenic print / Impresión cromogénica
13 ¹⁵/₁₆ × 13 ⅞ in. (35.4 × 35.3 cm)
2022.05.44

P. 134
Barrio Portrait, H Avenue Cuadra, Douglas, Arizona, 1978
Chromogenic print / Impresión cromogénica
9 ¹/₁₆ × 9 ¹/₁₆ in. (23 × 23 cm)
82.77.64

P. 100
Boda de Luz, Douglas, Arizona, 1978
Digital image from color negative / Imagen digital a partir de negativo en color
Bernal archive, AG 182, Photographic materials, Box 14, Folder 7, Roll 4537, Frame 9
Vintage print: 82.77.76

P. 121
Dos Mujeres, Douglas, Arizona, 1978
Chromogenic print / Impresión cromogénica
14 × 14 ¹/₁₆ in. (35.6 × 35.7 cm)
2022.05.46

P. 119
El Show de Rosita, Barrio Anita, 1978
Digital image from color negative / Imagen digital a partir de negativo en color
Bernal archive, AG 182, Photographic materials, Box 14, Folder 7, Roll 4531, Frame 4
Vintage print: 2022.05.25

P. 19
Juanita Serrano with Santo Niño de Atocha, 1978
Digital image from color negative / Imagen digital a partir de negativo en color
Bernal archive, AG 182, Photographic materials, Box 14, Folder 7, Roll 4507, Frame 5
Vintage print: 2022.05.10

P. 153
Leon Speer's Barber Shop, Felix Valdivezo & Daughter Patricia, Lordsburg, New Mexico, 1978
Chromogenic print / Impresión cromogénica
9 × 9 ¹/₁₆ in. (22.9 × 23 cm)
82.77.83

P. 136
Los Vatos Locos, Douglas, Arizona, 1978
Chromogenic print / Impresión cromogénica
9 ¹/₁₆ × 9 ¹/₁₆ in. (23 × 23 cm)
82.77.84

P. 2
Martinez Brothers in Candy Store, Douglas, Arizona, 1978
Chromogenic print / Impresión cromogénica
9 ¹/₁₆ × 9 ¹/₁₆ in. (23 × 23 cm)
82.77.80

P. 20
Nanita Mendibles, Barrio Anita, 1978
Chromogenic print / Impresión cromogénica
9 ¹/₁₆ × 9 ¹/₁₆ in. (23 × 23 cm)
82.77.67

P. 118
Recámara de Blas y Pauline Flores, 1978
Digital image from color negative / Imagen digital a partir de negativo en color
Bernal archive, AG 182, Photographic materials, Box 14, Folder 7, Roll 4534, Frame 3
Vintage print: 2022.05.11

P. 114
Recámara de Catalina Olomos, Phoenix, Arizona, 1978
Chromogenic print / Impresión cromogénica
9 × 9 in. (22.9 × 22.9 cm)
2022.05.67

P. 140
Recámara de Mis Padres, Phoenix, Arizona, 1978
Chromogenic print / Impresión cromogénica
9 × 9 in. (22.9 × 22.9 cm)
2023.03.05

P. 123
Retrato de Boda Rosa, 1978
Chromogenic print / Impresión cromogénica
9 ¹/₁₆ × 9 ¹/₁₆ in. (23 × 23 cm)
82.77.74

P. 21
Rosie Siqueiros, Barrio Anita, Tucson, Arizona, 1978
Chromogenic print / Impresión cromogénica
9 × 9 in. (22.9 × 22.9 cm)
2022.05.24

P. 23
San Pedro Ranch, Animas, New Mexico, 1978
Chromogenic print / Impresión cromogénica
9 ¹/₁₆ × 9 in. (23 × 22.9 cm)
82.77.88

P. 22
San Pedro Ranch, Animas, New Mexico, 1978
Chromogenic print / Impresión cromogénica
9 × 9 ¹/₁₆ in. (22.9 × 23 cm)
80.45.5

P. 113
Señora Espinosa, Membrillo, Tucson, Arizona, 1978
Digital image from color negative / Imagen digital a partir de negativo en color
Bernal archive, AG 182, Photographic materials, Box 14, Folder 3, Roll 278, Lower Left Frame
Vintage print: 2022.05.4

P. 154
Untitled, 1978
Chromogenic print / Copia cromogénica
14 × 11 in. (35.5 × 27.9 cm)
97.46.39

P. 122
Untitled, 1978
Posthumous digital inkjet print from color negative / Impresión póstuma de inyección de tinta digital a partir de negativo en color
16 × 16 in. (40.7 × 40.7 cm)
Bernal archive, AG 182, Photographic materials, Box 20

P. 13
Untitled, 1978
Chromogenic print / Impresión cromogénica
9 × 9 in. (22.9 × 22.9 cm)
2022.05.12
—
(Not illustrated in this publication / No esta ilustrado en esta publicación)
Virgen de Guadalupe, Barrio Viejo, 1978
Chromogenic print / Impresión cromogénica
9 ¹/₁₆ × 9 ¹/₁₆ in. (23 × 23 cm)
82.77.81

PP. 94–95
4th Street Barrio, Douglas, 1979
Gelatin-silver print / Impresión en gelatina de plata
5 × 12 in. (12.7 × 30.5 cm)
2022.05.34

PP. 164–65
4th Street Barrio, Douglas, 1979
Gelatin-silver print / Impresión en gelatina de plata
5 × 12 in. (12.7 × 30.5 cm)
2022.05.38

P. 156
6th Street Barrio, Douglas, Arizona, 1979
Chromogenic print / Copia cromogénica
9 × 9 in. (22.9 × 22.9 cm)
97.46.45

P. 157
Anna Quiñonez, Douglas, 1979
Digital image from color negative / Imagen digital a partir de negativo en color
Bernal archive, AG 182, Photographic materials, Box 14, Folder 2, Roll C8709, Frame CM10
Vintage print: 2022.05.51

P. 139
El Gato, Canutillo, New Mexico, 1979
Chromogenic print / Impresión cromogénica
13 ¹⁵/₁₆ × 13 ⅞ in. (35.4 × 35.3 cm)
2022.05.42

P. 162
Hermanos, Chihuahuita, El Paso, 1979
Gelatin-silver print / Impresión en gelatina de plata
9 × 9 in. (22.9 × 22.9 cm)
97.46.28

P. 159
José Padilla, Panadero, El Paso, 1979
Gelatin-silver print / Impresión en gelatina de plata
9 × 9 in. (22.9 × 22.9 cm)
2022.05.37

P. 101
Juan Mejia, Marines, Douglas, Arizona, 1979
Gelatin-silver print / Impresión en gelatina de plata
9 ¹/₁₆ × 8 ¹⁵/₁₆ in. (23 × 22.7 cm)
97.46.5

P. 158
Loncheria Junior, 1979
Digital image from color negative / Imagen digital a partir de negativo en color
Bernal archive, AG 182, Photographic materials, Box 14, Folder 5, Roll C5501, Frame 11
Vintage print: 2022.05.17

P. 125
María Soto Audelo, Tucson, 1979
Gelatin-silver print / Impresión en gelatina de plata
9 × 9 in. (22.9 × 22.9 cm)
2022.05.31

P. 163
Mother and Son, 6th Street Cuadra, Douglas, Arizona, 1979
Gelatin-silver print / Impresión en gelatina de plata
9 × 12 in. (22.9 × 30.5 cm)
2022.05.30

P. 130
Naco Portrait, 1979
Gelatin-silver print / Impresión en gelatina de plata
9 ⁷/₁₆ × 6 ⅞ in. (24 × 17.4 cm)
2010.20.6

P. 135
Stephen Quiñonez, Douglas, Arizona, 1979
Gelatin-silver print / Impresión en gelatina de plata
9 × 8 ¹⁵/₁₆ in. (22.9 × 22.7 cm)
97.46.14

P. 137
Untitled, 1979
Chromogenic print / Impresión cromogénica
9 × 9 ¹/₁₆ in. (22.9 × 23 cm)
97.46.32

P. 15
Untitled (farmworker), late 1970s
Posthumous digital inkjet print from color negative / Impresión póstuma de inyección de tinta digital a partir de negativo en color
16 × 16 in. (40.7 × 40.7 cm)
Bernal archive, AG 182, Photographic materials, Box 20

P. 14
Untitled (female striker), late 1970s
Posthumous digital inkjet print from color negative / Impresión póstuma de inyección de tinta digital a partir de negativo en color
16 × 16 in. (40.7 × 40.7 cm)
Bernal archive, AG 182, Photographic materials, Box 20

P. 126
Cholos, Logan Heights, San Diego, 1980
Gelatin-silver print / Impresión en gelatina de plata
8 × 12 in. (20.3 × 30.5 cm)
2022.05.35

P. 97
Kennedy Cocio Altar, Tucson, 1980
Gelatin-silver print / Impresión en gelatina de plata
8 × 12 in. (20.3 × 30.5 cm)
2022.05.14

P. 172
La Pelona, Mexico, 1980
Gelatin-silver print / Impresión en gelatina de plata
8 × 12 in. (20.3 × 30.5 cm)
2022.05.19

P. 96
Milagros, Mexico City, 1980
Gelatin-silver print / Impresión en gelatina de plata
8 × 12 in. (20.3 × 30.5 cm)
2022.05.13

P. 155
*New Immigrants, Douglas,
Arizona*, 1980
Digital image from color neg-
ative / Imagen digital a partir
de negativo en color
Bernal archive, AG 182, Pho-
tographic materials, Box 14,
Folder 5, Roll C5500, Frame 4
Vintage print: 97.46.36

P. 17
*Quinceañera, Phoenix,
Arizona*, 1981
Gelatin-silver print / Impresión en gelatina de plata
8 × 12 in. (20.3 × 30.5 cm)
2022.05.29

P. 16
Santos y Television, Mexico,
1981
Gelatin-silver print / Impresión en gelatina de plata
6 × 9 in. (15.2 × 22.9 cm)
2022.05.32

P. 127
Dos Cholas, Tucson, Arizona,
1982
Gelatin-silver print / Impresión en gelatina de plata
8 × 12 in. (20.3 × 30.5 cm)
2018.38.1

P. 129
Los Vatos, Del Rio Ballroom,
1982
Gelatin-silver print / Impresión en gelatina de plata
9 × 9 in. (22.9 × 22.9 cm)
2022.05.27

PP. 168–69
*Manuel Álvarez Bravo,
Coyoacán, México*, 1982
Gelatin-silver print / Impresión en gelatina de plata
4 15/16 × 11 15/16 in. (12.6 × 30.3
cm)
83.75.1
—
Retablo #3 El Pajaro, 1982
(Not illustrated in this publication / No esta ilustrada en
esta publicación)
Gelatin-silver print / Impresión en gelatina de plata
5 × 4 in. (12.7 × 10.2 cm)
2022.05.88

P. 178
*Untitled (Man in interior),
Havana, Cuba*, 1982
Digital image from black
and white negative / Imagen
digital de negativo en blanco
y negro
Bernal archive, AG 182, Pho-
tographic materials, Box 14,
Folder 11, Roll 440, Frame 9A

P. 183
*Untitled (Military Guard),
Havana, Cuba*, 1982
Digital image from black
and white negative / Imagen
digital de negativo en blanco
y negro
Bernal archive, AG 182, Pho-
tographic materials, Box 14,
Folder 11, Roll 435, Frame 8A

P. 177
*Untitled (School Girls),
Havana, Cuba*, 1982
Digital image from black
and white negative / Imagen
digital de negativo en blanco
y negro
Bernal archive, AG 182, Pho-
tographic materials, Box 14,
Folder 11, Roll 475, Frame 11

P. 182
*Untitled (Street scene with
women), Havana, Cuba*, 1982
Digital image from black
and white negative / Imagen
digital de negativo en blanco
y negro
Bernal archive, AG 182,
Photographic materials, Box
14, Folder 11

P. 181
*Untitled (Walking Woman),
Havana, Cuba*, 1982
Digital image from black
and white negative / Imagen
digital de negativo en blanco
y negro
Bernal archive, AG 182,
Photographic materials, Box
14, Folder 11, Roll 441, Frame
23A

P. 179
*Untitled (Woman with baby
and umbrella), Havana,
Cuba*, 1982
Digital image from black
and white negative / Imagen
digital de negativo en blanco
y negro
Bernal archive, AG 182, Photographic materials, Box 14,
Folder 11, Roll 475, Frame 19

P. 131
La Reina de Mi Vida, 1983
Gelatin-silver print / Impresión en gelatina de plata
12 × 8 in. (30.5 × 20.3 cm)
2022.05.16

P. 133
*Cruisin' Cholas, Tucson,
Arizona*, 1984
Gelatin-silver print / Impresión en gelatina de plata
8 × 12 in. (20.3 × 30.5 cm)
2022.05.18

P. 187
*Polaroid Vendor, Figueroa
Street, Los Angeles
Olympics*, 1984
Cibachrome print / Impresión
Cibachrome
14 × 17 1/14 in. (35.6 × 43.8 cm)
2022.05.57

P. 185
*Sisters, Archery, Long Beach,
Los Angeles Olympics*, 1984
Cibachrome print / Impresión
Cibachrome
14 × 17 1/14 in. (35.6 × 43.8 cm)
2022.05.58

P. 186
*Volunteers, Rowing, Lake
Casitas, Los Angeles
Olympics*, 1984
Cibachrome print / Impresión
Cibachrome
14 × 17 1/14 in. (35.6 × 43.8 cm)
2022.05.59

P. 190
*Untitled (Boardwalk), Los
Angeles*, 1984
Gelatin-silver print / Impresión en gelatina de plata
8 × 12 in. (20.3 × 30.5 cm)
2022.05.76

P. 189
*Untitled (Lunch Stand), Los
Angeles*, 1984
Gelatin-silver print / Impresión en gelatina de plata
8 × 12 in. (20.3 × 30.5 cm)
2022.05.73

P. 191
*Untitled (Street Preacher),
Los Angeles*, 1984
Gelatin-silver print / Impresión en gelatina de plata
8 × 11 ¾ in. (20.3 × 29.8 cm)
2022.05.74

P. 188
*Untitled (Supermarket), Los
Angeles*, 1984
Gelatin-silver print / Impresión en gelatina de plata
8 × 12 in. (20.3 × 30.5 cm)
2022.05.72

P. 174
El Diablo, ca. 1985
Gelatin-silver print / Impresión en gelatina de plata
8 × 12 in. (20.3 × 30.5 cm)
2022.05.09

P. 173
*Granddaughter and Grand-
mother, Mexico City*, 1987
Gelatin-silver print / Impresión en gelatina de plata
8 × 12 in. (20.3 × 30.5 cm)
2022.05.33

P. 175
Cristo de la Calle, Mexico,
1988
Gelatin-silver print / Impresión en gelatina de plata
8 × 12 in. (20.3 × 30.5 cm)
2022.05.20

P. 52; fig. 19 (inset / recuadro)
Dia de los Muertos, 1988
Gelatin-silver print / Impresión en gelatina de plata
8 × 12 in. (20.3 × 30.5 cm)
2022.05.15

P. 201
Untitled, 1987; from the
series *Lubbock*
Chromogenic print / Impresión cromogénica
14 × 14 in. (35.6 × 35.6 cm)
2022.05.52

P. 197
Angelina, 1988; from the
series *Lubbock*
Chromogenic print / Impresión cromogénica
14 × 14 in. (35.6 × 35.6 cm)
2022.05.50

P. 203
Caridad Sanchez, 1988; from
the series *Lubbock*
Chromogenic print / Impresión cromogénica
14 × 14 in. (35.6 × 35.6 cm)
2022.05.45

P. 199
Helen, 1988; from the series
Lubbock
Chromogenic print / Impresión cromogénica
14 × 14 in. (35.6 × 35.6 cm)
2022.05.49

P. 200
Untitled, 1988; from the
series *Lubbock*
Chromogenic print / Impresión cromogénica
13 ¾ × 13 ¾ in. (34.9 ×
34.9 cm)
2022.05.41

P. 195
Untitled, 1988; from the
series *Lubbock*
Chromogenic print / Impresión cromogénica
14 × 14 in. (35.6 × 35.6 cm)
2022.05.43

P. 194
Untitled, 1988; from the
series *Lubbock*
Chromogenic print / Impresión cromogénica
14 × 14 in. (35.6 × 35.6 cm)
2022.05.47

P. 193
Untitled, 1988; from the
series *Lubbock*
Chromogenic print / Impresión cromogénica
14 × 14 in. (35.6 × 35.6 cm)
2022.05.39

P. 207
*Untitled (Dresser Top),
Douglas*, 1989
Digital image from color neg-
ative / Imagen digital a partir
de negativo en color
Bernal archive, AG 182, Pho-
tographic materials, Box 14,
Folder 5, Roll C6467, Frame 2

P. 204
*Untitled (Hands on Table),
Douglas*, 1989
Digital image from black
and white negative / Imagen
digital de negativo en blanco
y negro
Vintage print: 2022.05.63

P. 208
Untitled (Shoes), Douglas,
1989
Digital image from color neg-
ative / Imagen digital a partir
de negativo en color
Bernal archive, AG 182,
Photographic materials,
Box 14, Folder 5, Roll C6467,
Frame 15

P. 205
Untitled (Table Top), Douglas,
1989
Digital image from black
and white negative / Imagen
digital de negativo en blanco
y negro
Vintage print: 2022.05.64

LOUIS CARLOS BERNAL (born in Douglas, Arizona, 1941; died in Tucson, 1993) was a pioneering Chicano photographer active in the last quarter of the twentieth century, maturing as an artist in the wake of the 1970s civil rights era. After completing his MFA at Arizona State University in 1972, he joined the faculty of Pima Community College in Tucson, where he developed and led its photography program, and remained for the duration of his career. The Center for Creative Photography at the University of Arizona, Tucson, preserves the Louis Carlos Bernal Archive, containing fine prints and research materials that include project records, correspondence, clippings, writings, and publications.

ELIZABETH FERRER is a writer, curator, and arts activist. She is the former vice president of contemporary art and chief curator at BRIC in Brooklyn. Ferrer is the author of *Latinx Photography in the United States: A Visual History* (2021) and the monograph *Lola Álvarez Bravo* (Aperture, 2006). She is curator of the traveling exhibition of Bernal's work from the Center for Creative Photography, Tucson, set to open in 2024.

REBECCA SENF is chief curator at the Center for Creative Photography, Tucson. She is author of *Reconstructing the View: The Grand Canyon Photographs of Mark Klett and Byron Wolfe* (2012), *Betsy Schneider: To Be Thirteen* (2017), *Making a Photographer: The Early Work of Ansel Adams* (2020), and *Richard Avedon: Relationships* (2022).

LOUIS CARLOS BERNAL (nacido en Douglas, Arizona, 1941; fallecido en Tucson, 1993) fue un fotógrafo chicano vanguardista activo durante el último cuarto del siglo XX, madurando como artista tras la época de la lucha por los derechos civiles en los años 70. Después de recibir su MFA de Arizona State University en 1972, entró como miembro de la facultad de Pima Community College en Tucson, donde desarrolló y dirigió el programa de fotografía, y donde quedó como profesor a lo largo de su carrera. El Center for Creative Photography en University of Arizona, Tucson, preserva el Archivo de Louis Carlos Bernal, que contiene fotografías impresos y materiales de investigación que incluyen registros de proyectos, correspondencias, recortes de diarios, escritos, y publicaciones.

ELIZABETH FERRER es escritora, curadora, y activista del arte. Anteriormente fue vicepresidenta de arte contemporánea y directora de curaduría de BRIC en Brooklyn, NY. Ferrer es la autora de *Latinx Photography in the United States: A Visual History* (2021), así como la monografía *Lola Álvarez Bravo* (Aperture, 2006). Ella es la curadora de la exposición itinerante de la obra de Bernal del Center for Creative Photography, Tucson, programada para abrir en 2024.

REBECCA SENF es la directora de curaduría en el Center for Creative Photography, Tucson. Es la autora de *Reconstructing the View: The Grand Canyon Photographs of Mark Klett and Byron Wolfe* (2012), *Betsy Schneider: To Be Thirteen* (2017), *Making a Photographer: The Early Work of Ansel Adams* (2020), y *Richard Avedon: Relationships* (2022).

ACKNOWLEDGMENTS

My essay for this volume was made possible thanks to the generous contributions of many people who knew Louis Carlos Bernal, including members of his family, his students, and his artistic peers. Similar to the way strangers opened their doors to Lou and his camera, every individual I approached about him was quick to accept an invitation to talk, and the resulting conversations were long and informative. I learned so much—about Lou's charisma, his sly smile, and his humor. I also learned that he was a great athlete, an impeccable dresser and a neatnik, and such a good dancer that he could attract a crowd of onlookers. He could also be temperamental when he was preoccupied with his work, and highly demanding of his students. He touched so many lives in deeply meaningful ways, and he clearly left his mark on all who were graced with his presence.

First and foremost, I offer my great thanks to Louis Carlos Bernal's daughters, Lisa Bernal Brethour and Katrina Bernal, who spoke with me often and candidly. They shared a range of information and remembrances that painted such a vivid picture of their father. In donating the Bernal archive to the Center for Creative Photography, they also made this exhibition possible.

The Mexican photographer and photography historian Armando Cristeto Patiño made essential contributions to this project. Bernal met Cristeto Patiño in Mexico City in 1981, and they maintained a close relationship until Bernal's accident at the end of that decade. Cristeto Patiño, who has preserved an archive of correspondence, publications, and other materials related to Bernal, was always available to answer my questions or share letters and publications. I am deeply indebted to him.

Bernal's partner, the artist and activist-curator Marietta Bernstorff, now based in Oaxaca, Mexico, was also equally supportive of this project. Marietta began to discuss Bernal's importance with me in 2002, and I was able to draw fruitfully from information she provided in interviews at that time, as well as from more recent, lengthy virtual chats. She also shared personal photographs, writings, and remembrances that have greatly enriched my text.

Ann Simmons-Myers, the photographer who assumed Bernal's position at Pima Community College and who curated *Louis Carlos Bernal: Barrios*, an important exhibition of his work at Pima Community College in 2002, has been deeply supportive of this project and provided valuable advice and feedback. George Luna-Peña, a young scholar with a special interest in Bernal's life and work, assembled the richly informative chronology for this catalog. I am deeply impressed by George's research skills and by his dedication to this project.

At Aperture, an organization with which I've had a long relationship, I wish to single out Sarah Meister, executive director; Lesley A. Martin, creative director; Brendan Embser, senior managing editor of *Aperture* magazine and coordinating editor for this publication; and Noa Lin, editorial assistant, for their professionalism and hard work to bring *Monografía* to fruition. I would also like to thank copy editor Claire Voon, translators Elianna Kan and Enrique Pérez Rosiles, designer Duncan Whyte, and Aperture's production team, Andrea Chlad and Minjee Cho.

Numerous other individuals assisted with the development of this project. I offer my deep thanks to David Andres, director of Louis Carlos Bernal Gallery at Pima Community College (PCC), Tucson; Ernesto Esquer, laboratory specialist of photography at PCC; Chris Benson, photographer and former student of Bernal's; Jim Covarrubias and Joseph Sánchez, artists and cofounders of Ariztlán; Robert Buitrón, photographer and curator in Chicago; Terry Etherton, owner of Etherton Gallery, Tucson; Tom Eckert, sculptor in Tempe and former classmate of Bernal's; Roberto Gil de Montes, artist in La Peñita, Nayarit, Mexico; Lorenzo Hernández, collector and former gallerist in Pasadena, California; Jeff Smith, photographer in Tucson and former student of Bernal's; Antonio Solisgomez, writer in Tucson; Esperanza Valverde, Angeles; and Laura Anderson Barbata, New York.

Many staff members at the Center for Creative Photography at the University of Arizona had a hand in the development of the exhibition and catalog. I offer special thanks to CCP's chief curator Rebecca Senf, who acted as a sounding board, suggested resources and contacts, and continually expressed her enthusiasm for this project. At the Center for Creative Photography, I also offer many thanks to Aimee Baker, Lynn Richards, Audrey Williams, Dana Hemmenway, Bryanna Knotts, Meg Jackson Fox, Denisse Brito, Alex Moral, Emilie Hardman, Emily Weirich, Diana Chávez, Tess Christiansen, Leigh Grissom, JP Westenskow, Miles Scott, Staci Santa, Ashley Swinford, Emilia Mickevicius, Chris Schafer, and Gia Del Pino, as well as former CCP staff members Leslie Squyres and Megan Clancy, and Amy Smith, formerly of the University of Arizona Foundation. Andrew Schulz, vice president for the arts and dean of the College of Fine Arts at the University of Arizona, was deeply supportive of this project since its inception, and his enthusiasm for the Center and its initiatives provided great energy for our work on Bernal.

Louis Carlos Bernal: Monografía would not have been possible without the generous support of the Henry Luce Foundation, which has enabled the Center for Creative Photography to dedicate extensive resources to this publication and associated exhibition and public programs. The Foundation's stated aim—to empower institutions to challenge accepted histories, elevate underrepresented voices, and promote critical conversations—aligns deeply with this project devoted to a Chicano photographer deserving of a more central place in the discourse on American photography.

In closing, I wish to express my profound gratitude to my husband, Gilbert C. Ferrer. Before his recent passing, he supported my work on this project in many ways: by listening to my stories of Louis Carlos Bernal's life and times, with his words of encouragement during my many hours of research and weeks of writing, and especially with his genuine enthusiasm for Bernal's work. I dedicate this project to him.

Elizabeth Ferrer

Mi ensayo para este volumen ha sido posible gracias a la generosa contribución de muchas personas que conocieron a Louis Carlos Bernal, lo que incluye a miembros de su familia, sus alumnas y alumnos y sus colegas artísticos. Al igual que en su momento personas desconocidas abrieron sus puertas a Lou y a su cámara, todas las personas a quienes me dirigí para hablar de él aceptaron de inmediato mi invitación para conversar y las interacciones resultantes fueron largas e informativas. Aprendí tanto —acerca del carisma de Lou, su sonrisa traviesa y su humor. También me enteré de que era un gran atleta, que vestía de manera impecable y que era un bailarían tan talentoso que podía atraer a una multitud de curiosos. También podía ser temperamental cuando estaba preocupado por su trabajo y muy exigente con sus alumnas y alumnos. Afectó a muchas vidas de una manera profunda y significativa y queda claro que dejó su huella en quienes tuvieron la bendición de tenerlo cerca.

En primer lugar, quiero agradecer a las hijas de Louis Carlos Bernal, Lisa Bernal Brethour y Katrina Bernal, que hablaron conmigo con frecuencia y franqueza. Compartieron una amplitud de información y recuerdos que me dejaron un retrato vívido de su padre. Al donar el archivo Bernal al Center for Creative Photography (Centro para la Fotografía Creativa), también hicieron posible esta exposición.

El fotógrafo e historiador de la fotografía mexicano Armando Cristeto Patiño realizó contribuciones fundamentales a este proyecto. Bernal conoció a Cristeto Patiño en la Ciudad de México en 1981 y entre ellos había una relación estrecha hasta el accidente de Bernal a finales de esa década. Cristeto Patiño, que ha conservado un archivo de correspondencia, publicaciones y otros materiales relacionados con Bernal, estuvo siempre disponible para responder a mis preguntas o compartir cartas y publicaciones, por lo que estoy en deuda profunda hacia él.

Marietta Bernstorff, la compañera de Bernal, artista y curadora-activista radicada actualmente en Oaxaca, apoyó de igual manera a este proyecto. Marietta empezó a hablar conmigo acerca de la importancia de Bernal en 2002 y pude aprovechar de la información que me proporcionó en entrevistas que realicé con ella en México en aquella época, así como de largas charlas virtuales más recientes. También compartió fotografías personales, escritos y recuerdos que han enriquecido enormemente mi texto.

Ann Simmons-Myers, la fotógrafa que asumió el puesto de Bernal en el Pima Community College y que curó *Louis Carlos Bernal: Barrios*, una importante exposición de su obra en la galería de la universidad —renombrado la Galería Louis Carlos Bernal en ese entonces— en 2002, ha apoyado con esmero este proyecto y ha proporcionado consejos y comentarios valiosos. George Luna-Peña, un joven erudito con especial interés en la vida y obra de Bernal, elaboró la cronología para este catálogo, de gran riqueza informativa. Estoy profundamente impresionada con el talento investigatorio de George y por su dedicación a este proyecto.

En Aperture, una organización con la que he mantenido una larga relación, quiero destacar a Sarah Meister, directora ejecutiva; Lesley A. Martin, directora creativa; Brendan Embser, redactor gerente principal de la revista *Aperture* y editor coordinador de esta publicación; y Noa Lin, asistente editorial, por su profesionalidad y trabajo arduo para llevar a cabo *Monografía*. También quiero dar las gracias a la correctora Claire Voon, los traductores Elianna Kan y Enrique Pérez Rosiles, al diseñador Duncan Whyte y al equipo de producción de Aperture, Andrea Chlad y Minjee Cho.

Varias otras personas colaboraron en la elaboración de este proyecto. Ofrezco mi profundo agradecimiento a David Andrés, director de la Galería Louis Carlos Bernal en el Pima Community College (PCC), Tucson; Ernesto Esquer, especialista de laboratorio de fotografía en el PCC; Chris Benson, fotógrafo y ex alumno de Bernal; Jim Covarrubias y Joseph Sánchez, artistas y cofundadores de Ariztlán; Robert Buitrón, fotógrafo y curador en Chicago; Terry Etherton, dueño de Etherton Gallery, Tucson; Tom Eckert, escultor en Tempe y ex-compañero de clase de Bernal; Roberto Gil de Montes, artista en La Peñita, Nayarit, México; Lorenzo Hernández, coleccionista y ex galerista en Pasadena, California; Jeff Smith, fotógrafo en Tucson y ex-alumno de Bernal; Antonio Solisgomez, escritor en Tucson; Esperanza Valverde, Los Ángeles; y Laura Anderson Barbata, New York.

Muchos de los miembros del personal del Centro para la Fotografía Creativa de la Universidad de Arizona han participado en el desarrollo de la exposición y el catálogo. En particular, quisiera expresar mi agradecimiento a la curadora jefe, Rebecca Senf, que fungió como consejera, sugirió recursos y contactos y expresó continuamente su entusiasmo por este proyecto. En el Centro para la Fotografía Creativa, también doy las gracias a Aimee Baker, Lynn Richards, Audrey Williams, Dana Hemmenway, Bryanna Knotts, Meg Jackson Fox, Denisse Brito, Alex Moral, Emilie Hardman, Emily Weirich, Diana Chávez, Tess Christiansen, Leigh Grissom, JP Westenskow, Miles Scott, Staci Santa, Ashley Swinford, Emilia Mickevicius, Chris Schafer, y Gia Del Pino, así como Leslie Squyres y Megan Clancy, ex miembros del personal de CCP, y Amy Smith, ex miembro de la Fundación de la Universidad de Arizona. Andrew Schulz, vicepresidente de las artes y decano de la Facultad de Bellas Artes de la Universidad de Arizona, apoyó profundamente este proyecto desde sus inicios, mientras que su entusiasmo por el Centro y sus iniciativas aportó una gran energía a nuestro trabajo sobre Bernal.

Louis Carlos Bernal: Monografía no habría sido posible sin el generoso apoyo de la Henry Luce Foundation, que ha permitido al CCP destinar recursos importantes a esta publicación, así como a la exposición y programas públicos vinculados con ello. El objetivo declarado de la Fundación —potenciar a las instituciones para que desafíen las historias establecidas, eleven las voces marginalizadas y promuevan conversaciones críticas— se alinea profundamente con este proyecto dedicado a un fotógrafo chicano quien merece un lugar más central en el discurso sobre la fotografía estadounidense.

Para terminar, deseo expresar mi profunda gratitud a mi marido, Gilbert C. Ferrer, quien antes de su reciente fallecimiento apoyó mi trabajo en este proyecto de varias maneras: ya sea escuchando mis múltiples historias sobre la vida y la época de Louis Carlos Bernal o con sus palabras de aliento durante muchas horas de investigación y semanas de escritura, y sobre todo con su entusiasmo genuino por la obra de Bernal. Dedico este proyecto a él.

Elizabeth Ferrer

ILLUSTRATION CREDITS / CRÉDITOS DE ILUSTRACIÓN

All reproduction material is copyright Lisa Bernal Brethour and Katrina Bernal, unless otherwise noted.

IMAGES BY LOUIS CARLOS BERNAL:

pp. 2, 20, 23, 100, 123, 134, 136, 153: Center for Creative Photography, University of Arizona: Gift of the Mexican American Legal Defense and Educational Fund; pp. 4, 13, 14, 15, 16, 19, 21, 48 (top and left), 49 (bottom), 50 (top left), 50 (bottom left), 51 (left), 77, 78, 79, 80, 81, 83, 84, 85, 86, 87, 88, 89, 90, 91, 93, 94–95, 96, 97, 99, 103, 108, 113, 114, 115, 118, 119, 122, 125, 126, 127, 128, 129, 131, 133, 140, 157, 158, 159, 161, 163, 164–65, 171, 172, 173, 174, 175, 177, 178, 179, 181, 182, 183, 185, 186, 187, 188, 189, 190, 191, 193, 194, 195, 197, 199, 200, 201, 203, 204, 205, 207, 208: Center for Creative Photography, University of Arizona: Louis Carlos Bernal Archive; pp. 11, 22, 168–69: Center for Creative Photography, University of Arizona: Gift of the artist; pp. 17, 24, 104, 105, 107, 109, 111: Center for Creative Photography, University of Arizona: Purchase; pp. 98, 101, 117, 135, 137, 139, 154, 155, 156, 162: Center for Creative Photography, University of Arizona: Gift of Morrie Camhi; pp. 121, 130: Center for Creative Photography, University of Arizona: Gift of Helen Unruh; p. 167: Center for Creative Photography, University of Arizona: Gift of Dr. Gene Gary and Dorothy Gruver

ADDITIONAL CREDITS:

p. 47 (top): courtesy Lisa Bernal Brethour and Katrina Bernal; p. 47 (left): © Luis C. Garza; p. 47 (bottom): Center for Creative Photography, University of Arizona: Frederick Sommer Archive © Frederick and Frances Sommer Foundation; p. 48 (bottom): courtesy Arizona Historical Society: © Gene Magee; p. 49 (top): © Nyle B. Leatham; p. 49 (left): courtesy Lisa Bernal Brethour and Katrina Bernal; p. 50 (top right): courtesy Arizona Historical Society; p. 50 (bottom right): © Adam Avilla; p. 51 (top): Center for Creative Photography, University of Arizona: Purchase © Pedro Meyer; p. 51 (bottom): © Armando Cristeto; p. 52 (top): © Rubén Ortiz-Torres; p. 52 (bottom left): © Archivo Manuel Álvarez Bravo, SC; p. 52 (bottom right): courtesy Armando Cristeto; pp. 213–14: courtesy Lisa Bernal Brethour and Katrina Bernal; p. 215 (top left and top right): courtesy Lisa Bernal Brethour and Katrina Bernal; p. 215 (bottom left): Consejo Mexicano de Fotografia, A.C.; p. 215 (bottom right): © Armando Cristeto; p. 216 (top left and top right): © Armando Cristeto; p. 216 (bottom): © Robert C Buitrón archive; p. 232: © Graciela Iturbide

Todo el material de reproducción es copyright de Lisa Bernal Brethour y Katrina Bernal, a menos que se indique lo contrario.

IMÁGENES DE LOUIS CARLOS BERNAL:

p. 2, 20, 23, 100, 123, 134, 136, 153: Centro para la Fotografía Creativa, Universidad de Arizona: Regalo del Fondo Mexico-americano de Defensa Legal y Educación; p. 4, 13, 14, 15, 16, 19, 21, 48 (arriba), 48 (izquierda), 49 (abajo), 50 (superior izquierda), 50 (inferior izquierda), 51 (izquierda), 77, 78, 79, 80, 81, 83, 84, 85, 86, 87, 88, 89, 90, 91, 93, 94-95, 96, 97, 99, 103, 108, 113, 114, 115, 118, 119, 122, 125, 126, 127, 128, 129, 131, 133, 140, 157, 158, 159, 161, 163, 164-65, 171, 172, 173, 174, 175, 177, 178, 179, 181, 182, 183, 185, 186, 187, 188, 189, 190, 191, 193, 194, 195, 197, 199, 200, 201, 203, 204, 205, 207, 208: Centro para la Fotografía Creativa, Universidad de Arizona: Archivo de Louis Carlos Bernal; p. 11, 22, 168–69: Centro para la Fotografía Creativa, Universidad de Arizona: Regalo del artista; p. 17, 24, 104, 105, 107, 109, 111: Centro para la Fotografía Creativa, Universidad de Arizona: Compra; p. 98, 101, 117, ,135, 137, 139, 154, 155, 156, 162: Centro para la Fotografía Creativa, Universidad de Arizona: Regalo de Morrie Camhi; p. 121, 130: Centro para la Fotografía Creativa, Universidad de Arizona: Regalo de Helen Unruh; p. 167: Centro para la Fotografía Creativa, Universidad de Arizona: Regalo del Dr. Gene Gary y Dorothy Gruver

CRÉDITOS ADICIONALES:

p. 47 (arriba): cortesía de Lisa Bernal Brethour y Katrina Bernal; p. 47 (izquierda): © Luis C. Garza; p. 47 (abajo): Centro para la Fotografía Creativa, Universidad de Arizona: Archivo de Frederick Sommer © Fundación Frederick y Frances Sommer; p. 48 (abajo): Sociedad Histórica de Arizona: © Gene Magee; p. 49 (arriba): © Nyle B. Leatham; p. 49 (izquierda): cortesía de Lisa Bernal Brethour y Katrina Bernal; p. 50 (superior derecha): cortesía Sociedad Histórica de Arizona; p. 50 (inferior derecha): © Adam Avilla; p. 51 (arriba): Centro para la Fotografía Creativa, Universidad de Arizona: Compra © Pedro Meyer; p. 51 (abajo): © Armando Cristeto; p. 52 (arriba): © Rubén Ortiz-Torres; p. 52 (inferior izquierda): © Archivo Manuel Álvarez Bravo, S.C; p. 52 (inferior derecha): cortesía Armando Cristeto; p. 213: cortesía de Lisa Bernal Brethour y Katrina Bernal; p. 214: cortesía de Lisa Bernal Brethour y Katrina Bernal; p. 215 (superior izquierda): cortesía de Lisa Bernal Brethour y Katrina Bernal; p. 215 (superior derecha): cortesía de Lisa Bernal Brethour y Katrina Bernal; p. 215 (inferior izquierda): Consejo Mexicano de Fotografia, A.C.; p. 215 (inferior derecha): © Armando Cristeto; p. 216 (superior izquierda): © Armando Cristeto; p. 216 (superior derecha): © Armando Cristeto; p. 216 (abajo): © Robert C Buitrón archive; p. 232: © Graciela Iturbide

Louis Carlos Bernal: Monografía

By Elizabeth Ferrer
Essay by Rebecca Senf

Front cover:
Dos Mujeres, Douglas, Arizona, 1978

Managing Editor: Brendan Embser
Designer: Duncan Whyte
Production Director: Minjee Cho
Production Manager: Andrea Chlad
Assistant Editor: Noa Lin
Senior Text Editor: Susan Ciccotti
Copy Editor: Claire Voon
Proofreaders: Elianna Kan, Isla Ng

All texts translated from the English by Elianna Kan and Enrique
Pérez Rosiles.

Additional staff of the Aperture book program includes:
Sarah Meister, Executive Director; Lesley A. Martin, Editor at
Large; Michael Famighetti, Editor in Chief, *Aperture* magazine;
Emily Patten, Managing Editor, Books; Kellie McLaughlin, Sales
and Marketing; Richard Gregg, Sales Director, Books

This project was supported, in part, by a
grant from the Henry Luce Foundation.

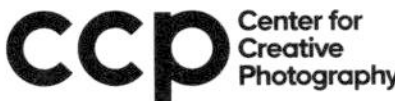

**HENRY
LUCE
FOUNDATION**

First edition, 2024
Printed by Midas in China
10 9 8 7 6 5 4 3 2 1

Library of Congress Control Number: 2023924166
ISBN 978-1-59711-557-5

Copublished by Aperture and the Center for Creative
Photography, University of Arizona, Tucson

ccp Center for
Creative
Photography

Center for Creative Photography
1030 N. Olive Road
Tucson, AZ 85719
ccp.arizona.edu

To order Aperture books, or inquire
about gift or group orders, contact:
orders@aperture.org

For information about Aperture
trade distribution worldwide, visit:
aperture.org/distribution

aperture

548 West 28th Street, 4th Floor
New York, NY 10001
aperture.org

Aperture is a nonprofit publisher dedicated to creating insight,
community, and understanding through photography.

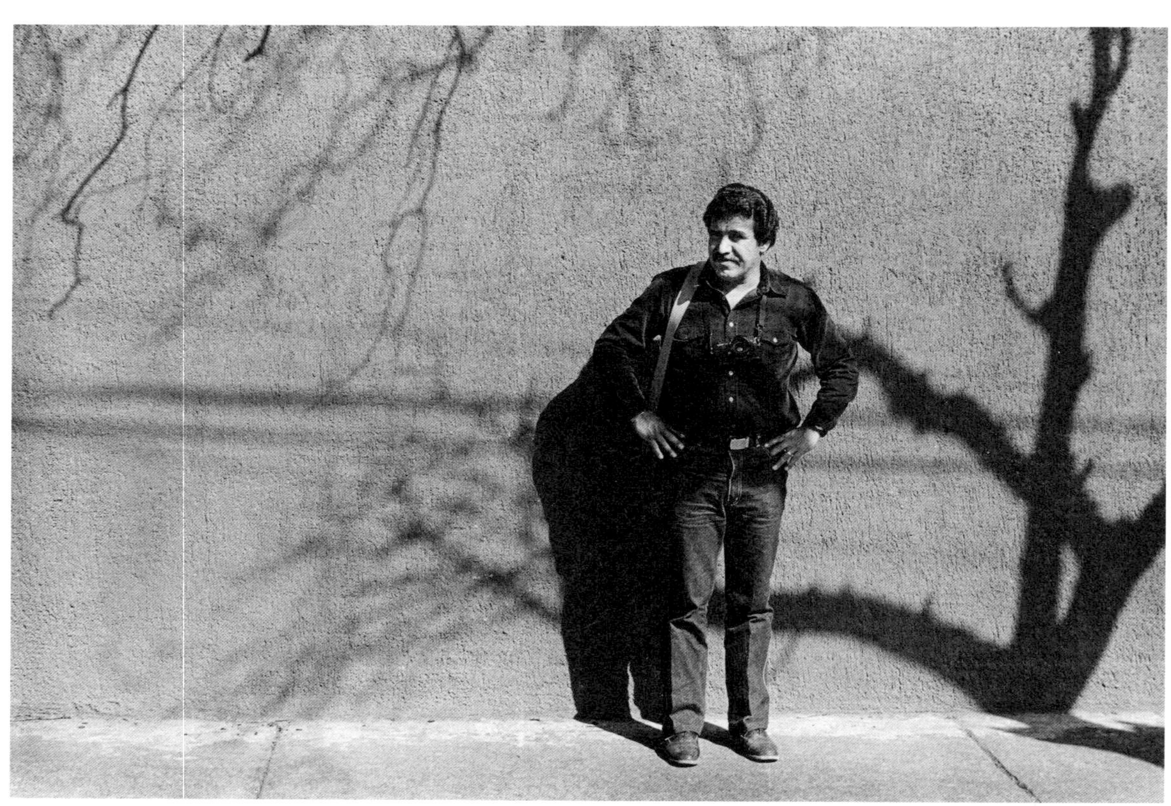

Graciela Iturbide, Louis Carlos Bernal, Mexico City, ca. 1980s